Remittances
Development Impact and Future Prospects

Editors
Samuel Munzele Maimbo
and
Dilip Ratha

THE WORLD BANK

ISBN 0-8213-5794-8
EAN-ISBN 978-0-8213-5794-1
e-ISBN 0-8213-5795-6

Library of Congress Cataloging-in-Publication Data

Remittances : development impact and future prospects / editors, Samuel Munzele
Maimbo, Dilip Ratha.
    p. cm.
  Proceedings of a 2003 conference organized by the Department for International
Development, IMF, and World Bank.
  Includes bibliographical references and index.
  ISBN 0-8213-5794-8 (pbk.)
  1. Emigrant remittances—Developing countries—Congresses. 2. Transfer
Payments—Developing countries—Congresses. 3. Developing countries—Economic
conditions—Congresses. 4. Finance—Government policy—Developing countries. 5.
Developing countries—Emigration and immigration—Economic aspects—Congresses. I.
Maimbo, Samuel Munzele. II. Ratha, Dilip.

  HG3877.R46 2005
  338.9'009172'4—dc22   2005045771

Cover photo: Corbis.

Table of Contents

BOXES

FIGURES

TABLES

Foreword

For too long, migrants have faced unwarranted constraints to sending money to family members and relatives in their home countries, among them costly fees and commissions, inconvenient formal banking hours, and inefficient domestic banking services that delay final payment to the beneficiaries. This book demonstrates that governments in developing countries increasingly recognize the importance of remittance flows and are quickly addressing these constraints. But as Maimbo and Ratha rightly contend, more needs to be done to maximize the development impact and potential that remittances offer.

This book, the first comprehensive study of remittances by the World Bank, is a timely addition to the economic literature, advancing the World Bank's dream of a world free of poverty and my personal conviction of the need to increase financial resources flowing to developing countries. For many countries, remittances are larger and more stable than foreign direct investment and in some cases, larger even than official development aid. Given the low rate of domestic saving and high government expenditure in many developing countries, external sources of finance, particularly remittances, have played a critical part in local economic development and poverty reduction strategies. Not only do remittances increase the consumption levels of recipient families—so that education and health care are not out of reach—they also, if conscientiously saved and aggregated, contribute to infrastructure development and investment for increased income in the long term.

However, as I welcome the publication of the book, I caution that remittances are not a panacea to development issues. Remittances complement efforts by governments in developing and developed countries, but are not a substitute for sustained assistance. Although remittances are now an important source of development finance, rising to over US$100 billion at the end of 2004, it remains the central responsibility of developing country governments to provide basic social services for poor people. And it remains the responsibility of donor governments to provide adequate assistance.

Development assistance is still required to fund those investments that cannot be financed by developing-country governments, by the private sector, or by remittances. Development assistance is also key to getting more out of remittances themselves—by supporting financial sector reform, for instance. Also, the growing importance of the remittances agenda presents a good opportunity for the international community to come together. To address the remittances issue effectively, we need a better understanding of migrants and their situations, the needs of recipient families, what new financial products remitters want, the changes needed in regulatory and monitoring mechanisms in the developed and developing countries, and the development climate within each developing country. No individual institution possesses all of this knowledge. I am therefore pleased that the World Bank is partnering with others on this critical agenda

The greater challenge, however, rests with developing countries themselves. It would be difficult to imagine progress on the remittances agenda without progress on financial sector reform, corporate governance, anticorruption efforts, and other related issues. Developing-country governments must take full ownership of the remittances agenda, as they do for their own development. Development is not something that can be done *to* people; it has to be done *by* them and *with* them.

The studies in this book identify and discuss the key challenges the development community and developing-country governments face in harnessing the benefits of remittance flows while respecting the fact that these are private, hard-earned incomes of poor people seeking to better their lives.

James D. Wolfensohn
President
The World Bank

Acknowledgments

The editors wish to acknowledge the invaluable contributions that many individuals made to the publication of this book:

The contributors who presented papers at the International Conference on Migrant Remittances: Development Impact, Opportunities for the Financial Sector and Future Prospects, organized by the Department for International Development and the World Bank in collaboration with the International Migration Policy Programme, on October 9–10, 2003, in London, and subsequently worked with the editors in revising their papers—Abdusalam Omer, Abul Kalam Azad, Admos O. Chimhowu, Antonique Koning, Barnabé Ndarishikanye, Caroline Pinder, Cerstin Sander, David C. Grace, Devesh Kapur, Gina El Koury, Ildefonso F. Bagasao, James P. Korovilas, Jenifer Piesse, John Page, Manuel Orozco, Nikos Passas, Norbert Bielefeld, Raul Hernandez-Coss, Richard H. Adams Jr., Roger Ballard—all added to the quality and depth of the study.

The participants who commented on the papers presented at the conference all ably represented their respective organizations and governments, notably African Development Bank, Asian Development Bank, Canadian International Development Agency, Department for International Development, Consultative Group to Assist the Poor, International Labour Organization, International Fund for Agricultural Development, International Migration Policy Programme, Inter-American Development Bank, Inter-American Dialogue, International Monetary Fund, International Organization for Migration, United States Agency for International Development, World Bank, World Council of Credit Unions, and World Savings Bank Institute.

We thank the staff members of the World Bank, the Department for International Development, and the International Migration Policy Programme, who either facilitated the 2003 conference or the subsequent publication of the proceedings, including Abayomi Alawode, Alessandra Roversi, Alexandre Casella, Anders Hjorth Agerskov, Boris Wijkstrom, Cesare Calari, Cristina Zara, David Stanton, Douglas Pearce, Elena P. Mekhova, Gauri Rani Deshpande, Ismail Radwan, James Quigley, Jan Wimaladhrma, Jennifer Isern, Joseph Del Mar Pernia, Kadija Jama, Marjorie Espiritu, Mamphela Ramphele, Margery

Waxman, Marilou Uy, Maryia Rasner, Radha Singla, Raul Hernandez-Coss, Richard Boulter, Robert Keppler, Rolf Jenny, Simon C. Bell, Syed Abul Kamal Md Abdul Hye, Syed Mesbahuddin Hashemi, Oriana Bolvaran, Jamie G. Olazo, Colleen Thouez, W. Paati Ofosu-Amaah, and Melina Cholmondeley, to whom we owe a special thank you for her unwavering support of this project.

Finally, but certainly not the least, we are grateful to our editorial team—Dana Vorisek, Melissa Edeburn, Monika Lynde, Nicola Marrian, and Stephen McGroarty. Their collective efforts have greatly strengthened the quality of the final product in your hands.

Contributors

RICHARD H. ADAMS JR.

Richard H. Adams Jr. is a consultant in the Poverty Reduction and Economic Management Unit of the World Bank. Prior to joining the World Bank, he worked as a research fellow at the International Food Policy Research Institute (IFPRI) in Washington, DC. Adams is the author of three books and has published extensively on the topics of poverty, migration, and remittances in such journals as *Economic Development and Cultural Change, Journal of Development Studies,* and *World Development.* Adams received his Ph.D. from the University of California, Berkeley.

ABUL KALAM AZAD

Abul Kalam Azad is joint director of Bangladesh Bank, the central bank of Bangladesh. He is currently working in the Foreign Exchange Policy Department of Bangladesh Bank, where his main job is to formulate policy proposals for enhancing the inflow of migrant workers' remittances to Bangladesh and facilitating their productive investment. Prior to Bangladesh Bank, Mr. Azad worked at the Bangladesh Red Cross Society, where he obtained extensive experience in managing cyclone, flood, and other natural disasters and serving disaster survivors. He has published a number of works on migrant remittances, banking, finance and insurance, and financial markets in refereed journals. He is a contributor to *Banglapedia,* the national encyclopedia of Bangladesh published by the Asiatic Society of Bangladesh in 2003. His current research interests include the impact of sending-costs on migrants' remittance flows to Bangladesh, migrant remittances and community development in Bangladesh, effective strategies for financial market development in Bangladesh, and migrant remittances and microenterprise development. Mr. Azad is a fellow of the Bank of England. He has participated in various conferences, seminars, and workshops on migrant remittances and other related issues at home and abroad. He received his MPhil degree in International Finance from the University of Glasgow, United Kingdom.

I. F. BAGASAO

I. F. Bagasao is president and executive trustee of the Economic Resource Center for Overseas Filipinos (ERCOF) in Geneva and the Philippines.

ROGER BALLARD

Roger Ballard is an anthropologist with a specialist interest in transnational networks that have their roots in the large-scale inflow of labor migrants into the United Kingdom from South Asia during the 1960s and 1970s. He has conducted extensive ethnographic fieldwork in and around South Asian ethnic colonies in the United Kingdom, as well as in settlers' villages of origin in northern India and Pakistan. He has recently had an opportunity to explore the ongoing dynamics of transnational networks, and to make an assessment of the differential impact of remittance transfers on patterns of economic growth between UK-based settlers' villages of origin on either side of the Indo-Pakistani border. Dr. Ballard's current academic post is director of the Centre for Applied South Asian Studies at the University of Manchester, UK.

NORBERT BIELEFELD

Norbert Bielefeld is deputy director of Payments Systems at the European Savings Banks Group (ESBG). In this capacity he has been assigned to the Secretariat of the newly formed European Payments Council. Mr. Bielefeld has also been elected chair of the Industry Issues Committee of the Global Payments Forum in Washington, DC. He began his career with Union de Banques à Paris. He then became finance manager at Clark Credit France, before creating Econocom Deutschland GmbH as finance director and ECS International Belgium S.A. as managing director. At SWIFT, the bank-owned telecommunications services company, he was successively head of marketing and customer support, senior manager new network services, and director of Payments Strategy and Banking Industry Initiatives. Mr. Bielefeld is a graduate of the Ecole Supérieure des Sciences Economiques et Commerciales, Paris, and a chartered accountant. He received further education at the University of California, Berkeley; Cambridge University, United Kingdom; and INSEAD, France.

ADMOS O. CHIMHOWU

Admos O. Chimhowu is a geographer at the University of Manchester. He teaches international development studies at the Institute for

Development Policy and Management, where he also co-directs post-graduate programs in economics and management of rural development, and environment and development. He has a Ph.D. in development planning and management. His research examines the impact of informal financial and other remittance flows as both drivers and pathways of local-level change and social transformation in rural Africa. He has also undertaken research on Mozambique, South Africa, and Zimbabwe and has taught rural development planning at the University of Zimbabwe.

GINA EL KOURY

Gina El Koury is the programme officer for Financial Services with the United Nations Development Programme for Somalia. For more than two years she has worked with initiatives supporting the Somali remittance sector, including the establishment of the Somali Financial Service Association, as well as initiatives involving the Somali Diaspora.

DAVID C. GRACE

David C. Grace is senior manager of the World Council of Credit Unions (WOCCU). He is responsible for the development of the International Remittance network (IRnet) service and its application in both developed and developing countries. Grace has been deeply involved in remittance briefings for both the U.S. and Mexican governments and has been widely interviewed as an expert on remittances by national and international media. He was previously with the Federal Reserve Bank of St. Louis, managing its financial services and information technology units. Grace holds a master's degree from Washington University in St. Louis and graduated with honors from St. Louis University.

RAUL HERNANDEZ-COSS

Raul Hernandez-Coss is a financial sector specialist working at the World Bank unit responsible for implementing anti-money laundering and counterfinancing of terrorism assignments in the Bank's Financial Market Integrity Department. He has been task manager for the Bank's involvement in the Asia-Pacific Economic Cooperation (APEC) Remittance Systems Initiative. In addition to presenting reports to APEC finance ministers in 2003 and 2004, he published the U.S.-Mexico and Canada-Vietnam Remittance Corridor studies, which present lessons on shifting from informal to formal transfer systems. He has organized two policy dialogues among APEC economies on remittances. Currently he is responsible for the Bilateral Remittances Corridor Analysis that includes preparation of several remittance corridors studies, among them Germany-Serbia, U.S.-Guatemala, U.K.-Nigeria, The Netherlands-Dutch Antilles, and Italy-Morocco. Before joining the Bank, he served at the Mexican Deposit Insurance Institute and the North American Free Trade Agreement Secretariat and provided legal services for Booz Allen Hamilton, the Bhutan National Bank, Datamonitor Inc., Caja España de Inversiones, and Caja Popular Mexicana. He earned a law degree from the Instituto Tecnológico Autónomo de México and a master's of international affairs from Columbia University.

DEVESH KAPUR

Devesh Kapur is an associate professor in the Department of Government at Harvard University. He also is a faculty associate at the Weatherhead Center for International Affairs and the Center for International Development at Harvard University and a nonresident fellow of the Center for Global Development in Washington, DC. His research interests focus on local-global links in political and economic change in developing countries, particularly India, focusing especially on the role of domestic public institutions and international financial institutions, and international migration. Current research projects include the design and performance of public institutions in India, the impact of international human capital flows on developing countries, and the political and economic impact of emigration and the Indian diaspora on India.

ANTONIQUE KONING

Antonique Koning is adviser of institutional relations at the World Savings Banks Institute (WSBI). She is responsible for relations with savings and retail banks in the Americas and the Caribbean and for relations between the WSBI and international organizations such as multilateral financial institutions and UN agencies. Before joining the WSBI, Antonique spent three years in El Salvador, where she developed and managed a microcredit program for women and farmers. She has several years of research experience as a research fellow of the London-based Overseas Development Institute, where she worked between 1994 and 1997 on issues related to trade and development.

JAMES P. KOROVILAS

James P. Korovilas is a senior lecturer in economics at the University of the West of England, Bristol. He has been involved in various research projects investigating the relationship between economic development and remittances in the southern Balkans. The research has focused on the impact of the various waves of Albanian economic migration in both post-Communist Albania and postconflict Kosovo. This research has resulted in various publications that consider the issues of remittances, migrant labor, and development, including "The Albanian Economy in Transition: The Role of Remittances and Pyramid Investment Schemes" in *Post-Communist Economies,* September 1999; "The Economic Sustainability of Post-Conflict Kosovo" in *Post-Communist Economies,* March 2002; and "People in Search of Work: Albanian Migrants in Greece" in *Europe, Policies and People: An Economic Perspective,* 2002.

SAMUEL MUNZELE MAIMBO

Samuel Munzele Maimbo is a senior financial sector specialist in the South Asia Region of the World Bank. Since March 2002, Maimbo has been leading the Bank's work on informal remittance systems. His publications on the subject include a joint IMF Occasional Paper titled "Informal Funds Transfer Systems: An Analysis of the Informal Hawala System," "The Money Exchange Dealers of Kabul: A Study of the Hawala System in Afghanistan," and "Migrant Labour Remittances in the South Asia Region." Before joining the World Bank, he worked as a senior bank inspector with the Bank of Zambia (1995–97), and briefly as an auditor with PriceWaterhouse. A Rhodes Scholar, Maimbo obtained a Ph.D. in public administration and an MBA degree from the University of Manchester and the University of Nottingham, respectively. He is also fellow of the Association of Chartered Certified Accountants, United Kingdom, and a fellow of the Zambia Institute of Certified Accountants.

BARNABÉ NDARISHIKANYE

Barnabé Ndarishikanye is a policy research analyst in the Canadian International Development Agency's (CIDA) Policy Branch and the coordinator of CIDA's Poverty Reduction Network. He is also responsible for the Population and Development file, and he is currently working on country programming risk assessment. He has master's degrees in international economics (Grenoble) and in agricultural economics (McGill University). His article on "Rural-Urban Migration and Agricultural Productivity: The Case of Senegal" was published in *Agricultural Economics* in 2004. He has published extensively on the root causes of civil war and extreme violence, using the case of Burundi as an example. Since July 2003, he has been leading research on migrant remittances from Canada.

ABDUSALAM OMER

Abdusalam Omer, Ph.D., is a programme manager for governance and financial services with the United Nations Development Programme (UNDP) for Somalia. He has led initiatives supporting the Somali remittance sector for over two years and established the first UNDP program supporting money transfer businesses. He is the author of the UNDP report "Supporting Systems and Procedures for the Effective Regulation and Monitoring of Somali Remittance Companies (Hawala)."

MANUEL OROZCO

Manuel Orozco is director of the remittances and rural development project funded by the Multilateral Investment Fund of the Inter-American Development Bank and International Fund for Agricultural Development. Orozco taught political science at the University of Akron, Ohio, and has researched migration and international relations issues for the Tomas Rivera Policy Institute. He has worked as a policy consultant for various organizations in the United States as well as in Central America, Asia, and Africa. He taught international relations in Costa Rica. His areas of interest include globalization, democracy, migration, conflict in war-torn societies, and minority politics. Orozco holds a doctorate in political science from the University of Texas at Austin, a master's in public administration and Latin American studies, and a bachelor's in international relations from the National University of Costa Rica. Among his recent publications are *International Norms and Mobilization for Democracy London* (Ashgate Publishers, 2002), "The Remittance Marketplace: Prices, Policy and Financial Institutions" (Pew Hispanic Center, Washington, DC, 2004), and "Mexican Hometown Associations and Development Opportunities (*Journal of International Affairs*, spring 2004, vol. 57, no. 2).

JOHN PAGE

John Page is chief economist for the Africa region at the World Bank and adjunct professor at the Nitze School of Advanced International Studies, Johns Hopkins University. He received his bachelor's degree in economics from Stanford University and his doctorate from Oxford University, where he was a Rhodes Scholar. He is the author of 3 books and more than 50 published papers on economic growth and development.

NIKOS PASSAS

Nikos Passas is professor of criminal justice at Northeastern University, Boston, specializing in the study of white-collar crime, corruption, organized crime, and international and transnational crimes. Since September 11, 2001, he has been conducting research into terrorist funding sources, trade diversion, hawala, and other informal value-transfer systems for the Financial Crimes Enforcement Network (Fin-CEN), U.S. Department of the Treasury, and the National Institute of Justice. He has published extensively in eight languages, and is the drafter of the *Legislative Guide to the UN Convention against Transnational Organized Crime* (2003).

JENIFER PIESSE

Jenifer Piesse is a reader in international finance at King's College, London, and a visiting professor at the University of Stellenboshc, South Africa. Her research interests include the institutional aspects of emerging- and developing-economy financial systems and the impact of research and development on growth and poverty reduction. She has published extensively, including papers on income distribution and household expenditure in South Africa and the relationships between the national capital markets in Sub-Saharan Africa. Her work on remittances examines the poverty-reducing effects of migrant labor. She is an associate of Women in Sustainable Enterprise Development (WISE).

CAROLINE PINDER

Caroline Pinder is director of Women in Sustainable Enterprise Development (WISE), an international consulting agency that operates as a global network of independent women consultants. Pinder's main areas of expertise are enterprise, social, and institutional development. She has spent 15 years working in Africa and Central and Eastern Europe, where she has conducted impact assessments for multilateral and bilateral international organizations using participatory methods to research sustainable livelihood and rights approaches. She has developed a framework for assessing the impact of business-enabling environment programs for the Department for International Development in the United Kingdom. Her work in Southern Africa has included reviews of the impact of remittances and the migrant labor system of the mining industry on rural households throughout the region.

DILIP RATHA

Dilip Ratha is a senior economist in the Development Prospects Group of the World Bank. He has worked extensively on international finance topics including determinants of official development finance, short-term debt and crisis, South-South foreign direct investment, and securitization of future receivables. He is considered among the top world experts on international migrant remittances. Prior to joining the World Bank, he worked in Credit Agricole Indosuez as a regional economist for Asian emerging markets. Before that, he taught macroeconomics at the Indian Institute of Management, Ahmedabad. He has a Ph.D. in economics from Indian Statistical Institute, New Delhi.

CERSTIN SANDER

Cerstin Sander is a private sector adviser with the Department for International Development in the United Kingdom. She has worked extensively on migrant remittances and money transfers and has produced topical studies, conference papers, and publications. She currently serves as editor of *Migrant Remittances,* a quarterly newsletter. She has worked on assignments in Africa, Asia, the Caribbean, Latin America, and parts of the former Soviet Union through consultancies and staff positions with the International Development Research Centre and as the East Africa Regional Private Sector Development Advisor to the Austrian Development Corporation. Her assignments have been in the areas of enterprise finance and private sector development, as well as institutional assessment, performance and evaluation, and socioeconomic and fiscal impact. She holds a master's from Queen's University, Canada.

Remittances: An Overview

International migrant remittances are perhaps the largest source of external finance in developing countries. Officially recorded remittance flows to developing countries exceeded US$125 billion in 2004, making them the second largest source of development finance after foreign direct investment. Remittances were certainly larger if flows through informal unrecorded channels are also included. As the development community continues the search for additional resources to finance the Millennium Development Goals, remittances—pro-poor and cyclically stable, compared to other capital flows—appear to be a promising source. Remittances also appear to be the least controversial aspect of the overheated debate on international migration. Both remitting and recipient countries are considering the long-term economic implications of these transfers.

A number of remittance initiatives are underway. The Sea Island G-8 Summit in June 2004, for example, called for "better coherence and coordination of international organizations working to enhance remittance services and heighten the developmental impact of remittance receipts" (U.S. Department of State 2004). The World Bank, the International Monetary Fund, and the United Nations have formed an interagency, intergovernmental technical group to improve remittance statistics. The Bank for International Settlements and the World Bank have formed a special task force on international retail payment systems, to improve transparency in remittance transactions. An interagency task force on remittances led by the U.K. Department for International Development and the World Bank has been in operation since the International Conference on Migrant Remittances: Development Impact, Opportunities for the Financial Sector, and Future Prospects held in London October 9–10, 2003. Regional development banks, bilateral aid agencies, and other international agencies have also started ambitious programs to collect information and facilitate remittance flows. Both source and destination countries are eager to understand these flows and their policy implications.

This book is an attempt to identify and discuss what is needed to develop policies, processes, and infrastructure to foster a development-oriented transfer of financial resources between migrants in developed economies and their families in developing countries. The book is intended for policy makers who legislate and regulate the financial sector, as well as for researchers and providers of remittance services. The information should be of special use to those who administer remittance services and to financial supervisors responsible for ensuring compliance with international money transfer codes and standards.

This book, however, does not attempt to cover all aspects of the policy debate on remittances. The choice of subject matter in part reflects the significance of selected topics, but in part also the scarcity of studies on other important topics.

We have tried to organize the chapters along precise and clear remittance-relevant themes. However, as is to be expected from a volume trying to capture an emerging and rapidly growing topic such as international migrant remittances, various chapters have overlapping themes and varying regional or country focus. We have therefore loosely organized the chapters according to five broad themes: remittance trends and determinants; maximizing the development impact of remittances; strengthening the formal financial infrastructure for remittances; increasing transparency in the informal financial infrastructure for remittances; and the complex interplay between migration, development, and remittances.

The beginning chapters focus on the emerging remittance flows and the development potential they offer. The chapters thereafter focus on the infrastructure for remittances and the challenges present in the provision of accessible, cost-effective, reliable, and speedy formal and informal delivery mechanisms for migrants sending funds home to their families. The final chapters focus on the implications for this notable economic phenomenon occurring between developed and developing countries.

REMITTANCE TRENDS AND DETERMINANTS

The recent revival in interest in migrant remittances is largely due to the sheer size these flows have acquired in recent years. That remittances are the second largest source of external financing in developing countries was first revealed by Ratha in an earlier version of chapter 1 of this volume. Chapter 1 shows that, in addition to being large, remittances are stable and may even be countercyclical during a growth slowdown in the recipient country. It also shows that remittances are more evenly distributed among developing countries than other sources of hard currency flows. Although top recipient countries are typically large countries such as India, Mexico, and the Philippines, remittances as a share of gross domestic product (GDP) or in per capita terms are large in small countries such as Tonga, Tajikistan, and Lesotho. Lebanon is among the top recipients in terms of remittances per capita.

Global flows of migrant worker remittances were estimated at US$182 billion in 2004, up 5.7 percent from their level in 2003 and 34.5 percent compared to 2001 (World Bank 2004). Developing countries received an estimated US$125.8 billion workers' remittances in 2004, registering an increase of nearly 48.7 percent compared to 2001.

Growth in remittances was especially strong—nearly 83 percent during 2001–2004—in low-income countries, notably India.

These official figures, however, represent only a portion of true remittances. Ratha discusses the pitfalls of using currently available remittance data and suggests ways to improve the definition and the collection of remittance data. Flows through informal channels such as *hawala* are believed to be large, but are not captured in official statistics. Also, a significant portion of flows through formal channels are believed to be excluded from official statistics because most countries do not insist on regular reporting of flows below predefined thresholds. Rich countries such as Canada and Denmark, for example, do not report any remittance data, and several poor countries either do not report or report inaccurate data. Even when remittance data are available, countries often classify them incorrectly. Many countries report workers' remittances as "other transfers." Sometimes it is difficult to distinguish remittance flows from, say, tourism receipts or from nonresident deposits. Finally, only a handful of countries report bilateral flows of remittances.

Sander and Maimbo (chapter 2) highlight this problem in the context of African countries. Their preliminary study of migrant remittances in Africa is based on a review of widely dispersed data and documentation. Remittance receipts to Africa since 1990 peaked in 1992 at US$10.7 billion and were at their lowest in 2000 (US$7.8 billion). For Sub-Saharan Africa, the share of global workers' remittances dropped from some 8 percent in 1980 to under 5 percent in 2004, reflecting the growth of flows to other regions rather than any absolute reduction in flows to Africa (Ratha 2003; Gammeltoft 2002).

Improving remittance data would require not only gathering information, but also studying the relationship between migration stock and remittance flows, remittance behavior of migrant workers in major remittance-source countries, and the way in which remittances respond to changes in the source and destination economies. One way forward, and perhaps the only way forward, would be to conduct surveys of remittance senders and recipients to find out the size of remittance flows, their sources and destinations, the channels used, and their ultimate uses. Major international coordination is necessary for improving the data on remittances.

Remittances are expected to show a steady increase well into the foreseeable future, as more people migrate in response to globalization and as income levels grow in labor-receiving countries. In particular, persistent income inequalities between source and destination countries, the increase in temporary and circular migration, and increasing South-South migration—all assisted by the low cost of travel—are contributing to increasing global migration.

MAXIMIZING THE DEVELOPMENT IMPACT OF REMITTANCES

That the increase in remittances is taking place at a time of declining official development assistance flows adds additional importance to the remittance debate and research. Policy makers are increasingly concerned with the impact of remittances on poverty and economic development.

Chimhowu, Piesse, and Pinder (chapter 3) adopt a community- and family-level approach to find that remittances enable better health care, nutrition, housing, and education. Spending patterns, however, depend on factors such as the strength of the migrant's kinship ties and intent to return to the country of origin. Migrants who intend to return tend to remit more than those who are permanently integrated into host countries, so remittances may slow as ties weaken with time. This argument supporting the remittance decay hypothesis remains anecdotal, however. While it is true that the propensity to remit (that is, the proportion of income remitted by a migrant may decline over time, it rarely vanishes, because first-generation migrants (and often even second-generation migrants) continue to send money to their original communities. Even if the propensity to remit declines, the remittance volume arguably increases with the sharp rise in income levels of migrants over time.

Remittances may help improve economic growth, especially if used for financing children's education or health expenses. Even when they are used for consumption, remittances generate multiplier effects, especially in countries with high unemployment. In many other countries, a large part of remittances are invested in real estate, reflecting both a desire of migrants to provide housing to families left behind, and a lack of other investment instruments in the recipient community. Whether remittances are used for consumption or buying houses, or for other investments, they generate positive effects on the economy by stimulating demand for other goods and services.

Roger Ballard, in chapter 4, Remittances and Economic Development in India and Pakistan, considers migratory flows from the Punjab region of Northern India and from Pakistan to the United Kingdom and the impact of remittances on the local economy in and around migrants' villages of origin. The development potential of the huge inflow of capital has not been adequately realized, not because of a lack of entrepreneurial skills among migrants and their kin, but rather because of structural obstacles at the local, national, and international levels. The combined impact of these obstacles has been to confine villagers' entrepreneurial activities to limited spheres, few of which provide adequate foundations for the emergence of sustainable patterns of economic development. Based on extensive fieldwork in settlements of

South Asians in the United Kingdom, as well as in settlers' villages of origin in India and Pakistan, Ballard offers some suggestions about how the spirals of "de-development" so often set off by the arrival of migrant remittances can be brought to a halt through carefully tailored "smart aid" designed to kick-start the neglected productive potential of the local economy in areas of heavy overseas migration.

Remittances may aid micro-finance institutions, and vice versa, especially when they serve the same customers. Azad (chapter 5) examines this link using the case of Bangladesh and reviewing the efforts of several countries to help their expatriates channel money into investments. Although the government continues to provide enhanced facilities for sending those remittances through banking channels, a large portion of migrant remittances move through informal channels. Bangladesh migrant workers are mostly semi- or unskilled, and their earnings are low compared to those of migrants from other countries. Pooling and redirecting these small amounts to microenterprise development would require establishment of "Diaspora Community Development Funds." The importance of Filipino diaspora groups and the investment role of their remittances are also explored by Bagasao in chapter 6. Ndarishikanye (chapter 7) focuses on how the formal money transfer market to Haiti, Jamaica, and Guyana is dominated by remitting companies, with Canadian banks playing a minor role in the industry; an unknown share of remittances is channeled informally.

Some authors (Chami, Fullenkamp, and Jahjah 2003) argue that remittances may reduce recipients' motivation to work and, thus, slow down growth (although reduced work effort by some individuals need not translate into low employment in an economy with a high unemployment rate). Others argue that remittances may increase income inequality in the recipient country because it is the rich who can migrate.

Also, as with all foreign currency inflows, too great a volume of remittances can result in currency appreciation, which may affect the competitiveness of exports. On the other hand, remittance receipts enable a country to pay for imports and repay foreign debt. The effect of remittances on country creditworthiness is easily evident in some countries: For example, for several years it was feared that Lebanon was vulnerable to a balance-of-payments crisis because its foreign debt stood at nearly five times the size of its exports. Yet, the fact that such a crisis did not materialize is sometimes attributed to large remittance flows. Remittances sent by members of the Lebanese diaspora are about as big as Lebanon's exports (about US$2.4 billion in 2002). The ratio of Lebanon's debt to exports is halved when remittances are included in the denominator. Brazil and other countries have been able to borrow from the international capital markets at lower interest rates and longer maturity by using remittances as collateral (Ketkar and Ratha 2004)

The last three chapters in the book highlight the complex interplay between migration, development, and remittances. Because migration is a complex and fluid phenomenon involving millions of individuals, its development impacts for both origin and destination countries depend on a variety of interacting factors. Migration, through the impact of remittances, is an integral part of the processes of development and globalization—with a potentially important role to play in the alleviation of poverty.

In policy circles it is often debated whether there may be ways to encourage the use of remittances for more productive purposes than for consumption or for purchasing land and houses. While such a question may be appropriate for official aid flows, it is not entirely appropriate for personal remittance flows. If it is true that senders and recipients rationally decide, given their economic environment and available investment instruments, to consume more and save less, it would be hard for policy makers to induce them to do otherwise. Indeed, forcing remittance recipients to save more and consume less, as Lesotho, Mexico, Turkey, and other countries have done in the past, reduces consumer welfare. Nevertheless, there may be ways to indirectly increase the development impact of remittances. For example, encouraging account-to-account remittance flows instead of cash transfers would result in increased saving by recipients (and senders) and better matching (by banks) of available saving and investment demand. Improving the investment climate in the recipient community would also encourage more investment.

The following policy questions arise in the context of remittances:

- How can the financial infrastructure supporting remittances be strengthened?
- How can policies regarding anti–money laundering and facilitating remittances be balanced?
- Should governments use fiscal incentives to attract remittances?

STRENGTHENING THE FINANCIAL INFRASTRUCTURE SUPPORTING REMITTANCES

Exorbitant fees—13 percent on average and frequently as high as 20 percent—charged by money transfer agents are a drain on hard-earned remittances (chapter 1). These fees especially affect poor migrants who remit only small amounts and are forced to pay proportionally more. Reducing remittance fees would significantly increase annual remittance flows to developing countries, especially to the poorest recipients.

The remittance cost typically involves three components: the true cost of sending money, the profit component, and the foreign exchange commission. It is difficult to see why remittance fees should increase, rather than stay fixed, with the amount of transfer. Anecdotal evidence suggests that the true cost of sending remittances is small. Informal channels, for example, regularly charge fees under 1 percent. It is reported that some formal agents in Hong Kong, China, charge a fixed fee of only US$2.50 to transfer funds to the Philippines. High costs are in part a result of inefficiencies in the regulatory framework. The profit component is high because many transfer agents have been able to charge high fees without the threat of competition. To some extent, competition in the remittance industry is hindered by ad hoc rules and regulations. For example, high collateral requirements (often in excess of US$1 million in some states in the United States) often deter new players who could compete effectively in some remittance corridors. Worse, collateral requirements and compliance with regulation vary widely from one state to another in the United States, discouraging many transfer agencies from expanding their operations across states. Some countries require transfer agents to obtain full banking licensing even when these agencies have no intention of providing banking services. Entry barriers also include lack of access to existing payment systems, which forces new entrants into the remittance market to build their own costly proprietary transfer systems. Frequently, large remittance service providers have persuaded the postal network, or large banks with extensive branch networks, to sign exclusive contracts that limit the access of competitors to these well-developed distribution networks. Fixing these problems would involve policy coordination—especially harmonizing regulatory and compliance requirements—between source and destination countries. It would also be helpful to find ways to harmonize payment systems and to increase access to existing payment systems. Use of electronic card-based products would also reduce costs of remittances.

The currency conversion fee, the third cost component mentioned above, is often in the range of 3 percent of the principal remittance amount. Banks with access to wholesale foreign exchange markets tend to charge a lower fee than money transfer operators, but banks also tend to benefit from the "float," the interest they earn by delaying delivery of funds. The foreign exchange commission can be high in countries that have exchange controls and a wide divergence between the official and the parallel exchange rate. In República Bolivariana de Venezuela in early 2004, for example, the foreign exchange commission was nearly 40 percent (the official rate was 1,920 bolivars per U.S. dollar, the free market rate was over 3,200 bolivars per U.S. dollar), implying a huge loss to remittance senders using formal channels.

Even with the existing cost structure, there may be potential to reduce average remittance costs by "bundling," that is, by enabling senders to remit more money but less frequently. In the above cost schedule, for example, if a person sends 150 euros (US$201) per month for a period of six months, the total remittance cost would be 10 percent or 90 euros (US$121). If, however, this person were able to send the entire 900 euros (US$1,207) in one transaction, the remittance cost would fall to just over 4 percent or under 40 euros (US$54). The difficulty, of course, is that many poor remittance senders typically do not have sufficient funds to be able to bundle remittances. Banks and microfinance institutions could play a role in alleviating such liquidity constraints and reduce the effective cost of remittances.

Unfortunately, a large number of migrants, especially those who are poor or undocumented, do not have bank accounts. Improving migrant workers' access to banking in the remittance-source countries (typically developed countries) would not only reduce costs of remittances, it would also lead to financial deepening in many receiving countries. It is observed, for example, that 14 percent to 28 percent of nonmembers who came to credit unions affiliated with the World Council of Credit Unions to transfer funds ended up opening an account. Using existing retail financial infrastructure, such as postal savings banks, commercial banks, or microfinance institutions in rural areas could facilitate remittance flows.

In chapter 8—Exploring the Credit Union Experience with Remittances in the Latin American Market—David Grace explores the experience of credit unions with remittances in the Latin American market, identifying several promising ways to reduce remittance costs. He notes, too, that growing interest in the remittance business on the part of financial institutions has increased the variety and efficiency of remittance services and products available to migrants.

Already, as a result of greater competition among financial institutions, transactions costs are lower and outreach has improved. Nevertheless, a significant portion of immigrants in host countries, as well as their families in home countries, remain "unbanked." Latino immigrants in the United States are four times more likely to be unbanked than the general population. Figures for other immigrant communities reveal similar patterns. This situation prevents migrants and their families from accessing a range of secure services including savings, credit, and insurance options offered by the financial system.

One of the major challenges confronting traditional financial institutions and other financial service providers is to integrate unbanked senders and receivers into the financial system. Several approaches discussed here include new products such as prepaid account options, expanded and more flexible card-based services for remittance recipients, increased access to automated teller machines, the IRnet service now offered by credit unions, and other modern payment systems. The large volume, both of money and potential new clients, makes it attractive to the private sector to find ways of providing these services, especially once the appropriate regulatory framework is firmly in place.

With regard to improved outreach, Grace notes that credit unions—relative newcomers to the remittance business—are generally well positioned to serve the unbanked because of their extensive networks of rural points of service. Research findings from Latin America show that credit union members are more likely to save some portion of the value of remittances received than those using other nonbank financial services such as money transfers. Also, and most significantly, the provision of remittance services by credit unions often results in the opening of depository transaction accounts and consequently integrates unbanked senders and receivers into the financial system. However, regulatory obstacles to credit union participation in the remittance business remain. Specific challenges include improving credit unions' access to central bank clearing and settlement systems.

As James P. Korovilas shows in chapter 9, Remittances and Pyramid Investment Schemes in Albania, however, the hard-earned remittances of migrant workers can vanish in corrupt, unregulated, and fraudulent investment markets, such as those that flourished in the first years of postcommunist economic change.

Better ways of protecting remittances is the focus of Barnabé Ndarishikanye in chapter 7, on remittances sent from Canada to Central America and the Caribbean. Canada is home to many citizens from developing countries and a destination for thousands of seasonal agricultural workers. Although migration to Canada is well documented, related remittances, and how they are processed and transferred, are largely unknown and poorly understood. This chapter reviews the procedures and services used by almost 400,000 immigrants from Central American and Caribbean countries to send money home. Too great a share of the remitted funds is absorbed by fees, pointing to the need for improved services and enhanced regulatory frameworks related to the remittance process.

Sander and Maimbo (chapter 2) also argue that throughout Africa, financial and monetary policies and regulations have created barriers to the flow of remittances and their effective investment. Restrictive licensing of money transfer services, for example, limits access to remittances and restricts the potential impact of remittances in many areas. Other regulations and policies create unattractive environments for investment and block improvements in financial services. Removing those obstacles—and broadening and adapting relevant financial products and services, such as savings and investment instruments— would boost remittance flows and raise their impact on development.

In chapter 10, Norbert Bielefeld and Antonique Koning, citing the case of a Spanish savings bank, call on individual market participants to deliver "end-to-end fair value."

One of the unanimous policy-related conclusions of the International Conference on Remittances—convened by the World Bank and the U.K. Department for International Development in London, October 9–10, 2003—was the desirability of developing a set of core principles to be satisfied by remittance systems that aim to provide "fair and certain value" to senders, recipients, and service providers within an appropriate policy, legal, and regulatory environment.

The proposed core principles for remittances have an important role to play within the international financial architecture. Several international initiatives to maintain financial stability have been completed or are underway. In 2004, the Committee on Payment and Settlement Systems (CPSS) of the Bank for International Settlements and the World Bank set up a task force to look into payment system issues. This task force builds on the Core Principles for Systemically Important Payment Systems (promulgated by the Bank for International Settlements in January 2001). In conjunction with the Technical Committee of the International Organization of Securities Commissions, the CPSS issued in November 2001 a set of Recommendations for Securities Settlement Systems. A new CPSS task force has started work to prepare core principles applicable to a wider range of payment systems. Based on the use of such core principles and recommendations, it is clear they enjoy strong and widespread international support. For example, the World Bank and the International Monetary Fund use core principles when advising their members on payments and securities systems. Although core principles sometimes contain precise technical language, they are expressed in the most general way to ensure that they may be useful in all countries and that they will be durable. Core principles are not intended as a blueprint for the design or operation of any specific system, but rather to suggest the key characteristics that should be satisfied by different systems to achieve a stated common purpose, such as that envisaged for international remittance systems—fair and certain value for end users.

In reaching these conclusions, the authors acknowledge that the connections between financial-service policies and the volume and channels of remittances are only partially understood. To date, those connections have been explored primarily in the context of foreign exchange controls, taxation, and state monopolies in financial services. Regulations directed at money transfer operators and transfer services in both sending and receiving countries have received scant attention, despite their clear impact on the availability and viability of services.

INCREASING TRANSPARENCY IN THE INFORMAL FINANCIAL INFRASTRUCTURE FOR REMITTANCES: STRIKING A BALANCE

The regulatory regime governing remittances has to strike a balance between curbing money laundering, terrorist financing, and general financial abuse, and facilitating the flow of funds between hard-working migrants and their families back home, especially for remittances through informal financial systems. It is not entirely clear that personal remittances (typically small) are an efficient way of laundering or illegally transferring sizeable amounts of funds. More important, informal channels owe their existence to the inefficiencies in the formal system: informal agents are cheaper, they work longer hours, they operate in remote areas where formal channels do not operate, they often have staff who speak the language spoken by the migrant customers, and they offer anonymity. Informal channels, however, can be subject to abuse. Strengthening the formal remittance infrastructure by offering the advantages of low cost, flexible hours, expanded reach, and language can induce a shift in flows from the informal to the formal sector. Both sender and recipient countries should support migrants' access to banking by providing them with identification tools. Encouraging funds to flow through formal channels, especially banks, would also help in tracking any illegal use of funds.

Although technology offers recipient countries an opportunity to make rapid strides in developing their remittance infrastructure, it also carries risks. The attacks of September 11, 2001, raised concern about the security implications of formal and informal remittance systems and their susceptibility to abuse by money launderers and financiers of terrorism. Some national financial regulators are reexamining regulations, and in some cases, developing tighter standards for registration, reporting, and disclosure for remittance service providers. In October 2001, the Financial Action Task Force agreed to Special Recommendations on Terrorist Financing, extending anti–money laundering requirements to remittance systems. In the face of increasing regulatory and supervisory oversight, it is important to determine the optimal legal and regulatory framework for remittances, and to ensure that tighter controls do not reduce availability or drive up costs of services for the poor.

In chapter 11, Samuel Munzele Maimbo and Nikos Passas review recent efforts to strengthen the regulatory and supervisory framework for informal funds transfer systems. Warning that regulatory theory related to remittances is still in its infancy and does not provide adequate guidance for policy makers faced with a highly innovative and growing remittance industry, Maimbo and Passas argue that a regulatory structure that is too detailed in its prescription of prudential requirements may stifle rather than promote the growth of innovative yet accountable and transparent remittance services. They urge that international and domestic policies now being developed should be flexible to allow for adjustment as experience is gained, and that the regulatory models adopted by the international community and national regulators should promote incentive-based regulation rather than regulation based solely on direct external interventions. Ideally, concerned stakeholders such as informal remittance service providers should be included in the regulation-making process. In the long run, broad financial sector policies that improve the quality of remittance services in the formal sector will be most effective in reaching the necessary balance between transparency and access.

The authors' position on the regulation of informal remittance service providers is gaining broader acceptance. Although reactions to informal transfer systems after September 11 focused initially on prohibition of everything that was unregulated, more nuanced approaches recognize the need to strike a balance between minimizing financial abuse and promoting cost-efficient and accessible transfer services.

In chapter 12 on regulation and supervision in Somalia, Abdusalam Omer and Gina El Koury emphasize that remittances, including those passing through informal channels, play a vital and life-sustaining role for millions of vulnerable people in poor countries, particularly in post-conflict countries and in situations where formal financial services and infrastructures are nonexistent. Remittance flows to Somalia are greater than total development assistance. Caution must therefore be exercised so that remittance options are not limited or access reduced in a manner that would adversely affect populations in recipient countries dependent on remittances for their survival.

The Somali example illustrates the importance of matching regulatory requirements with local and national capacities to ensure enforceability. Sometimes it will be necessary for the international community to help raise national capacities to supervise and enforce regulations. In situations where formal financial systems are virtually absent, such as Somalia and Afghanistan, regulations may have limited or counterproductive effects if complementary efforts are not made to develop financial infrastructure and supervisory capacity.

Protecting the flow of remittances is the focus of Raul Hernandez-Coss in chapter 13, A Proposed Framework to Analyze Informal Funds Transfer Systems. Because informal funds transfer systems have proven to be a resilient method of transferring value from one location to another, why shift from informal to formal systems? Hernandez-Coss offers some answers that indicate why such a shift to formal channels is not only possible but desirable. Hernandez-Coss urges the formal sector to learn from the success of informal systems and to move to provide similar services. Once legitimate flows, particularly migrant worker remittances, are moved into formal channels, they can continue to circulate. At the same time, law enforcement can better focus its efforts on the illegitimate flows left in the informal sector.

MIGRATION, DEVELOPMENT, REMITTANCES, AND THE USE OF FISCAL INCENTIVES

Labor mobility between source and destination countries is perhaps the most crucial and controversial means of increasing remittance flows to developing countries. It is beyond the scope of this book to present the full argument in the "migration for remittances" debate. The papers in the final section only begin the discussion.

Adams and Page (chapter 14) focus on the positive side of remittances resulting from migration, which they argue reduce poverty. Adams and Page use cross-country regression based on 74 countries and find that a 10 percent increase in the share of remittances in a country's GDP can lead to an average 1.2 percent decline in the poverty headcount. The robustness of this result has been verified using household survey data, by Adam's more recent work on Guatemala (Adams 2004), and Yang's study on the Philippines (Yang 2004).

In discussing the new transnational networks that have emerged from the consolidation of migration ties based on household-to-household relationships, Orozco (chapter 15) refers to the mobilization of migrants' (and their relatives') savings and investments at home (through the acquisition of land, property, or small businesses), which can spur economic growth in areas neglected by the public and private sectors.

In particular, he focuses on what he refers to as the Five T's—transfers, tourism, transportation, telecommunications, and nostalgic trade—and presents a range of development strategies for remittance-receiving developing countries as they establish their national remittance strategies.

The majority of developing countries offer tax incentives to attract remittances. The side effect of such incentives, of course, is that remittances may then be used for tax evasion and money laundering. Also, some governments provide matching funds for remittance-backed projects (as in Mexico's 3-for-1 program). Again, the side effect may be diversion of scarce budgetary resources to projects favored by nonresident nationals.

Many aid agencies are looking into using hometown associations (HTAs) to channel aid. While there might be limited potential for channeling any significant volume of official funds this way, there may be potential for using HTAs for promoting community financing of infrastructure or other collective funding for community priorities.

One effective policy measure to encourage remittance inflows is unification of exchange rates and elimination of the black market exchange premium. República Bolivariana de Venezuela offers an interesting example in this respect. With a black market premium of nearly 40 percent, the effective cost of sending remittances to Venezuela is nearly half the principal amount! Nonresident Venezuelans, therefore, are either discouraged from sending remittances, or they are sending them through informal channels.

From this discussion, we conclude that while formulating policies on remittances, policy makers should keep in mind that remittances are not public money. They are personal flows, and the decision of how they should be spent is better left to the remitters and recipients. Efforts to tax remittances or direct them to specific investments are likely to prove ineffective. Instead, policy makers should try to improve the investment climate in the recipient communities. Remittances are more effective in generating incomes and investment when they are supported by good policy and public infrastructure.

For that reason, we end the book with Kapur's chapter (chapter 16), which brings the book to a close with a critical scrutiny of the remittance debate by drawing attention to some conclusions that may prove simplistic or overoptimistic, particularly in light of the poor quality of available data on remittances. He rightly cautions that development economics is prone to fads and fashions, just as private capital is alleged to be. He contends that remittances strike the right cognitive cords—they fit in

> ... with a communitarian "third way" and exemplify the principle of self-help. People from poor countries can just migrate and send back money that not only helps their families, but host and recipient countries as well. Immigrants, rather than government, become the biggest provider of "foreign aid." The general feeling appears to be that such "private foreign aid" is much more likely to go to people who really need it. On the sending side it does not require a costly government bureaucracy; on the receiving side it is less likely to be siphoned into the pockets of corrupt government officials. It appears to be good for equity and for poverty and yet imposes few budgetary costs. What could be better? Are those hopes valid?

In debating answers to these questions, Kapur, like the authors of the previous chapters in the book, acknowledge that remittance flows play a significant role in augmenting private consumption and alleviating poverty in developing countries. However, there remain important aspects of the remittance debate that are less well understood. Rigorous data and research on the effects is surprisingly limited—this book is an effort to mitigate this handicap in this emerging dynamic aspect of development economics.

REFERENCES

Adams, R. 2004. "Remittances and Poverty in Guatemala." Policy Research Working Paper 3418, World Bank, Washington DC.

Chami, R., C. Fullenkamp, and S. Jahjah. 2003. "Are Immigrant Remittance Flows a Source of Capital for Development?" Working Paper No. 03/189, International Monetary Fund, Washington DC.

Gammeltoft, Peter. 2002. "Remittances and Other Financial Flows to Developing Countries." Working Paper 02.11, Centre for Development Research, Copenhagen, Denmark. http://www.cdr.dk/working_papers/wp-02-11.pdf.

Ketkar, S. and D. Ratha. 2004. "Recent Advances in Future-Flow Securitization". Paper presented at Annual Finance & Accounting International Conference - Managing Securitization for Lebanon and the MENA Region, December 3-4, Lebanese American University, School of Business, Beirut, Lebanon.

Ratha, Dilip. 2003. "Worker's Remittances: An Important and Stable Source of External Development Finance." In *Global Development Finance: Striving for Stability in Development Finance* (157–75). Washington, DC: World Bank.

U.S. Department of State. 2004. "G8 Action Plan: Applying the Power of Entrepreneurship to the Eradication of Poverty." The White House Office of the Press Secretary, Sea Island, Georgia, June 9.

World Bank. 2004. *Global Development Finance 2004: Harnessing Cyclical Gains for Development*. Washington, DC: World Bank.

Yang, D. 2004. "International Migration, Human Capital, and Entrepreneurship: Evidence from Philippine Migrants' Exchange Rate Shocks." Gerald R. Ford School of Public Policy and Department of Economics, University of Michigan, Ann Arbor, MI.

Part I
Remittance Trends
and Determinants

Chapter 1
Workers' Remittances:
An Important and Stable Source
of External Development Finance

Dilip Ratha

This chapter examines the relative importance of workers' remittances as a source of external financing for developing countries and discusses measures that industrial and developing countries could take to increase remittances. The main messages are:

- Remittance flows rank behind only foreign direct investment (FDI) as a source of external funding for developing countries. In 2004, workers' remittance receipts in developing countries exceeded US$126 billion, much higher than total official development assistance and private non-FDI flows, and more than half of total FDI flows to developing countries. Remittances to low-income countries were larger as a share of gross domestic product (GDP) or as a share of imports than were those to middle-income countries. Remittances also are more stable than private capital flows, which often move procyclically, thus raising incomes during booms and depressing them during downturns. By contrast, remittances are less affected by economic cycles in the recipient country. Remittances are expected to rise significantly in the long term, once sluggish labor markets in G-7 (Canada, France, Germany, Italy, Japan, the United Kingdom, and the United States) economies recover and new procedures for scrutinizing international travelers become routine.
- Remittances are often invested by the recipients, particularly in countries with sound economic policies. Improvements in policies and relaxation of foreign exchange controls in the 1990s may have encouraged the use of remittances for investment.
- By strengthening financial sector infrastructure and facilitating international travel, source (developed) and recipient (developing) countries could increase remittance flows, thereby bringing more funds into formal channels. The transaction costs of fund transfers often exceed 20 percent; reducing them by even 5 percentage points could generate annual savings of over US$6 billion for workers sending money home.
- Remittance flows to developing countries would rise with greater international labor mobility. Greater international migration, moreover, could generate substantial benefits to the world economy. One positive step in this direction is Mode 4 trade in the General Agreement on Trade in Services (GATS), which proposes greater temporary movement of individual service suppliers. However, developed countries remain wary of relaxing immigration policies for fear of exposing local workers to greater competition, incurring the fiscal costs of providing social services to migrants, encountering problems of cultural assimilation of migrants, and endangering national security. Developing

20

countries also remain concerned about the emigration of highly educated workers although they probably stand to gain more from greater international migration in the form of remittances and positive network effects on trade and investment.

The first section of the chapter analyzes trends and cycles in workers' remittances in developing countries and compares them to other sources of foreign exchange earnings—among them exports, private capital, and official flows. The next section examines the impact of remittances on growth, investment, and income distribution in recipient economies. The third section discusses means of strengthening the infrastructure for sending remittances. The fourth deals with international migration—the precondition for remittances. The final section outlines the near- and long-term outlooks for remittance flows to, and migration from, developing countries.

TRENDS AND CYCLES IN WORKERS' REMITTANCES IN DEVELOPING COUNTRIES

In 2004, remittances to developing countries from overseas resident and nonresident workers exceeded US\$126 billion, or 1.8 percent of GDP (tables 1.1 and 1.2).[1] Remittances were smaller than FDI inflows,

TABLE 1.1 WORKERS' REMITTANCES

	1999	2000	2001	2002	2003	2004 (est.)
All developing countries (US$billion)	73	77	85	99	116	126
East Asia and Pacific	11	11	13	17	20	20
Europe and Central Asia	11	11	11	11	13	13
Latin America and the Caribbean	18	20	24	28	34	37
Middle East and North Africa	13	13	15	16	17	17
South Asia	15	16	16	22	27	33
Sub-Saharan Africa	5	5	5	5	6	6
All developing countries (% of GDP)	1.2	1.1	1.2	1.6	1.7	1.8
East Asia and Pacific	0.7	0.7	0.6	0.9	1.0	1.0
Europe and Central Asia	0.9	0.9	0.9	1.0	0.9	0.9
Latin America and the Caribbean	1.0	1.0	1.2	1.6	2.0	2.2
Middle East and North Africa	2.2	1.9	2.3	2.3	2.4	2.4
South Asia	2.6	2.3	2.3	3.0	3.4	4.1
Sub-Saharan Africa	1.3	0.8	1.0	1.7	1.5	1.5

Sources: Author's calculations based on IMF *Balance of Payments Statistics Yearbook;* World Bank *World Development Indicators.*

TABLE 1.2 REMITTANCES RECEIVED BY
          DEVELOPING COUNTRIES, 2003

	All developing countries	*Low-income countries*	*Lower-middle-income countries*	*Upper-middle-income countries*
Total remittances (US$ billion)	116.0	36.7	54.9	24.4
Percentage of GDP	1.7	3.3	1.3	1.3
Percentage of merchandise imports	6.2	18.5	5.1	4.0
Percentage of domestic investment	6.7	15.3	4.8	7.1
Percentage of FDI inflows	76.4	228.0	55.1	67.6
Percentage of official flows	365.6	-	-	-
Outward remittances (US$ billion)	33.5	2.1	8.6	22.8

Sources: IMF, *Balance of Payments Statistics Yearbook,* 2004; World Bank, *World Development Indicators,* 2004.

but larger than international capital market flows during 1999–2004 (figure 1.1). For most of the 1990s, remittance receipts exceeded official development assistance.

Remittances are more significant in low-income countries than in other developing countries. In 2003, remittances to low-income countries were 3.3 percent of GDP and 18.5 percent of imports; in the upper-middle-income countries they were 1.3 percent of GDP and 4 percent of imports (figures 1.2 and 1.3). Although in nominal terms the top recipients of remittances included several large countries—China, India, Mexico, Pakistan, and the Philippines (figure 1.4)—remittances as a share of GDP were larger in smaller and poorer countries, including Haiti, Jordan, Lesotho, Moldova, and Tonga (figure 1.5).

The United States and Saudi Arabia are the largest sources of workers' remittances to developing countries (figure 1.6). Other top sources are France, Germany, and Switzerland. Although it is difficult to disaggregate the remittance data, anecdotal evidence suggests that developing countries may have received nearly US$18 billion in 2001 from the United States alone.[2] Until the mid-1990s, when its economic boom (driven by oil exports) subsided, Saudi Arabia was the largest source of remittance payments in the world (figure 1.7). It still is the largest source on a per capita basis. Several other developing countries (China, Malaysia, the Russian Federation) also figure among the top 20 source countries for remittances.

FIGURE 1.1 WORKERS' REMITTANCES AND OTHER INFLOWS

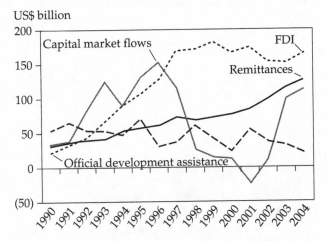

US$ billion

Sources: Author's calculation based on IMF *Balance of Payments Statistics;* World Bank staff estimates; *World Development Indicators* and *Global Development Finance,* various years.

FIGURE 1.2 REMITTANCES ARE HIGHER IN LOWER-INCOME COUNTRIES, 2003 (PERCENTAGE OF GDP)

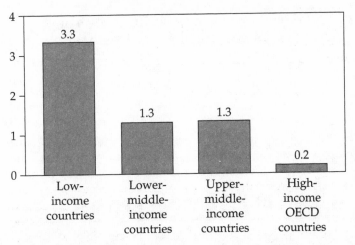

Sources: Author's calculation based on IMF *Balance of Payments Statistics;* World Bank staff estimates; *World Development Indicators* and *Global Development Finance,* various years.

Note: OECD = Organisation for Economic Co-operation and Development.

FIGURE 1.3 REMITTANCES ARE HIGHER IN LOWER-INCOME
COUNTRIES, 2003 (PERCENTAGE OF MERCHANDISE
IMPORTS)

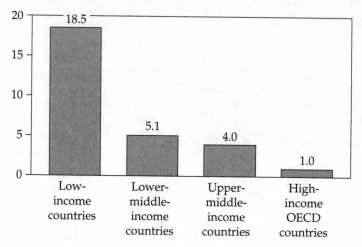

Sources: Author's calculation based on IMF *Balance of Payments Statistics;* World Bank staff estimates; *World Development Indicators* and *Global Development Finance,* various years.

Note: OECD = Organisation for Economic Co-operation and Development.

FIGURE 1.4 TOP 20 DEVELOPING-COUNTRY RECIPIENTS OF
REMITTANCES, 2003 (BILLIONS OF DOLLARS)

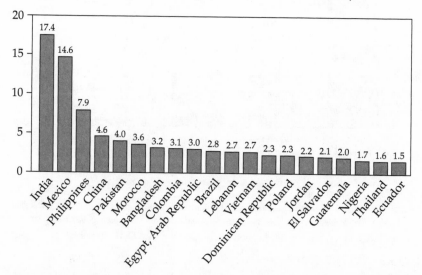

Sources: Author's calculation based on IMF *Balance of Payments Statistics;* World Bank staff estimates; *World Development Indicators* and *Global Development Finance,* various years.

FIGURE 1.5 TOP 20 DEVELOPING-COUNTRY RECIPIENTS OF
REMITTANCES, 2003 (AS PERCENTAGE OF GDP)

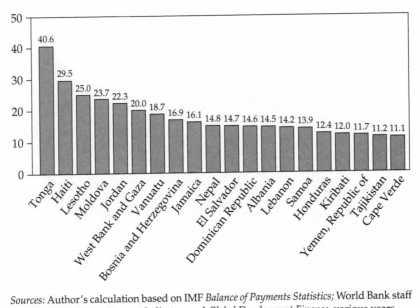

Sources: Author's calculation based on IMF *Balance of Payments Statistics;* World Bank staff estimates; *World Development Indicators* and *Global Development Finance,* various years.

FIGURE 1.6 TOP SOURCES OF OUTWARD REMITTANCES, 2003
(BILLIONS OF DOLLARS)

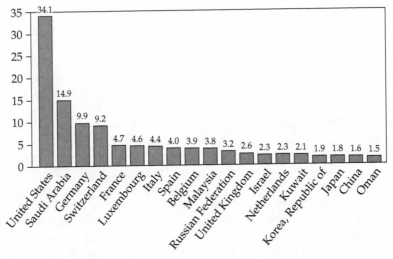

Sources: Author's calculation based on IMF *Balance of Payments Statistics;* World Bank staff estimates; *World Development Indicators* and *Global Development Finance,* various years.

Note: This figure shows remittance payments to developing countries as well as advanced countries.

Figure 1.7 Outward Remittances from the United States and Saudi Arabia (Billions of Dollars)

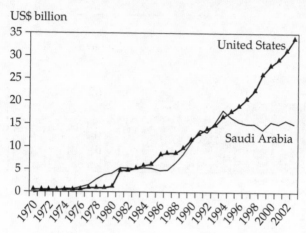

Sources: Author's calculation based on IMF *Balance of Payments Statistics;* World Bank staff estimates; *World Development Indicators* and *Global Development Finance,* various years.

Importantly, remittances were one of the least volatile sources of foreign exchange earnings for developing countries in the 1990s (see figure 1.1). While capital flows tend to rise during favorable economic cycles and fall in bad times, remittances appear to react less violently and show remarkable stability over time. For example, remittances to developing countries continued to rise steadily in 1998–2001, as private capital flows declined in the wake of the Asian financial crisis. Even the more stable components of capital flows—FDI and official aid flows—declined during 2000–2003, while remittances continued to rise.

Remittances intended for consumption by recipient households should be less volatile than those intended for investment, especially in low-income countries, where families of migrant workers depend on remittances as a source of income and may live at close to subsistence levels. Economic downturns often encourage workers to migrate abroad—and to begin transferring funds to families left behind.

Even when the purpose behind remittances is investment, remittances are less likely to suffer the sharp withdrawal or euphoric surges that characterize portfolio flows to emerging markets. Overseas residents are more likely to continue to invest in their home country despite economic adversity than are foreign investors, an effect that is similar to the home-bias in investment. This relative stability has encouraged some emerging market economies to use remittances as collateral against which to borrow on international capital markets on substantially better terms than they otherwise could (box 1.1).

BOX 1.1 SECURITIZING FUTURE FLOWS OF
WORKERS' REMITTANCES

In recent years, many emerging-market issuers have resorted to future-flow securitization to access international markets, often to avoid credit rationing in the face of deteriorating sovereign risks. Workers' remittances have been used quite frequently along with other future-flow receivables such as oil exports or credit card receivables. For example, in 2001 Banco do Brasil issued US$300 million worth of bonds (with five-year maturity) using as collateral future yen remittances from Brazilian workers in Japan. The terms of these bonds were significantly more generous than those available on sovereign issues. Rated BBB+ by Standard and Poors, these securities were several notches higher than Brazil's sovereign foreign currency rating, BB+ at the time. At 375 basis points, the launching spreads were lower than sovereign spreads.

Source: Ketkar and Ratha 2001.

Other countries, such as Mexico and El Salvador, have used future workers' remittance-backed securities to raise external financing. Assuming that about half of all recorded remittances pass through the banking system, and assuming an overcollateralization ratio of 5:1, developing-country issuers could potentially raise about US$7 billion a year using future remittance-backed securitization. However, developing countries should carefully weigh the trade-off between lower borrowing costs and longer maturities that securitized debt offers and the inflexibility associated with servicing such debt.

The high margins associated with remittances have attracted some significant FDI deals in developing countries. For banks, intermediating fund transfers between overseas workers to families back home is a high-margin business. Some authors estimate that remitters collected about US$12 billion in fees in 2001 (Maldonado and Robledo 2002). While the size of this business itself is attractive to banks, new customers who start a relationship with a bank initially for remittance purposes eventually bring in other business. The large and rapidly growing business opportunities associated with workers' remittances have attracted at least two major FDI deals in Mexico. Valued at US$12.5 billion, the Citigroup-Banamex deal in 2001 was the single biggest investment south of the border for any U.S. company (Latin Finance 2002). In December 2002, Bank of America and Santander Serfin announced a US$1.6 billion deal.

Despite greater stability overall, remittances do respond to dramatic changes in economic activity in recipient countries. They rose steadily in the Philippines as the investment climate improved in the early 1990s, becoming more volatile following the financial crisis in the late 1990s (figure 1.8). Similarly, Turkey's remittance receipts increased for most of the 1990s but suffered a decline as the economy slipped into crisis in 1999 and 2000 (figure 1.9). In both cases, the decline in remittances, and their volatility, were smaller than those of capital flows.

FIGURE 1.8 VOLATILITY OF REMITTANCES COMPARED TO PRIVATE FLOWS IN THE PHILIPPINES

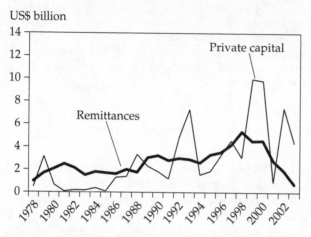

Sources: Author's calculation based on IMF *Balance of Payments Statistics;* World Bank staff estimates; *World Development Indicators* and *Global Development Finance,* various years.

FIGURE 1.9 VOLATILITY OF REMITTANCES COMPARED TO PRIVATE FLOWS IN TURKEY

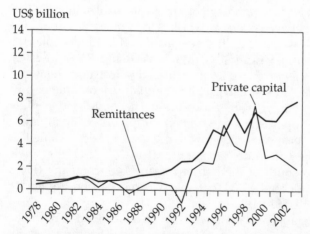

Sources: Author's calculation based on IMF *Balance of Payments Statistics;* World Bank staff estimates; *World Development Indicators* and *Global Development Finance,* various years.

Some evidence indicates that remittances have been increasingly used for investment purposes in developing countries, especially in low-income countries. As low-income countries lifted exchange restrictions and liberalized their current and capital accounts in the 1990s, remittance receipts rose sharply—and the volatility of remittances also rose (figure 1.10).[3]

Cross-country comparison reveals that remittances are affected by the investment climate in recipient countries in the same manner as capital flows—but to a much lesser degree. During 1996–2000, for example, remittance receipts averaged 0.5 percent of GDP in countries with a higher-than-median level of corruption (as indicated by the index of the International Corruption Research Group) compared to 1.9 percent in countries with lower-than-median corruption (table 1.3). Countries that were more open (as measured by their trade to GDP ratio) or more financially developed ($M2^4$ to GDP) also received larger remittances.

In contrast to capital flows, however, remittances were significantly higher in countries that were high risk (as measured by their *Institutional Investor* rating) and had a high level of debt relative to GDP.[5] This is consistent with the finding, mentioned earlier, that low-income countries, which are usually high risk, receive relatively more remittances as a share of GDP than do countries with higher incomes. In fact, in 1996–2000 remittances tended to be higher in poor countries that had lower-than-median growth rates, probably because most remittances to poorly performing low-income countries are for consumption. By

FIGURE 1.10 VOLATILITY OF REMITTANCES, BY COUNTRY GROUP, 1980S AND 1990S

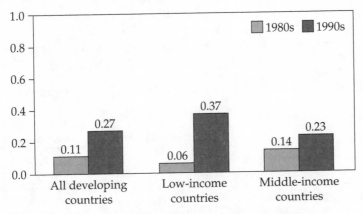

Sources: Author's calculation based on IMF *Balance of Payments Statistics;* World Bank staff estimates; *World Development Indicators* and *Global Development Finance,* various years.

Note: Volatility as determined by standard deviation divided by mean.

TABLE 1.3 INVESTMENT CLIMATE AND WORKERS' REMITTANCE RECEIPTS IN DEVELOPING COUNTRIES

Climate Indicator		Remittances as % of GDP
Corruption level	High	0.5
	Low	1.9
Inequality (Gini index)	High	0.9
	Low	1.5
Financial depth (M2/GDP)	High	1.2
	Low	0.9
Trade openness [(Exports+Imports)/GDP]	High	1.2
	Low	1.0
Indebtedness (Debt/GDP)	High	2.3
	Low	0.8
Country risk (based on *Institutional Investor* rating)	High	2.4
	Low	1.0

Sources: Author's calculation based on IMF *Balance of Payments Statistics Yearbook;* World Bank staff estimates; *World Development Indicators* and World Bank *Global Development Finance,* various years.
Note: High and low usually refer to above and below median for the concerned variable. The numbers used are the sum of remittances of all developing countries (except Lesotho) divided by the sum of GDP of the same countries. Average remittances and average GDP during 1996–2000 are used for each country included in these calculations.

contrast, middle-income countries with higher-than-median growth rates had higher remittances, presumably because remittances tend to behave more like investment flows in these countries (table 1.4).

As one would expect, remittance flows are affected by the economic cycles of the source countries. An upturn in the source country increases the income earned by migrant workers. It also attracts more migrants looking for better incomes.[6] For example, remittance payments from the United States surged in tandem with strong economic growth in the mid-1990s. Led by the information technology sector, the

TABLE 1.4 REMITTANCES AS A PERCENTAGE OF GDP, 1996–2000
percent

	Poor countries	Other developing countries
Higher-than-median growth rate	3.4	1.0
Lower-than-median growth rate	4.3	0.8

Sources: Author's calculation based on IMF *Balance of Payments Statistics Yearbook;* World Bank staff estimates; World Bank *World Development Indicators* and World Bank *Global Development Finance,* various years. Poor countries are defined as in World Bank 2002a.

boom caused the United States to revise its immigration policies to enable companies to hire more technology workers from abroad.[7] Remittance payments from Saudi Arabia rose during the oil boom years of the 1970s and early 1980s but declined in the mid-1980s as oil prices fell, the budget deficit mounted, and the government put limits on hiring foreign workers.[8]

Remittances may remain stable even during economic downturns in developed countries. The fiscal systems of most developed countries have automatic stabilizers that offer some income protection to migrant workers during economic downturns. Taylor (2000) found that public income transfer schemes in the United States resulted in increased remittances to Mexico. Other things being equal, immigrant households that received Social Security or unemployment insurance were 10 percent to 15 percent more likely to remit; their monthly remittances abroad (especially to Mexico) were US$150 to US$200 higher than those of immigrant households not receiving public transfers. Another reason for relative stability of remittances in the face of economic downturns in source countries may be that if migrant workers are forced to return to their home country, they might bring back their entire savings (which show up as migrants' transfers in the balance of payments statistics). This may have been the case in India during the Gulf War of 1990, which forced a large number of Indian workers in the Gulf to return home—without lowering remittances to India (figure 1.11).

FIGURE 1.11 INDIA'S REMITTANCE RECEIPTS
(BILLIONS OF DOLLARS)

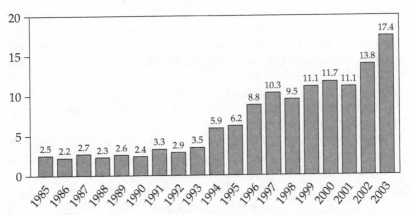

Sources: Author's calculation based on IMF *Balance of Payments Statistics;* World Bank staff estimates; *World Development Indicators* and *Global Development Finance*, various years.

ECONOMIC EFFECTS OF REMITTANCES

Remittances augment the recipients' incomes and increase their country's foreign exchange reserves. If remittances are invested, they contribute to output growth; if they are consumed, they generate positive multiplier effects. Thus, remittances offset some of the output losses that a developing country may suffer from emigration of its highly skilled workers.[9] Adelman and Taylor (1990) found that for every dollar Mexico received from migrants working abroad, its GNP increased by US$2.69 to US$3.17, depending on whether remittances were received by urban or rural households.[10] Remittances also more than offset the loss of tax revenue in most developing countries. For example, the net fiscal loss associated with Indian emigration to the United States was estimated at 0.24 percent to 0.58 percent of Indian GDP in 2001 (Desai, Kapur, and McHale 2001a), but remittances amounted to at least 2.1 percent of GDP in the same year. In the case of unskilled workers who emigrate to escape unemployment, remittances are likely to prove an even clearer net gain to the developing country.

Inward remittances are believed to have a positive impact on savings and investment. Household surveys in Pakistan indicated that in the late 1980s and early 1990s, the marginal propensity to save was higher (0.711) for income from international remittances than for domestic urban-to-rural remittances (0.490) or rental income (0.085) (Adams 2003 and 1998). Furthermore, such transfers provide the hard currency required for importing scarce inputs that are not available domestically. Remittances may serve as insurance policies against risks associated with new production activities (Taylor 1999). Some studies estimate that remittances from the United States are responsible for almost one-fifth of the capital invested in microenterprises in urban Mexico (Woodruff and Zenteno 2001).[11] Similarly, in Egypt, a large proportion of returning migrants in the late 1980s set up their own enterprises using funds brought back from abroad,[12] thereby creating "good" jobs (McCormick and Wahba 2003). Lucas (1987) estimated that in five Sub-Saharan African countries, emigration (to work in South African mines) reduced labor supply and crop production in the short run, but in the long run enhanced crop productivity and cattle accumulation through invested remittances.

The evidence about the impact of remittances on income inequality is mixed. Remittances augment incomes and can lift people out of poverty. Some studies argue that remittances may have had an equalizing effect on the distribution of income among socioeconomic groups in Mexico (Taylor 1999; Adelman and Taylor 1990). However, remittances may also raise inequality because rich workers are better able to pay the high fixed costs associated with international travel.[13] Indeed, household survey data from Pakistan reveal that the share of income originating from external remittances rose with the income groups—the group with the highest income received the highest share of income from external remittances (see table 1.5). Such patterns may be reinforced where remittances are exempted from tax.

Remittances do not necessarily go to countries with poor income distribution, however. During 1996–2000, remittances were nearly twice as high (1.5 percent of GDP) in countries that had relatively even income distribution (represented by the Gini index[14]) than in other countries (0.9 percent of GDP). Some studies argue that remittances increase urban-rural inequality, because they tend to finance investments in real estate or in enterprises in urban areas. McCormick and Wahba (2003) found that returning migrants in Egypt in 1988 tended to set up enterprises in greater Cairo; however, this may have been due to distortions in the economy that discouraged investments in rural areas.

STRENGTHENING THE INFRASTRUCTURE SUPPORTING REMITTANCES

Despite the clear welfare benefits of remittances, weaknesses in the financial sector and in government administration impose substantial transaction costs on migrant workers who send them. Easing such constraints could increase remittance receipts, while bringing a larger share of remittance payments into the formal financial system. Anecdotal evidence suggests that inefficiencies in the banking system—long delays in check clearance, exchange losses, or improper disclosure of transactions costs[15]—deter inward remittances.

The average cost of transferring remittances is in the range of 9.5 percent—and in some cases not detailed here exceeds 20 percent (figure 1.12). These charges, astronomical in comparison with the costs of bank

TABLE 1.5 INCOME FROM EXTERNAL REMITTANCES IN PAKISTAN BY INCOME GROUP, 1986–87 AND 1990–91

Quintile income group	Average per capita income (1986 constant rupees, 5-year average)	Percentage of per capita income from external remittances
Lowest	1,176	1.0
Second	1,721	1.7
Third	2,200	4.8
Fourth	2,876	7.2
Highest	5,261	13.8

Source: Adams (1998), based on a survey of 469 Pakistani households in 1986–87 and 1990–91.

FIGURE 1.12 AVERAGE TRANSFER FEE AND EXCHANGE RATE
COMMISSION FOR SENDING US$200, FEBRUARY 2002

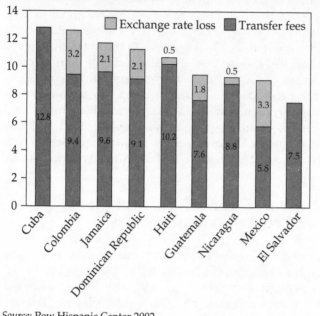

Source: Pew Hispanic Center 2002.

transfers among industrial economies, are largely due to the fixed cost of wire transfers combined with the fact that the average remittance transaction tends to be small, usually less than US$200. Bringing transactions costs down to below 10 percent would imply an annual savings of US$3.5 billion to overseas workers. No doubt a substantial portion of the savings would be remitted.

Improved banking sector technology could substantially reduce transactions costs by expediting check clearance, reducing exchange losses, and improving disclosure, especially in rural areas. One promising approach is to establish partnerships between leading banks and the government post office network in countries that do not have banks with extensive rural branch networks. Remittance activities may also be attractive for banks, as margins can be high.

Banks in many developing countries have not shown much interest in workers' remittances in the past, presumably because of cumbersome paperwork and lack of widespread branch networks. This is beginning to change, however. International efforts to crack down on money laundering and terrorist financing have affected remittances through the informal networks, and a large number of workers are looking for formal banking channels through which to remit funds. These developments, and the high margins associated with the business, have attracted some new entrants. For example, the International Remittance network (IRnet) has started offering a fund transfer service that links credit union cooperatives (such as of unionized agricultural workers) with Citibank branches in the United States and in receiving countries such as El Salvador, Guatemala, and Mexico. Reportedly, the cost of remittance through this new network is only US$6.50 per transaction, significantly lower than the costs of using informal networks.

Industrial countries should consider facilitating efforts to reduce the transactions costs of remittances to developing countries. The United States and Mexico already are collaborating to provide better financial services to Mexican migrants (including illegal immigrants), an effort that promises to significantly improve the migrants' access to and use of banking services, especially for wiring funds to families back home. Such policies—including measures to improve disclosure[16] in fund transfers—are likely also to benefit the source country (by generating more tax revenues) as well as banks (by generating fees for fund transfers and other banking services).

Recent surveys of migrants in Los Angeles and New York show that migrants are discouraged from opening bank accounts because of minimum balance requirements—and, to a lesser extent, by stringent identification requirements. When these obstacles are eased—for example, by accepting as valid forms of identification special documents issued by Mexican consulates (*matrículas consulares*) or the IRS individual taxpayer identification number (ITIN)[17]—immigrants can become the source of substantial banking business over and above wire transfers (box 1.2). In recent years, financial fairs have been held to promote remittances and encourage migrant workers to use the formal banking system (box 1.3).

FACILITATING INTERNATIONAL LABOR MOBILITY

Facilitating labor mobility between source and destination countries is perhaps the most crucial—and controversial—means of increasing remittance flows to developing countries. Even though world migration pressures have risen, the progress of globalization has been slower in the area of migration (Hatton and Williamson 2002; World Bank 2002b) than in trade (Findlay and O'Rourke 2002) and capital flows (Obstfeld and Taylor 2002).

The main concerns of developed countries regarding immigration center on

- local workers' fear of competition from migrants;
- the fiscal burden that may fall on native taxpayers for providing health and Social Security benefits to migrants;

Box 1.2 MEXICAN *Matrículas Consulares*
        BOOST REMITTANCES

For many decades, Mexican consulates have been issuing an identity card known as the matrícula consular to Mexican citizens living in the United States—legally or illegally. According to a study by the Pew Hispanic Center, 740,000 matrículas were issued in the United States during the first nine months of 2002. Designed originally to help police identify people involved in accidents, matrículas are increasingly recognized as proof of identity when opening accounts at U.S. banks. Some 66 banks (and 801 police departments in 13 U.S. states) now accept the matrícula as a valid identification document. According to a *New York Times* report, since November 2001 when the matrícula was first accepted, Mexicans had used them to open bank accounts with over US$50 million in deposits.

Several Central American governments are also considering such cards, which would help their migrant population obtain bank accounts and use banks to transfer funds cheaply and transparently. Guatemala has recently begun issuing a consular identification card to its 600,000 citizens in the United States. The Wells Fargo bank accepts the cards as proof of identity from people seeking to open an account.

Source: Pew Hispanic Center 2002.

- fears of erosion of cultural identity and problems of assimilation of immigrants;
- national security (especially after September 11, 2001).

On the first issue, increased labor supply due to immigration is widely thought to depress wages or raise the unemployment rate. Empirical evidence on this point is inconclusive, however, as researchers have been unable to isolate the effects of immigration from those of other factors such as differences (between local workers and migrants) in skills, sex, age, and professional education and experience obtained abroad (Coppel, Dumont, and Visco 2001). The dynamic nature of the problem has made it more difficult to assess the effects of migration on labor supply. For example, local workers may move to another location, and this may show up as lower employment in their original location, but it would be hard to attribute this fall in employment rate to immigration (see Borjas, Freeman, and Katz 1997; Borjas 1994). Some studies that distinguish between short- and long-term impact find that, while unemployment may increase in the short run in response to immigration, in the long run the overall rate falls permanently (Gross 1999). The effects of immigration on wages are found to have been negative, as expected, but small. Borjas, Freeman, and Katz

---

BOX 1.3 FINANCIAL FAIRS PROMOTE GOOD BANKING HABITS

Developing countries wishing to raise remittances from the United States can benefit from the experiences of the innovative "festivals of finances" that took place in Kansas City and Chicago in August 2002. Recognizing that migrant workers are a potential source of remittances, tax payments, and savings, the Community Affairs Office of the U.S. Federal Deposit Insurance Corporation staged the fairs in collaboration with the Mexican consulate, the Internal Revenue Service (IRS), and six private banks.

At the fairs, the Mexican consulate issued identification papers (matrículas) with photo and U.S. address to undocumented migrant workers from Mexico. The IRS collected back taxes from these workers and issued individual taxpayer identification numbers (ITINs) on the spot, sparing everyone the 6–8 weeks' wait. The tax payments entitled workers who were becoming legal residents to claim earned income tax credits—good for an average tax refund of about US$1,700 per year—once their papers were processed. The banks accepted the matrículas and ITIN as identification from migrants wishing to open bank accounts. Already legalized workers were able to receive earned income tax credit on the spot; some deposited their tax refunds in their newly opened bank accounts. The first fair attracted more than 400 migrant workers, and 96 new bank accounts were opened that day.

The documentation requirement for opening new accounts (according to section 326 of the USA Patriot Act) allows other forms of identification such as passports or even voter registration cards. Some financial institutions (for example, U.S. Bank, Kansas City and Second Federal Savings, Chicago) have started accepting voter registration cards as valid identification documents.

Source: U.S. Federal Deposit Insurance Corporation.

(1997) found that the 21 percent increase in the number of unskilled migrant workers in the United States during 1975–95 reduced the wage earnings of unskilled local workers by up to 5 percent (see also World Bank 2002b).

Although the potential adverse effect of immigration on unemployment and wages receives a lot of attention, immigration also generates many positive effects. First, migrant workers may relieve labor shortages in areas in which native workers do not want to work and where there are no substitutes to human labor (for example, caring for the elderly). Migration may thus increase productivity and moderate inflation, as was the case in the United States (especially in the technology sector) in the 1990s. Second, migrant workers tend to be more responsive to labor-market conditions than local workers; thus, migration may help soften labor-market rigidities and improve productivity

(Coppel, Dumont, and Visco 2001). Third, the multiplier effects generated by migrants' spending in the host countries should not be underestimated. Finally, the competition that less-skilled local workers in developed countries face from migrant workers is the same as the challenge posed to such workers by imports of labor-intensive goods from developing countries (Winters 2002).

On the question of whether immigrants are a net drain on the fiscal system in industrial countries, there is little disagreement among researchers and policy makers that skilled immigrants pay more in taxes than what they receive in Social Security from the state. Even in the case of unskilled immigrants, the fiscal costs, if any, are limited to the first generation; it is believed that the next generation earns and contributes more in taxes than the corresponding generation of native workers (Borjas 1994). Such costs are obviously reduced if migrant workers do not stay in the host country until they are eligible to receive Social Security. Some policy makers have suggested greater use of temporary unskilled workers (as in the Mexican guest workers proposal of U.S. Senator Phil Gramm).[18] However, enforcement of such revolving door policies may prove extremely difficult (Mattoo 2002).

The social costs of immigration, including cultural fears, crime, and national security, are not quantifiable and will continue to act as brakes against attempts to liberalize immigration laws in developed countries. However, the rising migration trend is unlikely to be reversed, because these costs have to be traded off against the benefits of letting in more immigrants at the margin (Winters 2002).

Considering the huge income gap between the rich and the poor countries, most economists and developing country policy makers see large benefits in greater international mobility of labor. Winters (2002) estimates that world welfare would increase by more than US$150 billion per year if developed countries were to increase their quotas of international temporary workers to 3 percent of their workforces.[19]

For developing countries, the benefits of migration—and its costs—are more obvious. Countries benefit from workers' remittances and from the rise in real wages (especially for unskilled and unemployed workers) that often occurs as emigration clears the labor market. On the negative side, the emigration of highly skilled workers has been linked to skill shortages, reductions in output, and tax shortfalls in many developing countries. Such burdens appear even heavier for countries whose educated workers emigrated in large numbers after receiving highly subsidized technical education. Carrington and Detragiache (1998) estimate that over one-third of individuals with tertiary education from Africa, the Caribbean, and Central America emigrated to the United States and Organisation for Economic Co-operation and Development (OECD) countries. Migration rates are also high in Iran, the Philippines, the Republic of Korea, Taiwan, and

Turkey. The International Organization for Migration estimates that for 40 percent of African countries, more than 35 percent of college graduates reside abroad (IOM 1999). Desai, Kapur, and McHale (2001b) discuss the emigration of a significant share of India's information technology professionals to the United States in late 1990s—these authors estimate that forgone income tax revenues associated with Indian-born residents of the United States amount to one-third of current Indian income tax receipts.

The negative effects of the emigration of highly skilled individuals are offset to some extent by inward remittances from migrant workers. Source developing countries may also benefit from network effects (that is, business contacts, investments, technological help, and so on) from their skilled and successful emigrants abroad (Desai, Kapur, and McHale 2001b). It is also debatable whether the skilled workers, had they not emigrated, would have been employed to their full potential given the imperfect work environment in many developing countries.[20] Finally, many skilled workers return to their home countries when the investment climate and work environment improve.

FROM CONTROLLING TO MANAGING MIGRATION

Bhagwati (2003) believes that developed countries should shift the focus of their immigration policies from control to management. The goal of such a shift would be to glean the shared benefits of greater international labor mobility while avoiding the undesirable effects of immigration quotas—chief among them the suffering of those trying to cross borders illegally and the abuse of illegal immigrants. For their part, developing countries could benefit by adopting a "diaspora approach" in dealing with the emigration of skilled workers, exploiting their potential as a source of capital, remittances, and other transfers; building networks for trade, tourism, investment promotion, and training youngsters at home; and otherwise harnessing migrants' knowledge, skills, and assets for economic development.[21] At the very least, developing countries could remove the hurdles that their nationals face in undertaking overseas travel.[22]

Immigration policies in developed countries are so complex that making a direct investment in a developing country is often less cumbersome than bringing in workers to a developed country (Mattoo 2002). To improve transparency in immigration policies, Bhagwati (2003) proposes a World Migration Organization that would codify immigration policies and spread best practices. Rodrik (2001) similarly proposes "multilateralizing" immigration rules so that two countries participating in a special arrangement to share workers would not generate adverse spillover effects on other countries.

One positive, albeit limited, step in this direction is the so-called Mode 4 of supplying services under consideration in the current round of the General Agreement on Trade in Services (GATS). The agreement proposes greater freedom for the "temporary movement of individual service suppliers."[23] Although little progress was made when this issue was first negotiated in the Uruguay Round, World Trade Organization (WTO) member countries now seem more willing to negotiate. However, the Mode 4 trade proposal is presently limited in scope to managers, executives, and professionals; thus, countries that are not significant foreign investors and those with unskilled workers are not going to benefit much from progress in the current negotiations.

PROSPECTS FOR REMITTANCE FLOWS TO DEVELOPING COUNTRIES

Remittance flows have shown remarkable stability over the last decade, and the rising trend evident in recent years is likely to continue, particularly remittance flows from nonresident or temporary workers. The search for lower costs is driving multinational corporations to hire overseas workers for cross-border jobs. This trend toward more mobility of temporary workers may be reinforced if progress is made on Mode 4 trade in services in the GATS negotiations. Improvements in transportation and communications will complement this trend.

Migration pressure is likely to continue to rise in the foreseeable future.[24] The most important factor in the rise is perhaps the aging of the population—and the implied surge in pension costs—in the developed nations (see, for example, United Nations 2000). Because skilled workers pay more taxes and need less support from state Social Security systems, future changes to immigration policies are likely to favor permanent skilled and temporary unskilled migrants (Desai, Kapur, and McHale 2001a).

In addition to differential changes in dependency ratios, Hatton and Williamson (2002) identify three historical economic determinants of world migration:

- Wide wage gaps between developed and developing countries
- High but falling costs of migration relative to the low incomes in developing countries
- The size of existing migrant stocks in receiving countries (which affects the extent of influx of friends and relatives).

In 1994, some 3.6 million persons were on the waiting list for admission to the United States (Hatton and Williamson 2002; Smith and Edmonston 1997). About 1 million people enter the United States legally and about 500,000 illegally each year; the numbers are similar, or perhaps a bit higher, in Europe.[25] Immigration to many Asian countries (Malaysia, the Republic of Korea, Taiwan [China], and Thailand) also surged in the 1990s. The number of asylum seekers grew as well—according to statistics from the United Nations High Commissioner for Refugees, there were 923,000 asylum applications worldwide in 2001, with about an additional 940,800 awaiting decision.

As the demand for migration has risen, so have payments to human traffickers (table 1.6). Fees range from US$200 to US$400 along the Mexico–Los Angeles route to US$35,000 between China and New York (table 1.6).

The fees paid to *coyotes*, professional people-smugglers along the U.S.-Mexico border, have doubled, tripled, or even quadrupled, depending on the services offered and the entry corridor (Cornelius 2001). Although this increase is due in part to stricter border enforcement (the budget of the U.S. Immigration and Naturalization Service for the 2002 fiscal year was US$5.5 billion, more than triple what it was in 1993; the size of the Border Patrol has more than doubled in size since 1993), it is also due to rising demand for migration.

Economic growth in some parts of the developing world, for example, East Asia and South Asia, may imply less migration pressure from these regions, but not from Africa. (The only factor that may moderate migration from Africa is the epidemic of HIV/AIDS.) South-South migration is likely to increase faster than South-North migration, as many quickly growing, newly industrial countries in the South are expected to attract more migrants than the industrial countries (Hatton and Williamson 2002). The induction of Central and Eastern European Countries (CEECs)

TABLE 1.6 PAYMENTS TO TRAFFICKERS FOR SELECTED
MIGRATION ROUTES

Migration route	U.S. dollars per person
Kurdistan–Germany	3,000
China–Europe	10,000 to 15,000
China–New York	35,000
Pakistan or India–United States	25,000
Arab states–United Arab Emirates	2,000 to 3,000
North Africa–Spain	2,000 to 3,500
Iraq–Europe	4,100 to 5,000
Middle East–United States	1,000 to 15,000
Mexico–Los Angeles	200 to 400
Philippines–Malaysia or Indonesia	3,500

Source: "Migrant Trafficking and Human Smuggling in Europe," International Organization for Migration, 2000 (as reproduced in *The Economist* 2002b).

into the European Union (EU) is also likely to increase migration from these countries into the older EU member states, with movements of temporary workers being almost certain to surge.[26]

However, in the next five to ten years, the positive outlook for remittance flows to developing countries is moderated by the sluggish labor markets in G-7 economies and tighter scrutiny of international travelers following September 11. These factors affect the overall value of remittance flows to developing countries; they also are likely to change the geographical composition of remittance flows. Given the geopolitical risks of war and conflict, developing countries in South Asia and the Middle East and North Africa that supply workers to countries such as Saudi Arabia and Kuwait are likely to experience declines in remittance flows. Increased migration from CEECs after the EU enlargement may crowd out migration from other countries. These declines are, however, likely to be dominated by the positive effects on remittance flows of greater labor mobility and progress in the GATS negotiations—depending on how quickly G-7 economies emerge from the economic downturn.

ANNEX 1A. SOURCES OF REMITTANCE DATA

In this study, workers' remittances are defined as the sum of two components: workers' remittances recorded under the heading "current transfers" in the current account of the balance of payments; and compensation of employees, which includes wages, salaries, and other benefits of border, seasonal, and other nonresident workers (such as local staff of embassies). Compensation of employees is recorded under the "income" subcategory of the current account. The main source of data for these items is the IMF's *Balance of Payments Statistics Yearbook* (item codes 2391 and 2310).

This broader definition of remittances is believed to capture the extent of workers' remittances better than the data reported under the heading of workers' remittances alone. In the Philippines, for example, remittances from overseas Filipino workers through the banking system are largely recorded under compensation of employees (which, strictly speaking, should include only remittances by temporary workers). In 2000, compensation of employees amounted to more than US$6 billion, whereas workers' remittances were just US$125 million. In contrast, in India, most remittances reported by authorized dealers are captured under workers' remittances (more than US$9 billion in 2000), while the compensation-of-employees figure (US$126 million in 2000) is known to be underestimated. In Turkey, workers' remittances exclude other current transfer credits such as "imports with waiver," that is, imports financed from the earnings of Turkish nationals living abroad; this item needs to be added to remittances.[27]

The above definition does not include transfers through informal channels—such as hand-carries by friends or family members or in-kind remittances of jewelry, clothes, and other consumer goods. These are believed to be significant in many countries, ranging from 10 percent to 50 percent of total remittances, but often are not recorded in the official statistics (Puri and Ritzema 1999). If and when they are recorded, it is not clear to what extent they reflect actual transfers rather than imports. For example, in recent years India has started recording as imports gold brought in by incoming international passengers, placing a contra item in the private transfers. Thus, data for private transfers in recent years show a slight decline, even though nothing substantial has changed.

The unrecorded portion of remittances may be heading down due to better technology and efforts to crack down on money laundering. These changes make it difficult to interpret current trends. For example, in the first nine months of 2002, remittances to Mexico were up 9.9 percent over the previous year—how much of this rise reflects better reporting and how much a rise in underlying activity is difficult to tell. More extreme is the case of Pakistan, which recorded a whopping US$2.4 billion in remittance receipts in fiscal year 2002, more than double the US$1.1 billion recorded a year earlier (table 1A.1). According to the State Bank of Pakistan (2002), the turning point was the international crackdown on informal money transfer businesses (especially in the United States and the United Kingdom after September 11, 2001); the other reason might have been the waning attraction of foreign exchange due to the appreciating value of the Pakistani rupee.

The definition does not include "other current transfers," either, which often reflect workers' remittances. This item, large in both Turkey and India, should be included in workers' remittances.

Remittances are supposed to be current transactions that do not involve transfers of ownership of assets. In practice, however, it may be

TABLE 1A.1 WORKERS' REMITTANCE INFLOWS TO PAKISTAN, 1999–2002 (MILLIONS OF U.S. DOLLARS)

Remittances	FY99	FY00	FY01	FY02
Total	1,060	984	1,087	2,389
From the United States	82	80	135	779
From the United Kingdom	74	73	81	152

Source: State Bank of Pakistan 2001, 2002.

difficult to identify or estimate such transactions. For example, remittances can be masked as capital inflows to take advantage of tax and other incentives. In many countries, nonresident deposits, although classified under the capital account, may in part reflect workers' remittances. For example, the nonresident rupee deposits in India are most likely remittances disguised as deposits—upon maturity, they do not return to the nonresident depositor, because the rupee is not convertible into hard currency.

As with most of the items in the global balance of payments, the estimates of remittances suffer from the fact that inflows and outflows reported by countries do not match. World inflows of remittances totaled US$111 billion in 2001—more than 7 percent higher than recorded outward flows (US$103 billion).

NOTES

1. Workers' remittances are known to be underestimated significantly in the IMF balance-of-payments statistics. If "other current transfers"—which cover food, clothing, consumer goods, medical supplies, gifts, dowries, payments from unfunded pension plans from nongovernmental organizations, and other categories—were also included, remittance receipts would amount to nearly US$150 billion in 2004. (See IMF's *Balance of Payments Manual*). A frequent practice in the literature is to include migrants' transfers in remittance receipts. Annex 1A discusses data issues relating to remittances.

2. One reason remittance flows data are not disaggregated by source or destination countries is that the financial institutions that act as intermediaries often report funds as originating in the most immediate source country. For example, the Philippines tends to attribute a large part of its remittance receipts to the United States because many non-U.S. banks route their fund transfers through the United States. Hsu (2002) estimated that over half (54 percent) of the remittances of the top 10 developing country recipients originated in the United States. Orozco (2002) suggests that more than 90 percent of remittance flows to Latin American countries originate in the United States. Harrison, Britton, and Swanson (2004) present one of the first attempts to estimate bilateral remittance flows.

3. For example, remittances rose sharply when countries allowed residents to hold onshore foreign currency deposits. Private transfers to Uganda increased from US$80 million in 1991 to US$415 million in 1996 in response to measures that permitted residents to open foreign currency accounts onshore (Kasekende 2000). In October 2002, Uganda's foreign exchange accounts deposits were 27.8 percent of all deposits.

4. Defined as notes and coins in circulation plus noninterest bearing bank deposits plus other retail deposits with banks and building societies.

5. See also Russell (1992, p. 277), Meyers (1998), and Elbadawi and Rocha (1992). El-Sakka and McNabb (1999) found that inflation had a positive and

significant impact on inflow of remittances, probably reflecting the need to boost family support in times of rising prices.

6. Swamy (1981) argues that the economic situation in the host country is the main determinant of the size of remittance flows to developing countries.

7. See Clark, Hatton, and Williamson (2002) and World Bank (2002b) for a description of changes in U.S. immigration rules and U.S. immigration trends. The increase in remittance flows to developing countries coincided with an increase in the migrant population in developed countries. Estimates suggest that migrant stocks in developed countries increased from 3.1 percent in 1965 to 4.5 percent in 1990 (Hatton and Williamson 2002); in all likelihood this trend continued through the 1990s.

8. Remittances intended for investment purposes may decline when the source country's economy is strong and rates of return are high. El-Sakka and McNabb (1999) found that remittance inflows to Egypt were lower when rates of return were higher in Arab source countries during 1967–91.

9. It is worth noting that the same skilled workers could be significantly less productive in a developing country (where the unemployment rate is higher and investment climate worse) than in an industrial country. See also Nayyar (1994).

10. Rural households tend to consume more domestically produced goods—and hence generate larger multiplier effects—than urban households.

11. Some governments are trying to encourage the use of remittances for investment purposes. For example, government agencies in Zacatecas in northern Mexico, give three U.S. dollars for every U.S. dollar contributed by migrants' associations for investment projects (*The Economist* 2002a).

12. The funds brought back by return migrants are reported as migrants' transfers in the balance of payments. Unfortunately, very few countries report such funds as a separate item. Presumably a large part of this item is already included in remittance receipts. The aggregate migrants' transfers to developing countries as reported in the IMF's balance of payments statistics were less than US$1.5 billion in 2000.

13. Adams (1993) found from Egyptian household survey data collected in the second half of the 1980s that the relationship between migration and income had an inverted U-shape, suggesting that middle-income individuals were migrating. The very poor do not migrate because they cannot pay the costs associated with international travel, while the very rich do not want to migrate. After adding land to income, he dismissed this view and concluded that it was the very poor who migrated because they had the most to gain (and they were able to meet travel costs by selling land).

14. Measures the extent to which the distribution of income among individuals or households within a country deviates from a perfectly equal distribution.

15. A survey by the Pew Hispanic Center (sponsored by the Multilateral Investment Fund of the Inter-American Development Bank) of 302 Latin American-born adults residing in Los Angeles and Miami found that remitters were troubled by the high cost of transferring funds due to flat fees and unfavorable exchange rates. Other concerns included delays in money being delivered to

the recipient. The survey revealed that nearly 83 percent of those interviewed sent money through international money transfer companies such as Western Union or Moneygram, and only 9 percent through banks (Pew Hispanic Center 2002). The Bank of Mexico (1997) estimated that in 1995, 40 percent of remittances came in through money orders, 24 percent through wire transfers, 27 percent through other electronic means, and 8 percent through cash transfers. Lozano-Ascencio (1998), using surveys of migrants themselves, estimates that 15 percent of remittances enter Mexico as pocket transfers.

16. In 2001, the United States proposed to amend the Electronic Fund Transfer Act, requiring financial institutions and money transmitters initiating an international money transfer to prominently disclose the exchange rate used in the transaction, as well as the exchange rate prevailing at a major financial center of the foreign country as of the close of business on the previous business day; all commissions and fees charged; and the exact amount of foreign currency to be received by the customer in the foreign country (see www.ncua. gov, H.R. 1306-Wire Transfer Services).

17. An ITIN is required to open interest bearing accounts in U.S. banks. Without an ITIN, only checking accounts that do not pay interest can be opened.

18. Senator Gramm proposed that Mexican "guest workers" be hired on an annual or seasonal basis. A 15.3 percent payroll tax on their employers would pay for the worker's emergency medical care and an individual retirement account, which the worker could withdraw at the time of departure back to Mexico. See http://migration.ucdavis.edu/rmn/archive_rmn/oct_2001-10rmn.html. Similar proposals to make Social Security benefits portable, to encourage return migration, are being debated in Europe as well.

19. See also Rodrik's comments at the Conference on Immigration Policy and the Welfare State, Trieste, June 23, 2001.

20. Nayyar (1994) argues that the magnitude of emigration from India is small compared to the substantial reservoir of unemployed among the educated, and thus the macroeconomic impact is perhaps negligible.

21. Some authors argue that developing countries should try to tax their migrant workers abroad by basing their tax laws on nationality (as do the United States, the Philippines, and Eritrea) rather than residence. See Desai, Kapur, and McHale (2001a); Bhagwati (2003).

22. Such hurdles may include restrictions on or delays in issuance of passports, access to foreign exchange to undertake the initial travel, or simply lack of communication infrastructure that slows down job searches or results in delays in finalizing job contracts. Political instability often disrupts international migration. For example, the number of Mozambican workers in South African mines dropped by half before and after Mozambique's independence from Portugal in 1975. To some extent, this drop reflected mistrust of "leftist" workers by South African mine owners, but to a large extent it was also a result of disruptions in passport issuance by Mozambican authorities (Lucas 1987).

23. See Mattoo 2002 for a detailed discussion of various aspects of this issue. The other three modes of GATS are "cross-border supply" (that is, trade in

goods), consumption abroad (for example, tourism or study abroad), and commercial presence (for example, supplying services through a branch abroad).

24. The industrial countries may respond to rising migration pressure by relaxing immigration laws, in particular, by encouraging more temporary migration (akin to the U.S. H-1B visa).

25. According to recent survey of migration by *The Economist* (2002b).

26. A seven year delay before CEEC workers are allowed to work in the older member states has been proposed, similar to the "transitional period" arranged for Spain and Portugal when they entered in 1985. Several studies estimate that migration from these countries into the EU would rise to about 2-3 percent of the population of the sending country (Boeri and Brucker 2000), but others (Borjas 1999; Drinkwater 2003) estimate smaller numbers. There appears to be a consensus, however, that temporary movement of workers from these countries will increase significantly.

27. One of the techniques devised to cope with the deteriorating external imbalance was a form of foreign borrowing known as the "convertible Turkish Lira deposit" or "Dresdner Bank" scheme. The program, dating from the late 1960s, was designed to attract the savings of Turkish nationals working in foreign countries, as well as cash deposits that might have been earned through black market trade, smuggling, or fraudulent invoicing of imports and exports. According to the scheme, the Central Bank of Turkey offered interest rates on foreign exchange deposited in Turkish commercial banks 1.75 percentage points above the Euromarket rate while also guaranteeing the foreign exchange value of both principal and interest. Beginning in 1975, the program was broadened to allow nonresidents in general, not only Turkish nationals working abroad, to hold these deposits. Foreign exchange receipts from this source were transferred from commercial banks to the Turkish central bank and on-lent to government and state enterprises, with expansionary effects on the money supply. Inflation accelerated markedly (still with a fixed exchange rate), worsening the underlying disequilibrium in the external sector. Because the Dresdner deposits constituted short-term foreign loans, the maturity of Turkey's external indebtedness shortened steadily as the decade progressed, despite earlier rescheduling intended to spread out debt servicing over time. The scheme was withdrawn for a few years, but reintroduced in February 2001. At the end of 2001, such deposits by Turks living in Europe amounted to US$10 billion. See Barth and Hemphill (2000).

REFERENCES

Adams, Richard H., Jr. 1993. "The Economic and Demographic Determinants of International Migration in Rural Egypt." *Journal of Development Studies* 30(1): 146–67.

———. 1998. "Remittances, Investment, and Rural Asset Accumulation in Pakistan." *Economic Development and Cultural Change*, 47(1): 155–73.

———. 2003. "International Migration, Remittances, and Brain Drain: A Study of 24 Labor Exporting Countries." Policy Research Working Paper 3069, World Bank, Washington, DC.

Adelman, Irma, and J. Edward Taylor. 1990. "Is Structural Adjustment with a Human Face Possible? The Case of Mexico." *Journal of Development Studies* 26(3): 387–407.

Bank of Mexico. 1997. *The Mexican Economy: Dirección de Organismos y Acuerdos Internacionales.* Bank of Mexico: Mexico City.

Barth, Richard, and William Hemphill. 2000. *Financial Programming and Policy: The Case of Turkey.* International Monetary Fund, Washington, DC.

Bhagwati, Jagdish. 2003. "Borders Beyond Control." *Foreign Affairs* 82(1): 98–104.

Boeri, T., and H. Brucker. 2000. "The Impact of Eastern Enlargement on Employment and Wages in the EU Member States." Report to the European Commission. Brussels.

Borjas, George J., ed. 1994. "The Economics of Immigration." *Journal of Economic Literature* 32(4): 1667–1717.

———. 1999. "Economic Research on the Determinants of Immigration: Lessons for the European Union." Technical Paper 438, World Bank, Washington, DC.

———. 2000. *Issues in the Economics of Immigration.* Chicago, IL: University of Chicago Press.

Borjas, George J., R.B. Freeman, and L. F. Katz. 1997. "How Much Do Immigration and Trade Affect Labor Market Outcomes?" *Brookings Papers on Economic Activity* 1: 1-90.

Carrington, William, and Enrica Detragiache. 1998. "How Big Is the Brain Drain?" Working Paper WP/98/102, International Monetary Fund, Washington, DC.

Clark, Ximena, Timothy J. Hatton, and Jeffrey G. Williamson. 2002. "Where Do U.S. Immigrants Come From, and Why?" NBER Working Paper 8998, National Bureau of Economic Research, Cambridge, MA. www.nber.org/papers/w8998.

Coppel, Jonathan, Jean-Christophe Dumont, and Ignazio Visco. 2001. "Trends in Immigration and Economic Consequences." OECD Economics Department Working Paper 284. Paris. www.oecd.org.

Cornelius, Wayne A. 2001. "Death at the Border: Efficacy and Unintended Consequences of U.S. Immigration Control Policy." *Population and Development Review* 27(4): 661–85.

Desai, Mihir A., Devesh Kapur, and John McHale. 2001a. "Sharing the Spoils: Taxing International Human Capital Flows." *International Tax and Public Finance* 11(5): 663–693.

———. 2001b. "The Fiscal Impact of the Brain Drain: Indian Emigration to the U.S." Paper presented to the third annual NBER-NCAER conference, December 17–18, Harvard University, Cambridge, MA.

Drinkwater, Stephen. 2003. "Go West? Assessing the Willingness to Move from Central and Eastern European Countries." Department of Economics, University of Surrey, UK.

Economist. 2002a. "Emigration from Latin America." February 21.

Economist. 2002b. "The Longest Journey: A Survey of Migration." November 2.

Elbadawi, I. A., and R. Rocha. 1992. "Determinants of Expatriate Workers' Remittances in North Africa and Europe." Policy Research Working Paper WPS 1038, World Bank, Washington, DC.

El-Sakka, M. I. T., and Robert McNabb. 1999. "The Macroeconomic Determinants of Emigrant Remittances." *World Development* 27(8): 1493–1502.

Findlay, R., and K. H. O'Rourke. 2002. "Commodity Market Integration 1500–2000." In *Globalization in Historical Perspective,* ed. M. Bordo, A.M. Taylor, and J. G. Williamson. Chicago, IL: University of Chicago Press.

Gross, D. M. 1999. "Three Million Foreigners, Three Million Unemployed? Immigration and the French Labor Market." IMF Working Paper WP/99/124, International Monetary Fund, Washington, DC.

Harrison, Anne, Tolani Britton, and Annika Swanson. 2004. "Working Abroad—the Benefits Flowing from Nationals Working in Other Countries." Paris: OECD.

Hatton, Timothy J., and Jeffrey G. Williamson. 2002. "What Fundamentals Drive World Migration?" NBER Working Paper 9159, National Bureau of Economic Research, Cambridge, MA.

Hsu, Jeffrey. 2002. "Immigrant Remittances." Wilson College, Princeton University, Princeton, NJ.

IMF (International Monetary Fund). various years. *Balance of Payments Statistics Yearbook.*Washington, DC: IMF.

———. 1993. *Balance of Payments Manual.* Washington, DC: IMF.

International Organization for Migration (IOM). 1999. "Return of Qualified African Nationals Programme." Fact Sheet. July. Sub-Regional Office for Central & East Africa, Nairobi, Kenya.

———. 2000. "Migrant Trafficking and Human Smuggling in Europe," International Organization for Migration (as reproduced in *The Economist,* "The Longest Journey: A Survey of Migration," November 2, 2002.)

Jasso, Guillerma, Mark R. Rosenzweig, and James P. Smith. 2000. "The Changing Skill of New Immigrants to the United States: Recent Trends and Their Determinants." In *Issues in the Economics of Immigration,* ed. G. J. Borjas, 185–226. Chicago, IL: National Bureau of Economic Research.

Kamemera, David, Victor I. Oguledo, and Bobby Davis. 2000. "A Gravity Model Analysis of International Migration to North America." *Applied Economics* 32(13): 1745–55.

Kasekende, Louis A. 2000. "Capital Account Liberalization: The Ugandan Experience." Paper presented at the Overseas Development Institute, London, June 21.

Ketkar, Suhas, and Dilip Ratha. 2001. "Development Financing During a Crisis: Securitization of Future Receivables." Policy Research Working Paper 2582, World Bank, Washington, DC.

Latin Finance. 2002. "Mergers & Acquisitions: Betting Big on Mexico." February. Available at LatinFinance.com.

Lozano-Ascencio, Fernando. 1998. "Las Remesas de los Migrantes Mexicanos en Estados Unidos: Estimaciones para 1995." In *Migration Between Mexico and the United States: Binational Study, Volume 3, Research Reports and Background Materials.* Mexico City: Mexican Ministry of Foreign Affairs.

Lucas, Robert E. B. 1987. "Emigration to South Africa's Mines." *American Economic Review* 77(3): 313–29.

Maldonado, Andres, and Alejandra Robledo. 2002. "Sending Money Back Home." *McKinsey Quarterly* 4: 24–26.

Mattoo, Aaditya. 2002. "Introduction and Overview." In *Moving People to Deliver Services: Labor Mobility and the WTO,* ed. Aaditya Mattoo and Antonia Carzaniga, 1–20. New York and Oxford: Oxford University Press.

McCormick, Barry, and Jackline Wahba. 2003. "Return Migration and Geographical Inequality: The Case of Egypt." *Journal of African Economies* 12(4): 500–32.

Meyers, Deborah Waller. 1998. "Migrant Remittances to Latin America: Reviewing the Literature." Tomás Rivera Policy Institute, University of Southern California, and Inter-American Dialogue, Washington, DC. www.thedialogue.org/publications/meyers.html.

Nayyar, Deepak. 1994. *Migration, Remittances, and Capital Flows: The Indian Experience.* Delhi: Oxford University Press.

Obstfeld, M., and A. M. Taylor. 2002. "Globalization and Capital Markets." In *Globalization in Historical Perspective,* ed. M. Bordo, A. M. Taylor, and J. G. Williamson. Chicago, IL: University of Chicago Press.

Orozco, M. 2002. Statement to U.S. Senate Committee on Banking, Housing, and Urban Affairs. Oversight Hearing on "Accounting and Investor Protection Issues Raised by Enron and Other Public Companies." February 28. http://banking.senate.gov/02_02hrg/022802/orozco.htm.

Pew Hispanic Center. 2002. "Billions in Motion: Latino Immigrants, Remittances, and Banking." Presentation by the Pew Hispanic Center and Bendixen and Associates at a seminar organized by the Multilateral Investment Fund, Inter-American Development Bank, November 22.

Puri, Shivani, and Tineke Ritzema. 1999. "Migrant Worker Remittances, Micro-Finance, and the Informal Economy: Prospects and Issues." Working Paper 21, International Labour Organization, Social Finance Unit, Geneva.

Rodrik, Dani. 2001. "Comments at the Conference on Immigration Policy and the Welfare State." Paper delivered at the Third European Conference on Immigration Policy and the Welfare State, Trieste, June 23.

Russell, Sharon Stanton. 1992. "Migrant Remittances and Development." *International Migration* 30(3/4): 267–87.

Smith, J. P., and B. Edmonston. 1997. *The New Americans: Economic, Demographic, and Fiscal Effects of Immigration*. Washington, DC: National Academy Press.

State Bank of Pakistan. 2001. *Annual Report*. Karachi.

———. 2002. *Annual Report*. Karachi.

Swamy, Gurushri. 1981. "International Migrant Workers' Remittances: Issues and Prospects." Staff Working Paper 481. World Bank, Washington, DC.

Taylor, J. Edward. 1999. "The New Economics of Labor Migration and the Role of Remittances." *International Migration* 37(1): 63–86.

———. 2000. "Do Government Programs Crowd-in Remittances?" Tomás Rivera Policy Institute, University of Southern California, and Inter-American Dialogue, Washington, DC. www.thedialogue.org/publications/taylor.html.

United Nations. 2000. "Replacement Migration: Is It a Solution to Declining and Aging Populations?" Report no. ESA/P/WP 160, Department of Economic and Social Affairs, Population Division, New York.

Winters, Alan. 2002. "The Economic Implications of Liberalising Mode 4 Trade." In *Moving People to Deliver Services: Labor Mobility and the WTO*, ed. Aaditya Mattoo and Antonia Carzaniga, 59–92. New York and Oxford: Oxford University Press.

Woodruff, Christopher, and Rene Zenteno. 2001. "Remittances and Microenterprises in Mexico." UCSD Graduate School of International Relations and Pacific Studies Working Paper, University of California, San Diego.

World Bank. various years. *Global Development Finance*. Washington, DC: World Bank.

———. 2002a. *Global Development Finance: 2002: Financing the Poorest Countries*. Washington, DC: World Bank.

———. 2002b. *Globalization, Growth, and Poverty*. Policy Research Report. Washington, DC: World Bank.

———. 2003. *Global Economic Prospects and the Developing Countries 2003— Investing to Unlock Global Opportunities*. Washington, DC: World Bank.

World Bank. various years. *World Development Indicators*. Washington, DC: World Bank.

Yang, Philip Q. 1995. *Post-1995 Immigration to the United States*. Westport, CT: Praeger.

Chapter 2
Migrant Remittances in Africa:
A Regional Perspective

Cerstin Sander and Samuel Munzele Maimbo

U ntil recently, migrant remittances to developing countries were over-shadowed by other financial flows such as foreign direct investment (FDI) and official development assistance (ODA).[1] This picture is changing as the scope and relevance of remittances becomes recognized:

- Migrant remittances have grown rapidly and are now the second largest source of external flows to developing countries—ahead of ODA but still well behind FDI. Remittance flows to developing countries were 41 percent of FDI and 260 percent of ODA in 2001 (Ratha 2003).
- Migration to developed countries from the developing world continues to increase (Whitwell 2002).
- Remittance transfer services are under greater scrutiny because of heightened concerns about money laundering and terrorist financing since the attacks in the United States in September 2001.

Development agencies, including the World Bank, are increasingly recognizing the importance of migrant remittances and are focusing on how remittances contribute to development (Ammassari and Black 2001; Doorn 2002; El-Sakka and McNabb 1999; MIF 2003; Widgren and Martin 2002). This chapter focuses on what we know about remittances and their role in Africa—especially Sub-Saharan Africa—and on how the related financial infrastructure helps or impedes remittance flows.

Africa has a long history of domestic and intraregional migrant remittances. Since colonial times, when heads of rural households migrated to urban centers to earn wages to pay colonial taxes, workers have been remitting funds to their families. Migration and remittances have continued, primarily for economic reasons. In South Africa the mines, and in West and East Africa the cotton and tea fields, have long attracted workers from the surrounding region. In Zambia, men trekked to the copper mines on the copper belt or to southern Rhodesia (now Zimbabwe) to work on settler farms. The Zambian Tonga name for the monies they sent back was *mali a mbeleko* (money of the workers).[2] Similar indigenous terms exist in other parts of the continent. In Uganda, for example, the term "Kyeyo money"[3] is widely used to refer to money from the Ugandan diaspora.

In *Across Boundaries*, Mamphela Ramphele (1995) recalls how, in the 1940s, mine workers' remittances reached the intended households—a practice that may still be in use in some remote villages today:

I developed some understanding of the remittance patterns of several households because my father handled the village mail as one of his responsibilities as school principal. The mail arrived twice a week on the railway bus, which passed through Kranspoort on its

54

way to and from Alldays, farther west along the foot of the Sout-pansberg. The mailbag had to be fetched at about 10:30 am by one of the school boys and brought to the school for sorting. The post was then distributed at the end of school assembly when names of recipients of letters were called out, and their children or neigh-bors' children collected and delivered them. Registered letters were treated differently. Once notified, children were asked to alert their parents or neighbors, who had to come personally and sign for the registered items. The same applied to parcels. It was clearly a system based on trust, but sensibly tempered with safe-guards. (Ramphele 1995, p. 24)

Despite this long history of remittances, Africa has received the least attention—perhaps because Africa receives a relatively small share (15 percent) of total migrant remittances to developing countries. Surpris-ingly, all of Sub-Saharan Africa accounts for just 5 percent of the total flow (Sander 2003). Africa's inability to attract attention may also be the result of relatively high levels of domestic and intraregional migration and thus, as compared with other developing regions, fewer overseas migrants and a greater dispersion of African emigrants—especially those from Sub-Saharan Africa.

As this chapter highlights, remittances to Africa represent an important financial flow that has significant development impact. Moreover, actual flows are substantially higher than official data indi-cate, because many remittances remain unrecorded or unreported—partly a result of weak financial systems and services in much of Africa. Combined with financial policy and regulatory issues, this environment creates obstacles for the efficient transfer of remittances through formal money transfer services. It also limits the potential for remittances to make greater contributions to development—through investment, for example.

After first reviewing remittance volumes to Africa, especially Sub-Saharan Africa, compared with other developing countries, the chapter highlights migration patterns and trends that drive remittances. Using this as a backdrop, we examine the development impact of remittances, asking who receives remittances, how they are used, and what their macroeconomic effects are. Because money transfer services are a pri-mary means for sending remittances, a summary follows of remittance channels and of user preferences among the available financial services. This summary is complemented by an assessment of related financial sector policies and regulations and their effects on both the accessibility of money transfer services and the availability of options for investing remittances. The analysis identifies obstacles within the financial infra-structure and regulatory framework that impede remittance flows and thus their potential contributions to development. We conclude with research and policy recommendations.

REMITTANCE FLOWS TO AFRICA

Globally, migrant remittances to developing countries in nominal terms stood at US$80 billion in 2002, having more than doubled over the previous decade (from US$33.1 billion in 1991).[4] In contrast, remittances to Africa have grown little and declined in relative share.[5] In 2002, Africa received about US$12 billion in remittances, around 15 percent of global flows (figures 2.1 and 2.2). Split regionally, Sub-Saharan Africa received US$4 billion or 5 percent of the total, whereas the Middle East and North Africa combined received US$14 billion or 18 percent; North Africa alone accounted for about 10 percent (figures 2.3 and 2.4). In 2003, Sub-Saharan Africa received US$6 billion (5 percent of total global remittances) and the Middle East and North Africa US$16 billion (13 percent of total global remittances).

Remittance flows to Africa appear relatively small compared with flows to other developing regions; they are, however, heavily underreported, due partly to data gaps for African countries in international remittance statistics and partly to the high prevalence of informal remittance flows. Two factors contribute to the high level of informal flows: strong intraregional migration and weak financial infrastructure. Underreporting and unreported flows are particularly common in Africa.

The data used to illustrate these remittance trends is from the IMF's annual *Balance of Payment Statistics Yearbook* (IMF various years). Yet, however useful, the IMF data paint an incomplete picture because they lack information on approximately one-third of developing and transition countries (Gammeltoft 2002), the quality of reporting is inconsistent, and informal transfers are not included.

The impact of weak or absent financial systems, high rates of intraregional migration, and frequent physical transport of remittance monies suggest that informal remittances in Africa constitute a much higher share than typically found elsewhere in the developing world. Globally, estimates of migrant remittances to developing countries, including unreported international flows, run as high as US$200 billion—2.5 times higher than recorded flows (Sanders 2003). In Sudan, for instance, informal remittances were estimated to account for 85 percent of total remittance receipts (Puri and Ritzema 1999).

The strong and consistent flow of remittances to Northern Africa reflects patterns of regional migration to Europe and the Middle East. Of the total remittances to Africa over the past decade, 75 percent were received in North Africa, 13 percent in East Africa, and less than

FIGURE 2.1 REMITTANCES TO DEVELOPING COUNTRIES, 1970 TO 2001

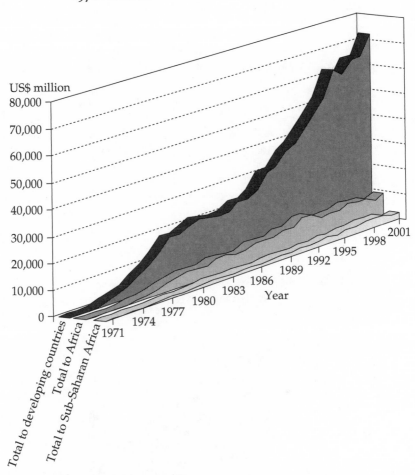

Source: Based on data from Ratha 2003.

10 percent each in Southern and West Africa (7 percent and 5 percent, respectively). Central Africa received less than 1 percent of the total remittances (figures 2.3 and 2.4).

Certain countries are clear frontrunners as either recipients or sources of remittance flows—their rungs on the remittance ladder reflecting in large part migration patterns. In 2001, the top five remittance-receiving countries in Africa were Morocco, the Arab Republic of Egypt, Tunisia, Sudan, and Uganda, in that order. Morocco and Egypt were the only African countries among the global top 20 remittance

FIGURE 2.2 TOTAL REMITTANCES TO AFRICA, 1990 TO 2001

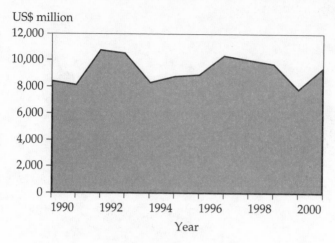

Source: Based on data from Ratha 2003.

FIGURE 2.3 REMITTANCES BY REGION, 1990 TO 2001
(PERCENTAGE SHARE OF TOTAL REMITTANCES TO AFRICA)

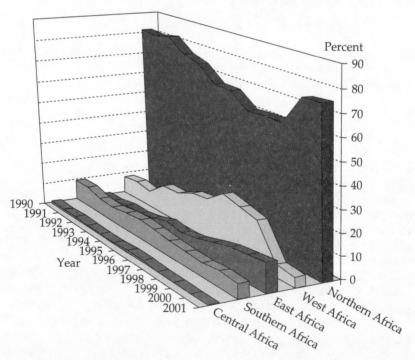

Source: Based on data from Ratha 2003.

FIGURE 2.4 REGIONAL DISTRIBUTION OF REMITTANCES
TO AFRICA, 2001

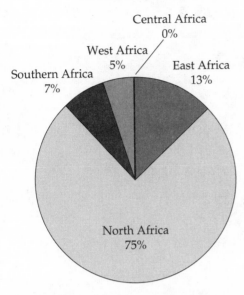

Source: Based on data from Ratha 2003.

recipients, occupying positions four and five, respectively.[6] Over the last decade, the single largest recipient in Sub-Saharan Africa was Nigeria,[7] followed by Lesotho, Sudan, Senegal, and Mauritius (figure 2.5).

MIGRATION AND REMITTANCES IN AFRICA

Remittances are inherently linked to migration. To devise policies that facilitate remittance flows and their developmental contributions, it is important to understand migration patterns and how migrants send and use remittances. As African migration has risen, one might expect to see a dramatic increase in remittance monies flowing to the continent, as has been the case in other regions with growing migration. Yet, the official remittance data for Africa do not show a rapid and proportional rise in remittances. The disparity is probably reflected in growth of unrecorded remittances—composed of uncaptured formal flows and flows through informal transfer channels.

While migration is not statistically correlated with remittances (see, for example, Buch, Kuckulenz, and Le Manchec 2002), it is the underlying reason for remittances. No direct correlation exists because each migrant or migrant group behaves differently when it comes to sending

FIGURE 2.5 TOP 15 REMITTANCE RECIPIENT COUNTRIES IN
SUB-SAHARAN AFRICA, 1990 TO 2001

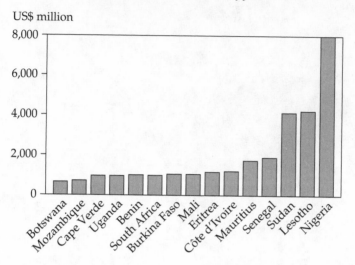

Source: Based on data from Ratha 2003.

Note: Annualized cumulative average, 1990–2001.

remittances; remittance patterns also change over the period of a migrant's absence from his or her home country. For instance, whereas some diaspora groups continue to remit into second and further generations, in other groups remittances decrease or stop after long absences from their country of origin, even among the original first generation migrants. The motives for migration, the choice of destinations, and the purposes and means for sending money home are important factors in understanding remittances, all of which should inform policy makers and providers of money transfer services.

Similar to the pattern in other developing regions, migration from Africa to the developed world is predominantly a strategy to reduce economic and political insecurities and to improve the livelihood of the migrant and the family left behind. The prime motivator for most African migrants is still economic, although war or political insecurity are increasingly more compelling and frequent factors prompting emigration. Refugees—many of whom are displaced to neighboring countries, especially to the Horn of Africa and parts of West Africa—are thus a key group of African migrants (IOM 2003, 2002; Whitwell 2002).

The major host countries in Africa are Côte d'Ivoire, Gabon, Botswana, and South Africa. Elsewhere, the principal host countries

are France, Italy, Saudi Arabia, and the United States. The main originating countries of immigrants are Mali, Burkina Faso, and Lesotho.

Migrant flows differ markedly between North Africa and Sub-Saharan
Africa. North Africans have tended to move overseas, mainly to Europe,
the Middle East, and, to a lesser extent, North America. In contrast, Sub-
Saharan African migrants have tended to stay on the continent, moving
intraregionally or domestically.[8] Their overseas destinations are mostly in
Western Europe, although even there the share of African migrants is relatively low, accounting for only 5 percent of the total migrant population
of the Organisation for Economic Co-operation and Development
(OECD) countries in 2002 (OECD 2002).

African migration patterns, long viewed as much more complex and
less consistent than those in Asia and Latin America, are undergoing
important transformations.[9] Key aspects of these transformations
include the following:

- Outmigration from Africa to developed countries has increased,
  even from Sub-Saharan Africa—a departure from the previously
  strong intraregional movements.
- More low-skilled laborers now migrate overseas—a migrant
  group that previously migrated largely on the continent.
- Intraregional migration of high-skilled professionals is increasing as
  professional opportunities improve in South Africa and elsewhere.
- Refugee flows are swelling due to renewed war and civil strife, as
  recently occurred in Côte d'Ivoire.
- Increasing numbers of women are migrating—a trend observed in
  other developing regions for some time but only recently in Africa.

Many of the top African remittance recipient and source countries
reflect these migration patterns—with some exceptions. Allocations of
remittance flows may be distorted due to the typically much higher
value of international remittance receipts per emigrant as compared
with intraregional or domestic remittances. Thus, the volume of remittance flows to a country with high overall emigration may still be
lower than those to a country with emigration that is lower but primarily to regions where economic activity and earning opportunities are
greater, usually off the continent. Moreover, the levels of remittances
tend to differ by migrant group and by factors such as the migrant's
intent and duration of stay. Another distortion is that refugee and
remittance flows do not readily match: refugees living overseas often
send money to family members who have found refuge in countries
neighboring their home countries or they send to a neighboring country when money transfer systems in the home country are unavailable
or unreliable.[10]

DEVELOPMENTAL EFFECTS OF REMITTANCES

Because remittances to Africa are highly underreported, their developmental effects are underestimated. Nonetheless, even the officially recorded flows suggest their developmental power and potential. Remittances constitute a major source of foreign exchange and influence the national balance of payments, often quite significantly. They also represent a substantial share of the gross domestic product (GDP) in many countries, often surpassing other significant financial sources—a surprisingly powerful macroeconomic outcome to attribute to simple fund transfers intended primarily to support families. For receivers, remittances are a vital source of income, with a crucial income-smoothing effect. Although remittances are mostly spent on consumption and household needs—including education and health—a small portion is invested in property, businesses, savings, or community capital. Altogether, remittances contribute to building human and social capital as well as capital assets.

Macroeconomic Effects

In macroeconomic terms, remittances constitute an important financial flow to Africa. Their economic effect is pronounced and significant, although the volume and relative share of remittances compared to other financial flows is smaller in Africa than in other developing regions. The significance of remittances also tends to be overshadowed because Africa—especially Sub-Saharan Africa—is statistically the most aid-dependent of all developing regions. ODA accounts for about one-half of all financial inflows to Africa, compared to a global average for developing countries of about one-tenth.[11]

Based strictly on officially recorded receipts, however, remittances represented 1.3 percent of GDP for Sub-Saharan Africa and 2.2 percent of GDP for the Middle East and North Africa in 2002. This closely mirrors the average developing-country ratio of remittances to GDP of 1.3 percent and even 2.5 percent ratio for South Asia, the highest of any region.

For individual countries, the ratio of remittances to GDP is much more pronounced. For instance, Lesotho in the 1990s received remittances from Basotho mine workers in South Africa that accounted for as much as 67 percent of GDP (IOM 2000). In other countries, foreign exchange reserves depend heavily on remittances. Somalia receives an estimated US$500 million annually from remittances,[12] four times the value of the main export, livestock (Ahmed 2000, cited in Ammassari and Black 2001). In 1998, Ghana's remittances constituted the fourth largest source of foreign exchange after cocoa, gold, and tourism (Schoorl and others 2000; Anarfi, Awusabo-Asare, and

Nsowah-Nuamah 2000). For many countries, remittances contribute substantially to the balance of payments. Remittances to Eritrea were 194 percent of exports and 19 percent of GDP in 1999; these same values in Cape Verde were 51 percent and 12 percent; in Comoros, 24 percent and 6 percent; in Egypt, 26 percent and 4 percent; and in Morocco, 18 percent and 5 percent (Rapoport and Docquier 2001).

Microeconomic Effects

Aggregate figures mask the significance of remittances for individual recipients and tell us little about how they are used and what benefits they bring. Case studies and survey findings, however, highlight the importance of remittances to recipient households.

Typically, remittances are income transfers from relatively richer to relatively poorer individuals and constitute a family welfare system that smoothes consumption, alleviates liquidity constraints, and provides a form of mutual insurance. Most remittances reach family members—especially spouses or parents—and many recipient households are headed by women.[13] Individual international transactions are typically about US$200 and are often received on a monthly basis.[14]

Remittances are used primarily for consumption and investment in human capital (education, health, better nutrition).[15] Investment in land, livestock, and housing is also relatively common but secondary to satisfying daily needs and meeting expenses related to human capital. Still less remittance money is used for investments in either savings[16] or in business, or to repay debt, such as a loan for the expenses of going abroad. Insecurity in the migrant's situation tends to be a main motivator for investment; the home-country context affects the type of investment made.[17]

The high proportion of funds used for general consumption is congruent with the idea of migration and remittances as part of migrants' strategies for reducing poverty and improving the quality of life of the migrants and their families. Consumption supported by remittances contributes to improved standards of living and educational opportunities. In Zimbabwe, for example, households with migrants were found to have less cultivated land than households without migrants, but slightly higher education levels (de Haan 2000).[18] In Burkina Faso, it was estimated that international remittances reduced the headcount of rural households in poverty by about 7 percent and of urban households in poverty by about 3 percent (Lachaud 1999).

Also important, and often more so than international flows, are urban-to-rural remittances, which are common in many parts of Africa. Although not captured in any remittance statistics, many more people benefit from domestic than from international remittances. Estimates suggest that this flow could contribute as much as three-quarters of nonfarm earnings in areas close to major cities and one-fifth of nonfarm earnings for more remote areas (de Haan 2000).

Communal Effects

While remittances are typically transfers between individuals or families, some migrants participate in diaspora, community, or church groups in their host countries that send collective remittances to the home communities. Often these remittances are collected through fundraising events and are applied to a range of investments, including building or renovating schools or churches.

Among African immigrants, the spectrum of community groups is wide. It includes associations, cultural or church groups, refugee groups, ethnic professional groups (for example, the Society of Black Lawyers), and even virtual groups that use the Internet as their organizing platform (Somali Forum, for one) (AFFORD 2000). Among the best documented examples are Malian and Senegalese groups in France that finance communal projects.[19] Other examples include Ghanaian migrants who participate in ethnic- and town-based associations. In the 1980s and early 1990s, for instance, some health institutions in Ghana survived on donations from such associations.[20] Some of these associations also assist in the transfer of individual remittances to help mitigate weak financial systems.

These developmental effects, macroeconomic and microeconomic, stem from migrants' private transfers of funds. An individual migrant's choices of whether and how much to remit, through what channel, and for what use are typically shaped by factors such as the economic and political stability or volatility in the home country, and by its policies on foreign exchange and taxation.[21] Remittance flows and investments are also shaped and impeded by weak financial infrastructures. The developmental effects of remittances depend on their continued flow and on the availability of investment opportunities, both of which depend, in turn, on financial services and infrastructure that are convenient and reliable for migrants and the recipients of their remittances.

FINANCIAL INFRASTRUCTURE FOR REMITTANCES

In much of Africa, the financial infrastructure is weak, and services reach few rural and low-income people—among the main recipients of remittances. Remittances through informal channels bridge gaps left by formal financial services,

A weak financial infrastructure impedes the efficient transfer of remittances through formal channels and limits the potential of remittances to spur development through investment. Given the high internal and intraregional emigration from Africa's rural and underdeveloped areas, many African migrants use informal channels because they lack access to viable formal financial services or because informal means are viewed as more efficient, familiar, trustworthy, or inexpensive. Access to reliable financial services at the sending and receiving ends is needed to increase fund transfer volumes. Access to ancillary financial services, such as savings instruments, is essential to facilitate investment of remittances.

Formal and Informal Remittance Channels

Remittances to and within Africa are transferred by both formal and informal means.[22] Both financial and nonfinancial providers offer services similar to those available in other parts of the developing world.

Formal channels include regulated money transfers through banks, foreign exchange bureaus, and dedicated money transfer operators (MTOs). Best known among the latter are Western Union and Money-Gram. Other services can be found in domestic or intraregional markets where bus, coach, or courier companies offer money transfer or transport services[23] as part of their regular service.

Informal systems of remittance transfers are common in Africa, as in other regions, such as Asia or the Middle East.[24] Often, money is carried from place to place by individuals, family and friends, or taxi and bus drivers. Other informal systems tend to be modeled on the hawala or *hundi* service networks or are single-destination services provided by individual business people.[25] The similarities between the informal systems in use in Africa, Asia, and the Middle East are probably due in part to longstanding trade and migration links.[26] Both the Indian diaspora and Somali refugee communities in East Africa, for instance, have long used such systems.[27]

Generally, the use of formal channels is higher in relatively robust and more liberalized economies with strong financial sectors. In Kenya, for example, bank transfer services are used more than in Tanzania and Uganda for domestic and intraregional money transfers, including remittances, because Kenya has a relatively well developed banking industry (Sander 2004). Informal channels tend to be used where the financial infrastructure is either absent (as in conflict or postconflict countries such as Somalia), weak, or distrusted (due to bankruptcies or other factors). Similarly, foreign exchange controls tend to lead to a higher use of informal channels. Conversely, in Uganda, the liberalization of the financial market—particularly of foreign exchange trade—and the legal use of foreign denominated accounts are said to have increased remittances through formal channels (see, for instance, Kasekende 2000 cited in Ratha 2003).[28] Failures of weak or distrusted banks and inefficiencies in the formal transfer system have resulted in unmet demand for reliable fund transfer options, a demand satisfied in part by informal services and increasingly by MTOs such as Western Union.

Access to Financial Services and the
Choice of Remittance Transfer Channels

A migrant's choice of remittance channels is influenced by many factors, including foreign exchange fluctuations and controls in the home country. Preferences for services can also vary by ethnic group or nationality. Some groups, such as Somalis, are said to have strong communal codes of trust that underlie and support active informal and familial remittance arrangements. Others lack this trust and prefer to use formal financial services whenever available. An observed loss of trust in informal arrangements may be an important trend in Africa that could affect user preferences for remittance services.[29]

A key factor in the choice of remittance services everywhere is accessibility. The concept of accessibility encompasses a person's awareness of a service as well its proximity and reliability. Subjective factors of familiarity and trust in a service can also play an important role, such as a preference for a service whose staff speak their language or share their cultural values. Such factors are often just as or more important than service cost.

Ready access at both the sending and receiving ends is another deciding factor in the choice of transfer services; lack of outreach of services, especially into rural areas, poses a great barrier. Many migrants need to send money to locations with weak or no financial infrastructure and from host-country financial institutions with little or no business history with the points of receipt. While African capitals and other urban centers offer fairly good access to money transfer services, rural regions tend to be much less well serviced because many formal remittance services do not have the requisite systems or outreach. For instance, only banks that are part of the Society for Worldwide Interbank Financial Telecommunication (SWIFT)[30] interbank transfer system or a similar system can receive international transfers. This limitation excludes many postal banks that may not be licensed to deal in foreign exchange (for instance in Kenya, Kenya Post Office Savings Bank can receive transfers but only as an agent of Western Union). Similarly, card-based systems with automated teller machines (ATMs) are expanding, but often these are not yet integrated into interbank networks and tend to be limited to urban centers.[31] Such constraints are costly to the sender and to the receiver.[32]

Post offices—prime service providers as far as access or outreach are concerned—are not as highly used as they could be because clients in many receiving countries view their services as inefficient and unfriendly. Clients in East Africa, for instance, report regular incidents of insufficient cash on hand or other delays in receiving funds. At the same time, in countries where post offices do operate effectively, such as Senegal or many parts of South Africa, post office money orders are a preferred option, especially for domestic remitters. However, not all post offices in South Africa can offer money orders because of the risk of robberies and related costs (Sander 2004; Sander and others 2003; Cross 2003; Nagarajan 2002; Sander, Millinga, and Mukwana 2001). A study of Sahelian[33] migrants sending remittances home from France, for instance, found that more than one-third sent remittances by hand, another third through post offices, and only 6 percent use banks (Russell-Stanton, Jacobsen, and Deane 1990).

Among the choices in formal financial services, MTOs are the most popular in many countries. Some migrant groups prefer MTOs to informal services due to their reliability and speed. Since its introduction in Senegal in 1995, Western Union has become a much-used service, although postal money orders remain a popular option in certain regions of the country (Sander and others 2003).

Filling the gap left by the traditional banking services, many MTOs and informal services are successful because they work with a market segment of migrants who are located in "micro-markets"—often certain cities or neighborhoods.[34] Informal channels sometimes provide not only efficient and speedy service and coverage in areas that lack banking infrastructure, they also offer innovative remittance methods designed to suit overseas workers' earnings patterns. In some instances this process of innovation has improved service levels and led to the development of new products within the formal sector. In Egypt, for example, several exchange companies now offer door-to-door delivery of money following the example of Philippine banks that successfully introduced and implemented the practice to stave off informal market operators (Buencamino and Gorbunov 2002; Azzam 2002).

Other services have contributed to satisfying demand for informal remittance channels in domestic and regional markets. For instance, in East Africa some courier and overland bus or coach companies provide money transfer or transport services for all kinds of private transfer activities, including migrant remittances (Sander, Millinga, and Mukwana 2001). These companies cover domestic and sometimes intraregional markets but do not extend services for international transfers.

Other international niche-market providers have begun to operate in markets such as Kenya and Senegal. For Kenyan migrants, a U.S.-based Internet service, Watuwetu, offers vouchers that can be redeemed at stores in Kenya; Leppe provides a money transfer service and delivery of staple products and key services to Senegal from France and the United States.[35] These vouchers and services highlight an important point: although remittances are normally monetary, some are in the form of goods (for example, foods and electronics) or services (religious ceremonies and airline tickets).

Although the focus of this chapter is on the financial infrastructure underlying money transfers, the presence of such services implies a demand and thus a desire of migrants to stipulate the use of the money, rather than leaving decisions entirely to recipients. This idea is worth exploring, because it suggests opportunities for diversified financial services linked to remittances, such as single transfer products with multiple payout or payment options, savings, or mortgages. It also underlines once again the migrants' search for alternative channels to overcome the limitations of formal money transfer services.

Regulatory and Policy Issues for Financial Services for Remittances

Regulatory and policy factors affect the availability and accessibility of formal money transfer services and thus the range of remittance-sending channels available to migrants (box 2.1). Because the prevalent money transfer services are limited to a pay-in and pay-out transaction, neither the migrant sending the remittance nor the receiver of the funds typically has easy options to save, invest, or build a cash-flow record that may be used, for instance, to build a financial history and client profile with a bank for a loan assessment.

Money transfer services are not consistently regulated, either in Africa or globally. In most cases regulation is handled by central banks. Regulation of money transfer services is often distributed over two departments in the central bank—bank supervision and foreign trade—especially if the latter oversees the foreign exchange bureaus.

Full commercial banks are generally licensed to deal in foreign exchange under their banking license. The same is not true of many postal banks, which operate under communications acts.

The licensing of dedicated MTOs varies by country. In some countries, only fully licensed banks can provide the service (Norway, for example), while in other countries dedicated licenses exist or have recently been introduced, such as in the United Kingdom in 2002.[36]

In Africa, MTOs such as Western Union often cannot be licensed directly. Instead they must operate as agents of banks and sometimes also through foreign exchange bureaus, although the latter tend to be subagents of bank agents. In either case, permission of the central bank is required (because the banking license requires separate authorization for additional services).

Box 2.1 THE EFFECTS OF REGULATION ON REMITTANCES

Regulatory factors can contribute to attracting, limiting, or deterring migrant remittance flows and their investment.

Factors that hamper the sending of remittances, especially through formal channels, include

- monetary policies, such as foreign exchange restrictions or the channeling of all foreign exchange dealings through the central bank or a state bank;
- financial sector regulations that affect the availability or outreach of financial services; for instance, when regulations require banks to open full branches rather than allowing for less costly service points; or restrictive licensing of MTOs that ties MTO services exclusively to banks.

Factors that hinder investment of remittances include

- restrictions on foreign exchange holdings, such as foreign-exchange-denominated bank accounts;
- denial of repatriation of savings;
- indirect taxation of remittances through exchange rate controls or by withholding portions of remittances;
- a narrow range of available financial investment products;
- administrative obstacles to setting up a business.

Source: Author discussions with regulators.

Central banks are generally more inclined to grant permission to operate money transfer services to a bank than to a foreign exchange bureau, although exceptions exist. The Bank of Uganda's Foreign Trade Department, for example, is generally supportive of granting permission to foreign exchange bureaus, whereas South Africa has stringent foreign exchange rules to protect its reserves and prefers to have only banks dealing in money transfers, particularly following its experience with Western Union and its former in-country agency, Union African Money Transfer, which failed to comply with foreign exchange control regulations. Banking regulations also tend to limit services to urban areas, because requirements to set up full branches in any new location often prove too costly in rural areas.

Overall, the nature and application of money transfer regulations in Africa tend to be conservative compared to some parts of Latin America, where regulations allow for varied points of sale of transfer services, including not only less-than-full bank branches but also services offered through retail businesses such as pharmacies or grocery stores.[37] Such flexibility allows for a broader outreach of money transfer services, although not necessarily better access to ancillary services such as savings or mortgages.

The uptake of innovations and service improvements through the use of new technologies for transfer services, such as mobile phones, may similarly be delayed in much of Africa—experience suggests that these could well receive a conservative assessment by African regulators. Moreover, such services may be limited to financial service providers despite the fact that a much broader outreach could be achieved with nonfinancial agents, such as retail businesses, as points of sale. The recent influence of the Financial Action Task Force (FATF) rules and processes has added weight to conservative views and to the cost of providing services. For example, the cost to service providers of complying with FATF's "know your customer" rule and service providers' tendencies to be too rigorous in regulatory compliance may harm the remittance environment.[38] The rule contributes to highly conservative assessments of licensing or authorization requests and to identification requirements that cannot be met by clients who have no official identification or proof of a physical address—common circumstances in Africa. In sum, the current experience indicates that these factors contribute to access to money transfer services and to broader financial services is becoming more limited for many remittance senders and receivers in Africa, as well as globally.[39]

CONCLUSIONS AND RECOMMENDATIONS

This analysis argues that remittances are an important source of supplemental finance for many African households and that their benefits—improved livelihoods, greater economic security, and increased human, social, and other capital—are indisputable. Remittance flows in Africa are substantial yet highly underreported due to weak data recording mechanisms and high levels of informal flows stemming partly from service gaps in the formal money transfer sector. Informal flows originating from domestic and intraregional migration are also high, but commonly unreported. With such high levels of unrecorded remittances, assessments of the developmental contributions of remittances are also underestimated.

The assessment of remittance uses, transfer channels, related financial infrastructure, and regulatory and policy environments has identified hurdles to remittance flows and their investment. The developmental contributions of remittances are hampered by weak financial systems with substantial limitations in both service outreach and product options. Obstacles embedded in the financial systems and policy environments in host and home countries limit the volume of remittances, divert them into informal channels, and discourage their use for savings and investment.

In all of this it is important to remember that remittances are a highly segmented flow, significant in aggregate terms but on an individual level even more important to the receiver of each relatively small transaction. Because remittances often compensate for the absence or shortage of social and welfare mechanisms, they constitute a developmental contribution that is different than, but indirectly complementary to, public interventions. As such, they should be facilitated. With this in mind, it is important to understand patterns and motivations, such as how remittances are sent and spent. Similarly, the hampering effects of current financial systems and services, as well as their regulations, need to be better understood, reviewed, and ideally reformed to facilitate and attract the transaction of remittances through formal financial services. This will require the dismantling of barriers that hinder the greater outreach of financial services and limit the range of available financial products and services.

The goals of collecting and analyzing data, and of translating findings into actions, could be facilitated by bringing together key stakeholders from policy making and regulatory bodies, financial service providers, and migrant groups to better assess flows, financial systems and services, related technologies, migration patterns, and motivations related to remittances. In the area of policies and regulations specifically, the connections between financial service policies and the volumes and channels of remittances are only partially understood. Regulations directed at MTOs and transfer services in both sending and receiving countries have received scant attention, despite their clear impact on the availability and viability of services. Similarly, the effects of policies and regulations on the availability of financial services and the range of products available and attractive to a low-income clientele requires more attention and, in some cases, reduced regulatory burdens to make them viable. The measures promoted by the FATF are one source of such regulations, as are conservative regulatory perspectives that tend to limit financial services to a narrow band of providers (primarily banks), to the exclusion of newer models of nonbank financial services and innovations in service delivery.

NOTES

1. This paper synthesizes the findings of a wider study conducted for the World Bank on migrant labor remittances in Africa. It is based on a review of existing documentation enriched with selected sources and information from key stakeholders (see Sander and Maimbo 2003). Migrant remittances are monies sent from one individual or household to another. International remittances are sent by migrant workers who have left their home country. Domestic remittances (or national remittances) are sent by migrant workers who left

their home village or town to work elsewhere in their home country. Most remittances are made in the form of cash rather than goods. The broad characterization of remittances as a "financial flow" is used throughout this chapter, although some authors consider remittances a capital flow (for example, Buch, Kuckulenz, and Le Manchec 2002). Workers' and migrants' remittances are used interchangeably in this chapter. Because some of the data used here have been culled from previous analyses, reference points, such as timeframes, change slightly throughout the chapter. To the extent possible, data are matched for consistency.

2. Other indigenous phrases for remittances used in Zambia are *kutumiza ndalama ku malo ya kunja* (sending money to countries outside); *kutimiza ndalama ky vyalu vinyaki* (sending money to other countries); and *ukutuma indalama ku fyalo fya kunse ya calo* (sending money to countries outside the country). Ghanaians in Twi will tell their family that they have sent money home, which literally translates as "I've made you money."

3. Kyeyo means broom in Luganda and other Bantu languages; the term refers to the migrants who, in the early days, often worked in jobs such as sweeping the streets. Today kyeyo refers to all migrants, many of whom are now professionals. Remittance inflows have overtaken export earnings from coffee, Uganda's main export commodity.

4. Data are based on the data set used by Ratha (2003). For 2003, the World Bank reports US$93 billion (World Bank 2003). In analyzing remittance flows, it is helpful to distinguish between cross-border (intraregional or international) and domestic (in-country) flows as well as between officially recorded and unrecorded flows. Most figures on migrant remittance volumes are based on officially recorded flows, meaning flows captured as part of the balance of payment data reported by each country to the International Monetary Fund (IMF). Officially recorded flows consist of the cross-border flows that regulated financial institutions report as part of international transactions to the central banks (IMF *Balance of Payment Statistics Yearbooks*; see also Ratha 2003 and Sander 2003).

5. Total remittance receipts to Africa, in nominal terms, over the past decade peaked in 1992 (US$10.7 billion) and were at their lowest in 2000 (US$7.8 billion). What lies behind such fluctuations or trends is hard to determine without a close analysis of changes that may have occurred in definitions for data collection, financial sector or monetary regulations, or availability of financial services.

6. Egypt was the largest receiver on the continent for the last decade until 2001 (in average nominal terms for the period 1990 to 2001).

7. Nigeria receives between 30 percent and 60 percent of remittances to the region (Orozco 2003).

8. Intraregional migration patterns are reflected in migrant stock data. Africa is home to about 9 percent of global migrants, compared to 6 percent in both Southeast Asia and Latin America and the Caribbean, 23 percent in North America, and 11 percent in Western Europe. Within Africa, Western and Eastern Africa have the largest share of the continents' migrant stock with 42 percent

and 28 percent, respectively (UN 2002; see also NOMRA 1998). South Africa and Côte d'Ivoire, in particular, have traditionally been key destinations for regional migration due to their economic strength, and in South Africa in large part due to the mining industry. As economies have shrunk and the 1999 coup in Côte d'Ivoire created an unsettled period, these patterns have changed. (See, for instance, McDonald 2000, on Southern African migration, and IOM 2003, on Côte d'Ivoire.)

9. Although global migration patterns have changed overall and tend toward growth and greater diversity, for the most part they remain true to trends set since the 1960s. Recent trends are in part due to complexities of labor mobility and migration-related policies. These include geopolitical changes such as the fall of the Iron Curtain and the emergence of "Fortress Europe," as well as aspects of globalization, including greater interdependence and relative ease of travel. See Whitwell 2002, on global and regional migration trends.

10. See also Gammeltoft 2002. In conversation with C. Sander, for instance, a Sudanese migrant mentioned how, due to lack of money transfer services in Sudan, remittances are sent by hand when possible and otherwise have to be picked up in neighboring capitals such as Kampala or Nairobi.

11. The proportion of remittances to total financial flows (public and private) amounted to the highest percentages in parts of North and West Africa. This reflects primarily countries such as Nigeria and Lesotho with ratios of remittances to aid of 7:1 and 4:1, respectively. In contrast, for countries such as Mozambique and Rwanda, remittances constitute only about 3 percent to 5 percent of total international flows (FDI, ODA, and remittances) (Gammeltoft 2002).

12. Another estimate for 2000 puts the figure at US$800 million to US$1 billion (Omer 2002).

13. See also syntheses and discussions such as Buch, Kuckulenz, and Le Manchec 2002; Rapoport and Docquier 2004; and Sander 2003.

14. Ratha (2003) quotes US$200 as a global average transaction value. This estimate is based on extensive research on remittances between the United States and Latin America, whereas remittances to African countries are less well researched. Anecdotally and based on a few case studies, the amount migrants send per transaction typically ranges between US$100 and US$1,000 for international remittances; intraregional and domestic remittances are generally much lower. This is logical, as income levels for migrants in industrial countries tend to be higher than for domestic or intraregional migrants. Regarding lower values for domestic remittance transfers, see Cross (2003) on South Africa, and Sander, Millinga, and Mukwana (2001) on Tanzania and Uganda.

15. See also de Haan 2000. In Ghana, for example, 70 percent of remittances is spent on recurrent expenditures (school fees, health care, and so on). Less than 30 percent is invested in assets such as land, cattle, or construction (Schoorl and others 2000). In Mali, 80 percent to 90 percent is spent on consumption, and there is almost no investment in local business (Martin, Martin, and Weil 2002).

16. Because land, livestock, and buildings are typical ways to invest and save in many migrants' home countries, the distinction is one of saving within the financial system.

17. For instance, investment in land rather than a financial investment if the currency is volatile or inflation is high. Insecurity as the motivator for investment is a point made by AFFORD (2000). Similarly, a study in Egypt in the early 1990s found that remittances were invested primarily in land, on which the economic rates of return were higher than in other areas (El-Sakka 1997).

18. Also see Martin, Martin, and Weil (2002).

19. See Martin, Martin, and Weil 2002 and Dieng 1998. Most documented and profiled, especially in the Anglophone literature, are the Hometown Associations (HTAs) of Latin Americans in the United States. One distinction highlighted between the Latino HTAs in the United States and associations of African migrants in France, such as the Malians, is that the latter often link up with municipalities and nongovernmental organizations, both in the host and home communities (see Grillo and Riccio 2003).

20. See Schoorl and others 2000, on the Ghanaian migrant experience. Similarly, Nigerian migrants make individual or pooled remittances through "home improvement unions" (IOM 2000).

21. See also El-Sakka and McNabb 1999, on macroeconomic determinants of migrant remittances.

22. See, for instance, Genesis 2003; Cross 2003; Sander 2003; and Sander, Millinga, and Mukwana 2001.

23. The distinction is that a transfer service records a financial transaction through a system of accounts and reconciliation, whereas a transport service involves the physical transport of the funds. See Sander, Millinga, and Mukwana 2001, where this distinction is made, and where transport services, such as coaches and courier companies, are described based on market research in Tanzania and Uganda. (See also Kabbucho, Sander, and Mukwana 2003 for Kenya.)

24. For a discussion of such systems see, for instance, El-Qorchi 2002; El-Qorchi, Maimbo, and Wilson 2003; Buencamino and Gorbunov 2002; and Jost and Sandhu 2000.

25. Hawala means "transfer" in Arabic; similar terminology is used in other languages. MTOs sometimes use company names that reflect similar ideas of transfer or gift. For instance, Al-Barakat, the name of a now defunct Somali MTO, means "blessing."

26. Some researchers suggest that the hawala system has followed immigration patterns of Indian migrants spreading to other regions of Asia, the Middle East, Europe, and North and South America (see Buencamino and Gorbunov 2002).

27. Eastleigh, a neighborhood of Nairobi, is known as "Mogadishu" and many money transfers home to Somalia are handled by informal Somali agents with radio or satellite phones but also by registered MTOs. Similarly, homes or businesses of Ghanaians, Ugandans, or of other nationalists living overseas are known addresses among migrants to provide transfer services out of a back

office or living room. (See Omer 2002; Kabbucho, Sander, and Mukwana 2003; and Sander 2003.)

28. Past weaknesses in data collection, however, do not allow for a good assessment. As of 2001, Bank of Uganda reported all residual foreign exchange transactions as workers' remittances. A more refined system in line with balance of payments definitions has been developed and is being tested (conversation with Bank of Uganda staff, February 2003).

29. Several recent studies on microfinance, savings, and money transfer in East Africa, for instance, have recorded a decline in trust in informal systems and also a heightened sense of insecurity due to theft and robberies. See Sander Millinga, and Mukwana 2001. Other information is based on research in East Africa as well as conversations with African diaspora in the United Kingdom. On Somali remittances and systems, see especially Omer (2002).

30. SWIFT is the industry-owned cooperative supplying secure, standardized messaging services and interface software to 7,500 financial institutions in 199 countries, headquartered in Belgium (http://www.swift.com).

31. The limited availability of bank branches and ATMs in rural towns is a big problem in South Africa. In the Eastern Cape, many rural branches had to close in the mid-1990s due to the general economic decline, the rise in violent bank robberies, and the spread of Internet banking among higher income groups—the latter undercut the need for an expensive, risky, local bank structure accessible to the poor. However, where available, ATMs are becoming increasingly popular as a way of getting around banking hours (Cross 2003; Genesis 2003).

32. A study in South Africa, for instance, estimated that as much as 40 percent of the total value of a remittance of 200 rand (approximately US$30) to a rural recipient could go toward banking charges and transport costs (Cross 2003).

33. People from the semiarid region of Africa between the Sahara to the north and the savannas to the south, extending from Senegal, on the west, through Mauritania, Mali, Burkina Faso, Niger, Nigeria, and Sudan, to Ethiopia on the east.

34. For instance, concentrations of Kenyan migrants can be found in Minneapolis in the United States and in Tottenham, north of London. To capture their business, MTOs have to be present in their neighborhoods. Western Union and its Kenyan agent, Kenya Post Office Savings Bank, for example, seek out these communities for marketing visits and events.

35. http://www.watuwetu.com; financial transfers are also available and in the process of being expanded; and http://www.leppe.com; "leppe" means "all" in Woloff, one of the main Senegalese languages. The motto is "le plus du transfer," that is, to offer more than money transfer as migrants need other services. Leppe offers delivery of staple goods, payment of bills, organization of religious ceremonies, and similar services.

36. See Sander 2003, for some examples of licensing provisions.

37. For instance, Brazil's provision for "correspondent banking" outlets.

38. The efforts of the FATF (http://www1.oecd.org/fatf/), working with country regulators around the globe to implement rules to prevent money

laundering and financing of terrorist activities, have had a noticeable effect on the financial industry, including money transfer services. A well documented example is remittances to Somalia and the closure of one of the MTOs, Al-Barakat, in November 2001, which led to crackdowns in neighboring countries, uncertainty, and most probably diversion to informal services (see Omer 2002). FATF's "know your customer rules," which require service providers to identify and document their clients, are costly and difficult to accomplish for many of the poor people who send and receive remittances (Sander 2003; Sander and Maimbo 2003).

39. See Genesis 2003, for South Africa; other comments are based on C. Sander's research in East and South Africa, including conversations with central bank staff members in Kenya and Uganda and examples of recent "service exclusions" in the United Kingdom and the United States.

REFERENCES

AFFORD (African Foundation for Development). 2000. "Globalization and Development: AFFORD's Submission to the UK Government Regarding Its Globalization and Development White Paper." London.

Ahmed, I. 2000. "Remittances and Their Economic Impact in Post-War Somaliland." *Disasters* 24(4): 380–89.

Ammassari, Savina, and Richard Black. 2001. "Harnessing the Potential of Migration and Return to Promote Development: Applying Concepts to West Africa." Sussex Migration Working Paper 3, Centre for Migration Research, University of Sussex, Brighton, UK.

Anarfi, J. K., K. Awusabo-Asare, and N. N. N. Nsowah-Nuamah. 2000. *Push and Pull Factors of International Migration: Country Report Ghana.* Luxembourg: Eurostat.

Azzam, Henry T. 2002. "Hawala: The Poor Man's Private Banking Vehicle Is Under Attack." *Jordan Times,* June 2, 2002. www.jordinvest.com.jo/pdf/weekly_lm.pdf.

Buch, Claudia M., Anja Kuckulenz, and Marie-Helene Le Manchec. 2002. "Worker Remittances and Capital Flows." Working Paper, Kiel Institute of World Economics, Kiel, Germany. www.uni-kiel.de/ifw/pub/kap/2002/kap1130.pdf.

Buencamino, Leonindes, and Sergei Gorbunov. 2002. "Informal Money Transfer Systems: Opportunities and Challenges for Development Finance." DESA Discussion Paper No. 26, Department of Economic and Social Affairs, United Nations, New York. www.un.org/esa/esa02dp26.pdf.

Cross, Catherine. 2003. "Migrant Workers' Remittances and Microfinance in South Africa." Study prepared for the ILO and TEBA Bank. Human Sciences Research Council, Pretoria.

de Haan, Arjan. 2000. "Migrants, Livelihood and Rights: The Relevance of Migration in Development Policies." Social Development Working Paper 4,

Department for International Development, London. www.dfid.gov.uk/pubs/files/sddwp4.pdf.

Dieng, Seydi Ababacar. 1998. "Les pratiques financières des migrants Maliens et Sénégalais en France." *Epargne sans frontières, Techniques financières du développement*, no. 5 (March/April): 7–22.

Doorn, Judith van. 2002. "Globalisation, Remittances, and Development." International Labour Organization (ILO), Social Finance Unit, Geneva.

El-Qorchi, Mohammed. 2002. "Hawala." *Finance and Development* 39(4). www.imf.org/external/pubs/ft/fandd/2002/12/elqorchi.htm.

El-Qorchi, Mohammed, Samuel Maimbo, and John F. Wilson. 2003. "Informal Funds Transfer Systems: An Analysis of the Hawala System." IMF Occasional Paper 222, International Monetary Fund, Washington, DC.

El-Sakka, M. I. T. 1997. "Migration Remittances: Policy Options for Host and Countries of Origin." Department of Economics, Kuwait University. www.cba.edu.kw/elsakka/remitt3.doc.

El-Sakka, M. I. T., and Robert McNabb. 1999. "The Macroeconomic Determinants of Emigrant Remittances." *World Development* 27(8): 1493–1502.

Gammeltoft, Peter. 2002. "Remittances and Other Financial Flows to Developing Countries." Centre for Development Research Working Paper 02.11. Copenhagen. www.cdr.dk/working_papers/wp-02-11.pdf.

Genesis. 2003. "African Families, African Money: Bridging the Money Transfer Divide." Report prepared for FinMark Trust by Genesis Analytics, Johannesburg, South Africa.

Grillo, Ralph, and Bruno Riccio. 2003. "Translocal Development: Italy-Senegal." Paper presented at the International Workshop on Migration and Poverty in West Africa, March 13–14, University of Sussex, Brighton, UK. www.geog.sussex.ac.uk/transrede/workshop/IWMP6.pdf.

IMF (International Monetary Fund). Various years. *Balance of Payments Statistics Yearbook*. Washington, DC.

IOM (International Organization for Migration). 2000. *World Migration Report*. Geneva.

———. 2002. "Migration for Development in Africa (MIDA): Remittances from Migrant Workers from Some ACP Countries." Geneva.

———. 2003. "Facts and Figures on International Migration." *Migration Policy Issues*, No. 2.

Jost, Patrick, and Harjit Singh Sandhu. 2000. "The Hawala Alternative Remittance System and Its Role in Money Laundering." Lyon: Interpol. www.interpol.int/Public/FinancialCrime/MoneyLaundering/Hawala/default.asp.

Kabbucho, Kamau, Cerstin Sander, and Peter Mukwana. 2003. "Passing the Buck—Money Transfer Systems: The Practice and Potential for Products in Kenya." MicroSave-Africa, Nairobi.

Kasekende, Louis A. 2000. "Capital Account Liberalization: The Ugandan Experience." Paper presented at the Overseas Development Institute, June 21, London.

Lachaud, Jean-Pierre. 1999. "Envoi de fonds, inégalité et pauvreté au Burkina Faso." Working paper, Center for Development Economics, University of Bordeaux IV: Bordeaux.

Martin, Philip, Susan Martin, and Patrick Weil. 2002. "Best Practice Options: Mali." Cooperative Efforts to Manage Emigration (CEME), University of California, Davis.

McDonald, David, ed. 2000. *On Borders: Perspectives on Cross-Border Migration in Southern Africa.* Southern African Migration Project/Idasa. Cape Town and New York: St. Martin's Press.

MIF (Multilateral Investment Fund). 2003. "Transitional Communities: International Experiences in Remittances." Inter-American Development Bank, Washington, DC.

Nagarajan, Geetha. 2002. "Going Postal to Deliver Financial Services to Microclients." *ADB Finance for the Poor* 4(1): 5–8.

NOMRA (Network on Migration Research in Africa). 1998. "International Migration and Africa: Trends and Prospects for the 21st Century." Final Report of the Regional Meeting of Experts. Gaborone, Botswana, June 2–5. Paris: UNESCO. unesdoc.unesco.org/images/0011/001185/118566eo.pdf.

OECD (Organisation for Economic Co-operation and Development). 2002. "Trends in International Migration." OECD Annual Report, Paris.

Omer, Abdusalam. 2002. "Supporting Systems and Procedures for the Effective Regulation and Monitoring of Somali Remittance Companies (Hawala)." United Nations Development Programme, Somalia.

Orozco, Manuel. 2003. "Worker Remittances in an International Scope." Inter-American Dialogue Research Series, Washington, DC. www.iadialog. org/publications/country_studies/remittances/worldwde%20remit.pdf.

Puri, Shivani, and Tineke Ritzema. 1999. "Migrant Worker Remittances, Micro-finance, and the Informal Economy: Prospects and Issues." Working Paper 21, Social Finance Unit, ILO, Geneva. www.ilo.org/public/english/ employment/finance/papers/wpap21.htm.

Ramphele, Mamphela. 1995. *Across Boundaries: The Journey of a South African Woman Leader.* New York: Feminist Press at the City University of New York.

Rapoport, Hillel, and Frédéric Docquier. 2004. "The Economics of Migrants' Remittances." In *Handbook on the Economics of Reciprocity, Giving and Altruism,* eds. L. A. Gerard Varet, S. C. Kolm, and J. Mercier Ythier. Amsterdam: North Holland.

Ratha, Dilip. 2003. "Worker's Remittances: An Important and Stable Source of External Development Finance." In *Global Development Finance: Striving for Stability in Development Finance,* 157–75. Washington, DC: World Bank.

Russell-Stanton, Sharon, Karen Jacobsen, and William Stanley Deane. 1990. "International Migration and Development in Sub-Saharan Africa." World Bank Discussion Papers, Africa Technical Department Series 101, World Bank, Washington, DC.

Sander, Cerstin. 2003. "Migrant Remittances to Developing Countries—A Scoping Study: Overview and Introduction to Issues for Pro-Poor Financial Services." Report prepared by Bannock Consulting for Department for International Development, London. www.livelihoods.org/hot_topics/docs/Remitstudy.pdf.

————. 2004. "Passing the Buck in East Africa: The Money Transfer Practice and Potential for Services in Kenya, Tanzania, and Uganda." MicroSave-Africa, Nairobi. www.microsave.org.

Sander, Cerstin, and Samuel M. Maimbo. 2003. "Migrant Labour Remittances in Africa: Reducing Obstacles to Developmental Contributions." Africa Region Working Paper 64, World Bank, Washington, DC. www.worldbank.org/afr/wps/wp64.htm.

Sander, Cerstin, Altemius Millinga, and Peter Mukwana. 2001. "Passing the Buck—Money Transfer Systems: The Practice and Potential for Products in Tanzania and Uganda." MicroSave-Africa, Nairobi. www.microsave.org.

Sander, Cerstin, Issa Barro, Mamadou Fall, Mariell Juhlin, and Coumba Diop. 2003. "Etude sur le transfert d'argent des émigrés au Sénégal et les services de transfert en microfinance." Prepared for the International Labour Office (ILO/BIT), Social Finance Unit, Geneva.

Schoorl, J. J., L. Heering, I. Esveldt, G. Groenewold, R. F. van der Erf, A. M. Bosch, H. de Valk, and B. J. de Bruijn. 2000. *Push and Pull Factors of International Migration: A Comparative Report.* Luxembourg: Eurostat.

UN (United Nations). 2002. "International Migration 2002—UN Migration Wall Figure." Department of Economics and Social Affairs, Population Division, United Nations, New York.

Whitwell, Chris. 2002. "New Migration in the 1990s: A Retrospective." Working Paper 13, Centre for Migration Research, University of Sussex, Brighton, UK.

Widgren, Jonas, and Philip Martin. 2002. "Managing Migration: The Role of Economic Instruments." Expert Working Paper Series on Migration-Development Links, Centre for Development, Copenhagen. http://www.cdr.dk/migdevwall/papers/ManagingMigration.doc.

World Bank. 2003. *Global Development Finance: Striving for Stability in Development Finance.* Washington, DC: World Bank.

Part II
Maximizing the Development Impact of Remittances

Chapter 3
The Socioeconomic Impact of Remittances on Poverty Reduction

Admos Chimhowu, Jenifer Piesse, and Caroline Pinder

Remittances, one of the most visible outcomes of migration, have recently attracted much attention. Most empirical studies on the impact of remittances on poverty tend to be narrowly defined and restricted to formally transmitted monetary assets sent to households and community projects, rather than on physical and social assets (Gammeltoft 2002). Little has been done to develop a framework to assess the effect of remittances on poverty reduction. In particular, there is no generic body of theory that encapsulates assessment of such impacts, although Stark (1991) and Russell (1992) note the emergence of ideas coalescing around what is known as the "new economics of labor migration," which have been increasingly prevalent since the 1980s.[1]

THE NATURE OF REMITTANCES AND THEIR ROLE IN POVERTY REDUCTION

Increasing evidence indicates that remittances involve much more than pecuniary assets (Ballard 2002; Clarke and Drinkwater 2001; Orozco 2002). Any study of their impact on poverty requires attention to forms of transfer that are often neglected. For example, food, clothing, medicines, gifts, dowries, tools and equipment, and a range of domestic consumer goods are frequently transported between the home country and the workplace. These goods can make up a significant part of household consumption, but are often difficult to quantify, particularly when moving between countries that border one another, such as South Africa and Zimbabwe. Also important is the use of family savings, frequently imparted by established migrants, to provide the initial funds that assist additional family members wishing to migrate. Finally, one of the most important forms of remittance is the transfer of human capital. Many migrants arrive in the host country as unskilled workers but are able to benefit through training and experience during their employment, enabling them not only to earn a higher salary and therefore increase the amounts they are able to remit, but also to return home and obtain higher earnings than when they left. Such capacity building is highly beneficial and provides an indirect but crucial contribution to remittance benefits. Again, however, the gains are difficult to identify, measure, and quantify.

While capital flows to developing countries have declined during the past decade, workers' remittances have become an increasingly important source of external funds in poor countries (table 3.1).

This chapter is based on a report for the UK Department for International Development by WISE Development Ltd., Chimhowu, Piesse, and Pinder (2003). A full copy is available at info@wisedevelopment.com.

TABLE 3.1 REMITTANCES RECEIVED AND SENT BY DEVELOPING COUNTRIES

2001 US$ billion *Receipts*	*All developing*	*Low-income*	*Lower-middle-income*	*Upper-middle-income*
Total remittance receipts	72.3	19.2	35.9	17.3
Percentage of GDP	1.3	1.9	1.4	0.8
Percentage of imports	3.9	6.2	5.1	2.7
Percentage of domestic investment	5.7	9.6	5.0	4.9
Percentage of foreign direct investment flows	42.4	213.5	43.7	21.7
Percentage of total private capital inflows	42.9	666.1	44.9	20.2
Percentage of official flows	260.1	120.6	361.7	867.9
Other current transfers[a]	27.2	6.1	14.0	7.1
Remittances + other current transfers	99.5	25.3	49.9	24.4
Total remittance payments	22.0	1.2	1.7	19.1
Excluding Saudi Arabia	6.9	1.2	1.7	4.0

Source: IMF, Balance of Payments Statistics Yearbook 2001; World Bank, World Development Indicators 2001.
a. Other current transfers include gifts, donations to charities, pensions to retired expatriates, and so forth.

Most countries, and all regions, benefit from remittance transfers, although as a share of GDP the greatest impact is in the Middle East and North Africa, and South Asia (table 3.2).

The Sub-Saharan African countries, with some of the highest levels of poverty, receive the lowest absolute level of remittances. This suggests that international migration is not an option for the poorest households, which lack the initial funds to travel, perhaps have the lowest standard of health and nutrition, and have few support networks. Thus, the chance to find well-paid overseas employment and subsequently send remittances home is low. At the same time, however, the region is subject to considerable levels of in-country and interregional migration. Because remittances stemming from such migration are particularly difficult to measure, no definitive conclusions can be drawn concerning the relative importance of remittances in this region. (See also chapter 2.)

Several features of remittances differentiate them from other international investment flows. Remittances play a central role in the total income available to recipient households and communities. They also appear to be more stable than other international flows. For example, when private capital flows declined following the Asian financial crisis

TABLE 3.2 REMITTANCES RECEIVED BY DEVELOPING COUNTRIES,
BY REGION, 1999–2002

Region	1999	2000	2001	2002	1999	2000	2001	2002
	US$ billion				*As percentage of GDP*			
Total	67	66	72	80	1.2	1.1	1.3	1.3
East Asia and Pacific	11	10	10	11	0.7	0.7	0.6	0.6
Europe and Central Asia	8	9	9	10	0.9	0.9	0.9	1.0
Latin America and the Caribbean	17	19	23	25	1.0	1.0	1.2	1.5
Middle East and North Africa	12	11	14	14	2.2	1.9	2.3	2.2
South Asia	15	13	14	16	2.6	2.3	2.3	2.5
Sub-Saharan Africa	4	3	3	4	1.3	0.8	1.0	1.3

Source: IMF, *Balance of Payments Statistics Yearbook 2002;* World Bank, *World Development Indicators 2002.*

in 1997–98, remittances continued to rise steadily or at least remained constant. Both private capital flows and foreign direct investment to middle- and low-income countries move cyclically, depending on market conditions and the availability of attractive investment opportunities. The result can be increased investment during upturns in the economy—and the reverse during downturns. Even aid contributions may be subject to influences derived from changes in the international political environment. However, because economic recession and low domestic employment opportunities may induce more workers to migrate to increase the resources available for families at home, remittances are relatively insensitive to cyclical swings. Regional and international differences in relative wage rates will have the same effect. The independence of remittances from business cycles provides a means of income smoothing and may help poor and vulnerable households recover from unexpected crises.

The stability of remittance income is likely to be a function of the purposes for which the funds are intended. For example, remittances used for consumption by receiving households may be less volatile than those used for investment (see chapter 1). Where remitters have knowledge of the domestic household income and can estimate the shortfall between received income and expenditure, they can ensure that additional funds remain at a sufficient level to meet the needs of the household. Migrants tend to increase remittances in times of economic hardship or crisis for their families, particularly in low-income countries where households are living close to subsistence levels. Inflation in the home country has been shown to have a positive and significant impact on the inflow of remittances (Bracking 2003), reflecting the need for increased support for families when prices are rising. As money remittances are devalued, the benefits of other forms of transfers, such as domestic goods, medicines, and food become increasingly attractive.

By comparison, remittances transferred for investment purposes can be more volatile, although still less so than funds that make up portfolio holdings in emerging markets. Migrants' perceptions of risk in their home countries is not the same as that of foreign investors, an effect similar to the "home bias" phenomenon noted in investment patterns (World Bank 2002a). Some evidence suggests that remittances are used for investment purposes, particularly in low-income countries. For example, Woodruff and Zenteno (2001) estimate that remittances from the United States account for 20 percent of the capital invested in microenterprises in urban Mexico.

Remittances tend to be significantly higher in countries that are high risk and that have a high level of debt to gross domestic product (GDP). This is consistent with the fact, expressed in table 3.1, that low-income countries, which are more likely to be high risk, receive more remittances as a share of GDP than middle- and high-income countries. Remittances tend to be higher, and more uniform, in low-income countries, because they are more frequently used for consumption than for investment. Where cash remittances are sufficiently large, they may weaken the exchange rate of the home country, further depressing the economy and providing even more reason to migrate.[2]

Two further aspects of migration and remittances that bear on the discussion to follow are urban-rural drift and the potential negative effects of household and government dependency (Ballard 2002).

During the process of structural transformation, labor moves from rural economies to centers of manufacturing and services, increasing the migration from predominantly rural areas to the cities. However, migration to urban employment, whether on a local or global scale, can result in a reduction in the supply of available agricultural labor before sufficient levels of agricultural productivity have been achieved. This may have a devastating effect on food production that can often not be offset by remittance receipts at the household level.

The scale and character of the flows of value, people, and information can result in an inflow of capital to emigrant areas that is much greater than the local population could otherwise have expected to accumulate, even through movement to nearby cities. These windfalls are in the nature of a large marginal gain, even if the migrant intends to return. However, apart from any resulting inequality within the family or community, and the social instability that such inequality may cause, the inflows may create a culture of dependency that minimizes or neutralizes the benefits of economic gains. An analysis of the contemporary literature suggests that critics of policies that encourage remittances claim a negative impact on developing countries (Osili 2002). The implication is that the additional income from remittances becomes embedded within structures that perpetuate poverty in the developing countries and can promote economic stagnation rather than economic growth. Where the primary result of remittances is a level of economic dependence, and where the only rational strategy for labor is to migrate, the local community will not benefit but rather will lose resources. When that happens, long-term poverty reduction is unlikely.

A slightly different view of dependency holds remittances responsible for creating dependent relationships between the sending and the receiving countries (Portes and Borocz 1989). That view emphasizes macroeconomic relationships and the global structures within which goods and services move. Within countries, remittances are seen to generate inequality among households (Adams 1991). They also can threaten macroeconomic stability for countries with low GDP (Jones 1998).

At the national level, dependence on migration and remittances does not release governments from the responsibility to create jobs and provide a welfare net for those truly in need. Not all families have members that are able or willing to migrate; even if they do, they may not be able to depend on regular and sufficient levels of remittances to support the family. Relying on remittance support is not a substitute for poverty-reduction programs and economic growth.

THE USES OF REMITTANCES: CONSUMPTION VERSUS INVESTMENT EXPENDITURES

The analysis of remittance expenditure is frequently prefaced by an examination of the motivation for migration and subsequent remitting behavior. Three strands of literature are relevant here. First, the risk-sharing motive suggests that remittances are part of a risk-management strategy (Stark 1991; Stark and Lucas 1988). The remittances provide benefits to both the migrant who intends to return home and the recipient household, providing security and the maintenance of a sufficient income in the event of external shocks. Shocks may be a loss of employment on the part of the remitter or drought in the case of a rural beneficiary. Remittances are thus a mutual benefit—a contract between remitter and recipient. Thus conceived, remittances are a constant premium that is not affected by the number of remitting migrants from the same family or the poverty status of the receiving household. Any altruistic behavior is seen as coincidental to personal self-interest. One of the main problems of this approach, however, is that it assumes that the migrant is a rational economic being, whereas emerging evidence (Hadi 1999; Kannan and Hari 2002; Yang 2003) shows that family bonds of trust—not simply economic expedience—play an important role in the decision to remit.

Second is the view that remittances fulfill an obligation to the household, one based on affection and responsibility toward the family. The migrant is simply part of a spatially extended household that is reducing the risk of impoverishment by diversifying across several activities (Banerjee 1984; de Haan 2000; Agrawal and Horowitz 2002). Viewed this way, migration is a family decision. The migrant uses established networks for both potential employment opportunities and the transfer of funds and other resources. When motivated by altruism, remittances can vary depending on the number of household members that migrate and the poverty status of the receiving household, although it has been noted that poorer households receive a greater proportion of their total income from remittances than do nonpoor ones.

The third model is a combination of the previous two, in which altruism and self-interest both are determinants in the decision to migrate and remit (Ballard 2001; Clarke and Drinkwater 2001). While migrants are motivated by self-interest, that self-interest usually is conceived within the context of existing kinship ties, although there are gender differences. De la Cruz (1995) has observed that male migrants are more likely to follow self-interest, whereas female migrants remit more out of altruism.

However, whatever the motivation to migrate and remit, the uses to which the remitted funds are applied differ in their potential to reduce poverty and create economic security for the household and community. Remittances that are part of productive investment tend to have an impact on long-term poverty reduction, resulting in less vulnerability at both the household and the community level. There may also be a reduction in interhousehold inequality. Conversely, if remittances are used in local consumption, they may have only short-term significance and may well increase interhousehold inequality.

The decision to use remittances for consumption or investment is a function of several factors, not least of which is the pattern of control of household resources. This is particularly relevant with respect to the social aspects of remitting behavior and will be discussed further in the next section. However, it is clear that the role of the remitter in the household, and whether he or she intends to return home in the future, has a major influence on the decision to consume or invest funds that are received. Migrants who remit funds to build a house or start a business when they return are likely to be displeased to see their earnings spent on consumer goods while they are away.

A number of surveys from a range of countries have found fairly consistent results. The bulk of remittances, up to 80 percent in some regions, is spent on consumption and welfare, while only a small amount is invested in land, housing, or new productive investments (Gammeltoft 2002; Taylor 1999). Clearly, expenditure on land and housing creates employment, as does spending for consumption, education, and welfare. However, it has been found that for the long-term economic growth of a community, new productive investment is the critical factor (Ballard 2001). Apart from increasing disposable incomes and thus creating a spillover effect by raising the effective demand for local goods and services, invested remittances play a central role in developing local capital markets and productive infrastructure (Ballard 2002; Keely and Tran 1989).

The literature on remittance use is summarized in table 3.3. Note that whatever the motivation for remitting, the patterns of remittance use are not significantly different. However, the distinction between consumption and investment is not as straightforward as table 3.3 suggests. Some consumption patterns do have long-term influences on poverty, such as expenditure on health and education; clearly, these can be considered investment in human capital. Even pure consumption expenditures that appear solely to benefit individual households have secondary effects if production enhances the local economy. In some countries, special government schemes encourage the use of remittances to promote retail trade. For example, in the Philippines, special tax-free and duty-free shops have been set up to provide gift packs to local relatives of migrants.

TABLE 3.3 REMITTANCE MOTIVATION AND USE

Motivation	Consumption	Productive investment
Risk sharing	• Remittances help household cope with risks. • Cash receipts are used to purchase daily food and luxury consumables or to purchase locally available essential services (health, education). • Ensures the household functions day to day (Dreze and Sen 1989).	• Remittances help households manage idiosyncratic risks. • Investment in liquid assets such as livestock, agricultural implements, and new technologies help households to cope better in future (Lucas and Stark 1985).
Altruism	• Goods and gifts are sent to the household to fulfill altruistic obligations to the family (Agrawal and Horowitz 2002).	• Remittances are used to expand available capital assets. • Indirect benefit to the household, but long-term benefit to the wider community (Adams 1991; Martin 2001; Skeldon 2002).

From the discussion of the uses of remittances, three main issues emerge. The first is that there is a gender difference in remittance use. Female remitters are more likely to contribute to household consumption needs as a risk-reduction strategy, whereas males invest in productive activities or risk management. Explanations for this vary, but a contributing factor may be the observation that female migrants tend to settle in the host country for the long term while male migrants often intend to return home or are following international labor demand. Second, remittances sent through organized groups or associations tend to be used to mitigate natural disaster risks (also known as "covariate" risks, or those that affect a large number of people at the same time) and tend to be of long-term productive benefit to the local community. Although not benefiting directly, households of remitters experience better local amenities through such activities (Meyers 1998; Ratha 2003). Finally, apart from remittance declines caused by cyclical fluctuations in migration prospects, voluntary remittances from individual migrants progressively decrease over time as the migrant becomes more integrated in the host country (Gammeltoft 2002; Taylor 1999).[3]

The implication is that whereas the use of remittances for risk coping is an important factor in preventing families from falling into a livelihood crisis, it is investment in risk management that is likely to have a sustained impact on poverty. Thus, policies that enable organized group remittances to be transferred in a secure and cost-effective way, while at the same time allowing individual remittances to continue to be used to mitigate idiosyncratic risks, will provide the greatest benefit to recipient developing countries.

THE SOCIAL AND COMMUNITY IMPACTS OF REMITTANCES

The previous sections focused largely on the economic aspects of remittance flows. This section considers the impact of gender, kinship, and generational differences on remitters and recipients. The impact of remittances on economic inequality within communities and households was noted above. However, because remittances can change social structures and cultural practices, the concept of "social remittances"—that is, transfers of ideas and attitudes, particularly when migrants return home—is receiving increasing attention. The impact of such social remittances, like the effects of financial remittances on social structures and values, is often ambiguous. For example, remittance income may enable girls to complete their schooling, rather than having to leave school early to work in the home or on the farm. The empowerment resulting in this type of social change can increase the aspirations of young women to continue education and training, leading to higher earnings in the future. Those are positive effects. However, a negative result can occur when migrants return with nontraditional attitudes that can cause disharmony in the family or community.

Other gender effects have been noted. Large numbers of remittance-receiving households are headed by women (Hadi 1999; Kothari 2002), many elderly. In households where decisions are made by women, including the allocation of financial resources, expenditure patterns can differ from those in male-headed households (Piesse and Simister 2003). Particularly salient is the important difference in choices concerning consumption versus investment. From the remitter's perspective, although regional variations exist, women make up a small but growing percentage of migrants and are generally considered to be the more reliable remitters in the short term. For this reason, single women are often selected by their families to undertake migration (de la Cruz 1995; Dostie and Vencatachellum 2002). Female migrants are also beginning to exert some influence in the use of their remittances while away from home, and researchers have noted evidence of female preferences for expenditure on welfare-enhancing consumption such as education for younger siblings and health care for parents (de la Cruz 1995; Yang 2003). Conversely, male migrants tend to remit money to savings accounts for themselves, or for investment on their behalf in land and housing for the future. Males are more likely to take home consumer goods for their own use, such as televisions and cars (Adams 1991).

With respect to the decision to return home, female migrants from cultures that curtail women's empowerment are less likely to return home than men from those societies or women from more equitable societies (Ballard 2001; DeSipio 2000; Hadi 1999). For those who do return, their status may be enhanced as a result of their financial contribution to the household, leading to better employment or marriage prospects or social standing within the community.

Intergenerational effects should not be ignored. Again, recognizing regional differences, the majority of migrants are younger than age 35, unmarried, and likely to be the oldest daughter or son of the household (Adger and others 2002; Taylor 1999). Receiving households are therefore more likely to be led by older relatives, usually parents or grandparents. Funds remitted are often used on education of siblings who may also migrate eventually, or on the health needs of elderly relatives (Yang 2003); indeed, the provision of health and education is frequently a large factor in the motivation to migrate. However, in some regions, it is more often parents, young and old, who are the emigrants, as in the communities of Central and Southern Africa that provide labor for the mining sector, or the export-processing zones that attract women into factories or seasonal agricultural work such as flower and fruit picking. They may leave behind teenage children, usually girls removed from school early, to care for remaining children.

Intergenerational and kinship ties may be permanently dislocated in situations in which migration is a long-term strategy for the household. The longer migrants stay away, the more likely they are to settle in the country where they work, establish a household, and raise a family there. This settlement process reduces their remittances to their country of origin, and successive generations are less likely to continue sending remittances. Frequently, the remittances cease altogether (Ballard 2002; DeSipio 2000). In other cases, successive generations of migrants actually increase the size of their remittances to the family in the country of origin as they obtain better-paid jobs than their migrant parents. This is more likely to occur where groups of migrants from the same community retain close links with their families and each other, sometimes joining associations that finance community-based projects rather than individual households (Clarke and Drinkwater 2001).

While these links provide economic support and help to maintain kinship ties for long-term or permanent migrants, they can increase inequality in the receiving community if some households are remittance recipients and others are not. As a result, a previously cohesive community can become divided, sometimes leading to conflict (Ballard 2002; Hadi 1999; Russell 1992). The impact on the migrant-sending community as a whole, and households within it, can vary from extreme dependence on the remittances, with consequent vulnerability to changes in legislation or work requirements in the host countries, to increased prosperity, both in absolute terms and relative to other communities in the area, especially when the remittances are used to finance productive investment such as businesses, houses, and infrastructure (Ballard 2001; Taylor 1999).

A FRAMEWORK FOR ASSESSING THE IMPACT OF REMITTANCES ON POVERTY REDUCTION

To assess the impact of remittances on poverty reduction, it is necessary to develop a framework that employs the widely accepted multidimensional concept of household poverty. In that concept, reducing poverty involves more than raising cash income and consumption levels; poverty reduction also includes building the capacity to accumulate assets that reduce vulnerability to financial shocks, and gaining access to entitlements such as education and health care that contribute to secure and sustainable livelihoods. Therefore, a medium-term time horizon is required to evaluate the extent to which remittances provide a path out of poverty. Such a horizon allows inclusion of the impact of remittances on empowering recipients and on recipients' ability to participate in social and economic institutions. Remittances alone are unlikely to lift people permanently out of poverty, but the interaction of remittances with other economic, social, and cultural factors may have the power to do so. Thus, the crucial task is to examine the marginal benefit of remittances to the household in the medium and long term and to develop policy interventions that increase the impact of remittances on households' economic and social status, thereby reducing their vulnerability to poverty.

However, a major constraint in the development of an inclusive framework for policy interventions is the legal status of migrants. Legal immigration usually implies better pay and conditions of employment in the host country. It also tends to result in a greater awareness of formal methods of funds transmission, which are generally cheaper and more secure than informal methods. These factors can affect both the volume and pattern of remittances. Conversely, illegal migrants are more likely to be less educated and skilled and to originate from poorer households. These individuals may be ineligible for work permits, or unable to use legitimate recruitment agencies, leading to a higher likelihood of exploitation. One challenge for donors and governments is to widen the funds transfer options available to illegal migrants, thereby enabling them to benefit from reduced transaction charges and thus encouraging remittances.[4]

As has been shown in the previous sections, conclusions concerning the impact of remittances can vary depending on the analytical approach adopted. Regardless of approach, however, empirical studies on the poverty effects of remittances have shown clearly that, apart from possibly increasing inequality and dependency, remittances make a powerful contribution to reducing poverty and vulnerability in most households and communities (table 3.4). The importance of investigating the different effects of remittances at different levels becomes apparent when noting that inequality induced by remittances varies depending on the level of analysis. For example, although remittances increase inequality at the local level, they transfer resources from developed to developing countries, thus reducing inequality at the international level. National-level impacts are more significant in countries with large numbers of migrants and low GDP. In such cases, studies show that macroeconomic instability resulting from remittance flows can increase poverty for the wider population (that is, those whose families lack remitting migrants). At the community level the impacts are mainly indirect—although in countries where migrants remit in organized groups the impacts can be direct and significant.

Any investigation of the impact of remittances is by necessity interdisciplinary, and methods and techniques used in the assessments should be plural and varied. The emerging consensus calls for an integrated approach encompassing qualitative life histories, conventional quasi-experimental designs that can be used in program evaluations, and econometric models to simulate impacts of remittances at the local

TABLE 3.4 KEY IMPACTS OF REMITTANCES ON POVERTY
AT DIFFERENT LEVELS

Recipient	Poverty-reducing impacts	Other impacts
Households	• Income and consumption smoothing (Kannan and Hari 2002) • Increased savings and asset accumulation (liquid and nonliquid assets); collateral for loans; liquidity in times of crisis (Hadi 1999; Lucas and Stark 1985) • Improved access to health services and better nutrition (potential for improved productivity (Yang 2003)) • Access to better education for longer, reducing child labor (Edwards and Ureta 2001) • Increased social capital and ability to participate in social groups and activities, savings clubs, money rounds, reciprocal labor pools (Orozco 2002) • Improved access to information (Adams 1991; Ballard 2001)	• Dependence on remittances leaves households vulnerable to changes in migration cycles • High share of remittances spent on nonproductive investment and short-term consumption gains (Ballard 2001) • Differential access to the additional resources according to sex or age (Dostie and Vencatachellum 2002; Kothari 2002) • Adoption of innovations not suitable for the local environment (Osili 2002)
Community	• Improved local physical infrastructure (Ahmed 2000; Alarcón 2002) • Growth of local commodity markets • Development of local capital markets, availability of new services: banking, retail and trade, travel, construction (Ballard 2002) • Development of new development institutions (Alarcón 2002; Ballard 2002; Meyers 1998)	• Initially can increase inequality between households (those with access to remittances and those without) • Distortions in local factor markets (especially land and labor) • Transmission of negative cultural practices that reduce local quality of life (Levitt 1996)

(Continues)

TABLE 3.4 KEY IMPACTS OF REMITTANCES ON POVERTY
AT DIFFERENT LEVELS *(Continued)*

Recipient	Poverty-reducing impacts	Other impacts
Community *(Continued)*	• Changes to cultural practices, especially attitudes toward girl children • Generation of local employment opportunities • Reduction of inequality between households, particularly for poor households	
National	• Improved foreign currency inflows, in some countries up to 9 percent of GDP (Martin 2001; Orozco 2002; Ratha 2003) • Employment creation as remittances are invested in the productive sectors (Puri and Ritzema 2003) • Increased human capital as migrants learn new skills and work practices (Leon-Ledesma and Piracha 2001)	• Fluctuations in exchange rates, especially for countries with low GDP (Amuedo-Dorantes and Pozo 2002) • Growth of parallel foreign exchange markets • Distortions in property markets (Bracking 2003) • Withdrawal of state welfare programs due to remittances
International	• Reduction in inequality among countries as remittances exceed official aid transfers in some regions (Ratha 2003)	• Dependence on unreliable sources of foreign exchange subject to cyclical fluctuations (Amuedo-Dorantes and Pozo 2002) • Potential for money laundering

household, community, and national levels. Longitudinal anthropological investigations based on multigenerational recipient households offer further possibilities, although it is often difficult in such studies to separate the impact of remittances from the cumulative effects of other development policies. Substantially more effects are recorded at the household level than at community, national, and international levels (table 3.5), confirming the dominance of voluntary individual remittances in household welfare.

TABLE 3.5 PRO-POOR MARKET DEVELOPMENT: EXAMPLES OF
          MONITORING INDICATORS TO BE USED IN ASSESSING
          REMITTANCE-RELATED INTERVENTIONS

Market characteristic	Domain of intervention	Indicator	Means of verification
Market and regulatory factors influencing volume of remittances			
Enabling framework	Economic policy	• Increased volume of remittances entering through formal banking system • Removal of taxes and other penalties on incoming currency • Economic stability	• Economic surveys and reviews • Surveys of banks and other transmitters
	Law and administration	• Transparent legal system underpinning financial services providers, leading to increased confidence to use formal systems	• Surveys of remitters and receivers • Analyses of banking systems • Review of civil service procedures regarding currency importation
	Political and social culture, governance	• Political stability • Measures taken to close opportunities for rent-seeking among civil servants • Extent of male-dominated institutions	• Governance analysis • Gender analyses
Market failure	International markets	• Instability of capital flows and currency valuations	• Economic reviews
	Market power, monopoly	• Degree of competition among banks and other financial service providers	• Sector reviews
	Information asymmetry	• Knowledge of currency regulations and enforcement mechanisms • Knowledge of transmission fees of range of providers	• Surveys of remitters and receivers
	Transactions cost	• Lower charges by banks for transmission of remittances • Contract enforcement mechanisms • Barriers to formal financial sectors	• Financial sector studies • Legal reviews
Market and regulatory factors influencing use of remittances for productive investment			
Adverse power relations, exclusion	Regulations anti-poor, anti-women, anti-youth; ethnic bias	• Female property rights limited, inheritance laws • Law favors formal enterprises • Time and complexity of business start-up procedures	• Gender analyses • Review of regulations and legislation

(Continues)

TABLE 3.5 PRO-POOR MARKET DEVELOPMENT: EXAMPLES OF
MONITORING INDICATORS TO BE USED IN ASSESSING
REMITTANCE-RELATED INTERVENTIONS *(Continued)*

Market characteristic	Domain of intervention	Indicator	Means of verification
Market and regulatory factors influencing use of remittances for productive investment			
Adverse power relations, exclusion *(Continued)*	Organizational bias	• Absence of gender awareness in service providers • Unionization • Weak and nontransparent procedures	• Gender analyses • Organizational and institutional analyses
	Social relations link to markets	• Indebtedness to banks and other formal financial service providers for loans to support migration • Indebtedness to recruiters and transporters of migrant labor • Intra-household control of cash	• Social surveys • Household, gender studies
	Market segmentation	• Barriers to accessing formal credit • Barriers to formal labor markets • Weak business development of services market	• Sector studies
Intermarket links	Risk management	• Limited reliable facilities for savings • Limited availability of insurance	• Sector and client surveys
	Linked markets	• Requirement for migrant labor in developed economies (by country and sector)	• Economic reviews

CONCLUSION

This chapter considered the nature and role of remittances in household income and the impact remittances may have on poverty reduction. While accurate data on the real volume of funds transferred are scarce, there is ample evidence that remittance flows are substantial, stable relative to other forms of development finance, and well targeted to vulnerable families, both as support during a crisis and as an income-smoothing mechanism. Expenditure patterns—particularly whether remittances are used for consumption or investment—determine whether the poverty-reducing effect of remittances is short term or long term, as does the control of spending decisions by different family members. The gender of both remitter and recipient is important, economically and socially, as are the migrant's expectations of returning home. Intergenerational and kinship ties also influence the extent to which migration and remitting are ongoing strategies of the household.

A number of conclusions can be drawn about the impact of remittances on poverty. First, remittances now form an important part of household livelihood strategies. Remittances contribute directly to raising household incomes, while broadening the opportunities to increase incomes. They also allow households to increase their consumption of local goods and services. However, available evidence suggests caution in drawing further conclusions on the extent to which remittances can be a broad strategy for poverty reduction. Remittances can be unreliable and hence can make specific contributions only at a particular moment in time. In the long term, they can cease altogether as migrants either return to the home country or are integrated into the host community.

Second, at the community level, remittances generate multiplier effects in the local economy, creating jobs and spurring new economic and social infrastructure and services, particularly where effective structures and institutions have been established to pool and direct remittances. Where these have been set up and encouraged, and where the state is supportive, remittances can make a difference, particularly in remote rural locations where state resources have not been effective (Alarcón 2002).

Third, at the national level, remittances provide foreign currency and contribute significantly to GDP. However, for countries with low GDP, remittance receipts can distort formal capital markets and destabilize exchange-rate regimes through the creation of parallel currency markets.

Fourth, remittances can redistribute resources from rich to poor countries. The increase in remittances, which now surpass official aid transfers to developing countries, reduces international inequality and promotes poverty reduction.

Future research will benefit from development of a multidimensional approach and a broadly based framework that is sufficiently flexible to treat the impact of remittances at four levels—individual, household, community, and national.

NOTES

1. See Stark (1991) for a good summary, particularly of the idea that voluntary migration and remittances are part of household-level strategies for managing and coping with idiosyncratic and covariate risks.

2. This follows from the relative form of purchasing power parity, where the change in the ratio of domestic prices of internationally traded goods in two countries is reflected in the change in the exchange rate.

3. Only voluntary remittances have been considered here, but there is increasing evidence of the importance of involuntary remittances, perhaps better referred to as forced migration, which includes refugees of various kinds, asylum seekers, and migrants who escape starvation and natural disasters (see Dostie and Vencatachellum 2002; Sparreboom and Sparreboom-Burger 1996; Taylor and others 1996).

4. Of course, many migrant workers choose informal remittance channels to avoid taxation or income tracing in their home countries.

REFERENCES

Adams, Jr., Richard. 1991. "The Effects of International Remittances on Poverty, Inequality and Development in Rural Egypt." Research Report 86, International Food Policy Research Institute, Washington, DC.

Adger, W., P. Kelly, A. Winkels, L. Huy, and C. Locke. 2002. "Migration, Remittances, Livelihood Trajectories, and Social Resilience." *Ambio* 31(4): 358–66.

Agrawal, R., and A. Horowitz. 2002. "Are International Remittances Altruism or Insurance? Evidence from Guyana Using Multiple-Migrant Households." *World Development* 30(11): 2033–44.

Ahmed, I. 2000. "Remittances and Their Economic Impact in Post-War Somaliland." *Disasters* 24(4): 380–89.

Alarcón, R. 2002. "The Development of Hometown Associations in the United States and the Use of Social Remittances in Mexico." Department of Social Studies, Colegio de la Frontera Norte, Tijuana, Baja California, Mexico.

Amuedo-Dorantes, Catalina, and Susan Pozo. 2002. "Remittances as Insurance: Evidence from Mexican Migrants." Paper presented at the Northeast Universities Development Consortium Conference, Williams College, Williamstown, MA. July 24.

Ballard, R. 2001. "The Impact of Kinship on the Economic Dynamics of Transnational Networks: Reflections on Some South Asian Developments." Centre for Applied South Asian Studies, University of Manchester, United Kingdom.

———. 2002. "A Case of Capital-Rich Under-Development: The Paradoxical Consequences of Successful Transnational Entrepreneurship from Mirpur." Centre for Applied South Asian Studies, University of Manchester, United Kingdom.

Banerjee, B. 1984. "The Probability, Size and Uses of Remittances from Urban to Rural Areas in India." *Journal of Development Economics* 16(2): 293–311.

Bracking, S. 2003. "Sending Money Home: Are Remittances Always Beneficial to Those Who Stay Behind?" *Journal of International Development* 15(5): 633–44.

Chimhowu, A., J. Piesse, and C. Pinder. 2003. "Framework for Assessing the Socioeconomic Impact of Migrant Workers' Remittances on Poverty Reduction." Report for Department for International Development, London.

Clarke, K., and S. Drinkwater. 2001. "An Investigation of Household Remittance Behavior." Manchester School of Economic Studies Discussion Paper, Manchester, England.

de Haan, A. 2000. "Migrants, Livelihoods and Rights: The Relevance of Migration in Development Policies." Social Development Working Paper 4, Department for International Development, London.

de la Cruz, B. 1995. "The Socioeconomic Dimensions of Remittances: A Case Study of Five Mexican Families." *Berkeley McNair Journal* 3(1).

DeSipio, L. 2000. "Sending Money Home . . . For Now: Remittances and Immigrant Adaptation in the United States." Tomás Rivera Policy Institute, University of Southern California, Los Angeles, and Inter-American Dialogue, Washington, DC.

Dostie, B., and D. Vencatachellum. 2002. "An Empirical Analysis of Compulsory and Voluntary Remittances Among Domestic Workers in Tunisia." Institute of Applied Economics Working Paper, Hautes Etudes Commerciales, University of Montreal.

Dreze, J., and A. Sen. 1989. *Hunger and Public Action.* Oxford: Clarendon.

Edwards, A. C., and M. Ureta. 2001. "Income Transfers and Children's Schooling: Evidence from El Salvador." Working paper, California State University. Long Beach, CA. http://www.csulb.edu/~acoxedwa/rem0607.pdf.

Gammeltoft, P. 2002. "Remittances and Other Financial Flows to Developing Countries." *International Migration* 40(5): 181–211.

Hadi, A. 1999. "Overseas Migration and the Well-Being of Those Left Behind in Rural Communities of Bangladesh." *Asia-Pacific Population Journal* 14(1): 43–58.

IMF (International Monetary Fund). 2001. *Balance of Payments Statistics Yearbook.* Washington, DC: IMF.

———. 2002. *Balance of Payments Statistics Yearbook.* Washington, DC: IMF.

Jones, R. 1998. "Remittances and Inequality: A Question of Migration Stage and Geographic Scale." *Economic Geography* 74(1): 8–26.

Kannan, K., and K. Hari. 2002. "Kerala's Gulf Connection: Emigration, Remittances, and Their Macroeconomic Impact, 1972–2000." Working Paper 328, Centre for Development Studies, Copenhagen.

Keely, Charles B., and Bao Nga Tran. 1989. "Remittances From Labor Migration: Evaluations, Performance, and Implications." *International Migration Review* 24(3): 500–25.

Kothari, U. 2002. "Migration and Chronic Poverty." CPRC Working Paper 16, Institute for Development Policy and Management, University of Manchester, United Kingdom.

Leon-Ledesma, M., and M. Piracha. 2001. "International Migration and the Role of Remittances in Eastern Europe." Studies in Economics No. 0113, Department of Economics, University of Kent, United Kingdom.

Levitt, P. 1996. "Social Remittances: A Conceptual Tool for Understanding Migration and Development." Working Paper Number 96, Center for Population and Development Studies, Harvard University.

Lucas, R. B., and O. Stark. 1985. "Motivations to Remit: Evidence from Botswana." *Journal of Political Economy* 93(4): 901–918.

Martin, S. 2001. "Remittances as a Development Tool." Institute for the Study of International Migration, Georgetown University, Washington, DC.

Meyers, B. 1998. "Migrant Remittances to Latin America: Reviewing the Literature." Tomás Rivera Policy Institute Working Paper, University of Southern
California, Los Angeles.

Orozco, M. 2002. "Worker Remittances: The Human Face of Globalization."
Working Paper, Multilateral Investment Fund, Inter-American Development Bank, Washington, DC.

Osili, U. 2002. "Remittances from International Migration: An Empirical Inves-
tigation Using a Matched Sample." Paper presented at the conference on
Understanding Poverty and Growth in Sub-Saharan Africa, Centre for the
Study of African Economies, Oxford University, March 18–19.

Piésse, J., and J. Simister. 2003. "Bargaining and Household Dynamics: The
Impact of Education and Financial Control on Nutrition Outcomes in South
Africa." *South African Journal of Economics* 70(7): 163–72.

Portes, A., and J. Borocz. 1989. "Contemporary Immigration: Theoretical Perspectives on Its Determinants and Modes of Incorporation." *International
Migration Review* 23(Fall): 606–30.

Puri, S. and T. Ritzema. 2003. "Migrant Worker Remittances, Micro-Finance,
and the Informal Economy: Prospects and Issues." Working Paper 21, International Labour Organization, Social Finance Unit, Geneva.

Ratha, D. 2003. "Worker's Remittances: An Important and Stable Source of
External Development Finance." In *Global Development Finance: Striving for
Stability in Development Finance,* 157–75. Washington, DC.: World Bank.

Russell, S. 1992. "Migrant Remittances and Development." *International Migration* 30(3-4): 267–87.

Skeldon, R. 2002. "Migration and Poverty." *Asia-Pacific Population Journal* 17(4):
67–82.

Sparreboom, T., and P. Sparreboom-Burger. 1996. "Migrant Worker Remittances in Lesotho: A Review of the Deferred Pay Scheme." Working Paper
16, ILO, Social Finance Unit, Geneva.

Stark, O. 1991. *The Migration of Labour.* Oxford: Basil Blackwell.

Stark, O., and R. Lucas. 1988. "Migration, Remittances, and the Family." *Economic Development and Cultural Change* 36(3): 465–81.

Taylor, E. 1999. "The New Economics of Labour Migration and the Role of
Remittances in the Migration Process." *International Migration* 37(1): 64–88.

Taylor, E. J., J. Arango, G. Hugo, A. Kouaouci, D. Massey, and A. Pallegrino. 1996.
"Migration and Community Development." *Population Index* 62(3): 397–418.

Woodruff, C., and R. Zenteno. 2001. "Remittances and Micro-enterprises in
Mexico." In *Global Economic Prospects.* Washington DC: World Bank.

World Bank. 2001. *World Development Indicators 2001.* Washington, DC.

World Bank. 2002a. *Global Economic Prospects.* Washington, DC: World Bank.

World Bank. 2002b. *World Development Indicators 2002.* Washington, DC.

Yang, D. 2003. "Remittances and Human Capital Investment: Child School-
ing and Child Labour in the Origin Households of Overseas Filipino
Workers." Littauer Center Working Paper, Department of Economics,
Harvard University.

Chapter 4
Remittances and Economic Development in India and Pakistan

Roger Ballard

Now that long distance movement by migrant workers in search of better wages has become such a salient feature of the global economy, recognition is dawning that migrant remittances—amounting to many billions of dollars per year—constitute "an important and stable source of external development finance" (Ratha 2003). Just what sort of development do these flows actually finance? How much of the benefits of these capital inflows filter down to the rural areas from which the vast majority of labor migrants are drawn? Or is a significant proportion of their value "harvested" by the urban elite who control—and disproportionately benefit from—their country's financial infrastructure? To the extent that capital resources do indeed arrive in migrants' villages of origin, how often are they invested in such a way as to promote sustainable economic development? And if the opportunities thrown up as a result of this capital inflow are all too often frittered away in house construction and property speculation, what policy initiatives should be taken to nudge migrant workers into investing their savings in more profitable ways?

It is with such issues in mind that this chapter explores the scale on which migrant workers from the Punjab region of Northern India and Pakistan who have settled in the United Kingdom have set about sending remittances to their villages of origin, as well the impact that the arrival of these funds have had on two small areas from which a large number of settlers have arrived in Britain: District Jullundur in Indian Punjab, and District Mirpur across the border in the Azad Kashmir region of Pakistan. As has been shown elsewhere (Ballard 1983, 1988, 1989, 1991, 2003, 2004a) there have been all manner of differences in the history and dynamics of emigration from the two areas. These differences have had, in turn, a far-reaching impact on patterns of remittance transmission back to settlers' villages of origin. While these funds have in both cases been earmarked by their senders as investment capital, the projects into which these funds have actually been invested have, in each case, been powerfully conditioned by a wide range of locally specific environmental, infrastructural, and politico-economic factors. There is no way that the developmental potential of migrant remittances, or the observed outcomes that have actually accompanied their arrival, can be analyzed or understood in the absence of a thorough understanding of the environmental, infrastructural, and politico-economic circumstances affecting the migrants and their families.

That said, however, in neither area has the most been made of the potential of the inflow of remittances, even if it is quite clear that the Jullunduris (who are mostly Sikh) appear to have done a better job of it than their Muslim counterparts from Mirpur. How is this broad pattern of underperformance best explained? This chapter's conclusion, based on careful ethnographic observation, is that the underutilization of the development potential of remittances has not been the outcome of a lack of entrepreneurial skills among migrants and their kin, nor of differing levels of entrepreneurial aptitude between Muslims and Sikhs. Rather, underperformance in general, as well as the different outcomes between the two areas is largely a consequence of the differing environmental, infrastructural, and politico-economic characteristics of the two districts, which have been further compounded by additional structural obstacles at regional, national, and international levels. Hence, it is largely such structural obstacles—which appear throughout the greater part of the developing world—that have caused entrepreneurial activities of the recipients of these capital inflows to be relatively limited in scope, so much so that often little or nothing has been made of an unprecedented opportunity to lay down more adequate foundations around which more sustainable patterns of economic development might be constructed. Indeed, in the worst-case scenario, in which the arrival of large volumes of migrant remittances leads to a local withdrawal from productive activities in favor of short-term opportunities available in an almost entirely remittance-driven service sector, a downward spiral of local "de-development"—powered by ever-greater levels of emigration to urban areas—can all too easily occur.

It is with such considerations in mind that the chapter closes with a discussion of the way in which these downward spirals might be brought to a halt and, better still, reversed, through a variety of carefully tailored "smart aid" initiatives. Designed, funded, and implemented so as to overcome the most serious obstacles to productive forms of entrepreneurship, the goal of such initiatives would be to kick-start the productive potential of local economies in areas from which high levels of long distance migration have taken place.

MIGRATION AND ECONOMIC DEVELOPMENT IN JULLUNDUR AND MIRPUR

Many villages in the Jullundur Doab have a long history of overseas migration, as the presence of now-crumbling stucco mansions built by returnees from British Columbia and California at the beginning of the twentieth century serve to testify. Emigration from this area rose sharply when Britain ran acutely short of labor during the long post–Second World War economic boom. When the flow of remittances from the United Kingdom peaked during the early 1970s, rural Punjab was by sheer happenstance enjoying the benefits of a green revolution. Thanks to the availability of new high-yielding seeds, the application of artificial fertilizer, intense irrigation, and the much more widespread use of agricultural machinery, crop yields were increasing by leaps and bounds. However, while these new techniques were primarily indigenously generated, their successful implementation required a fairly high level of capital investment, and in that respect local families whose kin had settled in the United Kingdom were well placed to take advantage of the new opportunities. Thus, while the initial collections of remittance funds were usually used to rebuild or extend the family home, most migrants were eager to remit funds for the purchase of tractors, the construction of tube-wells, and the acquisition of machinery to cope with dramatically higher agricultural yields. Such investments were extremely profitable. While remittance flows from overseas consequently added substantially to Jullundur's growing condition of prosperity, remittances did not *cause* Punjab's green revolution: rather they added welcome gilt to the locally devised gingerbread (Ballard 1983).

Although emigration from District Mirpur has even deeper historical roots, which can be traced back to the demand for stokers by British shipping companies when they switched from sail to steam in the 1880s, migration from this area to the United Kingdom did not peak until the late 1970s, and has continued on a substantial scale through the early years of the 21st century. However, while the scale of the remittance inflow into Mirpur has consequently been larger and longer-sustained than in Jullundur, investment in agriculture has been virtually nonexistent. Instead there has been a succession of massive booms in house construction and in the service sector in general, with the result that the landscape is now peppered with spectacular multi-storied houses, most of which are permanently locked up, but which stand as a public witness to their overseas owners' economic achievements. Despite the area's considerable agricultural potential—most particularly to supply fresh produce to the nearby cities of Islamabad and Rawalpindi—agricultural production is wasting away. Thus, in sharp contrast to Jullundur's productively grounded economic boom (which has manifested itself in small-scale industry as well as agriculture), the local economy in Mirpur has moved in precisely the opposite direction. To be sure it gives a superficial appearance of prosperity, but this is wholly confined to the remittance-driven service sector. Whenever remittance flows diminish, as has happened several times during the last few decades, the impact on the local economy is dramatic. Just as has happened in a range of other locations from which mass migration has taken place, Mirpur has become locked into dependency. Given the downturn in agricultural production, and the absence of any kind of manufacturing activity, its current wealth is built on a foundation that appears to be unsustainable in the long run. That is not simply the conclusion of a skeptical academic commentator. Most of the district's inhabitants are also well aware of the shallow foundations of the local economy, with the result that finding some way to move overseas remains the central objective of most young Mirpuris (Ballard 1983, 1988, 1989, 2004b).

EXPLAINING DIFFERING OUTCOMES

Making sense of these differences required a dual agenda. The first task was to establish the varying ways that members of each group reacted to the specific environmental, historical, political, and administrative characteristics of their localities, together with ways in which their strategies of transnational migration had been further conditioned by the specific impact of the differing conventions of family organization, kinship reciprocity, and marriage rules within each community. The second task was to explore the ways in which the internal dynamics of the migrants' transnational networks have conditioned the diverse strategies they devised to circumvent the huge range of exclusionary obstacles—from immigration controls to racial discrimination—they encountered. As numerous studies have shown, the effectiveness and efficiency of these network-driven strategies are among the principal keys to the success of all those involved in processes of transnational migration "from below,"[1] no matter where in the developing world they may have originated from (Portes 2004; Smith and Guarnizo 1998).

The assets transferred by these networks are a major resource for economic development, from wherever such transnational migrants originate (Ratha 2003). The willingness of migrant workers to divert a significant part—often the greater part—of their overseas earnings back home can only be understood as the outcome of a deep-rooted commitment to investment. However, if this is development aid, it is aid of a very specific character. In sharp contrast to country-to-country or business-to-business assistance, it entails the channeling of resources that have been dispatched by workers living in highly localized ethnic colonies in metropolitan cities through networks of their own construction to family resident in equally specific localities overseas. Such migrant workers are not investing in such abstract concepts as "Pakistan," "the Philippines," or "Sri Lanka." Rather their commitment is to the families, the neighborhoods, and the immediate communities from which they came.

On its face, such informal development aid appears comprehensively superior to that delivered by formal international agencies. Remittances arrive with no strings attached, incur no external debts, and deliver capital resources on a massive scale directly into the pockets of those who need them most. One of the most important reasons why economic development in such areas remains stalled is that peasant farmers lack access to investment capital. Yet one pattern is all too frequently observed: funds from overseas provide an immense boost to the service sector, most particularly in house construction, but the more productive sectors of the local economy, especially agriculture, begin to languish.

The short-term prosperity caused by the arrival of remittances in areas where many in the local population have become migrant workers is real enough and the consequences far-reaching—if far from straight-forward. Therefore, however welcome the sharply increased levels of prosperity may be, the networks the migrants establish, and the ever-escalating flow of persons, ideas, and financial resources through those networks, invariably precipitate sociopolitical tensions and contradictions. Those contradictions are no less severe in national and international contexts than they are locally. It is precisely because such entrepreneurial networks so often emerge from and are driven by those who stand far out on the global periphery that their successes soon begin to "undermine the center" (Addleton 1992), and thereby destabilize the established (and usually profoundly unequal) socioeconomic order that precipitated migratory activity in the first place.

THE LOCAL CONSEQUENCES OF REMITTANCE INFLOWS

The arrival of remittances on a large scale soon begins to upset the local status hierarchy. The vast majority of those who made up the early waves of Indian and Pakistani emigrants were young males from households of middle socioeconomic rank within their villages. Returnees soon found that they had acquired a great deal more power not only with regard to their parents, but also their wives and siblings who stayed at home. While those who found themselves sidelined usually swiftly began to devise countermeasures, tensions invariably began to erupt within recipient families as a result of the massive new inflow of wealth (Gardner 1995).

Families with access to such transnational links soon become massively advantaged, disrupting established socioeconomic hierarchies in their villages of origin. Richer families who had disdained sending their sons to work as mere laborers overseas swiftly abandoned their previous inhibitions, while the poorest families drew on their links with more affluent patrons, who were often willing to facilitate their clients' sons' passage overseas. Thus the reconfigured patterns of wealth and status in the village caused by the arrival of remittances were themselves a powerful spur to further emigration and the resulting processes of chain migration were self-fueling.

A useful way of envisaging these processes is as self-constructed escalators that reach upward from specific localities in the developing world to equally localized ethnic colonies in specific cities in the metropolitan world. Migrants—no less than remittances—move around the globe through tightly personalized networks. Access to such networks confers real privilege: each network provides its members with easy access to an escalatory process that can transport them swiftly and smoothly from a position of relative poverty to one of relative wealth (Ballard 2003). By the same token, each network also facilitates the transmission of a large volume of money back to the escalator's starting point. However, each such escalator is highly specific. Some merely stretch to the national capital, others to more distant destinations elsewhere in the developing world, while a select minority stretch into urban centers in one or another of the metropolitan economies of the developed world. While all these escalators offer those who stand on them access to entrepreneurial opportunities, it is those that reach right into the heart of the developed world that invariably offer migrant workers and their families the greatest range of opportunities.

NATIONAL CONSEQUENCES AND CONTRADICTIONS

Migrant remittances also precipitate contradiction at the national level, particularly when the inflow of funds grows sufficiently large to engage the attention of the national government. Given that virtually all governments in the developing world suffer from a severe deficiency of foreign exchange, the inflow of migrant remittances (once recognized) is invariably viewed as a godsend. Not only is the inflow of foreign exchange perceived as virtually cost-free, but because it appears to arrive with no strings attached it provides a wonderful opportunity to pursue all manner of national objectives. Several examples follow:

- *Boost national foreign exchange reserves* by encouraging further emigration in what are often explicitly described as programs of manpower export, and by reminding emigrants that they have a patriotic duty to invest their savings back home, often in specially designed government bonds and high-yielding savings accounts
- *Further enhance government revenue by taxing this income stream*, if not directly, at least by setting inflated rates for the issue of passports and visas, departure taxes, international telephone calls, and so forth, all of which are facilities used disproportionately by migrant workers
- *Draw the excess funds into deposits in the formal banking system*, thereby hugely improving its liquidity, because the volume of funds remitted in this way is often so large it cannot be soaked up in immediate expenditure by recipients

However, while all these measures can be expected to provide a major boost to national financial resources, they also pose a further set of questions: by whom, for what purposes, and to whose advantage is this inflow of financial resources actually deployed? Officials in the ministry of finance and the central bank make these decisions. What are their objectives, and what sorts of financial initiatives do they tend to favor? In exploring these complex issues it is worth distinguishing the domestic from the foreign exchange dimensions of the opportunities to which the inflow of remittances gives rise.

REMITTANCES AND THE
NATIONAL FOREIGN EXCHANGE ACCOUNT

In many of the world's poorest developing countries, migrant remittances are emerging as a major source of foreign exchange, often so great that it substantially exceeds the income generated by the export of goods and other services. When this is so, remittances play a major role in national finances and are often the only bastion against a radical devaluation of the local currency. Most governments take it for granted that protecting the value of the national currency is a vital policy objective, but it is worth asking just which segments of the national population reap the greatest benefits from the fulfillment of that objective. A fall in the international value of the local currency tends to have relatively little impact on most members of the rural population. Living in near-subsistence conditions, peasant farmers' propensity to purchase imported goods and services is minimal; to be sure, they might find that prices for their agricultural products would rise if the price of imported grain rose as a result of a fall in the external value of the local currency—provided that grain prices were not held down by the authorities in the name of "social justice." By contrast, elite lifestyles are heavily dependent on goods and services that must ultimately be paid for in foreign exchange—whether in the form of cars, televisions, health care for themselves, or education for their offspring. It is these interests, rather than those of the rural peasantry, that are disproportionately favored when migrant remittances are used by elitist national governments as a convenient means of maintaining their local currencies at radically overvalued levels.

That said, there is yet another crucial subtext to the role that migrant remittances play in such contexts. In an effort to conserve the outflow of foreign exchange, many developing countries impose strict exchange controls, so strict that local residents who lack political and official connections find it virtually impossible to gain access to foreign exchange. A black market soon develops, because migrants are keen to get a better rate of exchange on their remittances than that offered by institutions directly controlled by the national government. However, in assessing the significance of such markets it is worth remembering that they only exist—and are only designated as "black"—because they operate outside the formal procedures of the state, and they do so in countries where the greater part of commercial activity also takes place within the informal sector. There are few indications that the growth of the informal sector does much harm to the migrants themselves, or to the local economies of geographically and politically peripheral regions from which most of them are drawn. Indeed, in those parts of the world in which the center has disappeared—because the state has effectively collapsed (as is the case in both Somalia and Afghanistan in the early years of the 21st century)—the entire national economy now operates within the informal sector. In both cases migrant remittances provide a substantial part of system liquidity (Maimbo 2003).

REMITTANCES AND THE LOCAL DIMENSIONS
OF THE NATIONAL ECONOMY

While contemporary Somalia appears to be unique in the sense that remittances now form the national economy's sole source of foreign exchange, there are many other parts of the developing world in which the inflow of value from remittances is substantially greater than that accruing from the export of goods. Just where does all the money actually go? Who benefits most from its arrival?

At one level the answer to the first question is clear: it goes straight to the rural areas from which the majority of transnational labor migrants are almost invariably drawn. District Mirpur is one such area. To non-Mirpuri Pakistanis, the prosperity of such areas is evident, so much so that the emigrants' success elicits active feelings of jealousy, even among members of the urban elite. Returning migrants may be mocked for their bizarre behavior, such as importing wide-screen televisions and enormous refrigerators to villages that are hardly yet served with electricity connections. From the perspective of the urban elite, returning migrants have more money than they know what to do with. Overseas development specialists, who socialize primarily with members of the urban elite, may be tempted to incorporate these arguments into their professional judgments.

There is, of course, a substantial degree of common sense logic to such arguments: the living standards of the inhabitants of areas from which mass overseas emigration has taken place are significantly higher than those in areas from which emigration has not occurred. However, in assessing the significance of that condition of relative wealth, it should not be forgotten that emigration from such areas began and continues because of local poverty, and even more specifically the absence of resources such as roads, schools, hospitals, markets, and so forth. While remittances can provide high-tech solutions for some of these deficiencies—because four-wheel drive vehicles can cope with the absence of paved roads, generators with the absence of electrical mains, and mobile phones with the absence of land lines—

such remedies merely circumvent, but do nothing to resolve, the underlying deficiencies in the local infrastructure. Moreover, as long as such deficiencies are left unremedied, as is invariably the case as long as national government priorities are focused elsewhere, the prospect of returnees being able to make profitable investments in any sector of the local economy other than that driven by the arrival of further remittances will remain remote. The result in Mirpur—as in many other similarly placed localities around the globe—is a sharp decline in agricultural production (which has become increasingly unprofitable) in an area with an excess of investment capital looking for a home.

Although members of the urban elite may routinely describe labor migrants as illiterate, and the social and cultural milieu from which they are drawn as backward, emigrants from such areas have displayed extremely high levels of entrepreneurial ability in the course of gaining entry to, and making the most of, opportunities in the global labor market. Set in that context, the suggestion that those abilities simply evaporated the moment migrants returned to their home base makes little sense. A better explanation is that despite all their efforts to deploy their entrepreneurial skills on a more sustainable basis, they were largely stymied by local obstacles. An investigation of the structural constraints that the inhabitants of these areas continue to encounter—rather than allegations that migrants and their families lack the necessary entrepreneurial abilities to do any better—is more likely to provide meaningful explanations of observed outcomes.

If infrastructure development programs bypass areas from which high levels of overseas emigration has taken place on the grounds that they are "not poor," remedies to the underlying infrastructural deficiencies that caused migration in the first place will be further postponed. Because such areas host their own self-funded programs of manpower export and are consequently highly efficient producers of foreign exchange, there is little incentive for government intervention.

Such areas also provide a vital prop to the national banking system. Having invested heavily in new houses and other status symbols, the inhabitants of such capital-rich areas place their surplus funds on deposit in the local banks. Hence, while bank branches in capital-rich areas usually have huge sums on deposit, their loan portfolios are almost always insignificant—at least locally. Migrants' savings consequently serve as a means of financing loans to customers living elsewhere—most usually to members of the elite in distant cities. From this perspective, such banking structures emerge as engines of financial redistribution, drawing in deposits from the relatively poor and redistributing their developmental potential to members of the urban elite. Where the banks in question are nationalized, as is frequently the case, politically well-connected borrowers are not only the most frequent recipients of such bank loans, but their connections often enable them to avoid ever having to repay them. In such circumstances a temporary redistribution of wealth from the poor to the rich can often prove permanent.

If and when such mechanisms become established, they can divert a significant portion of the value transfers set off by migrant remittances into reinforcing the wealth and living standards of distant urban elites. The more extensive this process of diversion becomes, the more resources to improve local infrastucture in areas of high migration will decrease, and the greater the prospect that local cycles of capital rich underdevelopment will emerge. This trend can be expected to reinforce the local propensity to migrate.

This paradoxical outcome is grounded in two wholly unexpected developments, at least from an elite perspective. The first development is the dramatic success of members of an otherwise peripheral group in exploiting overlooked niches in the global labor market, and the second is their equally dramatic success in shipping their savings home on their own terms. Because all these initiatives have been conducted on an informal basis, the custodians of the formal sector tend to view the growing scale and vitality of these developments with suspicion and alarm. In much of the developing world, efforts to suppress the initiatives remain vigorous—the more so because migrant remittances have become a principal source of liquidity. In these circumstances, it is easy to see why efforts to divert remittances back into formal channels have come to be regarded as an urgent priority. Quite apart from fears about drug smuggling and terrorist finance, the informal economy quite directly "undermines the center," as Addleton (1992) puts it. However, to the extent that the center undemines the potential wealth of the periphery, it is invariably in migrants' interest to devise strategies with which to resist such tendencies.

INTERNATIONAL CONSEQUENCES

The global contradictions unleashed by migrant remittances are no less complex, partly because remittances are such a big business. Commissions on international money transfers through the formal banking system range between 8 percent and 20 percent, depending on the sum transmitted and its destination.

Because of the high commissions charged by the banks, the slow pace with which they transfer funds to their destination, and the difficulties that relatives so often experience in retrieving funds when they eventually arrive, migrants throughout the world have developed their own informal modes of money transmission (El-Qorchi, Maimbo, and Wilson 2003). The *hawala* system used by South Asian migrants—which has its roots in the banking system used by long-distance traders in the Indian Ocean region before colonization—is one of the largest and most sophisticated. From its hub in Dubai, the contemporary hawala system of informal value consolidation, settlement, and deconsolidation handles many millions of dollars worth of migrant remittances every day, providing its customers with cash payouts in the most remote destinations far more swiftly and reliably than does the formal banking system. Moreover, its commissions—normally little more than 1 percent—are far lower than those charged by any bank (Ballard 2004c).

Although a number of banks have begun to break into the remittance market, many have run into competition from less formally constituted value transmission agencies. In addition, they have encountered considerable logistical challenges because they often find the cost of making cash deliveries to remote rural areas using formal techniques to be prohibitive.

The ultimate outcome of the intensifying competition between formal and informal value transmission systems remains unclear. At present, *hawaladars* occupy a position of clear competitive advantage: they can fulfill the task more cheaply, expeditiously, and reliably than can the formal sector. The migrants' self-constructed networks challenge the established order. If the U.S. Treasury manages to enforce its regulatory objectives, informal value transfer systems may be eliminated, and migrants will have to bear the additional transmission costs. However, the success of migrants' strategies of transnational entrepreneurship in so many other contexts makes this unlikely.

REMEDIES: MAKING MORE OF THE DEVELOPMENT POTENTIAL OF MIGRANTS' REMITTANCES

Remittances clearly have the capacity to transform economic conditions in migrants' villages of origin. Migrants have devised strategies to circumvent the many obstacles they encounter in the course of their travels. In doing so, it is their self-constructed networks—composed of and devised by peers and ordered in terms of specific values, assumptions, and patterns of reciprocity—that have proved to be their greatest asset. Efforts by members of more formally constituted agencies to provide aid or assistance in such circumstances tend to meet with suspicion and resistance. Migrants' initial reactions to such schemes are often to subvert them to their own purposes.

A major part of the secret of success of migrant networks is that their members are constantly on the lookout for better, but overlooked or unrecognized, opportunities. Hence, while members of such networks are invariably wary of the good faith of outsiders, and sensibly skeptical of proffered advice, they rarely reject it out of hand: their principal criterion is whether and how it will work for them in their own particular circumstances.

Viable initiatives must not only recognize and respect, but actively seek to build on, the resources and strategic solutions that members of local networks have already devised and implemented. To have any chance of taking hold, all such initiatives must at the very least include three components:

- A comprehensive appreciation of the precise character of the constraints and opportunities within which members of the local population find themselves operating, given the historical, social, economic, political, cultural, and religious features of their immediate environment
- An equally rich appreciation of the strategic initiatives that members of the local population have *already* devised in the course of circumventing the worst of the obstacles confronting them, and of making the most of whatever opportunities they have so far been able to identify
- A willingness, and the ability, to assist local populations identify additional options that could supplement those already in place, while adding entrepreneurially valuable skills, insights, and understandings to those already in evidence

STRUCTURAL CONSTRAINTS ON THE
USE OF MIGRANT REMITTANCES

Several issues must be addressed at a global level. Most saliently, obstacles placed in the way of the speedy, reliable, and economically efficient delivery of migrant remittances to their destinations can only be regarded as unhelpful. Money laundering and terrorist financing cannot be ignored, but migrants and their remittances should not be penalized by efforts to contain terrorism and drug trafficking.

The fact that migrants have found it necessary to move elsewhere in search of a better future underlines a crucial dimension of their predicament. No matter how strongly they may be committed to the betterment of conditions in their home base, the obstacles that cluster around them there are invariably far more deeply entrenched than those they encounter overseas—otherwise there would be no need for mass migration. It is also worth noting that migrants' overseas-born offspring are much less interested in stimulating home-based development initiatives. Thus, the window of opportunity within which remittance-financed initiatives might be implemented is sharply time-limited.

Such reservations aside, just what shape might initiatives of this kind be expected to have? Insofar as infrastructural deficiencies are a major obstacle to progress, it is worth remembering that migrants have already begun to address these issues on their own accord (Ballard 2004b). Collective efforts to construct shrines and temples, to pave the streets of villages, and to build schools, clinics, and even hospitals can be observed in every locality from which large-scale overseas migration has taken place. However, the prospect that more substantial infrastructural projects—such as highways, bridges, dams, electricity grids, and so forth—might be funded through such network-based voluntary initiatives appears to be remote. No matter how great the collective benefits such initiatives might be expected to bring, they are of such a scale as to be unlikely to be funded by any agency other than the state. If national governments in the developing world continue to set their priorities elsewhere, other stakeholders such as private business may well intervene.

THE PROSPECTS FOR SMART AID

Deployed in and around the capital-rich islands created by migrant remittances from the developed world, so-called smart aid initiatives would have two complementary objectives: first, to remedy specific deficiencies in the local infrastructure, thereby removing key blockages to the area's inherent developmental potential; and second, to promote and support more sustainable—but network-friendly—local entrepreneurial initiatives.

It is unrealistic to expect that the removal of infrastructural blockages would be sufficient, in and of itself, to stimulate sustainable growth in an otherwise stagnant local economy. There is thus a need to complement such initiatives with efforts to identify novel, but more profitable, forms of income generation that make the most of local resources. For example, it might be that incomes could be radically improved if farmers abandoned the largely unprofitable cultivation of food grains in favor of higher value crops such as vegetables and fruit; however, such profits could only be realized if there was a ready market in neighboring urban centers, together with a transport infrastructure to ensure timely delivery.

It would not be practical for smart aid initiatives to run such fruit and vegetable farms, marketing agencies, and their associated distribution networks; instead, the objectives of the initiative would be to establish—largely on the basis of locality-specific empirical research—just which crops might best fill high-value slots in accessible markets and how those crops might best be cultivated, marketed, and distributed. From this perspective, the central aim of the initiative would be to research potential solutions and to test their economic viability, leaving implementation to local entrepreneurs.

CONCLUSION

Ratha (2003) has rightly insisted that migrant remittances are "an important and stable source of external development finance," and one whose potential for stimulating economic growth has been largely neglected by those who explore such issues from the top down. By contrast, millions of migrant workers working from the bottom up, who have for many years been sending billions of dollars of investment funds back to their home villages have not been so negligent. Even if only a small part of the developmental potential of these funds has yet been liberated, that is not for want of efforts by the migrants themselves, by their overseas-born offspring, or even by their relatives back home. Absolute poverty, lack of capital, and lack of entrepreneurial ability have not been the central obstacles to the generation of more sustained patterns of economic growth from these inflows. Rather, institutional, structural, and infrastructural constraints—in many cases the same constraints that provoked migration—account for the poor development results of these opportunities.

Few parts of the developing world—including its most economically and spatially peripheral regions—are still untouched by long-distance migration. At the same time, vicious cycles of de-development are emerging throughout the developing world, as evidenced by explosive patterns of urban growth, especially in the very poorest of countries. We are all stakeholders in the negative consequences of such outcomes, which further disadvantage those unfortunate enough to find themselves confined to the underdeveloped periphery, and so reinforce their propensity to migrate. If such migration proves unstoppable not only will metropolitan centers—in the developed and the developing world—become increasingly overcrowded, but as their rural peripheries are drained of their populations, their productive potential will steadily decline, further fueling the drive to migrate. As long as policy initiatives and institutional structures favor the metropolis over the periphery, the urban over the rural, and the formal over the informal, a vicious cycle of ever-greater concentration of people and resources in metropolitan areas, and a parallel process of de-development in the countryside, seems set to continue.

NOTE

1. Migration "from below" is brought about by local communities, the informal economy, ethnic nationalism, and grassroots activism, as opposed to transnational migration "from above," which is spurred on by transnational capital, global media, and emergent supra-national political institutions.

REFERENCES

Addleton, Jonathan. 1992. *Undermining the Centre: The Gulf, Migration, and Pakistan.* Karachi: Oxford University Press.

Ballard, Roger. 1983. "Emigration in a Wider Context: Jullundur and Mirpur Compared." *New Community* 11: 117–36

———. 1988. "The Political Economy of Migration: Pakistan, Britain and the Middle East." In *Migrants, Workers, and the Social Order,* ed. J. Eades, 19–48. London: Tavistock.

———. 1989. "Overseas Migration and Its Consequences: The Case of Pakistan." In *The Sociology of Developing Societies: South Asia,* ed. H. Alavi and J. Harriss, 112–120. London: Macmillan.

———. 1991. "Migration and Kinship: the Differential Effect of Marriage Rules on the Process of Punjabi Migration to Britain." In *South Asians Overseas,* ed. C. Clarke, C. Peach, and S. Vertovec, 210–249. Cambridge: Cambridge University Press.

———. 2003. "The South Asian Presence in Britain and Its Transnational Connections." In *Culture and Economy in the Indian Diaspora,* ed. H. Singh and S. Vertovec, 197–222. London: Routledge.

———. 2004a. "A Case of Capital-Rich Under-Development: The Paradoxical Consequences of Successful Transnational Entrepreneurship from Mirpur." In *Migration, Modernity and Social Transformation in South Asia,* ed. F. Osella and K. Gardner. New Delhi: Sage.

———. 2004b. "Remittances and Economic Development." In "Migration and Development: How to Make Migration Work for Poverty Reduction," House of Commons International Development Committee. London.

———. 2004c. "Delivering Migrant Workers' Remittances: The Logistical Challenge." *Journal of Financial Transformation* 12: 141–53.

El-Qorchi, M., S. Maimbo, and J. Wilson. 2003. "Informal Funds Transfer Systems: An Analysis of the Informal Hawala System." IMF Occasional Paper 222, International Monetary Fund, Washington, DC.

Gardner, Katy. 1995. *Global Migrants, Local Lives.* Oxford: Oxford University Press.

Maimbo, Samuel. 2003. *The Money Exchange Dealers of Kabul: A Study of the Hawala System in Afghanistan.* Washington, DC: World Bank.

Portes, Alejandro. 1997. *Globalization from Below: The Rise of Transnational Communities.* Princeton, NJ: Princeton University Press.

Ratha, Dilip. 2003. "Workers' Remittances: An Important and Stable Source of External Development Finance." In *Global Development Finance 2003.* Washington, DC: World Bank.

Smith, M. P., and L. E. Guarnizo, eds. 1998. *Transnationalism From Below.* New Brunswick: Transaction Publishers.

Chapter 5
Migrant Workers' Remittances:
A Source of Finance for Micro-Enterprise
Development in Bangladesh?

Abul Kalam Azad

Microenterprises are an ancient way of life for the rural poor, but only recently have they been recognized as an effective tool for employment, income generation, and long-term economic development through poverty alleviation. These tiny enterprises are self-financed by entrepreneurs from family savings. In impoverished societies, in which the poor are unable to accumulate even tiny amounts of start-up capital, moneylenders are reluctant to lend for fear of not being repaid. When they do lend, they charge high rates of interest. Given these difficult circumstances, the microenterprise sector remains overlooked by both formal and informal financial systems despite its potential for poverty alleviation.

Interest in this neglected sector grew in recent years with the emergence of microfinance institutions (MFIs) that have targeted microenterprise development as a potential mechanism for poverty reduction. Unfortunately, most MFIs are nongovernmental organizations (NGOs) funded—often insufficiently—by donor agencies. Lacking resources of their own to meet the increasing demand for micro credit, they offer very small credits to the very poor, taking back only small amounts of savings from their own borrower-members—insufficient to finance the existing financial needs of the microenterprise sector, let alone to help potential entrepreneurs establish new entities. Being neither banks nor part of a formal financial system, MFIs are registered under diverse laws,[1] most of which do not permit them to take public deposits.

In Bangladesh as elsewhere, microenterprises are a subset of the informal economy, with common elements of ease of entry, self-employment, small-scale production, labor-intensive work, lack of access to organized markets, and lack of access to traditional forms of credit because of supply deficits and the high cost of borrowing. Tiny, self-owned enterprises in urban and rural areas, they are neither registered nor required to be registered with fiscal or regulatory bodies. They are not covered by uniform regulations. Most employ fewer than 10 people, usually the entrepreneur's family members, and are operated out of the owner's home. Microenterprises are often the single source of family income for poor entrepreneurs. Local moneylenders, friends, and even relatives in many instances are reluctant to give or lend money.

Commercial banks are rarely interested in providing start-up capital, for the following reasons:

- Lending to small enterprises is perceived to be very risky. The uncertainties that face a small company—including high business failure rates and susceptibility to market changes and economic fluctuations—make banks reluctant to deal with these clients. Nonpayment, or even delayed payment, by a few major clients can cause the collapse of a small business.

- Banks show a distinct institutional bias toward lending to the larger corporate sector. In many cases there are links in director-ships, joint ownerships, and various other common financial dealings between banks and large enterprises.
- The administrative costs of lending to small enterprises are high, reducing profitability.
- Many small enterprises are unable or unwilling to present full accounting records and other documentation. In most cases such records simply do not exist, making it difficult to assess loan applications.
- Small borrowers are often unable to provide the collateral and security demanded by banks and other lending institutions.
- Enterprises in the informal sector lack legal status.

Parallel to the reluctance of banks to lend to small enterprises is the reluctance of these enterprises to borrow from banks. The formalities of obtaining bank finance, particularly the time and paperwork involved, are a formidable deterrent to smaller businesses. The majority of microentrepreneurs lack formal education, which, when compounded by problems of location and time, makes it difficult for would-be bor-rowers to comply with the requirements of banks and other formal financial institutions. In many cases, potential borrowers have to pay for the preparation of accounts or special studies on top of the cost involved in the numerous visits to the lending institution.

The result is a large gap between the demand for and supply of credit.

LINKING MIGRANT REMITTANCES TO MICROENTERPRISE DEVELOPMENT

The burgeoning volume of international migrants' remittances has emerged as a potential source of funds for development activities, including microenterprises, which are now part of the development strategy of many developing countries. Remittances—a portion of the wages of migrant workers earned in foreign countries and sent back to their home country—are a strong source of foreign exchange for labor-sending countries, used to pay import liabilities, improve the balance of payments, build foreign exchange reserves, service external debt, and enhance the viability of the recipient countries' external sector. On the domestic front, remittances increase the household incomes of migrants' families, improve living standards, enhance savings, and generally contribute to national economic growth.

However, against the backdrop of rural poverty, inefficient and insuf-ficient credit delivery, and poor public services in many developing countries, directing flows of remittances toward microenterprise development seems a complex task.

Despite difficulties, some receiving countries—among them El Salvador, Guatemala, Mexico, and the Philippines—have succeeded in establishing remittance-backed enterprises and various community development projects. The following examples provide some practical insights into the beneficial links between migrant remittances and microenterprise development.[2]

Channeling Remittances toward Microenterprise Development in Mexico

One of the largest constraints to private sector growth in developing countries is the lack of credit for seed capital and working capital for enterprises, particularly small and medium-size enterprises. Pooled remittances can provide such credit, thereby supporting the growth of enterprises in countries whose migrant communities send large volumes of remittances. Although living abroad, many migrants are interested in investing in enterprises in their home country, either to employ family members at home, earn additional income, or to prepare for their retirement or eventual return. Remittances channeled through so-called Hometown Associations (HTAs) and other self-help groups are responsible for almost 20 percent of the capital invested in microenterprises in urban Mexico. These types of investments on the part of remitters can reduce poverty significantly by expanding businesses in their home communities and generating jobs and income that would not otherwise exist. While the actual number of jobs created and the overall earnings will vary with the market environment, such investments can help provide economic momentum in struggling local economies.

National Financeria, Mexico

National Financeria (NAFIN), a development bank, has provided financial and technical support to more than 80,000 microentrepreneurs since 1994. It supports productive projects in Mexico using migrant workers' remittances. The NAFIN program offers several advantages to migrants interested in establishing or expanding an enterprise in their home country, including financial training and technical and marketing assistance. NAFIN has developed community investment funds that can be adapted to mobilize remittances for community-managed investments in microenterprises.

Enhancing the Impact of Collective Remittances in Mexico

Understanding the beneficial effects of their migrant communities abroad, several governments, including Mexico's, have initiated economic projects to attract and use collective remittances. Mexico's most successful program is a three-for-one matching fund to encourage emigrant investments in small-scale infrastructure and other community projects and programs.

In 1992, the Mexican state of Zacatecas initiated *Iniciativa Ciudandana 3x1*, in which money donated by emigrants is matched with funds from federal and state governments. The program was expanded to include municipal funds, and for every dollar donated an additional three dollars was provided from government sources. The money raised goes into a fund for development projects in communities with HTAs.

In 2002, emigrant groups and government authorities channeled US$16 million through the program. The amounts committed to the program by HTAs has increased so rapidly in recent years that, at times, the government does not have the budget to match the funds. Due to the success of the program, other states are implementing their own matching programs.

The Multilateral Investment Fund in Ecuador and Brazil

In addition to facilitating access by remittance recipients to financial services, the Multilateral Investment Fund (MIF) of the Inter-American Development Bank has led development efforts to link remittances to the development of small and medium enterprises.

In Ecuador, MIF has been working with the Banco Solidario to support microenterprises through lines of credit. One of the main objectives of the project is to facilitate the flow of remittances and make it easier for Ecuadoran migrants and their families to gain access to services, maintain savings, and engage in productive investments. In addition, the project is extending coverage of the formal financial system in Ecuador to the microenterprise sector, especially in rural areas, inducing more people, including remittance recipients, to use financial instruments, while demonstrating to financial institutions the feasibility of achieving attractive financial returns through medium- and long-term lending.

In Brazil, MIF has worked with Banco Sudameris de Investimento on a remittance fund for entrepreneurs (the Dekassegui Fund). The project aims to promote entrepreneurial activities by Brazilian temporary workers overseas who want to start businesses upon their return by creating a mechanism whereby a portion of regularly transferred remittance accounts can be put to more productive uses.

Unlad Kabayan, Philippines

Unlad is one of the few organizations in the Philippines that aims to mobilize migrant-worker resources for productive use and community development. It has mobilized pooled migrant savings, helped to identify appropriate investments, and facilitated credit applications with the objective of creating new jobs through sustainable businesses. Services available to migrants include

- savings accounts;
- investments in existing businesses;
- special start-up funds;
- skills training, logistical support, and networking.

In addition to these services, Unlad has implemented a social support program to educate and organize migrant workers.

The Investment Potential of the Indian Diaspora

To facilitate the development of enterprises in India, the Indian Investment Centre has developed mechanisms that enable Indian companies to collaborate with nonresident Indians (NRIs) to identify sources of capital and technology. The agency maintains an industrial information service that provides the status of industries and profiles for potential industrial projects. Furthermore, the agency's Web site provides nonresident Indians with answers to an expansive list of investment questions on bank accounts; repatriation of profits; and investments in securities, shares, company deposits, and property. The site also offers special facilities to NRI investors repatriating funds.

Lesotho's Deferred Pay Scheme

More than 60 percent of Lesotho's working population works in South African mines. The association of mine workers established a deferred pay scheme in 1974 to ensure that more money earned by Basotho workers was invested or spent in the domestic economy. The scheme was also meant to raise an appreciation among migrant workers for saving. A board of trustees—chaired by the principal Secretary of Labor and Employment and including representatives from Lesotho's central bank and Ministries of Employment and Labor, Agriculture, and Finance; and from South Africa's Ministry of Labor—administers the fund.

The regulations governing the scheme stipulate that any money in the fund not immediately required for repayment should be invested in Treasury bills or other security issues guaranteed by the government. A 1990 amendment decreased the percentage of deferred pay to 30 percent from the original 60 percent minimum requirement, allowing employees to voluntarily agree to a deferment of up to 50 percent. No deductions are allowed during the first and the last 30 calendar days of a contract, while two withdrawals per contract period are allowed, each not to exceed 50 percent of deferred pay in the employee's account. The board decides on the interest rate payable on the accounts at Lesotho Bank.

THE CASE OF BANGLADESH

Can Bangladesh build on some of the experiments described above? To answer that question, it is important to consider whether Bangladesh provides the environment and infrastructure needed to attract migrant's remittances for microenterprise development.

Bangladesh is a major labor-exporting country. Since its independence in 1971, more than 3 million Bangladeshis have gone abroad. Their cumulative remittances during 1976–2003 stood at about US$22 billion. The central bank estimates that in 2003 alone, the country received US$3 billion from expatriates. The trend in the country's receipts of migrant remittances has risen sharply in recent years (figure 5 .1).

FIGURE 5.1 MIGRANTS' REMITTANCES TO BANGLADESH, 1990–2003

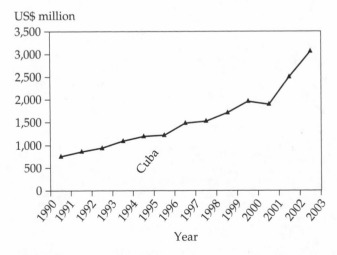

Source: Author's calculations using Bangladesh Bank (Central Bank of Bangladesh) Foreign Exchange Policy Department data.

The 3 million Bangladeshi migrants represent only 2.5 percent of the country's total population—a small percentage compared to other labor-sending countries. Migrants make up almost 9 percent of the population of the Philippines, and 15 percent of the population of Mexico. Thus remittances are small in comparison with overall economic activity, although they have exceeded the country's foreign exchange reserves since 1997 (figure 5 .2). Of the 3 million migrants, 2.5 million are semi-skilled or unskilled, with average monthly earnings under US$300, half or less than the earnings of Philippine and Mexican migrants. Siddiqui and Abrar (2003) estimate that a typical migrant remits 55.65 percent of his income and that remittances constitute 51.12 percent of the total income of recipient families.

Law and practice in Bangladesh strictly prohibit sending remittances through informal channels, such as *hundi* and *hawala*. Despite this prohibition, remittances received through banking channels, the only ones recorded in Bangladesh, are estimated to be no more than 46 percent of total remittances (Siddiqui and Abrar 2003). Another 40 percent is received through the informal hundi system (legislative prohibitions have failed to curb the attraction caused by its low cost and speed of delivery), about 5 percent through friends and relatives, and most of the remainder through migrant workers on visits home.

The state is the ultimate beneficiary of all foreign exchange earnings in Bangladesh; migrants' families receive the local currency (taka)

FIGURE 5.2 COMPARATIVE POSITION OF MIGRANT REMITTANCES
IN BANGLADESH, 1990–2003

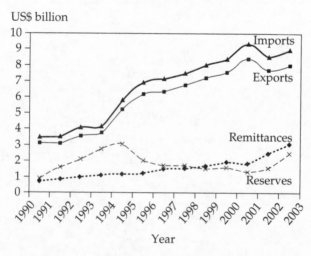

Source: Author's calculations using Bangladesh Bank (Central Bank of Bangladesh) Foreign Exchange Policy Department data.

counterpart of remittances, either directly or through their bank accounts. Currently, therefore, there is no mechanism for capturing and pooling the local currency equivalent of migrants' remittances.

Bangladeshi migrants may invest the taka counterpart of their foreign currency earnings in taka-denominated "wage earners' development bonds" bearing interest at 12 percent per year, higher than the rates offered on other government bonds and savings certificates. The interest earned is tax-free. Proceeds are convertible to foreign exchange and are transferable abroad.

The balances of foreign currency accounts maintained with commercial banks in Bangladesh are the migrants' money, freely convertible and transferable. Unless the balances are cashed in or converted into local currency, they are not reflected in the economy and provide little opportunity to stimulate microenterprise or other income-generating activities.

Deposits kept by the migrants in "nonresident foreign currency deposit accounts" are interest bearing, often above the market rates for Eurocurrency. The interest earned is tax exempt. The accounts are renewable and may be maintained for an unlimited time, even after the account holder migrates. Account holders may withdraw money from their accounts at any time and convert it into Bangladesh taka. They have no incentive to forgo these premium interest receipts to invest in risky rural microenterprises.

None of the systems described in the previous section could be replicated in Bangladesh now. Lesotho's deferred payment scheme or a similar alternative holds potential, although pooling migrants' remittances would require major policy and structural changes. Operating such a scheme requires a central body, stringently accountable to the highest institutional authorities, to regulate overseas employment. If this body were to be responsible for channeling foreign currency to the financial market, major changes to the foreign exchange laws and regulations would have to be made. Once the necessary changes were made, mechanisms would have to be created to redirect the taka counterpart of remittances to the rural economy for investment in microenterprise. Institutions in remote rural areas would be needed to conduct the transactions. These institutions could be rural branches of national commercial banks, or MFIs that already have experience and operational skills. Existing laws, however, do not allow MFIs to be involved in formal financing.

Obviously, extensive research and consensus building would be necessary before such sweeping changes could be made. Among the questions that would have to be addressed in the consensus-building process are the following:

- Do expatriate Bangladeshis want to help poor Bangladeshi communities in need of credit?

- Are the foreign source incomes of Bangladeshi migrants sufficient to allow for savings after family expenses and the costs of migration are met? What incentives would motivate migrants' families to save more?
- Will elite migrants invest in micro- and small enterprises before and after their return home? Given that migrants and their families in rural areas feel superior to nonmigrants and their families, how can migrants and their families be motivated to engage in tiny enterprise activities with poor entrepreneurs in the same village or community?
- Can Bangladeshi migrants organize into collectives, cooperatives, and other self-help organizations in the country of employment that could more efficiently manage funds meant for savings and investment in their home country?
- Should greater effort be made to increase the inflow of migrant remittances by extending investment opportunities, easing official procedures for sending remittances, and increasing migration to foreign destinations?
- Can informal channels be opened to receive migrant remittances? If so, how would the informal flows be regulated and accounted for? How would compliance with anti-money laundering laws and regulations be monitored?
- Is it feasible to involve MFIs in handling the remittances of home-bound migrants?
- Do the authorities have the power to make the necessary reforms in policies affecting the management of remittances?

POLICY PROPOSALS

Linking migrant remittances with microenterprise development in Bangladesh will clearly not be easy. To minimize risk and vulnerability, the proposals reviewed in the following sections may be considered.

Adoption of a Microenterprise Development Program

To redirect migrant workers' remittances to microenterprise development initiatives, it may be necessary to adopt a nationwide microenterprise development program, financed exclusively through migrant remittances or in combination with other sources of funds, to pool and transfer remittances to specific destinations. Once such a program is established, the government could introduce financial instruments or strategies to rechannel remittances toward microenterprise development.

Development of Diaspora Links

Members of the diaspora communities in most instances are rich and well organized by virtue of their long stays abroad and higher income levels, but they maintain close cultural relations with their country of origin. If this relationship can be converted to concern for the social and economic well-being of remaining friends and family members, or to humanitarian concerns, business interests, professional aspirations, or even a desire to return home some day, the country of origin stands to benefit enormously. Diaspora communities have the money, time, and intellectual resources to help reduce poverty, contribute to the expansion of the private sector, and enhance global competitiveness in their country of origin. Establishing and strengthening links to the diaspora can potentially make resources available for poverty alleviation activities such as microentrepreneurship development.

One way to mobilize diaspora communities is through the development of indirect investment vehicles that become a part of the portfolios held by individual investors. While such "retail" diaspora investors may invest in financial instruments to contribute to the economic development of their country of origin, they also wish to achieve a reasonable return on their investment to meet their own financial goals. Financial instruments targeting diaspora investors can include private equity funds or debt instruments such as business loans or sovereign bonds. Although the actual scale of individual investments may vary, the pooled resources can result in significant amounts of foreign direct investment and government financing. In addition to serving as a crucial source of financing, these instruments can encourage larger individual investments, adding to the depth of otherwise shallow financial systems and helping inject more advanced skills into the local financial sector.

Under the trusteeship of the Bangladesh government, a "diaspora investment fund" could be launched and communicated to the Bangladeshi diaspora as an investment opportunity with suitable incentives. Such a fund would merit confidence if managed by the Investment Corporation of Bangladesh. Profits could be channeled to microentrepreneurs or elsewhere.

A charitable rural development fund could be created to allow the diaspora to help the rural poor, perhaps under the leadership of the central bank or the Palli Karma Sahayak Foundation, the apex institution for the microfinance market. A high-powered committee or board of trustees would be entrusted with the management of the fund, with profits channeled to microenterprise and other income-generating activities through MFIs.

Involvement by MFIs

Although commercial banks may be better equipped to tap into financial and money transfer systems and provide sophisticated services to remittance recipients, they may not be able to serve the needs of poorer clients, particularly in rural areas, with their existing infrastructure. In this case, these banks may link smaller, down-market financial institutions to reach the unbanked poor. Increasing the involvement of MFIs in the intra-country delivery of local currency portion of Bangladeshi international migrant remittances is a promising means to expand financial access to the poor, particularly in rural areas that lack access to the larger commercial banks. MFIs could devote their attention to tapping remittances received through informal channels. They could also be allowed to undertake surveys to estimate the volume of informal remittances, including in-kind and other nonmonetary remittances, with a view toward eventually replacing those unauthorized informal channels.

Banks could engage NGOs and MFIs as partners in tapping the potential of the microcredit market and leverage their infrastructure and relationships toward delivering microfinance services. Using a wholesale linking model, banks could provide credit to intermediary MFIs for on-lending to microentrepreneurs. In this way, the problem of undercapitalization of MFIs would be reduced and the unused capacity of MFIs applied toward delivering new financial services. The banks would consolidate and restructure microfinance activities, fueling expansion of the microfinance market and overcoming current constraints to scaling up.

Remittance-Backed Bonds

Remittance-backed bonds permit countries to leverage diaspora funds to raise external financing for development. In recent years, emerging-market issuers have used the securitization of future flows of foreign exchange to avoid credit rationing in the face of deteriorating sovereign risk ratings. Banks that receive large amounts of wire transfers from workers and companies abroad issue the bonds. The funds backing the bonds are deposited in an offshore account before being converted into local currency to pay the recipients.

The investment instruments currently available for expatriate or migrant Bangladeshis are government-backed, with proceeds appearing in government accounts as public debt. The government could introduce bonds backed by migrant remittances, the local currency counterpart of which would be transferred to a fund for microenterprise development. Such government-sponsored bonds, if well managed, could be very attractive to migrants.

Special Migrants' Bond

Nationalized and private commercial banks may be allowed and encouraged to issue special bonds or saving schemes for migrants. The banks could lend these funds to microenterprise initiatives through their own networks of branches. Alternatively, banks could make MFIs their working partners in the rural areas for operating microfinance activities. The MFIs would act as loan service agents, and collaborate with social entrepreneurs to establish greenfield MFIs. Under such an arrangement, each bank or group of banks could build up a microfinance loan portfolio by accumulating the remittances they receive from migrant workers and creating a network that could eventually distribute a range of financial services throughout rural areas. In this way the commercial banks would be able to benefit from the potential of the microfinance sector.

Cooperation between MFIs and commercial banks has the potential to improve access to financial services for migrants and their beneficiaries, thereby creating formal banking relationships to provide greater financial security, reasonable returns, liquidity, and a greater capacity to leverage funds for productive activities. Financial institutions are more comfortable lending to remitters who use their services because a regular stream of remittance payments can represent a form of collateral. In some cases, recipients could use future remittances as collateral for lower lending rates.

CONCLUSION

This chapter has explored the possibility of linking and diverting migrant remittances toward microenterprise development in Bangladesh, thereby enhancing their productive uses. Although this approach is now being used in Latin America and elsewhere, its success has yet to be confirmed. Migrant workers' remittances are a strong source of foreign exchange earnings for Bangladesh, but Bangladeshi migrants are mostly semi- or unskilled workers whose earnings are low. They tend to be risk averse, and investing in microenterprises and other rural activities is not attractive to them. Pooling and redirecting these small amounts to microenterprise development is further hindered by lack of infrastructure for channeling them. Although the government continues to provide enhanced facilities for sending these private transfers through banking channels, a large portion still moves through informal channels.

Despite these difficulties, Bangladeshi diaspora communities may be willing to take part in the development of their country if the right instruments can be created to attract their interest. Various investment opportunities might be offered, along with incentives for unilateral contributions. Successful establishment of diaspora community-development funds for Bangladesh, headed and managed by trustworthy people, may be a useful option. Such funds could be created by the government and managed by the country's central bank, the Palli Karma Sahayak Foundation, or another similarly respected entity.

The successful investment of remittances has the potential to revitalize antipoverty activities in Bangladesh.

NOTES

1. In Bangladesh, NGOs and cooperatives are registered under five acts. Most are registered under the Societies Registration Act of 1860, which is administered by the Department of Social Welfare. Others are registered under any of the following: (a) as voluntary social welfare agencies (under the Registration and Control Ordinance of 1961); (b) as nonprofit companies limited by guarantee and licensed under Section 28 of the Companies Act of 1994; (c) as trusts under the Trust Act of 1882 or the Charitable and Religious Trust Act of 1920; or (d) as cooperatives under the Cooperative Societies Ordinance of 1984 (ordinance no. 1 of 1985). In the case of MFIs receiving foreign grants, the NGO Affairs Bureau, established under the Foreign Donations (Voluntary Activities) Regulation Ordinance of 1978, must clear the release of funds.

2. Some of the examples mentioned are drawn from Johnson and Sedaca 2004.

REFERENCES

Johnson, Brett, and Santiago Sedaca. 2004. "Diasporas, Émigrés, and Development: Economic Linkages and Programmatic Responses." Study prepared for the Trade Enhancement for the Services Sector (TESS), U.S. Agency for International Development, Washington, DC. http://www.tessproject.com/products/special_studies/emigre_pop.htm.

Siddiqui, Tasneem, and Chowdhury R. Abrar. 2003. "Migrant Worker Remittances and Micro-Finance in Bangladesh." Working Paper 38, Social Finance Programme, International Labour Organization, Geneva.

Chapter 6
Migration and Development: The Philippine Experience

I. F. Bagasao

The Philippines is one of the two highest migrant-sending countries in the world, and the highest in Asia, with almost 9 percent of its 82.8 million population living and working overseas. Remitting close to US$7 billion a year, Filipinos have tremendous potential for translating these net inflows to increased productive capacity. This chapter is based in part on consultations with Filipino communities in Europe on the ways in which they maximize their earnings and resources to improve their economic standing and the quality of life of their families.

Remittances are a more constant source of income to developing countries than other private flows and foreign direct investment, and decisions by migrants to submit a share of their income to their country of origin are affected less by international financial and market crises than by the decisions of private investors and speculators (Gammeltoft 2002). This chapter first briefly discusses data on Philippine migration and remittances, modes of remittance, and monitoring systems. It attempts to examine the impact of remittances on the development of the country and its citizens, and then describes the concerns, issues, and costs of migration, insofar as they are perceived to affect the ability of the country to leverage these remittances to contribute to its long-term growth and development. It then seeks to assess how government and the private sector, including civil society organizations, have attempted to harness migrant resources for more productive use.

THE CURRENT STATE OF REMITTANCES FROM OVERSEAS FILIPINOS

As of December 2001, an estimated 7.4 million Filipinos worked overseas. These people are classified into those who have permanent status, temporary or contract-based workers, and irregular workers or those who are working in other countries without the proper work documentation. Sea-based workers are estimated at 255,269, which is about one-fourth of the worldwide merchant marine population.

From the US$103 million recorded in 1975, about the time the Philippines started its overseas employment program, annual remittances as of 2002 almost reached the level of US$7 billion. There seems to be no letup to the migration of Filipinos, now recorded at more than 800,000 annually, or about 2,500 daily. The amount of remittances is expected to increase, given the new demand from North America, Japan, and the United Kingdom for professionals, such as nurses, caregivers, and others in medical-related fields, who earn higher wages than their less skilled counterparts.

Cost, speed of transfer, and exchange rates are the principal factors that affect the mode of remittance used, depending on the circumstances surrounding the transfer. Western Union, which uses Philippine commercial and rural banks and even pawnshops as conduits, appears to be the transfer agent of choice when time is of the essence, especially for medical or other emergencies when migrants do not mind the high transfer costs.

FORMAL AND INFORMAL MONITORING
MECHANISMS FOR REMITTANCES

The Philippine central bank (Bangko Sentral ng Pilipinas, or BSP) records and monitors formal remittances by virtue of its supervision over commercial banks, financial institutions, and their subsidiaries. Money changing centers do not fall within its monitoring mandate. Moreover, although remittances flow through commercial banks, BSP is not authorized to divulge the amounts received by individual banks, and commercial banks show no willingness to reveal these amounts.

BSP authorities state that remittance statistics do not reflect remittances going through informal channels, such as remittances brought by migrants themselves when they come home, money sent through friends, and amounts that are sent through informal money channels. Informal remittances are not susceptible to an accurate count. Nevertheless, the Survey of Overseas Filipinos conducted by the Philippine National Statistics Office (2003), which included 41,000 households, showed that of the 822,000 overseas Filipino workers (OFWs) who send cash remittances, 554,000 or 67.4 percent used banks, while 27.6 percent used informal channels or what is commonly known as "door-to-door" delivery channels. Another 2.4 percent remitted through an agency or local office, while the rest remitted through friends, co-workers, or other means.

With regard to the source, BSP cautions that the remittance data does not reflect the actual source country of the remittance due to the common practice of channeling remittances through correspondent banks that are often located in the United States. Because banks attribute the origin of funds to the most immediate source, the true origin is hard to verify.

Informal remittances consist of money sent by migrant workers and permanent residents through friends, relatives, and visitors who are going home, or money brought by migrants themselves who are homeward bound. It also includes transfers made through agents who engage in door-to-door transactions. The costs of goods or gifts sent by migrants to their families back home, as well as goods purchased by them from duty free shops upon their arrival at Manila, form part of informal remittances.

Undocumented migrants who are often not willing to open bank accounts for fear of exposing their status, or who may not be allowed to open bank accounts in their foreign workplaces, are most likely to use the informal channels.

Aside from surveys, one may appreciate how extensive these informal channels are by simply observing the long lines of people transacting with money changers usually found in shopping malls and population centers. In addition, the amount of duty free purchases by overseas Filipino visitors who are given the privilege to shop free of duty within 48 hours of arrival in the Philippines also provide a gauge of the extent of informal remittances.

SOURCES, BENEFICIARIES, AND USES OF REMITTANCES

The remittances captured by BSP from formal channels emanate from contract-based land and sea workers and go directly to their families. The amounts, frequency, and intervals vary by occupation and the level of wages in the foreign workplaces. In 2000, over 17 percent of Philippine households had at least one family member working abroad; 64 percent of these households were located in urban areas and 36 percent in rural areas (de la Cruz 2003). The remittances they received were used primarily for the following purposes:

- basic household necessities
- payments of debts contracted to underwrite migration expenses
- education of children
- medical expenses or emergencies
- land purchases, or home construction or improvement
- purchase of appliances or other durables
- savings and investments in microenterprises

Aside from remitting to their families, individual migrants as well as an estimated 12,000 regional, social, civic, and other migrant Filipino associations, have long been raising funds to underwrite small infrastructure projects and other humanitarian causes in the Philippines, such as building schools, hospitals, churches, water wells; funding of medical missions, medicine, and amelioration of calamities; and support of street children and orphans, churches, and others. The Commission on Filipinos Overseas, a Philippine government agency attached to the Department of Foreign Affairs, has run a 10-year program called Linkapil that has mobilized over a billion pesos (approximately US$18 million) from overseas Filipinos in North America, Australia, and Europe. This money has been used by various community projects in the provinces, in accordance with a needs profiling system that Linkapil devised, and probably represents only a small fraction of ongoing philanthropy by the extensive Philippine diaspora.

Some Philippine civil society organizations, such as the Asian Migrant Center, Unlad Kabayan, and Atikha, help migrants to prepare for their eventual return to the Philippines through migrant reintegration programs. These organizations help migrants form savings groups in places like Hong Kong, Japan, and Italy. The groups then invest the accumulated savings in enterprises of their choice within their hometowns. These programs, which promote value formation, the culture of savings, entrepreneurial skills, and even the participation of migrants' families in small enterprise, have attracted not only Filipinos but migrants of other nationalities as well, in preparation for the migrants' return to their home countries (Department of Foreign Affairs 2002).

THE IMPACT OF MIGRATION ON PHILIPPINE DEVELOPMENT

Migration in the Philippines affects the country at both the family level and the national level.

Impact on Families

Admittedly, the economic standing of many Filipino families has improved because their overseas breadwinners earn many times what they can earn in the Philippines. Over the years, a significant proportion of Filipino families have relied on foreign remittances or income from abroad as a main source of income. In 1997 the Family Income and Expenditures Survey revealed that 6.2 percent of Filipino families derived their main source of income from remittances. This translates to a total of 881,263 families who receive income from overseas (Go 2002).

Impact on the Nation

Although economists have pointed out that remittances have gone more toward consumption than increasing the productive capacity of the country, consumptive behavior does have a multiplier effect, particularly when used for education, health, and housing, which contribute to development (Lamberte 2002). Migration also eases the burden on the government of dealing with a high unemployment rate, which in the late 1990s hit 12.4 percent, while remittances act as a buffer for the country's balance of payments deficits and its reserves in times of crisis. Between 1990 and 1999, remittances contributed an average of 20.3 percent to the country's export earnings and 5.2 percent of gross national product (Go 2002).

There may be factors that affect the country's ability to leverage migrant inflows for growth and development or even deter the government from addressing the basic growth fundamentals. These factors may be the result of the effects of migration itself or the country's difficulty in solving its internal economic and political problems or in improving its global competitiveness.

The Philippines has to deal with its own economic, political, and social problems, the most prominent of which are lack of effective governance, a long-festering secessionist war in the South, and unstable government policies that seem to favor the perpetuation of power groups and the elite. It is also of no help that one-third of the Philippine budget is reserved for external debt service, and its products are beaten in the marketplace by cheap imports.

Despite its benefits, migration may also have perpetuated inequitable growth and spawned a culture of dependence on remittances. Inflows of remittances might allow postponement of painful but necessary reforms in governance, in improving income distribution through direct equity measures, and in facing up to the need for population control. Migration thus begets more migration, like a giant snowball that expands geometrically with its circumference—that is, until the opposite forces of economic growth at home reach sufficient strength to offset it. International Labour Organization studies indicate that the migration transition only occurs once a country crosses a threshold of about US$5,000 per capita income. Therefore, unless the Philippines slows down the growth of its population, its economy will have to grow at a rate of 10 percent a year until 2024 if it is to reach that threshold. Unfortunately, the Philippine population is growing at twice the rate of the Asian region as a whole, while the savings rate remains half that of its successful neighbors (Abella 2002).

The question also remains of whether the benefits of migration compensate for the costs to the sending country, such as emigration of the most capable, and the social disruption of families. The drain of so much human capital from a sending country, often the best and the brightest, reduces the country's capacity for long-term economic growth and human development. In the OECD countries as a whole, there are around 3 million migrants with a tertiary education. It has been suggested that if it costs about US$20,000 to educate someone to this level, the total wealth transferred from poor countries to rich is roughly now around US$60 billion (Stalker 2003).

WHAT TO DO?

Over the past 20 years, the Philippines has gradually built up legislation designed to tap the resources of its extensive diaspora. These laws invariably contain incentives and privileges for expatriates to invest, donate, purchase real property, or open a local enterprise in areas that normally are reserved for Filipino citizens. The latest of these laws—

the August 29, 2003, Republic Act No. 9225, otherwise known as the Dual Nationality Act—allows overseas Filipinos to participate in Philippine elections and to hold dual citizenship. (Before this act was passed, former Filipinos who lost their citizenship through various means were allowed to reacquire Philippine citizenship. The Dual Nationality Act now enables them to adopt Philippine citizenship without being considered to have abandoned their foreign citizenship.) Unfortunately, no monitoring system has been designed to measure how effective these laws have been in attracting expatriate capital, and there also is no extensive evidence showing that large numbers of migrants have taken advantage of these incentives. On the contrary, many potential returnees have decided to abandon plans of retiring, working, or investing in the Philippines after becoming disenchanted with its bureaucracy and unstable government policies.

Nevertheless, the strong desire to help is there and emigrants can still play an important role in contributing to the development of the Philippine economy apart from the remittances they send to their families, especially through activities initiated by the private business sector and civil society organizations to develop a viable business, savings, and investment environment. To have a significant impact on development, migrant savings, investments, and philanthropy programs must reach certain economies of scale and a critical mass. These attributes can be achieved only if savings and investments are organized and managed professionally to ensure that they are employed in industries or infrastructure that are urgently needed to improve productivity, address production and market inefficiencies, and help producers improve and find markets for their products. This will help improve the country's savings rate, which, at 20 percent is one of the lowest in the region. Savings and investment decisions made by migrants are usually made individually, and all too often, are based on incomplete and unreliable data. Studies indicate that such decisions result in a large number of small enterprises run by migrant family members that fail or have little significant impact on productivity.

New programs should be focused on the countryside, where about 60 percent of the Philippine poor live and where most of the migrants originate. Most migrants save in big commercial banks, instead of rural-based banks, thus migrant money is used mostly to service large accounts of the big banks.

Some potential prospects may address these imperatives, leveraging migrant remittances to serve as engines of growth. These programs present a fresh alternative to the traditional trickle-down approach and to the excessive dependence on foreign investment.

While reducing the costs of remittance transactions would greatly help to increase migrants' disposable income and possibly attract them to invest in their home country, more needs to be done. The potential increase in incomes resulting from the reduction in transfer fees still needs to be efficiently harnessed to have a significant impact on the development of their home countries. Multilateral institutions and international agencies need to coordinate with host country governments, perhaps following models such as the Mexican example, in which consular identification cards issued by the Mexican government have come to be accepted by banks as identity cards, thus allowing workers to open accounts and enabling them to remit formally.

The following section describes some pilot initiatives being undertaken by local government units supported by civil society organizations, which are aimed at harnessing the development impact of remittances.

Promotion of Trade and Investment by Local Government

Certain local government units (LGUs) are taking the initiative to attract expatriates to visit and explore trade and investment possibilities within their original home territory. With the help of international institutions and agencies as well as nongovernmental organizations (NGOs) and private financial institutions, they are engaged in building their capabilities and skills in promoting trade, investment, and tourism to outside visitors through the organization of trade and tourist promotion overseas, and the passage of local investment and incentive ordinances to be implemented by an investments office. In 2003, for instance, the province of Bohol organized more than 300 of its expatriates, currently living in North America, who came to visit their original hometowns and participate in an investment-matching forum with substantial results. Several other LGUs have shown interest in this model and are planning to replicate it.

Raising Revenues for Rural Infrastructure

LGUs are improving their skills in local governance, and are beginning to learn how to raise revenues independent of the national government, using powers granted to them by a 10-year-old decentralization law. In 2003, about 10 LGUs raised funds through bond issues at the local level to build public markets, ports, wharves, resorts, convention centers, and other rural infrastructure. These endeavors were accomplished with the help of a financial management firm that pioneered the use of LGU bonds for local development. While these bond issues were normally underwritten by commercial banks, a special security is being designed with overseas Filipinos as potential investors of bonds issued by their own home provinces or regions to finance urgently needed public projects such as processing plants, post-harvest facilities, hospitals, farm to market roads, and other strategic infrastructure.

Campaigns for Migrant Savings and Investments
in Microfinance Banks and Institutions

Some have questioned whether there is a role for microfinance institutions in linking informal remittances to development (Puri and Ritzema 1999). Absolutely. Microfinance reaches out to marginalized people and others in the informal sector whose only coping mechanism may be engaging in microenterprise. Migrants or their families could save or invest in microfinance banks or institutions and still manage a rate of return comparable to what commercial banks offer. Moreover, a one-year investment of about 100,000 Philippine pesos (approximately US$2,000), given the usual two microfinance cycles of six months each, could in one year support about 20 microentrepreneurs. Linking migrants and their families to microfinance institutions also provides migrant families with business mentoring and access to capital, which may be precisely what an absentee migrant needs to make sure that the money he or she remits is used productively and not wasted. A network of microfinance institutions and rural banks is designing such a system and marketing it abroad. The Philippine government has been relatively supportive of the microfinance industry by exempting microfinance banks from the moratorium on the opening of new banks or branches, along with other incentives.

Advocacy for a Partnership between Overseas Filipino Economic
Initiatives, Local Governments, and Development Agencies

To facilitate capital and capability buildup, and to improve local governance, advocacies and systems are being put together to pilot partnership projects between overseas Filipinos potentially wishing to save in, invest in, or donate to their hometowns, with LGUs putting up financial incentives, tax breaks, or support services, and funding or development agencies participating with an equivalent amount that may be used for capacity building or funding. Three such projects have been initiated by overseas Filipinos or migrants who have returned. Furthermore, development agencies are beginning to show interest in putting up counterpart money to match funds pooled by migrants for use in microlending, to be used in building capacity or other support for microentrepreneurs.

CONCLUSION

While studies point to remittances as supporting terrorist activities at home or elsewhere, or being used in money-laundering operations, the bulk of remittances are sent by migrants to support the basic needs of their families. Unreasonable and arbitrary scrutiny may lead to higher remittance costs, lead more people to the informal sector, and, more important, result in delays that affect the survival of migrants' families.

Novel programs being introduced in the Philippines on good governance, transparency, and accountability (by multilateral institutions such as the World Bank and others, in partnership with local development agencies) are a welcome development. Such initiatives check possible abuses in government and facilitate the delivery of much-needed funds to intended beneficiaries. The Philippines and other developing countries need more such programs that minimize intermediaries and allow institutions to be in direct touch and therefore able to personally know the real needs, concerns, and issues relating to poverty alleviation. There is indeed a link between poverty and migration; we need to empower migrants and recognize their contributions to the development not only of their countries of work, but also to their countries of origin.

REFERENCES

Abella, Manolo. 2002. "Filipinos are Bound to Be a Global People." Address delivered at Outstanding Overseas Filipino Awards, Manila, November 21–22.

Bangko Sentral ng Pilipinas (BSP). Annual reports available at http://www.bsp.gov.ph/resources/special_publications/default.htm.

de la Cruz, Josaias. 2003. "OFW Savings and Investments in Microfinance." Paper presented at the ERCOF Conference, Silang, Cavite, Philippines, July 16–18.

Department of Foreign Affairs (Philippines). 2002. "Final Report on Empowering Overseas Filipinos." Manila.

Durano, Marina. 1999. "Finance and Development Issues Arising from the Asian Crisis—A View from the Philippines." New York: Global Policy Forum. http://www.globalpolicy.org/socecon/ffd/durano99.htm.

Gammeltoft, Peter. 2002. "Remittances and Other Financial Flows to Developing Countries." Centre for Development Research Working Paper 02.11. Copenhagen. http://www.cdr.dk/working_papers/wp-02-11.pdf.

Go, Stella. 2002. "Migration, Poverty and Inequality: The Case of the Philippines." Department of Behavioral Studies, De La Salle University, Manila.

Lamberte, Mario. 2002. "Investments of OFWs in Rural Banks." Paper presented at the ERCOF International Conference, Davao, Philippines, April 10–12.

OFW Journalism Consortium. 2003. OFW Journalism Handbook. Overseas Filipino Workers Association: Manila http://www.theofwonline.com/ .

Philippine National Statistics Office. 2003. "Survey on Overseas Filipinos." Manila.

Puri, Shivani, and Tineke Ritzema. 1999. "Migrant Worker Remittances, Micro-Finance, and the Informal Economy: Prospects and Issues." Working Paper 21, International Labour Organization, Social Finance Unit, Geneva.

Stalker, Peter. 2003. "Proceedings of the NOVIB Experts Meeting on Migration, Globalization and Development." Netherlands, March 13–14.

Chapter 7
Remittances from Canada
to Central America and the Caribbean

Barnabé Ndarishikanye

Between 1980 and 2002, Canada became home to 4.2 million migrants as an average of 181,000 people entered the country each year (CIC 2002). The rate of immigration to Canada accelerated during the 1990s, with a total of 2.9 million immigrants arriving during the decade. By 2001, 5.4 million Canadians or 18.4 percent of Canada's total population had been born outside the country. Immigration was the main source of population growth in Canada between 1996 and 2001, accounting for more than one-half of growth (Statistics Canada 2001).

Most immigrants come from the developing world and countries in transition. Between 1991 and 2001, 58 percent of Canadian immigrants came from Asia and the Middle East, 20 percent from Central and Eastern Europe, 11 percent from Latin America and the Caribbean, 8 percent from Africa, and 3 percent from the United States. In 2002, the same proportions prevailed (CIC 2002).

Close to 400,000 immigrants from Central American and Caribbean countries entered Canada between 1980 and 2001. They came mostly from Jamaica (21.5 percent), Guyana (16 percent), Haiti (13 percent), El Salvador (12.6 percent), and Trinidad and Tobago (11 percent). Immigration of Mexicans is recent and represents 6 percent of the total. The share of migrants from Guatemala, Honduras, and Nicaragua does not exceed 5 percent for each country. Remittances represent a significant source of revenue for all these countries (figure 7.1).

Along with migrants, some 18,500 seasonal agricultural workers from Mexico and the Caribbean spend 17 to 20 weeks in Canada each year. Based on the number of workers needed by Canadian farmers, sending-countries select temporary workers and issue legal travel documents; Canada provides work permits. Housing is provided, and the employers may retain up to six Canadian dollars per day as a food charge. The seasonal workers are paid in cash or by check in Canadian dollars; the checks are accepted by farmers' banks.

Except for Mexican workers, 25 percent of the earnings of seasonal workers are withheld and sent to their home country, where the money is made available to the worker's family while they await the worker's return. More than Can$11 million is transferred annually to seasonal workers' families (table 7.1).

MIGRANT REMITTANCES TO SELECTED CENTRAL AMERICAN AND CARIBBEAN COUNTRIES

For the countries covered by this research, global remittances increased significantly from 1990 to 2002. They increased sixfold in El Salvador (from US$336 million to US$1,996 million), elevenfold in Guatemala (from US$119 million to US$1,320 million), ninefold in Honduras (from

FIGURE 7.1 REMITTANCES AS A PERCENTAGE OF EXPORTS IN SELECTED CENTRAL AMERICAN AND CARIBBEAN COUNTRIES, 1990–2001

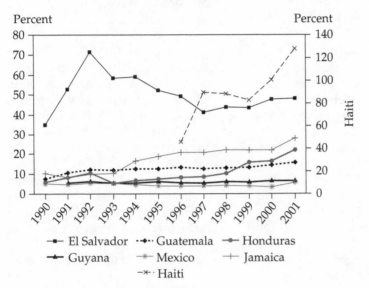

Percent (left axis) / Percent (right axis)

Legend: — El Salvador ··◆·· Guatemala —●— Honduras —▲— Guyana —*— Mexico —+— Jamaica —×·· Haiti

Source: IMF, *Balance of Payment Statistics Yearbook,* various years; World Bank, *Global Development Finance 2003;* for Haiti, M. Orozco 2002.

TABLE 7.1 SEASONAL AGRICULTURAL WORKERS FROM MEXICO AND THE CARIBBEAN, 2000–2002

	Mexico			Caribbean		
	2000	2001	2002	2000	2001	2002
Workers	9,265	10,709	10,779	7,438	8,063	7,756
Number of weeks	19.9	19.9	19.9	16.9	16.9	16.9
Hours per week	45	45	45	45	45	45
Hourly wage	$7.5	$7.5	$7.5	$7.5	$7.5	$7.5
Earnings per worker	$6,716.25	$6,716.25	$6,716.25	$5,703.75	$5,703.75	$5,703.75
Total earnings	$62,226,056	$71,924,321	$72,394,459	$45,424,492	$45,989,336	$44,238,285
25 percent mandatory transfer				$11,356,123	$11,497,334	$11,059,571

Source: Human Resources Development Canada 2003.
Note: Monetary unit is Canadian dollars. Participating countries: Barbados, Jamaica, Mexico, Trinidad and Tobago; and member states of the Organisation of Eastern Caribbean States: Antigua and Barbuda, Dominica, Grenada, Montserrat, St. Kitts and Nevis, St. Lucia, and St. Vincent and the Grenadines.

US$53 million to US$585 million), and fourfold in Mexico (from US$2.5 billion to US$9.8 billion). They doubled in Guyana (from US$21 million to US$44 million) between 1991 and 2001 and quadrupled in Jamaica between 1990 and 2001 (from US$229 million to US$940 million) and in Haiti between 1996 and 2001 (from US$152 million to US$600 million) (figure 7.2).

Remittances represent an average of 11 percent of GDP in El Salvador during the 12-year period under study, having grown from 7 percent to 14 percent. The same average is about 10 percent in Haiti, having increased from 5 percent to 16 percent between 1996 and 2001. Remittances represent an average of 8 percent of GDP in Honduras and Jamaica, and 6 percent in Guyana. Although Mexico is the second largest receiver of remittances in the world, the share of remittances in the country's GDP is negligible (figure 7.3).

The ratio of remittances to exports of goods and services in Haiti is around 90 percent, having increased from 46 percent to 128 percent between 1996 and 2001 (see figure 7.1). It also increased for Guatemala (from 7 percent to 16 percent), Honduras (from 6 percent to 22 percent), and Jamaica (from 10 percent to 28 percent) between 1990 and 2001. The ratio of remittances to exports is around 6 percent in Guyana and 5 percent in Mexico.

FIGURE 7.2 REMITTANCES TO SELECTED CENTRAL AMERICAN AND
CARIBBEAN COUNTRIES, 1990–2002

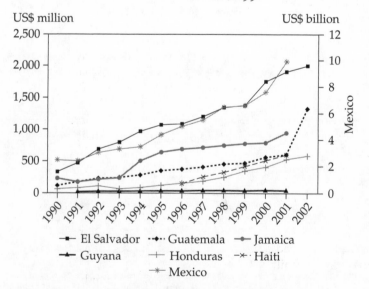

Source: IMF, *Balance of Payment Statistics Yearbook,* various years; World Bank, *Global Development Finance 2003;* for Haiti, M. Orozco 2002.

FIGURE 7.3 REMITTANCES AS A PERCENTAGE OF GDP IN
SELECTED CENTRAL AMERICAN AND CARIBBEAN
COUNTRIES, 1990–2001

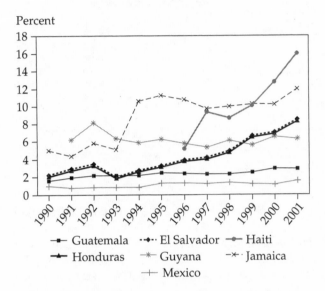

Source: IMF, *Balance of Payments Statistics Yearbook,* various years; World Bank, *World Development Indicators,* various years, and *Global Development Finance 2003.*

MONEY TRANSFERS THROUGH REMITTING COMPANIES

The formal money transfer market to Guyana, Haiti, and Jamaica is dominated by remitting companies, with Canadian banks playing a minor role in the industry; an unknown share of remittances is channeled informally. The analysis of these three countries, for which sufficient data is available, illustrates remittance characteristics between the two regions.

Haiti. Six companies act as principal remitters for the Haitian population in Canada. Most of the funds (95 percent) go to Haiti, the remainder to the United States. CAM Transfert is the clear leader in the market, followed by Unitransfer, and, some distance behind, Bobby Express. The other three companies—SOCA Transfert, Meli Melo Transfert, and Western Union Money Transfer—are relatively minor players.

CAM Transfert, established in Canada in 1985, services about Can$13 million annually in more than 38,000 transactions (table 7.2). Bobby Express, opened the same year, handles 7,500 transactions totaling about Can$1.58 million.

Three companies are involved in remittances in kind: CAM Transfert, Bobby Express, and SOCA Transfert. In these transactions, the remittance company either sells goods to remitters and delivers them

TABLE 7.2 AMOUNTS TRANSFERRED TO HAITI BY SURVEYED
COMPANIES, JULY 2003

Company	Number of transactions per month	Amount per transaction	Number of transactions per month, peak seasons	Amount per transaction per month, peak season	Number of transactions per year	Amount serviced per year
CAM Transfert	4,000	$150	8,000	$300	38,400	$12,600,000
Unitransfer	1,000	$150	2,000	$300	20,000	$10,000,000
Bobby Express	500	$150	1,000	$300	7,500	$1,575,000
SOCA Transfert	250	$75	400	$150	3,450	$348,750
Meli Melo Transfert	300	$150	500	$200	4,200	$705,000
Total					73,550	$25,228,750

Source: Discussions with managers.
Note: Monetary units are Canadian dollars. Peak seasons are at the end of December, at Easter, and in August.

in Haiti or acts as an intermediary between the remitters and participating stores.

CAM Transfert and Bobby Express have their own warehouses in
Haiti. A migrant based in Canada can buy goods in Canada using the
price board displayed in the company's lobby. CAM delivers the goods
to the receiver, just as it does for money.

Typical goods are rice, peas, sugar, milk powder, smoked meat, fish,
oil, and wheat flour. Each month, some 100 people send prepackaged
bags of individual commodities of 50 pounds each, increasing to 100
pounds in the peak season. Given that each bag is worth roughly
Can$20, the total value of remittances in kind serviced by CAM Trans-
fert is around Can$2 million per year. Bobby Express offers a similar
service, but on a smaller scale.

SOCA Transfert uses a catalogue of goods, mostly home furniture,
provided by participating stores located in Haiti. The company acts as
an intermediary between the sender and the stores and delivers the
goods to the beneficiary.

Jamaica. In addition to Western Union Money Transfer and Money-
Gram, three major funds-transfer companies serve Canada's large
Jamaican community. They are Rapid Remittances, Jamaica National
Building Society (JNBS), and Victoria Mutual Building Society (VMBS),
all based in Toronto's "Little Jamaica," in the district of York.

JNBS and VMBS were established in Canada in 1991 and 1992,
respectively. Both companies sell property in Jamaica and transfer
migrants' money to relatives there. Instead of opening a remittance
company of their own, they use the Bank of Nova Scotia, a Canadian
charter bank. JNBS and VMBS maintain accounts at the Bank of Nova
Scotia into which Jamaicans wishing to make remittances deposit
money. Remitting individuals then bring a record of the transaction to

JNBS or VMBS. There, they complete sending forms with the required instructions. The company verifies that the funds are available in the remitter's account at the Bank of Nova Scotia before proceeding with the transfer. Amounts sent range between Can$200 and Can$300 per transaction. JNBS estimates the number of transactions at 400 per month, while VMBS reports 75 (table 7.3).

Both companies see an increase in the number of transactions and average amount remitted at back-to-school time (August), before Christmas, and around Easter.

In November 2002, the Canadian Office of the Superintendent of Financial Institutions (OSFI) ordered the two companies to cease using the Bank of Nova Scotia as a charter bank. In the OSFI's view, money transfers represent a net loss of deposits for banks, which should not specialize in exporting funds that could be saved in Canada. In addition, to avoid potential money laundering or other criminal activities, banks are required to know their clients and cannot delegate this authority to a third party. OSFI gave the two Jamaican companies six months (from April 2003) to cease using the Bank of Nova Scotia or comply with the Foreign Bank Act. Becoming a foreign bank in Canada requires assets of at least Can$5 billion, or 20 billion Jamaican dollars. JNBS's total assets amount to 34 billion Jamaican dollars, or Can$6 billion. VMBS's assets are much smaller.

To continue its main activity of transferring money for mortgage payments and savings in Jamaica, JNBS created a remittance company, Jamaica National Money Transfer. In 2004, VMBS created a remitting branch, Canada Overseas Inc.

Guyana. One company serves the Guyanese community in Canada. Laparkan opened in Canada in 1993 and now has offices in Toronto and agencies in Montreal, Halifax, Winnipeg, Ottawa, and Edmonton. Laparkan channels 90 percent of the money it handles to Guyana; the remainder goes to Barbados, Jamaica, and Trinidad and Tobago.

The amount per transaction ranges from Can$150 to Can$200, reaching Can$400 in September, Christmas, and Easter. The number of

TABLE 7.3 AMOUNTS TRANSFERRED TO JAMAICA BY SURVEYED COMPANIES, JULY 2003

Company	Transactions per month	Amount per transaction per month	Transactions per month in peak season	Amount per transaction per month in peak season	Total transactions per year	Total amount serviced per year
JNBS	400	$250	800	$800	6,000	$2,820,000
VMBS	75	$250	200	$400	1,275	$408,750
Total					7,275	$3,228,750

Source: Discussions with managers.
Note: Monetary units are Canadian dollars.

clients per month varies between 200 and 300, and at least doubles in peak seasons. Thus, the minimum amount serviced per year is Can$750,000, while the maximum is Can$1,260,000. The number of clients varies from 3,000 to 3,600 per year.

Beside remittances in cash, Guyanese migrants living in Canada send goods to their relatives through Laparkan. Each month, an average of 300 boxes leave the country for Guyana, with a declared value of around Can$2,000 each. During peak seasons the shipment volume reaches 600 to 800 boxes per month; hence the Guyanese community living in Canada sends home goods worth Can$1.8 million to Can$4.8 million. The total annual value of remittances, including both money and goods, ranges between Can$2,550,000 and Can$6,060,000.

Western Union Money Transfer. Created in 1851, Western Union specializes in electronic transfer, credit card, telegraph, and facsimile services. In 1995 it became a division of Denver-based First Data Company, a large credit-card processor. In 2001, Western Union's global remittances were US$52 billion, dwarfing those of its nearest rivals, PayPal (US$6.2 billion), and MoneyGram (US$5.2 billion) (Rawe 2003).

Approximately 10 percent of the company's remittance business originates from Canada—about US$5.2 billion (nearly Can$8 billion). About two-thirds of that amount is remitted to the Caribbean, Central America, and South America.

THE PROS AND CONS OF REMITTANCE SERVICES

Remittance companies earn profits two ways: First, they charge a fee per transaction. Second, they realize gains on currency exchanges that often are not disclosed to customers.

The fee per transaction is fixed for any amount falling below certain thresholds. Western Union, for example, charges Can$14 to send less than Can$100, Can$18 to send between Can$101 and Can$200, and so on (table 7.4).

JNBS and VMBS charge relatively low fees because they manage mortgages for clients and earn interest on deposits made at the Bank of Nova Scotia. As of 2005, the two companies work with MoneyGram and their own representatives in Jamaica. Bank of Nova Scotia planned to open its own remitting company.

Remitting to Haiti is more expensive than to Jamaica and Guyana. The larger companies charge between 10 percent and 16 percent of the amount sent. For instance, CAM Transfer charges 12.5 percent for a Can$100 remittance if the recipient is located in a Haitian city and Can$15.80 for delivery to a rural area. SOCA Transfert and Meli Melo Transfert have competitive fees but do not serve a large market.

TABLE 7.4 THE COST OF SENDING MONEY, JULY 2003

Cost per Transaction for Ranges of Remittances

Company	$50 to $100	$101 to $200	$201 to $300	$301 to $400
Western Union	14	18	20	22
VMBS	10	15	20	25
JNBS	10	14	14	22
CAM Transfert	10	10 to 16	16 to 24	24 to 32
Bobby Express	12	12 to 24	24 to 36	30 to 48
SOCA Transfert	8	8 to 16	16 to 32	32 to 48
Meli Melo Transfert[a]	3	0	0	0
Laparkan	10	15	20	25

Source: Discussions with company managers.
Note: Monetary units are Canadian dollars.
a. No charges for large amounts of dollars to be delivered in Haitian gourdes.

Despite high fees and hidden costs, remitting companies offer the advantage of being close to the clients at both ends of the channel. They are quick, flexible, and reliable.

The companies that handle remittances to Haiti are based in Montreal in the neighborhoods where most businesses owned by Haitian immigrants are located. The companies have distribution centers in Haiti's major cities and throughout the countryside. CAM Transfert, for example, has 14 collection agents in Montreal, including barbershops and food stores frequented by the community members. Its 11 offices in Haiti pay out remittances quickly. SOCA Transfert has 10 collection agents in Montreal and two in Ottawa. In Haiti, it has an office in each of the major cities and a paying agent in small towns. Meli Melo Transfert has six offices in Haiti. In areas it cannot reach, it rents the service of Point Transfer, a U.S.-based remittance company with 15 distribution centers in Haiti.

JNBS has 23 offices in Jamaica and 23 collection agents in Canada. VMBS has 15 offices in Jamaica, Rapid Remittances has 24. Upon receiving funds, the companies deduct a mortgage payment, if appropriate, and deposit the remainder in a savings account or deliver it to the intended recipient.

Distribution for JNBS and VMBS is handled by the MoneyGram network, with which the companies have signed distribution agreements. The whole process, from depositing the remittances to reaching the beneficiary, takes less than 30 minutes in urban areas and does not exceed 12 hours even in rural areas.

In Guyana, Laparkan distributes 60 percent to 70 percent of total remittances (the remainder being handled by MoneyGram, Western Union, and small companies) and has arrangements with 65 postal offices that distribute money and packages to recipients across the country. The companies usually deliver the remittances the same day and in no case later than the end of the next day. Delivery methods vary slightly from one company to another, but all offer speed, convenience, flexibility, and reliability. Cars, motorcycles, bicycles, horses, and donkeys may be used depending on the final destination.

Competition is fierce among the companies. SOCA Transfert advertises heavily on Radio Haiti and offers discounts during peak seasons. Others, like JNBS and VMBS, build client trust through social activities in Canada and Jamaica. For example, VMBS provides financial support to New Hope Children's Home, the National Prayer Breakfast, the Women's Centre Foundation of Jamaica, and the Association of Street People. In Canada, VMBS organizes an annual seminar on marriage and family and funds university scholarships and grants.

MONEY TRANSFER SERVICES
OFFERED BY CANADIAN BANKS

Canadian banks are not deeply involved in helping migrant workers send money back to their countries of origin. However, a few initiatives are being piloted, and some local bank agencies offer remittance services.

Canadian banks charge on average Can$80 to transfer money. It takes at least 48 hours for the transferred amount to reach the destination account in a correspondent bank or the bank specified by the client. For instance, the National Bank of Canada corresponds with the Banque de l'Union Haitienne, the Universal Bank, and the Société Caraibéenne des Banques in Haiti; and with Citibank and the Capital & Credit Merchandize Bank in Jamaica.

Such a high fee attracts only large transfers, usually Can$3,000 or more. Migrant remittances are usually far below that level. Moreover, because banks prefer to transact business with other banks, a bank account is required to transfer money.

Buying a money order at a cost of Can$15 is also an option for sending money abroad, but it can take many weeks for the user to receive the money. Once users receive the money order by mail, they must take it to a bank, which sends it to a collection house, such as Chase Manhattan Bank, to verify that the funds are available. Depending on the quality of the postal services and banking system in the recipient's country, this process may take up to six months (Cameroon) or four weeks (Bangladesh).

On a small scale and for a Can$2 fee, Haitians buy money orders from the Caisse Populaires Desjardins and send them to Haiti, where they are accepted in cooperatives and corresponding banks. The requirement to have a bank account limits the potential of this channel.

Some local agencies offer remittance services as a response to high demand from a neighboring immigrant community. In such cases, individuals open an account in a Canadian bank and another in their country of origin. Senders make deposits in the account in Canada; they then communicate the list of deposits to the receiving end, along with amounts and payment instructions.

In some developing countries where automated teller machines exist, migrants living in Canada give debit cards to their relatives along with a corresponding personal identification number. Money withdrawn abroad is actually a remittance, although it is recorded as spending abroad by the account holder.

SERVICES FOR SEASONAL AGRICULTURAL WORKERS

The Bank of Nova Scotia operates in 28 countries in Central America and the Caribbean. It has 200 branches in the Caribbean, including 43 in Jamaica, 5 in Guyana, and 3 in Haiti. It controls the Scotia Bank Inverlat in Mexico, which has 400 branches throughout that country.

The Bank of Nova Scotia has set up a remittance program tailored to seasonal agricultural workers from Mexico. It is well-positioned to offer the same service to temporary workers from Caribbean countries.

Since the mid-1990s, the government of Mexico has encouraged foreign banks to help Mexican workers remit money. The Bank of Nova Scotia, having bought the Inverlat Bank, responded by designing a money transfer model designed for 10,000 Mexican seasonal agricultural workers who come annually to Canada. The model allows seasonal workers to send to their relatives an amount not exceeding Can$1,000 per week at a flat cost of Can$9.99 per transaction.

In Mexico, the government selects the workers and issues them identification relevant to a financial institution. Then a bank employee introduces them to the transfer mechanisms using a plastic card, labeled MiPagio (my payment). The card bears the worker's unique identification number, bank-account information, and a notice that it is valid only for transfers with the Bank of Nova Scotia. Workers give a duplicate copy of the card to their relatives.

Seasonal workers present the MiPagio card to a Scotia Bank agency, along with cash or a check, specifying the amount they wish transferred. If the check belongs to another bank dealing with the employing farmer, the Scotia Bank does not hold the money for collection purpose. Instead it uses the ScotiaDirect service, which allows it to verify funds availability within a short time. The next morning, reports of deposits are available in the 400 branches of Scotia Bank Inverlat in Mexico. Workers' relatives can withdraw money using their own MiPagio cards.

In 2002, 1,000 workers were registered and around 100 were pioneering this system. With more advertising and enough time for registration, both in Mexico and in Canada, the program could be used to a greater degree.

The Caisse Centrale Desjardins has been serving Mexican temporary workers since July 1997. At a fixed cost of Can$20, workers can send any amount they wish. The corresponding bank in Mexico, Banca Serfin, applies no additional charges to transfers made in Canadian dollars. In 2003, the service made 1,500 transfers totaling more than Can$2 million.

POLICY ISSUES

Lack of data on remittances in Canada. Canada does not prepare official estimates of migrant remittances. Statistics Canada includes in its annual household survey a question on gifts of money, pensions, and charitable donations that Canadian households send to the rest of the world. Each year between 1997 and 2001, such transfers represented Can$89 per household. Given that there are over 11.5 million households in the country, this proxy estimate suggests transfers of slightly more than Can$1 billion. It would be interesting to include a question specifically on remittances in the annual household survey.

Since September 11, 2001, for security purposes, remittance companies and financial institutions involved in money transfers to the rest of the world must report to the Financial Transactions Reports and Analysis Centre (FINTRAC). FINTRAC, Statistics Canada, and the Canadian International Development Agency (CIDA) could collaborate to design an appropriate system for collecting, storing, and sharing data on remittances.

Lack of regulations. In Canada, the Office of the Superintendent of Financial Institutions promotes and protects the legal framework within which banks, credit unions, and similar organizations operate. Because it does not regulate remittance companies, the use of exchange-rate differentials to generate revenue may remain hidden from consumers, and many companies have no incentive to address complaints from consumers.

CONCLUSION

Canada is home to many citizens from developing countries and a destination for thousands of seasonal agricultural workers. The prospect of being able to contribute to family budgets by sending money home is a compelling reason to migrate.

While migration to Canada is well documented, related remittances are largely untracked and poorly understood. Consequently, the development contribution of remittances from Canada has yet to be explored. However, the need for improved infrastructure services and an enhanced regulatory framework related to the remittance process is clear.

Evidence shows that microfinance can play a key role in reducing poverty and raising productivity and CIDA is developing a microfinance strategy. For many years, the agency has worked with and supported microfinance institutions—such as Proshika, Grameen, Bancasol, and credit unions in many developing countries in Africa—as well as Canadian nongovernmental organizations. To facilitate migrant transfers, CIDA could use its microfinance strategy to support program activities on remittances, such as supporting partnerships of migrant associations, credit unions, remittance companies, and commercial banks. The inclusion of money transfer programs would give concrete form to the international attention focused on making remittances work for the poor.

NOTE

The authors are grateful to the organizations that provided comments: Banque Nationale du Canada, Bank of Nova Scotia, BMO Banque of Montreal, Royal Bank of Canada, CIBC, Caisses Populaires Desjardins, Caisse Centrale, Développement International Desjardins, CAM Transfert, Bobby Express, SOCA Transfert, Meli Melo Transfert, Regroupement des Organismes Canada-Haïtiens pour le Développement, Statistics Canada, Office of the Superintendent of Financial Institutions, Jamaica National Building Society, Victoria Mutual Building Society, Laparkan, Jamaica Information Service, Gestion et conseil en coopération internationale.

REFERENCES

CIC (Citizenship and Immigration Canada). 2002. "Citizen and Immigration Statistics." Ottawa, Ontario. http://www.cic.gc.ca/english/pub/index-2.html#statistics.

Human Resources Development Canada. 2003. "Foreign Workers." Ottawa, Canada.

Orozco, M. 2002. "Remittances to Latin America and Its Effect on Development." Inter-American Dialogue, Washington, DC.

Rawe, Julie. 2003. "The Fastest Way to Make Money." *Time Canada*. June 23.

Statistics Canada. 2001. "Census of Population." Ottawa, Canada.

———. 2002. "Census of Population." Ottawa, Canada.

Part III
Strengthening the Formal
Financial Infrastructure
for Remittances

Chapter 8
Exploring the Credit Union Experience with Remittances in the Latin American Market

David C. Grace

Credit unions have traditionally been founded to correct a market failure—the lack of financial services for individuals of modest means. Today, developed countries have well developed and broadly accessible financial systems for most individuals, with the exception of newly arrived immigrants. Conversely, in many developing countries, market failures still exist for financial services; thus developing countries are a source of growth for newly formed credit unions. By providing remittance services, credit unions in developing countries have the opportunity to interact with potential members and capture savings from their communities.

In the late 1990s, the World Council of Credit Union's (WOCCU) member credit unions in Central America encouraged it to explore ways in which to facilitate the transfer of funds from credit unions in the United States to Latin America. The project was formalized in July 1999, and WOCCU's International Remittance network (IRnet®) service was launched to enable credit union entrance into the remittance business on both the sending and distributing sides of the transactions, with the end goal of increasing membership in credit unions. As of September 2003, 190 credit unions in 36 states with 850 points of service in the United States were using the service to send money to 42 countries on five continents. On the distributing end of transactions in Latin America, WOCCU works with two commercial money transfer companies and credit union national associations in El Salvador, Guatemala, Honduras, Jamaica, Mexico, and Nicaragua to provide remittance services.

As financial intermediaries offering a range of savings, credit, and related financial products to their members, credit unions are well positioned to influence the remittance market. Over 40,000 credit unions and their 90,000 points of service broadly disbursed in 85 countries provide one of the largest physical infrastructures of any financial network in the world to handle such payments.

This chapter seeks to provide resources to practitioners and donors, and offers a clear description of how the remittance market works based on experience gained from current remittance operations. A description of how and why credit unions have begun offering remittances, an analysis of their current and potential impact on the market in both the originating and distributing markets, and lessons learned for other financial institutions and development finance practitioners are presented.

MOTIVATION AND METHOD FOR OFFERING REMITTANCES

Credit unions engage in the provision of remittances for a variety of reasons, including to build relationships with existing or new clients, generate new sources of fee income, and as a means of providing a service to the community within which they operate.. These motivations are discussed below.

Motivation

Credit unions are not-for-profit financial cooperatives that have been operating for over 150 years. They can be found in nearly all parts of the world and serve 123 million members worldwide (WOCCU 2003). In general, when safe, sound, and efficient credit unions enter a market and offer lower-cost services, competition increases and prices fall (Emmons and Schmid 2001). Although credit unions are well positioned for the market, motivation for pursuing the market has been a combination of three factors.

Relationship Building

For sending institutions, the remittance services serve as a tool to reach new and growing immigrant markets while deepening relationships with existing immigrant members. Community demographics have changed so dramatically that in some cases not seeking to serve new immigrants is simply not an option if the institutions are to remain relevant. For distributing institutions, the act of distributing transactions brings individuals that are not already members into the organization on a repeated (often monthly) basis and presents the opportunity to attract these receivers as members and turn at least part of their remittances into savings.

New Source of Fee Income

The credit union involved generates income on each originating and distributing transaction. Credit unions consider the size of the international remittance industry—estimated to be at least US$72.3 billion in 2001 (Ratha 2003), with an estimated US$12 billion sent from the United States to Mexico in 2003—in their decisions to offer remittance services (Lugo 2003). Similar to most financial intermediaries worldwide, income from fees is a growing share of total income for credit unions.

Commitment to Communities

In many developed countries, credit unions offer remittance services as a way to reconnect to their founding mission of serving groups that otherwise would not have access to depository banking services.

The demographics of Latino immigrants in the United States who are most likely to send money to their home countries correlate well with the demographics of those Latino immigrants who are most likely to be unbanked. Approximately 69 percent of all Latino immigrants send money home to families—usually through nonbank providers charging exorbitant rates. Approximately 73 percent of Latino immigrants between the ages of 18 and 24 and earning less than US$20,000 per year are sending money home; 68 percent of Latino immigrants ages 18 to 24 earning less than US$20,000 per year are unbanked (Bendixen and Associates 2002). The primary reasons these individuals do not have accounts are that they do not feel they need an account (38 percent); they do not have the documentation that they believe is required to open an account (25 percent); or the process appears too complicated (9 percent) (Bendixen and Associates 2002). These data clearly demonstrate that reaching the core Latino money transmission sector in the United States equates to serving the underserved.

In contrast, in many developing countries 65 percent to 80 percent of the population has no access to depository financial services. Many of the existing members of credit unions may not have access to depository services if it were not for their credit unions (Westley and Branch 2000). Because receivers of remittances in Latin America are often members of low- to moderate-income groups, many banks are not actively seeking to open savings accounts for or provide credit to these clients (personal interviews 2000 and 2002). Yet, this clientele is already the core of credit union membership in these countries and new strategies by credit unions may not be required to connect to this type of potential member.

Method of Remittance Service

When WOCCU began investigating the methods for offering remittance services on a global basis, a range of options were evaluated based on efficiency, likelihood of adoption by users and credit unions, and technical fit with current operations. The four broad categories of options included card-based systems, account-based electronic transfers, international shared branching, and cash-based electronic transfers. In the five years through 2001, the growth area for credit unions working with WOCCU was concentrated on the cash-based model of electronic transfers. The majority of this section will address this methodology, so a brief review of the alternative methods considered is presented below.

Card-Based Systems

As technology has evolved, credit unions continue to monitor their remittance service strategies. While they encourage the use of automated teller machine (ATM) cards for remittances for some migrants, it remains a secondary strategy compared to cash payment at the point of sale for the following reasons:

- Receipt of money through ATMs does not facilitate savings and banking the unbanked as effectively as well-trained tellers who cross-sell the credit union's services.
- Immigrants in the host country must have a depository account and ATM card associated with an international network. Approximately 66 percent of Central American immigrants in the United States do not have a banking relationship (Bendixen and Associates 2002).
- The availability of international ATM networks in rural destination areas is limited, as is withdrawal size.
- While ATMs can be cost effective for remitters, programs from large U.S. banks to-date have been more costly than cash payments (Orozco 2002).

Account-Based Electronic Transfers

Nearly all 10,000 credit unions and 4,000 commercial banks operating in the United States have the capability to offer traditional account-based international wire transfers. Although financial intermediaries have been offering such services for decades this method has little penetration in family-based remittance transfers primarily because of the requirement for both the sender and receiver to maintain an account with a depository financial institution that has international correspondent relationships. In addition, these account-to-account transfers occur through traditional or established bank wire systems that were created for, and cater to, large-value commercial payments that originate through the Federal Reserve System's Fedwire and are carried across the SWIFT (Society for Worldwide Interbank Financial Telecommunication) messaging system. Because these systems are extremely flexible and ubiquitous in their ability to deliver payment to a vast number of banks worldwide, limited information is available to the originator of the transfer regarding the exchange rate at which the transaction will occur or the time by which payments will be received. These limitations have also created an environment in which many banks or credit unions in developed countries no longer actively promote such services because of previous negative experiences.

International Shared Branching

International shared branching refers to an integrated environment in which institutions allow individuals full access to their accounts in person and individuals can perform related banking services at facilities in a country other than his or her "home" branch. For example, a person who is a credit union member in Mexico could deposit or withdraw funds, apply for or make loan payments, and use associated services at a participating and distinct credit union in the United States. These services have not been implemented due to challenges in quantifying the potential return on investment for credit unions. However, there does seem to be some market for these services, because the availability of such a system would provide immigrants complete access to their home financial institution, eliminating the need to open an account abroad, manage funds across boarders in different institutions, and send money back to pay loans.

Cash-Based Electronic Transfers

Cash-based electronic transfers represent the most common, and a continually growing, method for transmitting money domestically and internationally. These transfers allow an individual to present cash or have an account debited at a sending institution, then cash is delivered to the recipient, or in some cases an account can be credited at a distributing institution abroad. WOCCU chose this as the optimal way to offer remittance services because of the popularity of this method with immigrants and the ease of implementation among a technologically diverse set of institutions; plus, the personal contact required for initiating and distributing transactions presents opportunities for gaining new members.

The limitation of this method is that to have significant presence or impact in the market a broad physical network is needed on both the origination and distribution sides, and a robust technological infrastructure is required to interconnect the participants. The importance of such a network is discussed further in the Lessons Learned section.

After selecting card-based electronic transfers as the preferred method, WOCCU began to identify and select potential alliance partners. As with selecting any strategic partner, key criteria included an institutional due diligence analysis encompassing license evaluation, determination of a similar cultural orientation (in this case, commitment to low-to-moderate income immigrant communities as demonstrated through transparent operations and low prices), and ensuring complementary business objectives. The primary complementary business objective was the need to combine a partner's technological network, on both the originating and distributing sides of a transaction, with the vast physical infrastructure that credit unions offer.

WOCCU, as a broker for credit union participation in remittances, and its chosen global strategic partner (Vigo Remittance Corporation) deem it essential that sending and distributing institutions meet minimum financial and operational standards to participate.

Requirements for Participation

Given the technology and method chosen for facilitating remittances, there are different operational requirements for credit unions on the originating and distributing sides of the transactions. The key difference is the ability to work with individual institutions on the originating side of transactions versus the need to work through networks of credit unions on the distributing side. By having broad networks on the distribution side, originating institutions can offer a convenient and consistent service with regard to price, exchange rates, and service to senders. Operationally, originating institutions can send the transaction information to centralized servers maintained by a network provider and settle the funds individually with the network provider. Conversely, a network of distributing organizations must identify a single centralized location within the network to receive information and funds for settlement from the centralized network provider on the origination side.

Potential requirements for distributing networks are described below:

- *A network of institutions that together offer a physical distribution system across a country.* The key element of a strong distribution network is the number of points of service it offers, with particular emphasis on immigrants' home regions. A single entity in the network contracts with the centralized network provider and subcontracts with the distributing institutions if they are separate organizations.
- *Applicable regulatory approval to offer money transmission services, and adherence to anti–money laundering guidelines.* Some governments allow only certain types of institutions to be engaged in money transmission or may require specific licensing to enter the market. Increasingly, regulatory requirements include adherence to the anti–money laundering principles of the Financial Action Task Force, or the USA Patriot Act if transactions pass through the United States.
- *A Central Financing Facility (cash management desk) with technical and operational capacity to manage the disbursement of funds and information.* Each institution offering remittance services must have its own account with the Central Financing Facility (CFF) through which funds are distributed. All funds are cleared through a CFF and settlement occurs between the CFF and each distributing institution. On behalf of the network, the CFF is also responsible for managing foreign exchange operations, if applicable. The management of foreign exchange includes informing the centralized network provider daily of the exchange rate that will apply for payments, and performing the exchange of currencies.

- *A reliable communications infrastructure through which information can be securely and efficiently distributed.* There must be a reliable system in place for communication between the national-level entity and the participating institutions. While different technologies may be used, a formal system capable of moving information through the network securely and efficiently needs to be in place. The level of automation and efficiency of the network affects the network's ability to grow the service.
- *A minimum level of financial performance, stability, and capacity to capture savings.* The cash-based methodology for offering remittance services requires distributing entities to make payment upon receipt of payment instructions; however, the settlement of funds between the originating and distributing institutions does not occur until the next business day. As a result, distributing institutions are providing overnight credit to originators (Herstatt risk) and need sufficient liquidity management capability to make payments immediately. To be in a position to make immediate cash payments to recipients, the institutions require a ready source of cash, such as member savings on deposit. Without the ability to attract adequate savings, the reliability of the remittance service becomes questionable if clients are requested to come another time while the institution looks for the required cash.
- *Strong customer service orientation that encourages recipients to continue using the service.* The bottom line accountability within the receiving country resides with the national regulatory body. This body must decide, within an acceptable range, the rigor with which it will hold individual distributing entities or branches to standards. Distributing entities should be open at least five days per week, have an external audit completed annually, have telephone and fax communication capabilities, and maintain a clearing account with the CFF.

ANALYSIS OF CURRENT AND POTENTIAL IMPACT

The most significant impact that the provision of remittance services by credit unions can have is to open more depository transaction accounts and integrate unbanked senders and receivers into the financial system. This impact does not diminish the interest in decreasing costs in the money transfer market but rather recognizes that lower costs in themselves are not sufficient to attract new clients. For example, if remittances were free but 50 percent of Mexican originators still relied on fringe banking services or put savings in the mattress, paid 1 percent to 3 percent to cash paychecks, lacked conventional credit histories, and utilized predatory lenders, the individuals would not be better off economically. As discussed above, credit unions on both the sending and receiving sides of the transfers are offering the product for similar reasons. The service enables credit unions to leverage their existing infrastructures to offer money transfers and develop new relationships. Much as checking accounts are offered at or below cost to build relationships for financial institutions, credit unions are able to offer remittance services as a relationship product with the expectation that income will be generated from such members on newly formed relationships that encompass savings, credit, and insurance products. This positioning of the product and the nonprofit status of credit unions enable them to undercut prices of the for-profit money transfer companies (as seen in table 8.1) and generate revenue on the relationships that can be built. In contrast, the major money transfer companies are publicly traded firms that must maximize their profits from the fees and a narrow set of products.

Impact in the Sending Country

Although the impact of remittances on developing economies that are dependent on these flows of funds for a significant portion of their exports is significant, the impact of including the originators of transactions in financial institutions should not be ignored because presence of an account is a significant determinant of the ability to accumulate basic individual financial assets in the United States (Beverly and Sherraden 2001). Relative to the rest of U.S. residents, immigrants, and particularly

TABLE 8.1 COST OF SENDING US$300 TO MEXICO FROM
CALIFORNIA, FRIDAY, MAY 17, 2002

Money transfer service	Exchange rate[a] fee (US$)	Fee charged (pesos to dollars)	Actual charge in Mexico	(US$)	Actual money received in Mexico[b] (US$)
IRnet	10	9.30	none	15	285
Bank of America (SafeSend)	10	9.20	none	18	282
MoneyGram	15	9.31	none	20	280
Western Union	14.99 (approximately)	9.26	none	21	279
WellsFargo (Intercuenta)	10	8.95	none	25	274
Citibank (C2it with Banamex)	14.99	8.92	none	31	269

Source: Greenlining Institute, San Francisco, CA.
a. Interbank exchange rate on May 17, 2002, was 9.46 pesos to US$1.00.
b. Actual money received is the initial $300 less the fee and the exchange rate loss (the difference between the interbank exchange rate and the offered exchange rate).

Latino immigrants, have lower incomes, are less educated, and are at least four times as likely to be unbanked (Bendixen and Associates 2002; U.S. Census Bureau 2002). The young, poor, and noncitizens are the Latino immigrants most frequently sending money home and also the immigrants who are most likely to be unbanked—reaching recent immigrants and the unbanked are inextricably linked.

The Federal Reserve Board's *1998 Survey of Consumer Finances* indicated that 9.5 percent of all families were unbanked (Kennickell, Starr-McCluer, and Surette 2002). Disaggregated and unpublished data from the survey also showed that 36 percent of Latino and 38 percent of Asian families were unbanked. Subsequent studies indicate that 44 percent of all Latino immigrants in the United States, or 6.38 million people, are unbanked today. Immigrants, as much as any other group in the United States, are disproportionally unbanked (Bendixen and Associates 2002).

Credit unions in the United States are trying to gain the confidence of immigrants by forging new relationships with immigrant community outreach centers, disclosing the actual exchange rate at the point of sale, and refunding a member's money and the fee paid if a problem occurs. These practices deliver on the promise of building trust between the provider and the user.

In addition to these transparent business practices and outreach efforts, credit unions in the United States offer remittance services at prices well below the competition for key markets such as Mexico and Central America (see table 8.2). For example, it costs only US$10 to send up to US$1,000 to El Salvador, Guatemala, or Honduras through participating credit unions.

Nonetheless, credit unions and other financial institutions have had limited success in penetrating the immigrant market with money transmission services. Part of this difficulty is immigrants' lack of awareness of the benefits of maintaining accounts, and part is due to infrastructure

TABLE 8.2 COST COMPARISON BETWEEN CREDIT UNIONS AND MARKET LEADERS

Amount sent to Guatemala	Cost		
	Market leader 1	*Market leader 2*	*Credit unions*
US$300	$25	$18	$10
US$500	$38	$30	$10
US$1,000	$65	$60	$10

Source: Surveys by WOCCU, October 2003.

challenges that financial institutions face in serving the market (lack of bilingual staff, limited hours of operations for a segment that conducts business in person, and inconvenient branch locations). Credit unions as prudentially regulated financial institutions have also been constrained relative to corner grocery stores offering remittance services by capital requirements and regulations restricting who they may serve. Many undocumented immigrants believe they cannot open an account because they lack the necessary documents to reside in the United States. In fact, as long as the undocumented individuals can provide secure photo identification authenticating their identity, they may open either a noninterest bearing account or obtain an individual tax identification number from the Internal Revenue Service.

The most significant impact that the 205 credit unions offering remittance services today has had is the market pressure and attention they have generated, not the capture of a significant portion of the business. In 2000, credit unions began offering remittances to Mexico at a flat fee of US$10 for sending US$1,000. Six months later a major bank in the United States, located in a market in which the new credit union offering was attracting significant press, began offering remittance services with the exact same pricing structure but a worse exchange rate. Three months later the largest retail-oriented bank in the United States began offering a card-based remittance solution with the same pricing structure but with additional fees. An additional four months later, the largest bank in the United States announced a remittance program to Mexico, again with a similar pricing structure, as an introductory offer.

While neither credit unions nor banks in the United States have been able to capture large shares of the market, their entrance nonetheless has changed the market. At the same time U.S. financial institutions were entering the market, Wall Street firms (for example, Celenet Communications, Sun Trust Banks Markets Group) were considering the impact new entrants would have on money transmitters' future profits and U.S. credit unions met with U.S. congressional representatives and the Fox administration of Mexico to highlight new alternatives for sending money. Although causality is unclear, the major money transmitting companies lowered their prices and exchange rates. During the first 18 months of the Fox administration, money transmission prices from the United States to Mexico dropped 32 percent (Orozco 2002).

Impact in Receiving Countries

While the market impact on the sending side of the transactions has been indirect, the influence in receiving countries is more direct and measurable. This influence has been felt in pricing, banking the unbanked, and capturing savings and market share.

WOCCU research conducted in November 2002 on Guatemalan and El Salvadoran credit unions reveals the following:

- *Credit union entry in the market lowers costs and creates competition.* In El Salvador, Guatemala, and Honduras credit unions are charging 40 percent below the market average for a US$200 transfer and 300 percent below the market leader for the average transfer (WOCCU data 2003).
- *Credit union distribution facilitates banking the unbanked.* Between 14 and 28 percent of the nonmember receivers of remittances at credit unions end up joining a financial institution for the first time (FEDECACES 2002; FENACOAC 2002).
- *Receiving remittances at credit unions encourages savings.* Thirty-seven percent of those individuals who are members of the credit union end up saving some part of their remittances. In addition, 10 percent of the value of the transfers sent is being deposited in a savings account at the receiving credit union compared with 1 percent to 4 percent being saved at other distributing institutions[1] (FEDECACES 2002; MIF and Pew Hispanic Center 2003).

Recipients of remittances generally have low incomes and are discouraged from saving as a result of receiving funds at department stores, or they are not eligible to open accounts at the banks disbursing the funds because of high minimum balances. It is estimated that 65 percent of Mexico's population does not have an account at a financial institution (Westley and Branch 2000). To the extent that receiving remittances at credit unions introduces individuals of all income groups to financial institutions, this program will increase the culture of banking within receiving countries and provide facilities for savings. As a result of utilizing the cash-based electronic transfer process for remittances, distributing credit unions that generally require photo identification and knowledge of the sender's name, amount, and transaction number of the receiver can also serve very low income individuals who lack identification if the credit union is made aware of this in the transaction's record. Notification of the transfer and any required information, such as a transaction number, is communicated between the sender and receiver. At times this notification can be prolonged if the receiver does not have a telephone and messages have to pass through acquaintances.

If remittances are received at safe and sound formal financial institutions that allow and facilitate saving part of each remittance, as opposed to remittances being distributed by commercial retail stores that encourage spending, individuals may be more likely to save. This ability to save by having funds deposited directly into an account can help individuals accumulate financial assets by easing the process of saving.

As of September 2004, credit unions in El Salvador and Guatemala were distributing approximately 55,000 transfers or over US$24 million per month after 36 months of being active in the market (WOCCU data 2004).

If remittances are sent or delivered by formal financial institutions should we also seek to "channel" remittances to productive uses? According to Puri and Ritzema (1999), with the exception of Korea, which has required the use of a specific facility as a condition of employment, Asian countries, including Bangladesh, India, Pakistan, the Philippines, Sri Lanka, and Thailand, have not been able to successfully channel remittances. They failed even when financial incentives were offered. Credit union data from Guatemala indicate that 80 percent of the transfers are used for consumption (FENACOAC 2002).

LESSONS LEARNED

Since WOCCU's International Remittance network (IRnet®) service was launched in 1999 to enable credit union entrance into the remittance business, WOCCU has learned the following lessons in the development of its remittance product.

- Listen to the market. Central American credit unions were the genesis of the product and WOCCU had to modify the design as it learned more about the market.
- There must be equal interest from providers on both sides of the transaction and strategic partners will likely be needed if choosing cash-based transactions, because barriers to entry are high.
- Remittances are a volume-based business; therefore systems that can efficiently process large volumes of transactions at low marginal costs are crucial if competitive prices are to be offered and revenue is to be generated.
- It is difficult for financial institutions seeking to serve Latinos to penetrate the origination side of the business in the United States.
- The remittance business is more competitive than microcredit in many markets. In the microcredit business, competition comes from local moneylenders or other nongovernmental organizations with limited resources. In money transfers the competition has significant resources.

Although these lessons are drawn from WOCCU's experience working with credit unions in the United States and Latin America and the Caribbean, WOCCU has found these lessons to be relevant as it has branched out to partner on remittances with other MFIs (microfinance institutions) and in WOCCU's own preliminary activities in the Polish and Filipino remittance markets.

On the surface, there are many similarities between the types of services and clients MFIs work with and the recipients of remittance transfers. These similarities include the following:

- small payment size
- close relationships to people of modest means and the poor
- broad networks, often in rural areas
- access to informal financial services
- need for trust and one-on-one interaction

CONCLUSION

From the outset, MFIs are likely to find that successfully providing remittance services will be more competitive than in the early days of microfinance. This process will require institutions to have networks and alliances in place to begin offering these services. While these challenges are formidable, there is tremendous opportunity to gain additional clients and help families combat the unsafe practices or usurious fees associated with the current options for sending money to friends or family back home.

There is much to be explored in cross-border marketing of remittance services, and there is yet to be a broad basis of experience with regard to offering associated financial products for remittances (remittance-day loans and insurance, for example). Greater analysis of the impact of remittances on account acquisition and savings mobilization needs to be examined. Even with these unanswered questions it seems clear that for there to be a sustainable and long-term impact from the provision of remittances, both originators and distributors should have the capacity to and the practice of encouraging senders and receivers to open depository accounts and, where possible, capture savings.

NOTE

1. The Central Bank of El Salvador has documented that only 1 percent of the value of the remittances received at non-credit union distribution sites is saved in a financial institution. Data from a 2003 survey from MIF and Pew Hispanic Center indicates 4 percent of transfers are being saved in El Salvador.

REFERENCES

Bendixen and Associates. 2002. "Survey of Remittance Senders: U.S. to Latin America. November/December 2001." Miami, FL: Bendixen and Associates.

Beverly, Sondra D., and Michael Sherraden. 2001. "How People Save and the Role of IDAs." In *Building Assets: A Report on the Asset-Development and IDA Field*, ed. Ray Boshara. Washington, DC: New America Foundation.

Emmons, William R., and Frank A. Schmid. 2001. "Membership Structure, Competition, and Occupational Credit Union Deposit Rates." *Federal Reserve Bank of St. Louis Review* 83(1): 41–50.

FEDECACES (Federación de Cooperativas de Ahorro y Crédito de El Salvador). 2002. Internal data.

FENACOAC (Federación de Cooperativas de Ahorro y Crédito y Servicios Varios). 2002. Internal data.

Kennickell, Arthur B., Martha Starr-McCluer, and Brian J. Surette. 2002. "Recent Changes in U.S. Family Finances: Results from the 1998 Survey of Consumer Finances." *Federal Reserve Bulletin* 86(January): 1–29.

Lugo, Luis Alfonso. 2003. "Fox Says U.S.-Mexico Remittances Hit High." Associated Press. September 24.

MIF (Multilateral Investment Fund) and Pew Hispanic Center. 2003. "Receptores de Remesas en Centro America." Guatemala City, Guatemala: Multilateral Investment Fund and Pew Hispanic Center.

Orozco, Manuel. 2002. "Attracting Remittances: Market, Money and Reduced Costs." Report prepared for the Multilateral Investment Fund of the Inter-American Development Bank. Washington, DC.

Puri, Shivani, and Tineke Ritzema. 1999. "Migrant Worker Remittances, Microfinance and the Informal Economy: Prospects and Issues." Working Paper No. 21, Social Finance Unit, International Labor Organization. Geneva.

Ratha, Dilip. 2003. "Workers' Remittances: An Important and Stable Source of External Development Finance." In *Global Development Finance 2003*. Washington, DC: World Bank.

U.S. Census Bureau. 2002. "Coming to America: A Profile of the Nation's Foreign-Born (2000 Update)." Washington, DC: U.S. Department of Commerce.

Westley, Glenn D., and Brian Branch. 2000. *Safe Money: Building Effective Credit Unions in Latin America*. Washington, DC: Inter-American Development Bank.

World Council of Credit Unions (WOCCU). 2001–2003. Internal data.

———. 2003. "2003 Statistical Report." Washington, DC: World Council of Credit Unions. https://www.woccu.org/pdf/stateng03.pdf.

Chapter 9
Remittances and Pyramid Investment Schemes in Albania

James P. Korovilas

The economic transformation of postcommunist Albania has had several features that are unique by Eastern European standards. During the 1990s, an enormous proportion of Albania's labor force worked abroad—an estimated 400,000 in Greece and Italy. These migrant workers play an important part in the Albanian economy because a large proportion of their earnings are transferred back home. Also unique to Albania is its rate of economic growth in the postcommunist era, which has outpaced that of all other transition economies. Finally, Albania witnessed the dramatic rise and collapse of a series of pyramid investment schemes during the period 1996–97 that were larger relative to the size of the economy than any previous schemes of this kind. This chapter investigates these three features of the Albanian economy in an effort to identify the link between foreign remittances, economic growth, and the pyramid investment schemes.

Since the disintegration of communism, most Eastern European countries have shared the experience of economic collapse followed by gradual recovery. The reasons for the collapse of the early 1990s, typified by plummeting production and hyperinflation, are well documented and uncontroversial. Output levels fell across Eastern Europe following the demise of central planning and the subsequent shortages of vital inputs. Hyperinflation in the early and mid-1990s was largely a result of monetary overhang from the communist era, coupled with the inability of postcommunist governments to implement suitable fiscal and monetary measures to control inflation.

In contrast to the lack of debate on the causes of the initial economic collapse in Eastern Europe, there is much debate over the reasons for economic recovery, and especially its pace. From the mid- to late 1990s, almost all of the countries of Eastern Europe experienced economic growth and lower inflation. However, the rate of economic recovery was not consistent across the region, with Poland and Albania, for example, far outpacing Hungary and Slovenia (table 9.1). Explanations for these disparities have focused on factors such as the pace of economic reform, the extent to which inflation has been controlled, the length of time spent under communism, and the degree of political stability. All of these factors are important in explaining the pace of economic recovery in most Eastern European countries, yet it is doubtful whether they can adequately explain the rapidity of economic recovery in Albania.

The Albanian economy from 1994 to 2002 experienced the fastest rise in real gross domestic product (GDP) in Eastern Europe. Gros and Steinherr (1995) demonstrated the link between the pace of economic reform and the speed of economic recovery in transition economies. This explanation of Albania's strong economic recovery is compelling, given that the pace of economic reform in Albania was rapid (EBRD 1998). Indeed, Hashi and Xhillari (1997) conclude that the success of the Albanian economy can largely be explained by the implementation of a

TABLE 9.1 ECONOMIC RECOVERY IN EASTERN EUROPE, 1994–2002
Percentage change in real GDP

	1994	1995	1996	1997	1998	1999	2000	2001	2002
Albania	8.3	13.3	9.1	–7.0	8.0	7.3	7.8	6.5	6.0
Bulgaria	1.8	2.9	–9.5	–5.6	4.0	2.3	5.4	4.0	4.0
Czech Republic	2.2	5.9	4.3	–0.8	–1.0	0.5	3.3	3.3	2.5
Hungary	2.9	1.5	1.3	4.6	4.9	4.2	5.2	3.8	4.0
Poland	5.2	7.0	6.0	6.8	4.8	4.1	4.0	1.0	1.0
Romania	3.9	7.1	3.9	–6.1	–5.4	–3.2	1.8	5.3	3.5
Slovenia	5.3	4.1	3.5	4.6	3.8	5.2	4.6	3.0	2.7

Source: EBRD 2002.

comprehensive privatization program. These factors form an important part of the overall explanation for the recent success of the Albanian economy, but the fact cannot be ignored that Albania only recently emerged from a long period of isolationist central planning and possessed few of the advantages enjoyed by more successful transition economies. It is, therefore, unlikely that Albania's recent economic success can simply be explained by its adoption of an appropriate set of government policies. The role that factors specific to Albania have played in the country's recent development must also be considered. For instance, a large proportion of Albania's population work abroad and send money back home. This chapter seeks to show that these remittances are substantial and are playing an important role in the economy's development.

A unique feature of the Albanian economy in the late 1990s was the rise and failure of several fraudulent pyramid investment schemes. Although such schemes have also appeared in other transition economies, the Albanian experience is unique. Albania's pyramid schemes were significantly larger, relative to the size of the domestic economy, and led to a greater degree of political and economic turmoil when they eventually collapsed. In 1995–96, pyramid investment schemes attracted total deposits equivalent to roughly half of Albania's GDP. This establishes a link between the flow of remittances and the rise and fall of these schemes.

BACKGROUND OF REMITTANCES IN ALBANIA

The fall of communism in Albania marked the end of one of Europe's most repressive political regimes of the twentieth century. Prior to 1989, Albanian citizens were subject to severe restrictions on their movements. Travel between the different regions of Albania required official approval, and travel to restricted areas such as border regions was strictly forbidden. Foreign travel was almost totally restricted, with only diplomats and members of the government having the opportunity to see the outside world. So great was the desire of the Albanian government to shield the population from the "corrupting influence" of the outside world, that it even took the extreme precaution of ensuring that Albanian diplomats were unable to speak the language of their host country, imagining that this would prevent them from being seduced by capitalist propaganda.[1]

In the early 1990s, Albanians witnessed a wide range of political and economic changes. In the political sphere, the government relaxed its control on foreign travel, finally abolishing all restrictions. However, trying legitimately to leave a country that had no previously negotiated reciprocal travel agreements proved to be difficult, especially because no country was willing to issue travel visas to large numbers of destitute Albanians (Hashi and Xhillari 1997). Despite these bureaucratic restrictions, the desire of ordinary Albanians to leave their country increased rapidly, perhaps due to access to Italian television channels that previously had been jammed. At the same time, the collapse of central planning led to widespread unemployment. This unemployment, coupled with chronic food shortages afflicting the country, provided the degree of desperation sufficient to force people to accept the risks involved in leaving their home country to find work abroad.

To understand the effect on the Albanian economy of the remittances sent home by emigrant Albanians, both the number of Albanians working abroad and the size of their remittances need to be calculated. Most publications dealing with this phenomenon are in agreement over the number of Albanians working abroad; an annual average of 400,000 men and women were employed in either Greece or Italy between 1992 and 1996.[2] Because Greece is far more accessible than Italy, and far less hostile to illegal immigrants (there have never been immigration detention camps in Greece), it is not surprising that roughly 90 percent of Albanian emigrants chose to search for work in Greece rather than risk incarceration or forced repatriation in Italy. Lazaridis and Romaniszyn (1998) argue that migration from Albania to Greece is partly a result of historical links between the two countries and partly because of the ease with which illegal immigrants can cross the largely unguarded Greek-Albanian border.

The vast majority of Albanian immigrants had no desire to remain in Greece for the long term, but simply wished to work for a few years to support themselves and send money back home to support their families in Albania. Initially most Albanian workers in Greece were driven by desperation and thus had modest subsistence requirements. However, they soon realized that the ready supply of well-paid casual work presented them with the opportunity to work for a few years and accumulate substantial sums (by Albanian standards).[3] After working in

Greece for several years and accumulating a sum of capital, many Albanians would return home and invest their money in an effort to acquire long-term security (Lianos, Sarris, and Katseli 1997). For example, many of Albania's new private businesses, such as petrol stations, were established with money earned by migrant workers in Greece.[4] Albanian workers in Greece had a great incentive to send a large proportion of their earnings back to Albania. Migrant workers with dependent families were responsible for the consistent but small flow of remittances, and those returning to live in Albania would often transfer a large sum, which either could be invested or used to establish a small business.

To estimate the impact of these remittances on the Albanian economy, it is necessary to calculate their total value, but there is no consensus on the size of this figure. In contrast to the agreement on the number of Albanians working abroad, estimates of the total annual value of remittances injected into the Albanian economy vary widely. The most conservative estimate is from the International Monetary Fund (IMF), which puts the annual inflow of remittances at US$200 million (IMF 1994). At the other extreme, a *Financial Times* survey on Albania offers the much higher figure of US$400 million (Done 1997). Because the various sources do not explain how they have arrived at their estimates, it is difficult to judge their credibility. In the absence of reliable data, it is worth putting these figures to the test by comparing them with an independent calculation of the total value of remittances, based upon reasonably reliable information about Albanian migrant workers.

CALCULATING THE SIZE OF REMITTANCES

The pattern of economic migration between Albania and Greece has remained relatively consistent over time. In the early years of Albanian economic migration (1992–99), Greece was the obvious country of choice for Albanians seeking to improve their economic prospects. In more recent years (1999–2004), Albanians increasingly migrated to the more prosperous countries of northern Europe, such as Germany and the United Kingdom (King and Vullnetari 2003). This change in the pattern of Albanian migration can be explained in several ways. First, Albanians working in Greece experienced significantly increased levels of prosperity, which, in turn, opened up the opportunity for international travel and made it possible for Albanians to be more ambitious in their choice of destination (Korovilas 2002). Second, the war in Kosovo in 1999 enabled ethnic Albanians from Kosovo to claim asylum in northern Europe. A significant number of Albanians from Albania were able to enter countries in northern Europe by claiming that they were from Kosovo. The extent to which this occurred is not known.

Despite these changes in the pattern of Albanian migration and a significant increase in the size and dispersion of the Albanian diaspora in recent years,[5] for the period 1992–1999, the pattern of Albanian migration, particularly to Greece, was relatively stable. In Greece in 1998, the documented migrant population (that is, those who applied for a permit to work) was estimated to be almost 400,000. The majority of the documented migrant labor force is from Albania, and constitutes almost 80 percent of incoming migrants (Psimmenos and Georgoulas 2002).

The following calculation for the total value of remittances entering Albania from the diaspora is based on the pattern of migration that existed prior to 1999. Although the distribution of the Albanian diaspora has changed, strong evidence supports the view that the remittance behavior of Albanian migrants remains relatively constant, regardless of their country of residence.[6] Therefore, assuming that the total number of Albanian economic migrants is relatively consistent over time, it can also be assumed that the following calculation for remittances is not significantly affected by changes in the distribution of the Albanian diaspora.

To calculate the total size of migrant remittances entering Albania, the average value of remittances for an economically active migrant worker is needed; then this figure is simply multiplied by the number of economically active Albanians working abroad. To obtain detailed financial information about the Albanian diaspora, a series of interviews were conducted with Albanian economic migrants in Greece. The interviews were conducted over three years from 1998 to 2000, using semi-structured, in-depth interviews. These interviews were designed to collect a wide range of economic data, which then allowed for cross-checking, to ensure that the key data on remittances was reliable. The population of Albanian economic migrants in Greece is geographically dispersed. However, the Albanian diaspora in Greece is concentrated in certain sectors of the labor market, specifically agriculture and construction (Korovilas 2002). To ensure that the interview samples were representative of the entire population, the following methodology was used: Two sample areas were defined, one in the urban sector and one in the rural sector. Within these two sectors, individuals were selected using a random stratified sampling technique, ensuring that the correct proportions of the main income groups were represented in the sample. The initial set of interviews conducted in 1998 contained a sample of 60 individuals. A series of follow-up interviews were conducted in 1999 and 2000. Individuals covered in the first set of interviews were re-interviewed in 1999 and 2000 to ensure that the information was consistent over two years. The results from the two follow-up interviews revealed no significant change over this period in either the level of income or the level of savings (remittances) in the sample group.

The sample data revealed that the average daily wage over the sample period was US$22, with an average monthly wage for the sample period of US$440. (The average monthly wage is calculated by multiplying the average daily wage by the average number of days worked per month.[7]) The figure for total remittances from the Albanian diaspora in Greece is calculated by multiplying the figure for average monthly remittances, in this case US$200, by the number of Albanians who were economically active (about 400,000). The sample data revealed that three-fourths of the sample were economically active. Therefore, assuming the sample is representative of the population, this yields an economically active population of 300,000 and a value of total monthly remittances entering Albania from Greece of US$60 million (300,000 migrants × $US200). This then gives a figure of US$720 million for annual remittances entering Albania from Greece.

These results suggest that the average level of remittances for Albanians in Greece is equivalent to 45 percent of total earnings. In the context of global flows of remittances this figure is rather high; however, this is explained by the unique nature of economic migration between Greece and Albania. Research on migrant remittances by Buch, Kuckulenz, and Le Manchec (2002) establishes the fact that the level of remittances is largely determined by the needs of the family. In this study of Albanians working in Greece, the survey data suggest that a large proportion of Albanians are not supporting family in Greece, instead they are making a vital contribution toward alleviating the poverty of their families in Albania, therefore creating a set of circumstances in which the flow of remittances needs to be maximized. Furthermore, the flow of migrant remittances between these two countries is also affected by the fact that Albanians are still not fully integrated into Greek society. "Home" is often seen as being in neighboring Albania, not in Greece; therefore there is a tendency to invest in Albania and not in Greece (Korovilas 2002).

The purpose of the calculation of remittances is to provide strong evidence that the official estimates for the size of total remittances are far too low. Official estimates for the value of remittances entering Albania for the years 1999 and 2000 range between the IMF's estimate of US$300 million (Jarvis 1999) and the Albanian central bank's estimate of US$400 million (Piperno 2003). If the basic assumptions of this chapter's calculations are correct, the official estimates for the total value of remittances must be far too low, even if a reasonable margin of error is allowed. This disparity between the survey results and the official estimates of remittances can be explained by the fact that the flow of remittances between Greece and Albania occurs largely within the informal sector. For example, a significant proportion of remittances are transferred using informal courier services. Also, only 16 percent of total remittances entering Albania are deposited in the formal banking sector, making it impossible to accurately monitor the flow of remittances entering Albania (Piperno 2003). Furthermore, at least 17 percent of remittances are saved outside the formal banking sector as idle cash balances, rendering them untraceable because idle cash balances have no effect on the domestic economy (Piperno 2003).

This chapter's calculation for the total value of remittances entering Albania from the Greek diaspora assumes that a typical Albanian worker in Greece should be able to save at least US$2,400 per year. To prove that this is possible hard evidence needs to be found that a typical Albanian migrant worker can amass annual savings of this magnitude. This task proved to be difficult, because illegal migrant workers are frequently robbed or deported, making them wary and reluctant to reveal information about their savings. The solution to this problem was to obtain information from a reliable independent source about the amount of money saved by Albanian workers.

Albanian workers in Greece save their money in several different ways. Some regularly save small amounts, which are then taken to Albania by couriers for a commission. This is a popular way of transferring funds, especially for those who are supporting a family in Albania.[8] However, it is difficult to establish how much money is being transferred by this method, because no records are kept. For those people without dependents in Albania, the preferred method of saving is to accumulate a large sum of money while working in Greece and to take it with them when they return to Albania. People who saved and transferred money in this way would be in an ideal position to provide precise information about the average propensity to save of Albanian workers in Greece, because they could reveal exactly how long they had worked and exactly how much they had saved in that time. However, most Albanians in Greece do not bank their savings, which makes them very unwilling to disclose information about their savings, because they fear betrayal and have much to lose.

In 1999, the author gained privileged access to details of bank accounts held by two Albanians who had worked in southern Greece for three years and had steadily accumulated all their savings in the local branch of the National Bank of Greece.[9] The two Albanians were involved in domestic construction and were relatively skilled in a number of trades. In August 1998, after working in Greece for three years, they withdrew all their savings from the bank, closed their accounts, and returned to Albania. The bank's records revealed that they had withdrawn a collective total of US$72,000.[10] To obtain a figure for the annual savings per person, the total is divided by six to obtain the astonishing figure of US$12,000. This example proves that it was possible for Albanian workers in Greece to save and to transfer sums of money considerably larger than those suggested by other sources. These two Albanians were probably much more fortunate than the majority of their compatriots in Greece, because their skills allowed them to command better wages, and they were continuously employed. However, their example suggests that the figure derived earlier for average annual savings is not unreasonably high; indeed, it is probably too modest.

This analysis clearly demonstrates that annual remittances entering Albania from Greece between 1999 and 2000 amounted to at least US$720 million. Calculating the value of the total remittances from the entire Albanian diaspora is beyond the scope of this research; however, if the value of remittances from the non-Greek Albanian diaspora are included, the total figure would clearly exceed US$720 million per year. Having demonstrated that the total value of remittances entering Albania is at least US$720 million, the effect of remittances on the Albanian economy can now be examined.

THE EFFECT OF REMITTANCES
ON THE ALBANIAN ECONOMY

In 2000, the gross domestic product of Albania was US$2.7 billion (EIU 2000). The inflow of hard currency in the form of US$720 million in annual remittances had a significant effect on the economy of posttransition Albania.

Put simply, a substantial inflow of hard currency reserves enables an economy to behave in any of the following ways: to spend more than it produces; to invest more than it saves; or to import more than it exports (Nafziger 1997). Lack of reliable information on domestic levels of production and consumption prevents an investigation of this feature of the Albanian economy. However, there is sufficient information on the other two features—investment and imports—for this investigation to focus on. If the flow of remittances into Albania was indeed as large as suggested, there should be some evidence of this in Albania's economic indicators. Whether there is evidence that Albania imported more than it exported will be considered first.

Albania's current account for the period 1996–2000 shows some interesting anomalies (table 9.2). The value of annual imports greatly exceeds the value of annual exports, yet this disparity is not captured in the current account. For example, in 2000, the value of imports exceeded the value of exports by US$700 million, but the current account recorded a deficit of just US$130 million, implying US$570 million in unaccounted for current account credits. The Economist Intelligence Unit (EIU) explains these figures by suggesting that the current account deficit was partly financed by running down reserves, but mainly financed by the inflow of remittances from Albanians working abroad (EIU 2000). The EIU figures suggest that reserves increased by US$6 million in 2000, and

TABLE 9.2 ALBANIA'S MAIN ECONOMIC INDICATORS, 1996–2000
US$ million

	1996	1997	1998	1999	2000
Annual inflation (%)[a]	12.7	32.1	20.9	0.9	0.5
Exports of goods	244	159	208	275	300
Imports of goods	922	694	812	938	1,000
Current account	–107	–272	-65	–156	–130
Reserves	281	309	349	369	375
Exchange rate (Albanian leks per U.S. dollar)	104.5	148.9	150.6	137.7	143.1

Source: EIU 2000.

a. Percentage increase in consumer price index from previous year.

remittances for 2000 are estimated at US$349 million. Leaving aside the fact that reserves actually increased during 2000, the official figure for the size of remittances is clearly insufficient to balance the current account, leaving a US$221 million shortfall. Although the EIU gives figures for the size of total remittances in 2000, there is no indication of how the figures were calculated and no explanation of the US$221 million shortfall in the current account.

Remittances from Albanians working abroad are technically classed as an invisible credit on the Albanian current account. The shortfall in the current account figures is clearly coming from somewhere, and it most likely consists of invisible items that are difficult to identify. Although this supposition appears plausible, the Albanian economy has few invisible earnings other than remittances. The two main areas in which a country such as Albania might have invisible trade surpluses are in tourism and services. The tourist industry in Albania is not well established, with earnings being far too small to be significant. As for services, Albania has an underdeveloped banking and financial services sector and is a net importer of these services (EIU 2000). Earnings from services and tourism are thus unlikely to be large enough to fill the gap in the current account figures, so it is safe to assume that this gap was being filled by flows of remittances. It seems equally safe to conclude that the EIU's figures underestimate the value of total remittances.

The main credit items of Albania's capital account, such as foreign direct investment (FDI) and international aid, can be accounted for. However, the main debit items, such as capital flight, are difficult to account for; but all that is required for the present analysis is to establish that Albania's capital account was not in surplus to such an extent that it would counterbalance the deficit on the current account. The largest credit item on the capital account is FDI, which averaged US$90 million between 1996 and 2000 (Datastream International 2000).

Although this is a significant figure given the size of the Albanian economy, it is clear that, when other official transfers are added and capital account debits such as capital flight are subtracted, the capital account could not have been in surplus to the extent needed to offset the visible trade deficit.

If the current account was indeed in deficit to the extent indicated by the EIU, a depreciating exchange rate and rapid inflation should be expected. In reality, the exchange rate against the U.S. dollar was relatively stable after 1996, and inflation over that period was at one of the lowest rates recorded in the transition economies (EBRD 2002). From this analysis, it is safe to conclude that the Albanian current account was not as substantially in deficit as the EIU suggests and that there were considerable invisible earnings from foreign remittances. These remittances had the effect of balancing the current account, thereby offsetting inflationary pressure and preventing a depreciation of the Albanian lek.

Foreign remittances helped stabilize the Albanian economy throughout the posttransition period. Remittances also provided much of the foreign exchange that was needed to import food and other essential goods. The extent to which the Albanian economy relied on imports is demonstrated by the fact that, in 2000, imports of nonagricultural goods were dominated by basic goods such as cement, copper pipes (for plumbing), and building bricks (INSTAT 2000). These basic building materials, which elsewhere are rarely imported owing to their low value and high transport cost, were vital to rebuilding Albania's crumbling infrastructure.

Several inferences can be drawn from the observation that the Albanian economy was importing far more than it was exporting. First, the assumption that remittances were large enough to fill the gap in the current account supports the idea that remittances were indeed much larger than officially recognized. Second, by filling the gap in the current account, remittances permitted relative economic stability without the occurrence of a balance-of-payments crisis. Third, remittances provided the hard currency needed to import the building materials and capital goods that were vital to Albania's economic recovery.

THE PYRAMID INVESTMENT SCHEMES

In January and February 1997, the Albanian economy was thrown into chaos by the collapse of several so-called pyramid investment schemes.

Annual remittances between 1998 and 2000 were calculated in this chapter to be at least US$720 million, and just over half of this sum can be accounted for by spending on imports. To explain what happened to the remainder of the remittances entering Albania, it is worth taking a closer look at Albania's several pyramid investment schemes.

The collapse of the pyramid investment schemes in January and February of 1997 was an important event, with both political and economic repercussions. When the total value of investments made in these schemes is considered, the significance of both their rise and subsequent collapse becomes clear. At the height of their popularity during 1995 and 1996, pyramid investment schemes attracted total deposits estimated to be between US$1 billion and US$1.3 billion, roughly equal to half of Albania's GDP for 1996. [11]

The rise of pyramid investment schemes has two important implications for this analysis of the effects of remittances on the Albanian economy. First, it can be demonstrated that the emergence of pyramid investment schemes was driven by the inflow of remittances. Second, such schemes were so large that one needs to ask how the population of Albania, with a GDP per capita of only US$800 in 1996 (Done 1997), managed to deposit such enormous sums of money in these schemes. The obvious answer is that their growth was financed by money from remittances, although this cannot be confirmed until other possible sources of money have been considered.

During 1995 and 1996, about US$1.3 billion was deposited with the various schemes. Although there is evidence of people selling their assets to invest in the schemes, there is far more evidence of people depositing money they had already accumulated. Almost every account of the collapse of pyramid investment schemes begins with a case study of a particular individual who lost his or her entire savings in a deflated investment scheme (Pettifer 1997). It seems reasonable to assume that, before the rise of such schemes in 1995, Albanian households had accumulated substantial monetary balances. To assume otherwise would be to suggest that household disposable incomes had increased dramatically since 1994, and there appears to be no evidence to support this.

The sample group interviewed between 1998 and 2000 revealed the following information about the link between remittances and pyramid investment schemes: from the sample of 60 Albanian migrants interviewed, 10 percent had invested money directly in pyramid schemes with an average investment of US$16,000. The examples from the sample follow a familiar pattern—people accumulated substantial monetary balances, then deposited them with one of the many pyramid investment schemes.

Popular demand encouraged the formation of investment schemes that could offer generous rates of return. It is worth considering whether the Albanian banking sector could have provided an alternative to the pyramid schemes. By looking at interest rates and the rate of inflation between 1994 and 1996, this possibility can be explored. Real interest rates were negative in 1994, before the rise of pyramid investment schemes, but were positive during 1995 and 1996, when these schemes were at the height of their popularity (table 9.3). Real interest rates were negative in 1994 because the Albanian government was operating some form of financial repression, holding interest rates below the market-clearing level (World Bank 1994). Thus, while it is evident that household savings could have been protected from inflation by depositing them with one of the Albanian banks, the rate of return was still far lower than the rates being offered by the pyramid investment schemes.

The Albanian banking system was still underdeveloped, with limited presence outside the capital city of Tirana (EIU 1997). Therefore, even though it offered positive real rates of return on deposits in 1995 and 1996, it was not accessible to a population requiring immediate access to savings. Although depositing savings in a bank may have provided protection from inflation, depositing money with a pyramid scheme provided income to meet daily expenses. Glenny (1997) refers to a case where US$9,000 was deposited with Vefa, the largest of the schemes, at a monthly interest rate of 10 percent. This provided the depositor with a monthly income of US$90, with the expectation that the principal would be preserved, should it be needed in the future.

If the pyramid schemes were financed by money from sources other than remittances, why does there appear to be no mention of these sources? As stated earlier, there are many documented cases of people investing money from prior savings and from the sale of assets, but there do not appear to be any recorded accounts of people who lost money that came from other sources. The most likely answer to this question is that many Albanians who lost money in pyramid investment schemes were involved in some form of illegal activity, and were therefore reluctant to reveal the initial source of their savings. Salome (1997) notes that pyramid investment schemes were financed by money from several sources, including remittances, diversion of EU loans to buy tractors, drugs and arms trafficking, and other criminal activities—including violating United Nations sanctions by smuggling goods into the former Yugoslavia. Of these four activities, only remittances are legal; therefore, the possibility that people involved in the other activities might claim that the money they lost in pyramid investment

TABLE 9.3 INFLATION AND NOMINAL AND REAL INTEREST RATES
percent change per year

	1994	1995	1996
Consumer price inflation	23	8	12
Deposit rate on savings (annual average)	15	16	19
Implied real interest rate	−8	8	7

Source: EBRD 1997.

schemes was derived from remittances has to be taken into account. This would explain why most of the documented accounts are of people who claim to have lost money earned while working abroad. Evidence supports the hypothesis that illegal activities were taking place. Trafficking in both drugs and arms is generally acknowledged to be a major source of revenue, especially in the relatively lawless and anarchic southern region of the country (Glenny 1997). Sanctions-busting was also widespread during the war in the former Yugoslavia, enabling Albanians to make handsome profits by selling petrol and diesel to Serbia. However, sanctions-busting and its associated profits came to an end in November 1995 when sanctions were lifted. A portion of the money invested in pyramid investment schemes no doubt came from these illicit activities, yet it is almost impossible to determine the size of that portion because there is no accurate information on earnings from illegal activities in Albania.

The money deposited in the various pyramid investment schemes clearly came from several sources. The absence of reliable figures makes it impossible to determine accurately the amount from each source, leaving educated guesswork as the only option; suffice it to say that a substantial portion may have come from remittances, with the remainder, in unknown proportions, from the sale of assets, other savings, and various types of illicit activities.

The pyramid investment schemes that plagued the Albanian economy in 1997 were the result of a combination of coinciding factors. The evidence suggests that a significant flow of remittances were entering Albania during the time when pyramid investment schemes were becoming established in 1996. The evidence also suggests that 26 percent of total remittances were saved, often as idle cash balances, thereby creating a buildup of savings over time.[12] Furthermore, there is evidence that Albanian economic migrants deposited significant volumes of their accumulated savings with pyramid investment schemes, which were in turn allowed to develop in an environment that lacked an appropriate level of financial regulation (Jarvis 1999). It is relatively easy to demonstrate how these various factors coincided and created a situation in which accumulated savings were drawn into fraudulent pyramid investment schemes. However, it is much harder to explain why Albanians were prepared to invest such large sums of money in schemes that were offering clearly unsustainable rates of interest. There are a range of possible explanations for why people were drawn into pyramid investment schemes. For example, Vickers and Pettifer (1997) claim that Albanians lacked appropriate experience with the fraudulent facet of free market capitalism, which in turn was a function of Albania's history of economic and cultural isolationism during the communist era. However, interviews with Albanians who lost significant amounts of money in pyramid schemes give a different explanation for this phenomenon. When Albanians who lost money were asked why they invested in pyramid investment schemes that were clearly unsustainable, they mainly claimed that they were driven by peer pressure and they invested their money fearing that they would be left out if they did not participate.

AFTER THE COLLAPSE OF THE PYRAMIDS

The figure of US$720 million calculated here for the total annual flow of remittances into Albania measures more than a quarter of the Albanian GDP in 1996. Clearly, remittances have played an important role in both stabilizing and fostering rapid growth in the Albanian economy. The balance-of-payments figures produced by EIU indicated a significant gap in the current account that, in the absence of an equally large surplus in the capital account, would have suggested a severe balance-of-payments deficit. During that time, however, the Albanian economy exhibited low inflation and currency stability, neither of which is consistent with such a large deficit. By including remittances as a credit on the current account, an overall balance can be achieved. This is consistent with Albania's main economic indicators, which never suggested that the country was suffering from the adverse effects of a significant balance-of-payments deficit.

Albania's several pyramid investment schemes played a key role in fueling economic growth. At the height of their popularity, these schemes had the effect of channeling savings into consumption, thereby raising consumer spending. The collapse of several large schemes in 1997 marked the beginning of a temporary collapse in the Albanian economy, triggering a wave of popular unrest. Anger was directed both toward the pyramid schemes and the government of President Sali Berisha, believed to be closely linked to several schemes. The economic collapse of 1997, with its associated popular unrest, caused a significant degree of economic disruption and resulted in a sharp reversal of Albania's rapid economic growth.

Despite the considerable political and economic disruption that occurred in 1997, by 1998 the Albanian economy was back on the road to economic recovery, with economic growth running at an annual rate of 8 percent in 1998 (EIU 2000). The most likely explanation for this second remarkable recovery is that the collapse of 1997 triggered a new wave of emigrants seeking work in Italy and Greece. This flow of migrant workers out of Albania not only boosted the number of Albanians working abroad, but also substantially increased the flow of remittances. It would seem that both the current and future success of the Albanian economy is highly dependent upon foreign remittances.

Ultimately, the only lesson that we can draw from the Albanian experience is as follows: the coincidence of various factors, such as a large volume of accumulated savings, an underdeveloped financial sector, and a complete lack of appropriate financial regulation can result in the type of financial disaster experienced by Albania in 1997. The key policy implication from this research is the need to ensure that the financial sector of a country receiving large volumes of remittances is appropriately regulated.

NOTES

1. Author's interview with Kosovar Consul in the Embassy of Kosova, Tirana, 1996.

2. Figures on the number of Albanians working in Greece and Italy are almost identical in a number of publications (IMF 1994; Done 1997; World Bank 1994).

3. In 1995, the daily wage for casual labor in Greece was half of the average monthly wage in Albania (Mancellari, Papapanagos, and Sanfey 1997).

4. Author's interviews with owners of petrol stations and other small businesses, Albania 1996.

5. The 2001 census gives a figure of 600,000 for the total number of Albanians living abroad (INSTAT 2002).

6. Interviews with Albanian migrants in Bristol, U.K., in 2002-2003 indicate a pattern of remittances similar to the pattern of remittances exhibited by Albanian migrants in Greece.

7. The average number of days worked per month did not vary according to the level of skill of the worker.

8. Information gained from interviews with Albanian migrant workers in Athens, September 1998.

9. Staff members at the National Bank of Greece were willing to provide this information on the understanding that it would be used only for academic purposes. Reliable information indicated that all deposits were made in person by these two Albanians, and that they were the only migrant workers in the area.

10. Transcript from National Bank of Greece's records of savings accounts, July 1997.

11. Because the majority of deposits with pyramid investment schemes were made during 1995 and 1996, by halving the total amount deposited, a rough figure of average annual deposits can be obtained, accepting that the majority of deposits were made in 1996.

12. Piperno 2003. Remittances entering Albania: 26 percent saved, 52 percent consumed, 22 percent invested.

REFERENCES

Buch, Claudia M., Anja Kuckulenz, and Marie-Hélène Le Manchec. 2002. "Worker Remittances and Capital Flows." Working Paper, Kiel Institute of World Economics, Kiel, Germany.

Datastream International. 2000. Database.

Done, K. 1997. "Foundations Exposed by Pyramids' Collapse." *Financial Times*, February 19.

EBRD (European Bank for Reconstruction and Development). 1995. *Transition Report*. London,

———. 1997. *Transition Report*. London: EBRD.

———. 1998. *Transition Report*. London: EBRD.

———. 2002. *Transition Report*. London: EBRD.

EIU (Economist Intelligence Unit). 1997. *Albania: Country Report, 2nd and 3rd Quarters*. London: EIU.

———. 2000. *Albania: Country Report, October*. London: EIU.

Glenny, M. 1997. "Heart of Darkness." *New York Review of Books* 44(13).

Gros, D., and A. Steinherr. 1995. *Winds of Change*. London: Longman.

Hashi, I., and L. Xhillari. 1997. "Privatisation and Transition in Albania." Working Paper 004, Staffordshire University, UK.

IMF (International Monetary Fund). 1994. "Economic Review: Albania." Washington, DC: IMF.

INSTAT (Albanian Institute of Statistics). 2000. *Albania in Figures*. Albanian Institute of Statistics, Tirana.

———. 2002. *Albania in Figures*. Albanian Institute of Statistics, Tirana.

Jarvis, C. 1999. "The Rise and Fall of Pyramid Schemes in Albania." *IMF Staff Papers* 47(1). http://www.imf.org/external/pubs/ft/fandd/2000/03/jarvis.htm.

King, Russell, and Juli Vullnetari. 2003. "Migration and Development in Albania." Working Paper WPC5, Development Research Centre on Migration, Globalisation, and Poverty, Brighton, UK.

Korovilas, J. 2002. "People in Search of Work: Albanian Migrants in Greece." In *Europe, Policies, and People: An Economic Perspective*, ed. Sue Hatt and Frank Gardner, 172–187. Hampshire, UK: Palgrave Publishers.

Lazaridis, G., and K. Romaniszyn. 1998. "Albanian and Polish Undocumented Workers in Greece." *Journal of European Social Policy* 8(1): 5–22.

Lianos, P., A. Sarris, and T. Katseli. 1997. "Illegal Immigration and Local Labour Markets: The Case of Northern Greece." *International Migration* 34(3): 449–84.

Mancellari, A., H. Papapanagos, and P. Sanfey. 1997. "Job Creation and Temporary Emigration: The Albanian Experience." *Economics of Transition* 4(2): 471–91.

Nafziger, W. 1997. *The Economics of Developing Countries*, 3rd edition. Upper Saddle River, NJ: Prentice Hall.

Pettifer, J., 1997. "Pyramid Schemes Teach Albanians a Harsh Lesson." *The Wall Street Journal Europe.* January 28, 1997, 10.

Piperno, F. 2003. "Remittance Enhancement for the Local Development in Albania: Constraints and Opportunities." Centro Studi di Political Internazionale (Center for International Political Studies) Working Paper 4/2003, Programma MigraCtion, Rome.

Psimmenos, I., and S. Georgoulas. 2002. "Migration Pathways: A Historic, Demographic and Policy Review of the Greek Case." Report prepared for the research project "Does implementation matter? Informal administration practices and shifting immigrant strategies in four member states" (IAPA-SIS), funded by the European Commission, Research DG. KEKMOKOP, Panteion University.

Salome, L. 1997. "Free Market Teaches Painful Lesson." *Atlanta Journal,* March 16, B4.

Vickers, M., and J. Pettifer. 1997. *Albania: From Anarchy to a Balkan Identity.* London: Hurst.

World Bank. 1994. *Albania: Building a New Economy.* Washington, DC: World Bank.

Chapter 10
International Remittances: Delivering Fair Value

Norbert Bielefeld and Antonique Koning

This chapter discusses what should be accomplished by key stakeholders in society—sooner rather than later because of the continued, steady inflow of migrants—to enhance the provision of remittance services to migrant workers and their families and relatives.

GETTING FAIR VALUE FROM REMITTANCES

Both individuals and nations deserve to get maximum value from the remittances migrants send home. However, information and power imbalances often prevent that value from being obtained.

Key Issues from the Customer's Perspective

Remitting migrants face a number of hurdles, even before initiating a transaction.

Access to market information. In a new environment, speaking a new language, and with limited time for such activities, new migrants who wish to begin sending remittances to their families have little opportunity to research and compare the alternatives that exist on the market. They often rely on the experience of colleagues, who may themselves be ill-informed.

Access to banking services. Migrants who enter a new country illegally and work illegally may not be willing or able to open accounts with established financial institutions. Even if they are able to do so, they may find it difficult to reach the institution using public transportation. Yet another hurdle is the availability of banking services at hours that match the requirements of the migrant population. These barriers and more force migrants to resort to alternative channels, often involving cash, which not only raise security and control issues but also create opportunities for criminal activity.

Access to transaction information. Remitters have little notion of the end-to-end cost of every transaction. Usually they are aware of the transactions fee charged up front, but the foreign exchange rate and the commission applied, as well as the transactions fee levied at the beneficiary's end may not be revealed. Remitters may be unaware that an average transaction may cost up to 25 percent of the original amount they present (generally in cash) to the remittance agent. This may be more efficient than official development assistance, where as little as 50 cents on the dollar reaches the intended beneficiary, but that is little solace for the individuals directly concerned.

Access to redress procedures. When a banking service is not fully executed, the customer should have right of redress. This is all the more important when the customer is entrusting to a service provider savings that are so essential for the remitter and the intended beneficiary. In the area of remittances three common problems arise during execution:

194

- Unauthorized deduction of fees and commissions (of which the customer may be unaware, as noted above)
- Delays in the completion of transactions (a problem not only because of the criticality of the amount for the intended beneficiary, but also because a delay may also—intentionally or accidentally—result in a lower amount being made available to the intended beneficiary because of a fluctuation in the exchange rate)
- The nonremittance of the instructed amount to the intended beneficiary

In all these situations (of which the last is obviously the most critical), the remitting migrant (or the intended beneficiary) usually has little opportunity to complain if an informal channel has been used. However, even when formal channels are used, the level of genuine assistance provided to resolve problems has often been criticized.

From the perspective of the intended beneficiaries the range of issues is quite similar. Do beneficiaries really have access to market information, with a fair chance to compare and choose the more competitive and highest quality channel? Is there a choice of banking services? What do they know about the conditions under which the transaction has been executed? Can they seek and obtain redress when the expected remittance does not arrive, arrives very late, or arrives heavily discounted by unexpected fees?

These are critical issues for those who must send remittances to enable their family and relatives to live.

Remittances also raise critical macroeconomic issues, ranging from determining how to multiply the monetary effects of remittances to how to keep them out of the criminal stream.

Macroeconomic Issues

An untapped lever for economic development. It is generally accepted that remitted funds properly invested in a developing economy may have an impact that is three times their initial amount. The challenge then becomes to ensure that this potential is fully realized. The first objective, of course, is to ensure that a greater share of the funds remitted actually reaches the intended recipient, by bringing down transactions fees. A second objective is to move away from cash-to-account and cash-to-cash transactions toward account-to-account remittances. Doing so would bring a range of macroeconomic benefits to recipient countries:

- The deposit base of local (often rural) financial institutions that house the accounts would be broadened. These deposits could then be employed to finance local projects, with reimbursement pegged to known, sustained flows of income from abroad, thus

minimizing risk of default and subsequently lowering interest rates for borrowers and intermediaries.
- Arbitrage opportunities could be provided, whereby the acquisition of assets in developing countries would be financed by liabilities incurred by remitters in developed countries, in hard currency, and at the much lower interest rates prevailing in such countries.
- Official, guaranteed channels for steady flows of remittances in hard currency would be created, thereby benefiting the national balance of payments. Such flows, which may represent a significant portion of gross national product, would reassure foreign partners and investors, provide a foundation for interest income, and support sound planning of public finances.

An unrecognized opportunity for social integration. The uncertain legal status of many migrant workers confines them to the margins of the societies in which they live and work. From a macroeconomic point of view the consequences are that

- the value added they generate has only a limited leverage effect (compared to what its potential is—contributions to taxes, for example);
- their reliance on cash locks them outside the banking sector; it not only reinforces their marginalization but also prevents them from accumulating savings that would benefit the national economy.

A feeder into illegal activities. The remittance business has several characteristics that attract the attention of criminals:

- Remitters quite often live or work illegally in their country of residence, so they are operating outside the normal protections of the law
- A significant portion of the remittance business is conducted in cash, which is fungible and untraceable, making it suitable for theft or money laundering purposes
- Some of the channels used to repatriate funds into beneficiary countries are based on techniques (such as compensating payments or barter) that may foster criminal activities and assist in disguising them

A CHALLENGE TO SOCIETY AND A NEW DEAL IN REMITTANCES

The challenge to policy makers and decision makers in developed and developing economies alike is significant because of the numbers involved—numbers of people as well as volume of capital—but the challenge cannot be ignored. Complex now, it can only grow in complexity because it touches so many facets of social organization, regulation, practices, and habits at local, national, and international levels.

As a consequence, the questions raised by remittances are multiple, and the responses may appear conflicting: Yet the sheer numbers of individuals affected require the options to be considered carefully:

- Should the remittance business be regulated?
- Who should bear the burden of such regulation?
- What balance of public and private initiative will enhance conditions for remitters and beneficiaries?
- How can competition be fostered in the remittance business?
- Is it possible to encourage established financial institutions to enter the remittance business?
- Should an infrastructure for efficient remittance transactions be created by public intervention?
- How might the system move away from cash remittances without imposing extra costs on the remitters and beneficiaries?
- How might remittances be moved beyond mere transactions and established as a foundation for sustainable economic development?

Clearly, the world of remittances is ripe for a new deal. Not only do toiling remitters and their families deserve it, but the global community stands to benefit as well. This new approach should involve the following steps: formulating policy, motivating players, and delivering value.

Formulating Policy

Regulators and international organizations need to define, agree on, and communicate their policies in the field of international remittances. Such policies should be structured along four main lines.

Overseeing the evolution of market structures and monitoring performance. Overseers, regulators, and international organizations should take a keen interest in analyzing the structure of the remittance market and its evolution, promoting their view of the related problems, establishing benchmarks for proper functioning, and monitoring the performance of players from a macroeconomic perspective. Their objective should be to ensure sufficient and genuine competition around a set of principles governing transparency and minimum service levels. In exceptional situations where competition is insufficient, the public sector should be prepared to supplement the private sector.

Establishing and enhancing the legal and regulatory framework. Where necessary, the legal framework (both international and national) should be enhanced to enable migrants to access a core set of banking services and to ensure a minimum level of certainty and redress in remittance services. Regulation should maintain three goals: First, remittance services should be provided by regulated (licensed) institutions, although supervision of remittance institutions may take different forms, particularly in developing countries, and flexibility in implementation—along clearly formulated principles—will be required so as not to stymie essential financial flows. Second, the settlement of international remittance transactions should occur through secured systems (Lamfalussy-compliant net settlement systems,[1] or real-time gross settlement systems). Third, new reporting requirements (by providers or end customers) should not add to the cost burden for remitters.

Setting standards and defining infrastructure. The definition and implementation of worldwide (open, not proprietary) standards for the execution of international remittances will ensure that costs remain low and will foster competition. Although policy making should remain neutral from a technical perspective, minimal guidelines for communication security and messaging standards, as well as operational rules, should be defined. These would allow market players (including new entrants) to have access to a choice of solutions based on a common, core infrastructure.

Encouraging and facilitating the market. An essential dimension of policy making would be to bring the topic of international remittances out of the closet and into the boardrooms of financial institutions. This should be achieved by establishing the importance of the topic from a macroeconomic perspective, by highlighting the opportunities for individual players, by promoting a stable and certain legal and regulatory framework so as to prompt players to act, by making market incentives available to potential players, and, if necessary, demonstrating leadership by becoming active as a player.

The World Savings Banks Institute (WSBI), on behalf of its members worldwide, has already publicly committed itself to participating in the formulation of policy. The WSBI is intent on playing a leading role in the remaining two pillars of the approach to remittances.

Motivating Players

The normal activity of overseers and regulators is probably not enough to motivate existing and potential players in the field of international remittances. Deliberate efforts by the international and national organizations that support and represent financial institutions are likely to be necessary. These organizations will play a pivotal role in drawing their members' attention to this important market, developing market research and qualifying opportunities, establishing (or facilitating) the formation of partnerships, and sometimes assisting in the selection and implementation of technical solutions.

Delivering Value

Value is the realm of individual market participants, acting in a competitive environment, yet establishing partnerships to deliver the expected end-to-end product. Wherever possible, these market participants should be financial institutions, or at least institutions subject to forms of oversight that are accepted at the international level. For the remitting customer, end-to-end value means the certitude of being able to initiate remittances at a lower cost, with full transparency of end-to-end charges, a guaranteed execution time, and a clear procedure for redress. For the receiving customer it means the certitude of higher receipts, predictable income, a clear redress procedure, and access to financial services, in particular loan facilities.

Policy makers and potential service providers alike should understand that the real objective of involvement in remittances cannot be simply to enhance the transactions business (that is, the business of transferring funds from A to B), but to create the conditions under which remitters and their beneficiaries will have access to needed financial services in a sustained manner. These include not only the services that accompany the evolution from a cash-based to an account-based relationship, but also all savings, lending, and insurance services that can provide benefits to this segment of the population.

For participating financial institutions, delivering greater value to their remittance customers should also bring rewards.

The originating bank will have the ability to differentiate its products to potential remitters (by offering the "ethical" approach), access to marketing assistance (community-based) from receiving banks, a clear dispute-resolution mechanism, greater customer retention, and cross-selling opportunities.

The receiving bank will benefit from the existence of a standardized framework for establishing and managing relationships with remitting banks, higher receipts for their account-based customers, more predictable cash management at the financial-institution level, lower processing costs, differentiated positioning with regard to other receiving banks and money changers, enhanced customer retention and broadening of product-acceptance opportunities, and a clear dispute-resolution mechanism.

THE MIGRANT STRATEGY OF ONE SPANISH SAVINGS BANK

For a savings bank there are several reasons to get involved in the remittance business. To begin with, the senders and beneficiaries of lower-value payment transactions are part of the natural client base of savings and retail banks—mainly households and very small to medium-size enterprises. Many savings banks rightly see opportunities to reach out to the market segment represented by remittance senders and receivers, thereby expanding their businesses and raising income from related services. The fact that the banks can take advantage of existing experience and infrastructure and build on economies of scale is stimulating, and cross-selling opportunities look attractive.

It is in the interests of savings banks everywhere to provide access to financial services in the regions in which their clients operate. Although remitters in developed countries use banks more than do recipients (and remitters) in developing countries, the rate of use is still under the average level in the sending country, implying plenty of room for growth. In Spain, for example, studies have found bank-use rates for the migrant community ranging from 50 percent to 80 percent depending on the country of origin of the migrants.

Participating in the remittance business allows savings banks to enhance remittance flows and their macroeconomic impact by reducing costs and offering additional services that make more productive use of remitted funds.

La Caixa's Strategy toward Migrant Customers

La Caixa, the largest savings bank in Spain, is a financial leader specializing in retail banking. It has a national network of more than 4,500 branches and close to 7,000 automated teller machines (ATMs) that allows it to operate 24 hours a day, 365 days a year. The bank completes nearly 200 million transactions per year, and 2 million clients use its Internet banking services. La Caixa has delivered 6.5 million banking cards.

In 2002, La Caixa made a strategic decision to get involved in the remittance business. The decision reflected the bank's philosophy, which is based on three main tenets: first, to serve the client—and the migrant community in Spain was identified as a target market; second, to adapt to the needs of the client with tailor-made financial products and other services; and third, to integrate the client into the banking system. This last goal is probably the most important part of the strategy because it reflects La Caixa's interest in including migrants in their client base, with full access to all banking products and services.

In Spain, as elsewhere in Europe, the migrant population is growing. In 2015 migrants are expected to be more than one-quarter of the entire population. Official figures for 2003 indicated the presence of 2.67 million

immigrants, of whom 22 percent were Europeans. (See table 10.1 for estimates of non-European migrants.) Immigrants, therefore, made up nearly
6.3 percent of Spain's population, an increase of 35 percent from the year
before. If estimates of nonrecorded migrants are counted, Spain had
around 2.4 million non-European migrants at the end of 2003, mainly
from Latin America, North Africa, Eastern Europe, and China.

Of the 2.4 million migrants, it is estimated that some 1.5 million have
a bank account in Spain. Although not all make use of the services
available to them, the numbers are significant. These trends and operating experiences in the community convinced La Caixa of the opportunities involved in responding to the basic requirements of migrants.

Responding to the demand for remittance services was a way to
gain access to a desired market segment. Remittance-receiving countries presented opportunities to reach out to populations previously
unbanked. The profiles and financial needs of those people make them
potential clients, even though it is the remittance service that initially
attracts them to the bank on both the sending and receiving side.

In partnership with banks in migrants' countries of origin, La Caixa
undertook market research to identify the special needs of migrants. A
summary of the research done in the Colombian and Spanish markets
appears in table 10.2.

Remittance Services

To respond to the needs and interests of the migrant community in
Spain, La Caixa created a money transfer system based on specially
designed products and services accessible in all of the bank's branches
and ATMs throughout the country, and on a range of cooperation
agreements with banks in the migrants' countries of origin.

TABLE 10.1 OFFICIALLY RECORDED MIGRATION FROM OUTSIDE
THE EUROPEAN UNION TO SPAIN, 2002

Country of origin	Number of migrants in Spain	Percentage of total
Ecuador	390,119	14.6
Morocco	378,787	14.2
Colombia	244,570	9.2
Romania	137,289	5.1
Argentina	109,390	4.1
Peru	55,881	2.1
Bulgaria	52,812	2.0
China	51,203	1.9

Source: Instituto Nacional de Estadisticas (INE) 2003.

TABLE 10.2 PROFILING REMITTANCE SENDERS AND BENEFICIARIES
IN SPAIN AND COLOMBIA

	Sender	Beneficiary
Priorities	• Transaction fee • Security	• Timeliness of transaction • Security
Other important factors	• Accessibility of transaction points • Duration of transaction • Exchange rate	• Conditions and requirements for obtaining the money transferred (simple processes, little information and documentation required) • Amount finally received
Profile	• Migrant workers employed in the informal sector • Little spare time (work up to 90 percent of their time) • Intention to legalize, stay in country, and continue to earn for personal benefit and for family at home	• Direct family members of the migrant • Receive remittances to cover mortgage payments, reimbursement of travel loan, basic needs, or investments • Generally no significant stable income, time is not an issue • Interested in obtaining additional bank products

Source: Results of survey of families of Colombian migrants in Spain, Banco Caja Social,
April 2002.

Remittances with a free personal message. La Caixa began to put remittance transfers on a more structured footing with the establishment of an infrastructure of call centers in Spain and in receiving countries in 2002. As part of the service, the call centers inform the beneficiaries by telephone when a transfer arrives; a personal message can also be included. This personal touch is much appreciated by clients on both ends.

In 2003, La Caixa originated around 20,000 transactions per month, with an average value of US$500. The number of transactions grew at a rate of around 20 percent per month.

International money transfer card. La Caixa also introduced an international money transfer card. The card offers an electronic solution in places without branches and gives access to La Caixa's extensive ATM network even outside normal office hours. This greatly improves the convenience of service delivery because clients can access the services whenever they want and as close to them as possible. This convenience responds to the finding that migrants' time is a valuable asset. The card allows migrants to transfer money to their families through partner banks of La Caixa as well as conduct withdrawal and deposit transactions as with any other bank card.

La Caixa benefits as well. First, the card assists in identifying the client; second, it stimulates the use of new technology (with only three clicks people can send their money); and third, it reduces branch involvement in transactions because the call center provides all information and assistance to the remitters. Spanish law permits anyone with an international identity card to open a bank account, with no additional documents required. The only condition for obtaining a money transfer card is opening an account with La Caixa, for which there is no charge and no minimum balance requirement. The cost of the card itself is 3 euro (US$3.99) per year, although there are promotional campaigns in which even this cost is waived.

The card was first issued in November 2002 and by March 2003, 15,000 international money transfer cards had been issued with an estimated 20 percent of all remittance transfers sent through ATMs.

Additional services. La Caixa offers additional services designed specifically for migrants. Repatriation insurance (SegurCaixa Repatriación) offers repatriation of the body in case of death. The insurance is easily accessible because it does not require a medical test and the premium is reasonable (around 6 euro [US$7.98] per month). In the case of Moroccan immigrants, the service is even offered for free to clients who transfer money from La Caixa through Banque Centrale Populare. The insurance provides 30,000 euro (US$39,942) for the beneficiary and up to 3,000 euro (US$3,994) for the cancellation of credit card balances held with La Caixa. There are two additional options, one that also insures against accidents and the other extending coverage to repatriated direct family members.

Partner Banks in Immigrants' Countries of Origin

La Caixa has so far negotiated agreements with partner banks in receiving countries that allow them to optimize service delivery. The criteria La Caixa maintains for selecting partners are not the same for all countries, but in general depend on the following factors:

- Coverage of the bank in the national territory
- Reputation, solvency, and stability
- Technological capacity that allows the bank to offer quality service delivery within a reasonable time
- Retail bank orientation with, for instance, microcredit programs that allow for the creation of banking products and services related to transfers

As of 2004, La Caixa had agreements with 15 partner banks in 11 countries; the agreements are specifically designed to facilitate remittance transfers (table 10.3). Each agreement has specific characteristics adapted to the nature of the financial sector in that country, the competition, and the needs of the migrant population and their families back home.

Banking the Unbanked

To stimulate the use of banks by immigrants, La Caixa offers a preferential rate for money transfers made by account holders (for example, 9 euro (US$12) instead of 12 euro (US$16) for a transfer to Latin America, 4 euro (US$5) instead of 5 euro (US$7) for a transfer to Morocco). Experience shows that migrant customers generally send three to four remittances before opening a bank account. After six to eight months (or transfers) they tend to apply for a credit card. About a year after having opened a bank account, clients start requesting personal loans, and after two years a number of them apply for mortgages.

Interestingly, evidence shows that migrant customers, once they become clients of the bank, are among the most loyal and best clients, and tend to have excellent payment track records for mortgages or other loans. For instance, more than 30 percent of La Caixa's Peruvian customers make use of a payroll deposit service and more than 90 percent of Peruvian account holders have a debit card. Comparing these ratios within the banking market in Spain, this customer profile scores substantially better than the average customer.

It is strategically important that La Caixa offers its entire range of banking services to migrants in all branches throughout the country. All staff are trained to offer the products and services that are specifically designed for migrants, and a special portal on La Caixa's intranet informs staff about these products and services. Attention is paid to the culture and especially language of the migrant customers. La Caixa has brochures, guides, and contracts available in the appropriate languages. The bank employs people of 36 different nationalities, allowing them to address clients in the language of their home country. At the end of 2003, La Caixa had almost 350,000 migrant clients, representing 4.5 percent of the total clientele.

La Caixa and partner banks in receiving countries also use creative measures to build loyalty among customers using remittance services. They offer "frequent client bonuses" or lotteries with highly valued prizes such as flights to the home country, television sets, DVD players, cameras, and so forth.

TABLE 10.3 COOPERATION AGREEMENTS BETWEEN LA CAIXA AND ITS PARTNER BANKS

Country	Partner bank	Special characteristics of agreement
Argentina	• Banco Macro-Bansud	• Partner bank is one of the principal retail banks in Argentina, with nationwide coverage.
Bolivia	• Banco de Crédito de Bolivia	• Universal bank with about 50 offices throughout the country; affiliate of Banco de Crédito del Peru.
	• Bancosol	• Specialized microfinance bank.
Colombia	• Banco Caja Social	• Partner bank has more than 120 branches in Colombia serving lower income people. Bank also relies for the delivery of remittances on 160 branches of another bank in the same group.
Cuba	• Banco de Crédito y Comercio	• Second largest retail bank in Cuba, with around 300 branches.
Dominican Republic	• Bank BHD	• Partner bank has a call center in the bank and does home delivery of remittances. Share of the Dominican remittances market is 40 percent.
Ecuador	• Banco Bolivariano	• First partner agreement La Caixa established, operating through call center "Ecuagiros."
	• Banco Solidario	• Partner bank is a so-called ethical bank, specializing in microfinance. It provides advisory services to emigrants for investment of remittances.
Morocco	• Crédit du Maroc	• Repatriation insurance is offered to remitters and included in the transfer service charge.
	• Banque Centrale Populaire	• Partner bank is largest bank in Morocco; it specializes in retail banking and has 400 branches throughout the country.
Peru	• Banco de Crédito del Peru	• Partner bank is largest in Peru and has an affiliate in Bolivia.
	• Mibanco	• Specialized microfinance bank.

(Continues)

TABLE 10.3 COOPERATION AGREEMENTS BETWEEN LA CAIXA AND
ITS PARTNER BANKS *(Continued)*

Country	Partner bank	Special characteristics of agreement
Philippines	• Metropolitan Bank	• Partner bank offers remittance services in cash, to accounts, to other banks, deposit on a prepaid bankcard, and "home delivery." It is the largest bank in the Philippines with regard to assets, number of branches, ATMs, and employees.
Senegal	• Société General de Banque au Senegal	• Partner bank is the principal retail bank in Senegal, with 30 branches.
Venezuela, R. B. de	• Banco Canarias de Venezuela	• Partnership agreement especially focused on commercial relations between Spain and República Bolivariana de Venezuela.

Source: Author research.

Future Perspectives: Cross-Selling Opportunities and Partnerships

A significant part of the remittances sent by migrants through La Caixa goes toward repayment of mortgage or microcredits in the originating country. However, this is not yet done on a structured basis and La Caixa does not track the information. As of 2004, one of the services La Caixa was working on with its partner banks was called "specific purpose remittances." This service is intended to allow the remitter to predetermine the amount of the remittance to be devoted to cash disbursements, to a savings scheme for housing, or to a mortgage or other specific destinations within a program agreed on by the remitting and receiving bank. This service was to be launched with partner banks in Ecuador.

In March 2004, La Caixa and three of its partner banks, in cooperation with Visa International, introduced a new service that enables remittances to be sent by means of a prepaid card. The prepaid card is a new tool for sending remittances from La Caixa in Spain to any ATM connected to the Visa network in Ecuador, Peru, and Bolivia. Migrants can apply for the card in any of La Caixa's 4,700 offices, while beneficiaries of the remittances in Ecuador, Peru, and Bolivia can obtain the card in the branches of Banco Bolivariano, Banco de Crédito del Peru, and Banco Caja Social, respectively. For subsequent transfers, the prepaid card gets automatically credited as soon as the remitter makes a transfer, so no visits to the branches are required. The prepaid card works similarly to an ordinary Visa card and gives the beneficiaries access to their remittances 24 hours a day through the ATM network, as well as the possibility to purchase goods in shops. It is a fast and especially safe way to transfer remittances, due to the fact that the use of the card requires a personal identification number and the card can be canceled or replaced easily in case of theft or loss. Additionally, it is a modern payment instrument and has the potential to increase the banking of the population. The prepaid card was unique in the market because it was launched cooperatively by four financial institutions in different countries spread across Europe and the Americas. The cooperation with Visa International also included publicity campaigns.

It can be envisaged that a migrant worker obtains a loan from La Caixa in Spain to finance an investment in a house, or a microenterprise, or a small or medium-size enterprise in the country of origin. Repayment of this investment could be made by La Caixa to the partner bank, withdrawing the amount from the migrant's account. The advantage of this would be that the migrant could borrow at relatively advantageous terms (comparing interest rates in Spain with those in the home countries), and money otherwise transferred with a cost and non-predetermined destination is in this case immediately productively invested.

Such arrangements are still in the development phase because difficulties exist in the cross-border treatment of guarantees and collateral, and in the risk assessment. Public interventions to improve the legal environment for such cross-border arrangements (as well as incentives provided by guarantee schemes that could cover a part of the credit and country risk) need to be introduced.

In general, these kinds of "crossed" products and services respond to the interest expressed by many migrant workers to specifically identify the destination of a transfer, or a share of it, and thereby ensure its productive investment. To introduce these mechanisms, available technology has to be put in place. Public support for such investment may facilitate adoption of these systems and thereby contribute to increasing the impact of remittance flows.

CONCLUSIONS

The sheer size of the remittance market, and the fact that it affects people on five continents, is certainly a call to attention for policy makers.

A call to attention, however, should not be confused with a call to action: the private sector has shown, and reaffirmed, its willingness to fully play its role, with all its obligations and responsibilities, in the remittance sector. In the early months of 2005, the emerging dialogue between the public and private sectors has confirmed that

- there is a clear space for cooperation to formulate and implement policies that apply to the remittance business on a worldwide basis;
- there are, furthermore, two places where market players, both individually and in partnership with industry organizations, have to take the lead and enhance the value proposition for remitters and beneficiaries, from both transaction and end-to-end perspectives. The growing synergies between banks, money transfer companies, and other players will result in welcome additional financial products and services and enhance overall capacity to reach out to all countries and regions.

NOTE

1. These are payment systems designed to deliver the most effective and reliable means for processing international payments.

REFERENCE

Instituto Nacional de Estadisticas (INE). 2003. Migration Survey. http:// www.ine.es/buscar/results.jsp?query=migration&L=0.

Part IV
Increasing Transparency
in the Informal
Financial Infrastructure for
Remittances

Chapter 11
The Regulation and Supervision
of Informal Funds Transfer Systems

Samuel Munzele Maimbo and Nikos Passas

Each country should take measures to ensure that persons or legal entities, including agents, that provide a service for the transmission of money or value, including transmission through an informal money or value transfer system or network, should be licensed or registered and subject to all the FATF Recommendations that apply to banks and nonbank financial institutions. Each country should ensure that persons or legal entities that carry out this service illegally are subject to administrative, civil or criminal sanctions.

—Special Recommendation VI (FATF SP.VI) issued on October 10, 2001, by the Financial Action Task Force

Following the events of September 11, 2001, and in the overall framework of financial controls of terrorism, authorities around the world have been under considerable pressure to regulate and supervise certain informal funds transfer (IFT) systems. *Hawala*, in particular, a traditional IFT system, has been viewed as especially vulnerable to abuse by criminal organizations and militants (APG 2001; see also FATF 1997, 1999, 2001, 2002; U.A.E. Central Bank 2002).

Arguing that money or value transfer systems had shown themselves vulnerable to misuse for money laundering and terrorist financing purposes, the Financial Action Task Force (FATF) issued FATF SP.VI with the objective of increasing the transparency of payment flows. It recommended that jurisdictions impose consistent anti–money laundering and counterterrorist financing measures on all forms of money and value transfer systems. Financial regulators began the process of reexamining existing regulations, and in some cases, designing, developing, and implementing new financial regulations.

In the rush to create a regulatory and supervisory framework for informal remittances, practice has preceded comprehensive theoretical debate and empirical research. Consequently, fundamental concerns remain. Although well intended, this top-down route to regulation may have serious adverse effects, not only for the effectiveness of those regulations and the capacity of supervisors to implement them, but also for the flow of significant migrant labor remittances to developing countries. There is, therefore, a need for an even more concerted and systematic evaluation of the regulatory objectives, strategies, tools, and mechanisms that are being advanced in the international and domestic design, development, and implementation of regulatory and supervisory frameworks for informal funds transfer systems.

This chapter begins by defining the terms used to describe informal remitters and regulatory objectives, then seeks to identify the challenges that regulators and controllers face, and continues with an overview of regulatory practice developments, concluding with policy implications and concrete recommendations.

DEFINING THE REGULATORY OBJECTIVES

Although the FATF has adopted the term "alternative remittance systems" to describe "financial services, traditionally operating outside the regulated financial sector, where value or funds are moved from one geographic location to another" (FATF 2003b, p. 1), the term remains subject to definitional debate. This debate leads to varying regulatory implications.

In a 1999 report, Passas criticized the term for being inaccurate and misleading. He also criticized the then-prevalent term "underground banking" for the same reasons. Banking was rarely, if ever, involved in these transactions, which took place quite openly in many parts of the globe. The word "alternative" is also not well chosen, because it implies the existence of other mainstream or conventional remittance systems. This is clearly not the case in scores of regions in the global south, where informal remitters and financiers (with a variety of names but quite similar mechanics) have been operating for a long time—predating contemporary banking facilities, which remain inaccessible to millions of people in many countries. "Alternative," thus, is too ethnocentric a term to apply in this context. In many instances, value rather than money is transferred from place to place. The term "informal value transfer systems" (IVT systems) was introduced in 1999, to demystify and describe more accurately and inclusively the phenomenon under study (Passas 1999, 2003a).

The specific words used have significant regulatory policy implications. They define the transfer entities and instruments targeted by regulators, and in turn, define the response of market service providers, participants, and clients. Ill-defined terms and concepts may lead to unintended regulatory and supervisory effects.

Starting from the premise that IVT systems refer to mechanisms or networks of people facilitating the transfer of funds or value without leaving a trail of entire transactions, or taking place outside the traditionally regulated financial channels, two types of IVT systems are relevant. At one end are IFT systems, (see Maimbo 2003; El-Qorchi, Maimbo, and Wilson 2003), and at the other extreme are "pure" transfers of value in the form of goods for their monetary value. In between, there is a continuum of combinations, generally referred to as informal value transfer (IVT) methods (see Passas 2003a), but for which a clear categorization would be impossible.

First, IFT systems, which refer to financial transfers, have the following features:

- Encompass traditional ethnic fund and value transfer operations and businesses

- Are generally thought to have originated in the Indian subcontinent and in China, but have spread throughout the globe following waves of immigration and processes of economic globalization
- Are currently subject to regulations designed for so-called money services businesses, and their clients and services are, for the most part, well-established and known to their respective local communities

IFT system examples are hawala, *hundi, fei chien, phoe kuan,* and other similar services (including couriers). The underlying characteristic is that the transfer is originated, transferred, and delivered as a financial asset.

Next is the physical transfer of goods, which the sender purchases with the sole understanding that once the goods reach the recipient's jurisdiction, the remitter will sell them to acquire the monetary value that those goods represent. Except for the profit that might arise from the sale, the monetary value of the goods is what might otherwise have been transferred through the financial system. In its purest form, this is an inefficient method of transferring value.

In between, there are individuals, networks, and organizations that employ a variety of informal methods of transferring both money and value. It is this gray area that causes regulators the most concern because, for the most part, there appears to be a direct correlation between the degree of funds and goods commingling and the likelihood of a criminal intent to conceal or deceive. These methods show the following characteristics:

- no need for widespread networks of people
- most can be accomplished by a couple of individuals on an ad hoc or regular basis (hence the term "method" as opposed to "system" or "network")
- can involve the use of the formal financial system, but leave no trail for anyone wishing to monitor or reconstruct the transaction route

They are often part of legitimate or legitimate-looking trade transactions, which effectively obfuscate substantial value transfers. When there is a criminal intent to conceal, the transactions are usually combined with other offenses (such as tax evasion, subsidy fraud, embargo busting, capital flight, terrorist funding, or smuggling).

IVT method examples include legal processes such as in-kind payments or transfers, use of gift services, stored value, credit or debit cards, use of correspondent accounts, use of brokerage accounts, options or futures trading, electronic payments, or the illegal acts of invoice manipulation and trade diversion.

Although subtle, the distinction between IFT systems and IVT methods is important, not just academic. It highlights the large variety of channels that can be used for the transfer of funds or value without leaving traces. Consequently, serious misconduct may also be perpetrated or facilitated by these channels, many of which involve regulated and formal sectors or institutions. Individually, these funds transfers are not necessarily illegal (with the exception of trade diversion). Rather, it is the combination of several of these transfer methods that should raise regulatory concern, along with the fact that illicit value transfers can be hidden behind other apparently legitimate and ordinary transactions. As stressed below, this distinction also draws attention to possible unintended effects of authorities seeking to regulate IFT (for example, displacement from IFT systems to IVT methods).

IDENTIFYING THE REGULATORY CHALLENGES

As explained in detail elsewhere in this chapter, there are many varieties of IFT (hawala-like) transactions and ways in which the books can be balanced.[1] Certain common characteristics create obstacles to law enforcement efforts, such as

- a general absence of long-term recordkeeping and "know your customer" practices, which blocks investigative trails;
- mixing IFT with other activities;
- concern about unintended and collateral damages;
- the difficulty of knowing for sure whether a policy related to IFT is actually producing the intended effects.

Absence of a Transparent Transaction Audit Trail

Because transactions are informal and the operations are typically low-overhead, recordkeeping by IFT operators is mostly a short-term exercise that lasts until the accounts with counterparts are balanced. Transparency is lacking because most transactions are conducted by telephone and fax machine. In some cases, Internet or telephone banking may be used to pay money to the ultimate recipient, but this is a double-edged sword. It may create some trail for investigators, but at the same time, IFT transactions can be lost in the massive numbers of other transactions.

Informality and a lack of regulation bring about a lack of standardization in the kinds of records each operator keeps. IFT ledgers are often insubstantial and kept in an idiosyncratic shorthand. Initials or numbers that are meaningful to the operators are useless if they reveal nothing about transactions, amounts, time, and the names of people or organizations. Personal ledgers are often destroyed quickly. In some cases, especially when people know that their clients are breaking the law, no notes or records are kept at all. In other cases, *hawaladars* may serve customers without asking too many questions about their true identity, the origin of their money, or the reason for the transfer. In such cases, even if the operators decide to cooperate with authorities, they will have no useful knowledge or information to share. Without records, a paper trail, or some documentary basis, there is little that investigators can pursue; as a result, their efforts to build a case against an IFT operator or his criminal customers will come to a dead end.

The opposite type of challenge is also possible. Contrary to conventional wisdom, some IFT operators do keep records even after the accounts have been balanced with counterparts overseas (and these records can go back for many years). In many cases in the United States, Europe, and South Asia, investigators end up finding masses of records, ledgers, or notes. The details include the sender, recipient, amount, exchange rate, commission charged, date, cash flow, and balances. Often records are kept in ways that are hard to decipher without the cooperation of those who created the records, perhaps because they are in foreign languages or use initials and codes. In other instances, third-party accounts of individuals or companies within the same country or abroad are also involved.

In the end, the paper trail does surface, but it is difficult to interpret and reconstruct accurately. The task of putting everything together both for investigators and, ultimately, for jurors, becomes more complicated; the acquisition of documents may require the cooperation of operators or controllers in multiple jurisdictions.

Business Combinations

An IFT system is not always an independent business. Some people run such an operation only on the side or as a free or extra service to clients (for example, in a travel agency or grocery store). The transfer of clients' money may be combined with gold, diamond, or other commodity deals. Innocent hawala and criminal activities alike can be concealed in the mass of other ordinary and unsuspicious transactions. For example, using different invoicing methods on exports or imports could assist operators in balancing their books; for instance, underinvoicing by $20,000 "pays" this amount to the computer equipment importer who will make profits higher by this amount upon resale of the goods. If the remittance amounts are not excessive, they can easily disappear in an otherwise legal trade (a $20,000 "mistake" in a $1 to $2 million trade is unlikely to raise eyebrows). Others may mix IFT with tourist businesses, wire transfer services, grocery stores, music or video stores, antiquity trade, farm exports, or jewelry shops. In other cases, "payments" are made for goods that are not delivered, described incorrectly in the invoice, or returned after delivery is recorded. The payment does not appear to be connected to any unusual or suspicious deal. In South Asia, gold movement across national borders is especially linked to hawala, either as a method of balancing accounts or as a reason hawala transfers are made.

IFT businesses also interface with financial institutions. (They may have bank or brokerage accounts, use foreign currency exchange, offer telephone and fax services, send wires, or engage in real estate deals.) This type of interface can multiply the usual difficulties that investigators face when they deal with correspondent or pass-through accounts, because it is hard to get information on the true beneficiaries of the transactions. For example, a currency exchange dealer in a given country can send and receive wire transfers for a hawala customer through one or more foreign banks. When the funds are booked into correspondent accounts at U.S. banks, identifying the parties to a given transaction is an onerous or even impossible task. The same challenges arise when accounts are held either by IFT operators or their clients in private banking departments.[2]

Detecting and proving criminal offenses and intent are more difficult when such commingling takes place. Even trained professionals will find it hard to detect an IFT operation. So, for businesses operating with a lot of cash or that involve high turnovers, it is easy to hide hawala-like deals.

Smart Targeting and Avoidance of Unnecessary Harm to Innocent Parties

A related challenge is how to target illegal acts perpetrated through IFT systems without affecting the numerous innocent customers who remit honest money back home to their families, and without unduly disrupting trade or harming legitimate enterprises. It is important to minimize "collateral damage" caused by unfocused or unfounded control actions.

Bank officials, credit card companies, brokerages, money exchanges, transmitters, and so on, must be familiar with IFT patterns, and recognize and report them as suspicious. However, such professionals are frequently unaware of the patterns or indicators of illegal IFT operations and unable to expose them for investigation.

By lending itself to money laundering and the hiding of proceeds of criminal activities, such as gold smuggling, human trafficking, illegal drugs and arms trade, terrorism, fraud, tax evasion, and corruption, IFT raises hurdles in law enforcement efforts to identify the beneficiary of amounts that are being transferred and to follow the money trail to the ultimate destination.

Supervisory and Policy Assessments

How can it be known if policies are working and are having a substantial impact? To the extent that the primary concern is terrorism funding or facilitation of other crimes, appearances may be deceptive. For instance, if some IFT activity is reported to be declining, it may be because former IFT dealers are switching to alternative activities (for example, commodity-based value transfers and other IVT methods) with which law enforcement agents are likely to be even less familiar. They may be aware of under- and overinvoicing practices, but private investigators and law enforcement agents have also encountered more sophisticated schemes, whereby the perpetrators engage in no eyebrow-raising activities (for example, trade diversion, which may involve the transfer of value without the physical movement of money or goods; see Passas 2003c for more details of this method).

Risks entailed by poorly thought-out policies include the following:

- Reduction of the positive economic impact of labor remittances at the local, regional, and national levels
- Criminalization of otherwise legitimate actors
- Higher human costs (such as families of immigrants not receiving desperately needed income)
- Alienation of large segments of the population from the government or those perceived as driving the national and international regulatory efforts
- Shift to IVT methods, such as incorrect invoicing or trade diversion

Authorities are currently attempting to regulate and render IFT systems more transparent (by having them register as "money service businesses," for example). When these efforts are not well formulated or the participants do not accept them, the intended shift from informal to formal institutions may not occur. Rather, a shift toward the use of IVT methods may result.[3]

The additional risk in such a case is that policy makers may know even less about IVT vulnerabilities and serious criminal abuse than they do about IFT. As a result, policy makers may be leaving the door open for more sophisticated value transfer methods that come with a higher capacity for voluminous amounts, and even may be providing incentives for operators and legitimate users to turn to such shady financiers. In other words, insensitive or unsuccessful regulatory frameworks can result in a criminalizing effect on people and funds that are absolutely legitimate. Instead of increasing the transparency of funds transfers and reducing crime, policy makers may find themselves encouraging the opposite result.

Moreover, from a prevention viewpoint, reducing the number of IFT operations may mean far fewer opportunities to monitor suspicious activities and gather valuable intelligence about planned crimes. To the extent that the reported nexus of hawala with terrorist funding is accurate, finding the right balance between the goal of intelligence gathering and that of shutting down hawala operations is no easy task.

DESIGNING AND DEVELOPING AN INTERNATIONAL REGULATORY FRAMEWORK

The task of introducing effective regulation is more complicated than one might think. To achieve the desired goals and avoid unintended consequences, regulation must be the end result of a careful process involving fact finding, understanding of local cultures and specificities, and consensus building. Measures that were recently introduced and considered positive in many jurisdictions are discussed below.

Licensing or Registration

The FATF calls for the "licensing or registration of persons (natural or legal) that provide money/value transfer services, including through informal systems" (FATF 2003b, p. 1). The definition adopted for regulatory purposes has a huge impact on the decision to license or register. In June 2003, the FATF issued a "Best Practices Paper" (FATF 2003a) for combating the abuse of alternative remittance systems. The paper adopted a broad definition of transfer systems, using the term "Money or Value Transfer service (MVT service)" to refer to

> [a] financial service that accepts cash, checks, other monetary instruments or other stores of value in one location and pays a corresponding sum in cash or other form to a beneficiary in another location by means of a communication, message, transfer or through a clearing network to which the MVT service belongs. Transactions performed by such services can involve one or more intermediaries and a third party final payment (FATF 2003a, p. 2).

In a deliberate attempt to include many possibilities, the paper also noted that MVT services may be provided by "persons (natural or legal) formally through the regulated financial system or informally through entities that operate outside the regulated system" (FATF 2003a, p. 2); that in some jurisdictions, "informal systems are frequently referred to as alternative remittance services or underground (or parallel) banking systems" (FATF 2003a, p. 2); and that often these systems have ties to particular geographic regions and are therefore described using a variety of specific terms, including hawala, hundi, fei chien, and the black market peso exchange.

As policy makers search for a global minimum standard, perhaps it is best to argue for a system that, at a minimum, requires registration and encourages licensing to fully comply with the other recommendations being proposed in the implementation package.

There are notable differences in what licensing and registration actually involve in various jurisdictions. In some, it entails a nominal fee or no cost to licensees, while in others it comes with the requirement to pay a substantial bond or fee. For many traditional and small or family-run IFT system operators, this can constitute an unbearable burden. It may be wise to either remove the licensing cost (the point is effective regulation, not to raise revenue), or reduce it and scale it to the volume of IFT business to be licensed (Passas 2003b).

Reporting Requirements

In line with the above debate, regulators have also tended to call for jurisdictions to introduce transaction reporting requirements in line with their current reporting requirements for financial institutions. This approach attempts to make formal institutions out of informal, alternate, or underground institutions; but they are very different financial creatures. Is it possible to design reporting requirements that are tailored to specific operating characteristics?

The U.S. Financial Crimes Enforcement Network (FinCEN) conducted a systematic study in an effort to develop a more complete picture of all IVT networks and mechanics, and their potential for abuse, and to recommend appropriate measures. The U.S. approach has been to require IFT system registration at the federal level (with FinCEN) and licenses at the state level. Failure to get a state license constitutes a federal felony carrying heavy sanctions. Under current laws, IFT systems also must employ customer identification procedures for certain transactions, maintain financial records for some time, and file currency transaction reports and suspicious activity reports.

According to the U.S. Treasury's report to the U.S. Congress, the Bank Secrecy Act and the Patriot Act provisions are sufficient for the regulatory tasks relative to IVT for the time being (see Secretary of the U.S. Department of the Treasury 2002). The report emphasized the need to continue monitoring the situation to see whether adjustments are necessary with respect to IVT. FinCEN and the U.S. Treasury Department also recognized the need for a more complete understanding of all types and mechanisms of IVT by controllers and lawmakers.

However, there has been no systematic assessment to date of the compliance rate for the new regulations. Some cases brought to light by law enforcement actions indicate continuing operations of unlicensed informal remitters. Given the inconsistent recordkeeping practices of IFT operators and their own customer identification practices, it is to be expected that at least some ethnic IFT operators probably have not registered. In addition, ledgers or notes maintained by such operators in code or shorthand, gaps in kept records, and little knowledge of customers' identity, the origin of their money, or the transfer reason would often constitute violations of U.S. regulations.

In most countries with formal rules about IFT, however, efforts have been primarily in the direction of communicating to remitters their duties and obligations. Trust is the core element of IFT operations. How and under what circumstances can service providers be expected to violate this trust and provide client information to the authorities? Attempting to guess the answer or simply applying IFT standards tailored to formal institutions does not seem to be the most appropriate way of constructing and implementing effective policy measures. A consultative process is necessary.

EFFECTIVE IMPLEMENTATION OF AN INTERNATIONAL REGULATORY FRAMEWORK

While the literature to date discusses the context or the conditions under which various recommendations could or should be implemented, there has been insufficient discussion on the preconditions to effective regulations.

In its examination of recent and ongoing regulatory practices, an IMF-World Bank study[4] noted that a two-pronged approach is required to achieve long-term financial sector development and minimize the potential risks of financial abuse and criminal activity (El Qorchi, Maimbo, and Wilson 2003). In countries where an informal hawala system exists alongside a well-functioning, conventional banking sector, it is recommended that hawala dealers be registered and keep adequate records in line with FATF recommendations. Efforts should be made to improve the transparency level in these systems by bringing them closer to the formal financial sector without altering their specific nature. In conflict-afflicted countries without a functioning banking system, requirements beyond basic registration may not be feasible because of inadequate supervisory capacity.

Simultaneously, the regulatory response should address weaknesses that may exist in the formal sector. Formal and informal financial systems tend to benefit from each other's deficiencies. Policy makers should address economic and structural weaknesses that encourage transactions outside the formal financial systems, as well as the weaknesses in the formal financial sector itself.

The IMF-World Bank study emphasized that just prescribing regulations will not ensure compliance. Regulators need to have the appropriate supervisory capacity to enforce the regulations and to provide incentives toward compliance with the regulations; compliance is likely to be weaker where there are major transaction restrictions in the formal financial system. It cautioned that the application of international standards needs to address specific domestic circumstances and legal systems, and concluded that policy makers should acknowledge the existence of practical reasons, from the customer's viewpoint, to resort to these methods rather than formal banks for international payments. As long as such drivers exist, the hawala and other IFT systems will continue to exist, so addressing IFT will require a broader response, including well-conceived economic policies and financial reforms, a well-developed and efficient payment system, and effective regulatory and supervisory frameworks.

The June 2003 FATF best practices paper outlined several guiding principles for the implementation of Special Recommendation IV that recognizes the complexity of the task facing regulators.

- *In certain jurisdictions, informal MVT services provide a legitimate and efficient service.* The services are particularly relevant where access to the formal financial sector is difficult or prohibitively expensive. Informal MVT services are available outside the normal banking business hours. Furthermore, money can be sent to and from locations where the formal banking system does not operate.
- *Informal MVT services are more entrenched in some regions than in others.* Underground banking is a longstanding tradition in many countries and predates the spread of western banking systems in the nineteenth and twentieth centuries. These services operate primarily to provide transfer facilities to neighboring jurisdictions for expatriate workers repatriating funds. However, underground banking's staging posts are no longer confined to those regions where they have their historical roots. Accordingly, informal MVT services are no longer used solely by persons from specific ethnic or cultural backgrounds.
- *MVT services can take on a variety of forms that, in addition to the adoption of a risk-based approach to the problem, point to the need to take a functional, rather than a legalistic, definition.* Accordingly, the FATF developed suggested practices that would best aid authorities to reduce the likelihood that MVT services will be misused or exploited by money launderers and terrorism financiers.
- *Government oversight should be flexible, effective, and proportional to the risk of abuse.* Due consideration should be given to mechanisms that minimize the compliance burden without creating loopholes for money launderers and terrorist financiers and without being

so burdensome that it in effect causes MVT services to go "underground," making them even harder to detect.

- *It is acknowledged that in some jurisdictions informal MVT services have been banned.* Special Recommendation VI does not seek legitimization of informal MVT services in those jurisdictions. However, the identification and awareness-raising issues noted may be of use for competent authorities involved in identifying informal MVT services and for sanctioning those that operate illegally.

These principles were largely influenced by extensive research that was undertaken by the Asia Pacific Group, FinCEN, the IMF, and the World Bank. In the months leading up to the February 2003 FATF Interpretive Note and the June FATF Best Practices Paper, these institutions were engaged in various policy research papers on various aspects of IFT.

CONCLUSION

The IMF–World Bank paper noted that the application of international standards needs to pay due regard to specific domestic circumstances and legal systems. It should also be understood that IFT is not the only or most important financial vehicle used by terrorists, nor even the most vulnerable to abuse.[5] Efforts should be made to improve transparency levels in these systems by bringing them closer to the formal financial sector without altering their specific nature, although such efforts may encounter significant legitimate difficulties.

The National Institute of Justice report (Passas 2003c) also draws attention to wider public and other policy implications, emphasizing that, because IFT systems serve millions of legitimate and mostly poor recipients of remittances in the global South, it is vital that authorities

- explore ways of offering additional channels for fund transfers;
- assist financial institutions;
- ensure continuation of vital services and minimum disruption;
- improve institutional or official methods offering similar services;
- provide adequate supervision to ensure compliance;
- reduce economic and other asymmetries (which are the root causes for IFT systems and for terrorism).

Once such policies are implemented, cracking down on criminal IFT uses will become an easier task.

Experience also suggests that regulation is most effective when those subject to it participate in its formulation or regard it as appropriate and legitimate. If the jurisdiction adopts the FATF special recommendations, the target institutions must be involved in a dialogue that accommodates their interests, concerns, and specific institutional characteristics. Thus, efforts should be made to engage IFT operators and their clients in a consultative process conducive to a consensus on what measures and steps are desirable and necessary. It is essential to seek a two-way dialogue—a practice frequently used with other businesses and sectors.

Once a consensus-building consultation is complete and before a regulatory framework is installed, each jurisdiction must undertake a comprehensive awareness-raising campaign. Further, if these campaigns are to work, it is essential to recognize the following:

- The focus should be on identifying and, if necessary, creating positive incentives for the operators to become active participants in the implementation of a regulatory and supervisory structure.
- In some cases, the operators are highly trained and well-educated individuals. Some are former bankers and well aware of the concerns that are shared by regulatory and law enforcement agencies.
- Although operators are often geographically dispersed and engaged in a variety of businesses, they tend to be aware of their competitors. In some cases, such as Afghanistan, they might even have an informal association or recognized leadership. Generally, the leader may be someone who has been in the business in the area the longest or who provides wholesale settlement services. Awareness campaigns are best advised to seek out such informal bodies or leaders and work with them in each community or area.
- Although terrorist financing concerns are of the greatest importance given the obvious consequences that they present, awareness campaigns ought not to focus on this risk exclusively. By doing so, the campaigns risk creating a level of unease or discomfort that may discourage operators from working with regulators.

NOTES

1. This section draws on the Passas report to the National Institute of Justice (NIJ) (Passas 2003c) and a paper he prepared for the U.S. Financial Crimes Enforcement Network (FinCEN) in 2002.

2. Concerted regulation and supervision of wire transfers in the formal sector is a recent phenomenon; along with the general IFTS control difficulties are problems with regulating correspondent accounts, private banking, commodities trade, online payments, and so forth.

3. It is worth noting that despite some claims made in the press about the methods that the September 11, 2001, hijackers used to transfer their funds, all available evidence points to their use of banks, wire services, credit card accounts, and other regulated remitters. So while terrorism funding may occur

through IFTS, there is little reason to believe that militants prefer to use this method, or that IFTS are more vulnerable than the regulated sector.

4. The IMF-World Bank study examined the (a) historical and socioeconomic context within which hawala has evolved; (b) operational features that make the system attractive for both legitimate and illegitimate purposes; (c) fiscal and monetary implications for informal hawala-remitting and hawala-recipient countries; and (d) current regulatory and supervisory responses.

5. See Maimbo 2003 and Passas 1999.

REFERENCES

APG (Asia-Pacific Group on Money Laundering). 2001. "Report for the Fourth Typologies Workshop of the Asia/Pacific Group on Money Laundering." October 17–18, Singapore.

El-Qorchi, M., S. Maimbo, and J. Wilson. 2003. "Informal Funds Transfer Systems: An Analysis of the Informal Hawala System." IMF Occasional Paper 222, International Monetary Fund, Washington, DC.

FATF (Financial Action Task Force). 1997. "1996–1997 Report on Money Laundering Typologies." Appendix to FATF Annual Report. Paris: OECD.

——. 1999. "1998–1999 Report on Money Laundering Typologies." Appendix to FATF Annual Report. Paris: OECD.

——. 2001. "2000–2001 Report on Money Laundering Typologies." Appendix to FATF Annual Report. Paris: OECD.

——. 2002. "2001–2002 Report on Money Laundering Typologies." Appendix to FATF Annual Report. Paris: OECD.

——. 2003a. "Combating the Abuse of Alternative Remittance Systems: International Best Practices." [Special Recommendation VI] June 20. Paris: OECD.

——. 2003b. "Interpretative Note to Special Recommendation VI: Alternative Remittance." February 14. Paris: OECD.

Maimbo, S. M. 2003. "The Money Exchange Dealers of Kabul: A Study of the Informal Funds Transfer Market in Afghanistan." Working Paper 13, World Bank, Washington, DC.

Passas, N. 1999. "Informal Value Transfer Systems and Criminal Organizations: A Study into So-Called Underground Banking Networks." The Hague: Ministry of Justice (Netherlands).

——. 2000. "Facts and Myths about 'Underground Banking'." In *Cross-Border Crime in a Changing Europe,* ed. P. C. van Duyne, V. Ruggiero, M. Scheinost, and W. Valkenburg. Tilburg and Prague: Tilburg University and Prague Institute of Criminology and Social Prevention.

——. 2003a. "Financial Controls of Terrorism and Informal Value Transfer Methods." In *Global Organized Crime: Trends and Developments,* ed., D. Siegel, D. Zaitch, and H. van de Bunt, 149–158. Dordrecht: Kluwer Academic Publishers.

————. 2003b. "Hawala and Other Informal Value Transfer Systems: How to Regulate Them?" *Journal of Risk Management* 5(2): 40–60.

————. 2003c. "Informal Value Transfer Systems, Money Laundering, and Terrorism." Report to the National Institute of Justice and Financial Crimes Enforcement Network, Washington, DC.

Secretary of the U.S. Department of the Treasury. 2002. "A Report to the Congress in Accordance with Section 359 of the Uniting and Strengthening America by Providing Appropriate Tools Required to Intercept and Obstruct Terrorism Act of 2001." Washington, DC: U.S. Department of the Treasury.

U.A.E Central Bank. 2002. "Abu Dhabi Declaration on Hawala." Abu Dhabi. May 16.

Chapter 12
Regulation and Supervision in a Vacuum: The Story of the Somali Remittance Sector

Abdusalam Omer and Gina El Koury

Stepping out of the single-engine airplane onto the dirt landing strip, one immediately notices the emptiness. The emptiness emanates from a country lacking the things ordinarily found in other places. Just as in many developing countries, there are few tarmac roads and cars to see, few school bells ringing, and the silence that bodes of ill health. The emptiness here on this landing strip, however, far exceeds the normal picture of a developing country. Something larger is missing here: a central government. The lack of a central government creates an unimaginable void—a void where police, military, and other emergency services are unheard of; where schools and health facilities do not exist for the public at large; where communications of all sorts go unregulated; and where there is no single body to identify its people to the outside world. To further exacerbate the situation, there are no central or commercial banking institutions to facilitate trade, enable investment, monitor currency, direct the economy, or get money to people who are in need. These missing elements drive the need to engage an ever-increasing diaspora in sending money home.

Since the collapse of the state in 1991, Somalia has been without a central government and a central bank. During Siad Barre's regime, from 1969 until 1991, Somalia had a largely centralized economy. Therefore, the central government's collapse meant the closure of all the banks as well as the failure of courts, schools, hospitals, sanitation services, electrical and water facilities, communications networks, and other public services. These closures translated into mass unemployment and emigration, which were compounded by the violent civil war that began immediately after the regime's overthrow. As of early 2005, the civil conflict has yet to be fully resolved; there were only tentative steps toward a political settlement.

Nevertheless, several private initiatives are acting to stem the tide of poverty, emigration, and lawlessness. The impact of the civil war and the absence of a central government have not diminished the Somalis' sense of community and entrepreneurship. New enterprises are replacing old ones; commercial airlines are being established; the telecommunications industry is flourishing; educational and health institutions have started materializing in many parts of the country; and the financial sector is reorganizing to meet the growing demands of its customers. Thus, private sector developments have become the engine that drives employment and the economy in its entirety, facilitating financial transactions, providing social services, and contributing to peace and stability in lieu of a functioning state.[1]

This is the unique situation in Somalia today, and it requires a unique perspective. In light of the current global political context regarding financial institutions, this chapter aims to recognize the critical utility of the Somali remittance sector and explore the methods by which it can

continue to function. It also proposes to identify the vital steps necessary to ensure that the remittance sector is in line with international regulations and has the capability to meet ever-changing requirements.

DEVELOPMENT OF THE SOMALI REMITTANCE SECTOR

The remittance sector is among the leading private initiatives in Somalia today. Somalis remit approximately US$700 million to US$1 billion
annually from more than 40 countries. This figure, collected through
research with the various remittance companies as well as from individual households and businesspeople inside Somalia, represents
funds remitted for daily subsistence, investment purposes, and trade
facilitation. To put it in perspective, the total remitted to Somalia annually dwarfs the total amount of aid from the international community,
including food (see figure 12.1).

The remittances members of the Somali diaspora send to their
impoverished family members each year provide food, shelter, clothing,

FIGURE 12.1 OFFICIAL DEVELOPMENT ASSISTANCE AND
REMITTANCES TO SOMALIA, 2001–2002

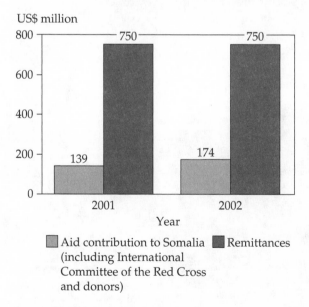

Sources: "A Report on Supporting Systems and Procedures for the Effective Regulation
and Monitoring of Somali Remittance Companies (Hawala)," August 2004; SACB (Somalia Aid Coordination Body) *Donor Annual Reports,* 2001, 2003.

schooling, health care, and other necessities. Remittances are the major source of income for most Somalis (see figure 12.2). This support extends beyond the boundaries of Somalia proper, into the Somali inhabited regions in the Horn of Africa, so the number of Somalis who rely on remittances for their livelihood is much bigger than the actual figures indicate.

Investment and trade in Somalia rely heavily upon the receipt of remittances. In addition to sending money individually to family members, migrants also send money collectively to invest in businesses, community services, and real estate development. These funds are critical to keeping the Somali economy afloat, as remittances are the largest source of hard currency for the country.[2] Because there is no formal banking sector, remittance companies provide a means by which money can facilitate trade internationally and investment and subsistence domestically. In the absence of a banking sector, Somali remittance companies transfer funds both domestically and internationally and provide basic savings and checking facilities for their customers inside Somalia.

The 10 years since 1995 have seen tremendous growth in the remittance sector, which has existed in Somalia for over four decades. Until the mid-1990s, the remittance system was highly informal, similar to the traditional *hawala* system, and relied on personal relationships as well as community and familial trust to ensure its success. It has always been the fastest, cheapest, and surest way to send money to any location inside Somalia, because many banks could not reach rural

FIGURE 12.2 MAJOR INCOME SOURCES IN SOMALIA

Source: Report No. 1, Somali Watching Brief 2003: Socio-Economic Survey 2002.

areas, would take several days or even weeks to transmit the money, and would charge a high fee. Remittances largely came from the diaspora in the Persian Gulf States; these people sent either money or high-value consumer goods, which were later sold with a portion of the sale going to the trader bringing the goods.

The rise of remittance transmissions during the course of the recent civil war, which has produced an increasing number of emigrants from Somalia; the post–September 11 context; and the expanse of countries from which remittances are sent, have forced the remittance sector to formalize its operations. Although Somalis still rely on the remittance system's trust, simplicity, and cost-effectiveness, remittance companies have rapidly begun to function much more like the banks that are so desperately needed inside their country, particularly because it is the only way to remit money to Somalia.

In addition, the expansion of telecommunications and trade in Somalia has facilitated the sector's growth. Remittance companies now have better access to remote parts of the country and more reliable services because they have communications with all of their agents. The remittance sector has also fulfilled the needs of local businesspeople in these times of insecurity. Without any public protection services, actual transportation of funds would face serious risks, such as banditry, fires, and other risks encountered during times of conflict. Remittance companies, however, allow businesspeople to move money throughout the country for purposes of trade by transferring funds through their complex computerized financial networks—not through physical means.

This brief background on the growing remittance sector is necessary to understand the challenges that it faces today. More significantly, the background identifies the willingness of Somalis to adapt to changing financial environments and, therefore, the obligation to help the sector overcome these obstacles to ensure that this lifeline of funds from the diaspora continues to reach Somalia.

CHALLENGES FACING THE REMITTANCE SECTOR

In the wake of the 2001 terrorist attacks on the United States, host country regulators as well as banking institutions increased their oversight of their clients, particularly through anti-money laundering and terrorist financing legislation. In November 2001, Al-Barakat, the largest Somali remittance company at the time, was closed in the United States and its assets were frozen worldwide based on allegations associated with terrorism.[3] The Al-Barakat closure compounded an already difficult situation for the Somali remittance sector and precipitated a crisis of confidence in the sector. The trust factor that is essential in the remittance business was called into question. Financial and government regulatory institutions experienced increased difficulties, and Somali remittance companies felt a sense of vulnerability in the changing environment after September 11. The cumulative effect has been to accelerate the growth and formalization of an otherwise rudimentary system. As a result, contrary to expectations and despite the frozen funds, Al-Barakat's closure has had a minimal impact on the delivery of remittances to individual Somali families and businesses because other remittance companies quickly filled the void.

Somalia poses unique challenges to any financial institutions already in operation or planning to operate there. The major problem is the country's vast insecurity. This insecurity causes problems for the various remittance company agents who are responsible for collecting and distributing hundreds of thousands of dollars on a daily basis. To counter this problem, the remittance companies are forced not only to hire their own protection, which is only a makeshift solution, but also to employ intensive screening procedures for their staff and their customers.

For example, all companies have hundreds of employees stationed throughout the country. Potential employees are assessed on their knowledge of the geographical regions, financial procedures, telecommunications skills, and computer abilities. Once the necessary job qualifications are fulfilled, the potential employees are then screened for proof of identity, which is increasingly difficult in a country lacking a central government and thus any recognized form of official identification. To fulfill this requirement, in addition to providing any identification documentation and educational records that the individual may have, the companies have to identify the individual's clan and community and use references from neighbors, family members, elders, and other community leaders to prove the prospective employee's identity, trustworthiness, and reliability. Finally, to protect themselves against theft or other legal violations by the prospective employee, the remittance companies require the individual to provide collateral, sometimes personally, but usually through a family member who has money or businesses, of several thousand U.S. dollars. Once the collateral is provided and the employee is hired, the individual is prohibited from conducting transactions above the amount of the collateral. Therefore, should something go awry, the company has a way to claim back its money and insure its customers against any losses. Because there is no government to impose and enforce laws and regulations, the companies have to shield both themselves and their customers from potential harm. Their enforced innovativeness in protecting themselves against insecurity has unknowingly brought them into compliance with the global sphere of financial regulations, particularly concerning the "know your customer" and "know your processes" methods of anti-money laundering and terrorist financing regulations.

The security problem highlights another major obstacle to operating inside Somalia: the lack of a central bank. Without a central bank, there is no money supply management and, therefore, no new currency production to meet the increased infusion of funds into the economy. This leads to counterfeit production of money and new money that various local administrations throughout the country produce. This infusion of new currency, which is not backed by a central bank, national reserves, or other securities, produces vast inflation and has to be monitored carefully by the remittance companies. To defend themselves against currency fluctuations, which are largely determined by local markets and political activities, the remittance companies deal only in United States dollars. They will exchange money for their customers, but will only remit and distribute dollars. Nevertheless, the currency problem remains a constant issue, particularly when large sums of money must be converted into the Somali shilling.

The central bank traditionally has other critical functions, specifically regarding regulating, monitoring, and setting national fiscal policy. Because these functions are also lacking, the remittance companies operate, albeit successfully, in a virtual vacuum. They use a free market, demand-driven economy. By doing so, they have prevented price fixing from occurring and monopolies from forming; developed strong competition, thereby improving services and reducing prices; and expanded their customer base. For instance, when Al-Barakat was still operating, it was the largest Somali remittance company. There were many other players in the market, but due to Al-Barakat's broad network both globally and inside Somalia, the others were unable to compete without charging higher fees. As such, several companies merged and others developed specialized market niches to compete against Al-Barakat. These actions were not only successful in preventing a monopoly, but also succeeded in responding to the ever-growing customer needs in the flourishing private sector. More significantly, however, when Al-Barakat closed, the sector as a whole had become so well developed that it immediately filled the gap, averting what would have otherwise been a humanitarian disaster. Despite the remittance sector's resilience, operating without domestic regulation and a central fiscal policy continues to prove difficult. As the companies are entering new international markets, they are blind to host country regulations and requirements, and unused to their thoroughness as well as the impact of the regulations on the economy as a whole.

Apart from general insecurity, the lack of a central authority poses many problems. With no central authority, there is no forum for diplomatic relations with other countries. Without diplomatic relations, the remittance companies have no body to advocate on their behalf, no leverage for imposing trade restrictions and regulations, and no accountability for the sector in the international arena. In addition, there is no central financial authority to participate in global financial forums, to sign and debate treaties, and to join international conventions and task forces to combat terrorist financing and money laundering, despite the willingness of the country's people. This void presents the Somali remittance sector negatively to the international community. Although central governments traditionally perform these functions, the sector, having recognized the tremendous significance of this advocacy, has recently begun to call upon the international community, particularly the United Nations Development Programme (UNDP), to assist in this area. Nevertheless, the sector still does not have a representative national body able to participate in global debates; this issue needs to be addressed.

To date, remittance companies have been individually dealing with these various problems. In doing so, they have begun to look at host country regulations for guidance in the formalization process. Because they have functioned in a lawless arena for over a decade, and even though they have increased the financial professionalism in their operations, they have yet to be on par with the formal financial institutions in the host countries in which they operate. They have, however, used the registration processes in several locales and the requirements that apply therein to create uniformity among their global operations, both individually and for the Somali remittance sector as a whole. This progress has led to increased recognition among host country regulators and a willingness to collaborate with the remittance companies to ensure their continuity.

In addition to conforming to individual host country regulations, the remittance companies are also made to comply with international financial regulations. The most significant body of international financial regulations is that of the Financial Action Task Force (FATF). Founded in 1989, with 33 current members, the FATF has become the leading intergovernmental body developing worldwide policies and regulations to tackle the problems associated with anti-money laundering and terrorist financing. Although the anti-money laundering regulations have been in place for a number of years, it was not until after September 11, 2001, when the compliance gap for money transfer businesses was identified, that the member countries began to heed the recommendations and enact new legislation or enforce existing legislation relating to their operations. This newly invoked legislation—mostly centered around identifying and reporting suspicious activity, management and ownership structures, licensing requirements, and auditing and accounting procedures—has been the most costly to the remittance companies, because it requires them to adopt higher diligence levels in their management and operation infrastructures than those used prior to September 11.[4]

Compliance with FATF best-practice recommendations, which include best practices for the 40 FATF recommendations on anti-money laundering as well as the eight FATF special recommendations on terrorist financing, is perhaps one of the most important compliance measures for any money transfer business. In this regard, the Somali remittance companies are making considerable progress. As mentioned earlier, several FATF recommendations have been implemented, either in full or in part, as a result of the requirements of the unique situation in Somalia, such as the "know your customer" requirements. There are, however, many recommendations relating to registration or licensing of money transfer businesses in their locales of operation. The remittance companies have made tremendous efforts to register or obtain licenses wherever they are in operation. In particular, nearly all are registered in the United Kingdom, with the United States federal government, and with the Minnesota state government (where there is a large Somali population). Many more companies are registered in various U.S. states and in various European countries, and some have even obtained licenses in the United Arab Emirates. A majority of the companies also have licenses or registrations pending with various host country regulators. Continual progress has been made since the imposition and enforcement of the regulations.

An important FATF registration recommendation relates to the need for remittance companies to maintain separate bank accounts from the other businesses owned by the proprietor, as well as the need for formal banking institutions to learn about and understand the remittance sector. This recommendation has been heeded by a majority of the remittance companies but, unfortunately, not by a majority of the banks. Although there has been an increase in its willingness to collaborate, the remittance sector still has many obstacles to overcome in conveying the inner workings of its systems.

Another major area of FATF recommendations relates to awareness-raising campaigns that both the host country authorities and remittance companies have launched. To this end, several companies have organized comprehensive staff training in various countries of operation. Although many companies have organized several different training opportunities, the focus has been on the United States, with the notion that if their staff can comply with the strict requirements of the USA Patriot Act, they are prepared for compliance with most international financial regulations. These sessions are often accompanied by a launch of a company's compliance manual (usually prepared by outside consultants or in-house legal counsel), which serves to raise awareness of the rules, and determine ways for the company to comply with the rules in their internal and external operations.

For the most part, host country authorities have not organized comprehensive training and compliance programs to assist the companies in mastering the financial regulations currently in place and to explain the expectations that the regulators have of the remittance companies.

However, the authorities are becoming increasingly cooperative, and some, such as the United Kingdom, distribute extensive training materials, including informative pamphlets and a video for use in internal company training sessions. In addition, at a 2004 UNDP workshop in the United Kingdom, many European regulators presented their country's regulations, made themselves available for individual consultations, and conveyed their interest in engaging with the Somali remittance sector in the future. All parties in attendance welcomed the cooperation as a sign of recognition of the unique situation of the Somali sector, which is struggling to achieve compliance, despite seemingly insurmountable limitations.

Some of the most widely publicized FATF best-practice recommendations relate to anti-money laundering regulations, specifically, customer identification requirements, recordkeeping requirements, and suspicious transaction reporting. Most remittance companies have comprehensive "know your customer" programs in place, and many use comprehensive databases to store and track customer information. In host countries, where a majority of the funds originate, identification is generally not a problem, as remitters possess legal documents from host countries. When a customer wants to remit funds, the remittance companies require the presentation of formal identification, and in some cases, the companies issue identification cards. To obtain a remittance company identification card, the customer has to provide the following information at a minimum: at least one, but sometimes two, official forms of identification as described in the host country regulations; several references; full contact information; clan affiliation; and a birth date. In addition, some companies have computerized customer identification systems and use thumbprints along with a photograph for customer identification. This information is then tied to a customer identification number, which is entered into the system to track all customer transactions. This form of identification is extremely helpful in Somalia where not all of the customers are able to provide a signature because of high illiteracy levels; this process is a considerable advance in accurately identifying, tracking, and recording client transactions.

Overall, the Somali remittance sector still has many needs, most of which relate to the lack of a central government. The sector must build its capacity to fulfill the international financial requirements for it to increase its current compliance level. The sector also needs domestic regulatory institutions to unify all remittance operations and reporting mechanisms, and to advocate on their behalf in the international arena. These overarching needs, which continue to grow, have started to become more manageable. The sector has begun several initiatives that, over several years, will lead them to a point of full compliance and put a domestic regulatory system in place.

REGULATION AND SUPERVISION IN A VACUUM

The first step the remittance sector took to convey and further compliance with host country regulations was to form the Somali Financial Services Association (SFSA). The SFSA is based on two principal activities: to act as a self-regulatory body for the Somali remittance sector until such time as a central authority is in place; and to play the role of a traditional association, working to meet its members' continuing needs through training, advocacy, networking, and information sharing. The association's self-regulation is envisioned as a short-term solution, lasting no more than five years, to provide sector supervision, regulation, and uniformity, and enabling its compliance with international financial regulations in the absence of central authorities in Somalia.[5] In addition to enhancing compliance with international rules and regulations, it will improve transparency and accountability, conduct advocacy both at home and abroad, and impose sectoral uniformity. Through these functions, the SFSA will be able to improve the skills of the sector's employees and impress upon the rest of the world the importance, both for fiscal and humanitarian needs, of the Somali remittance sector. Once central authorities are in place, the association will be in a position to entrust the policies, regulations, and monitoring mechanisms that the sector developed to the fledgling government to facilitate the smooth transition of this critical regulatory process. The SFSA would then remain indefinitely as an association committed to its members' advancement and to promoting the financial services sector.

Throughout the self-regulation process, the remittance sector, in accordance with the standards of the SFSA and with the international community's assistance, will continue to work to develop an environment conducive to the entry of a formal banking sector. A formal banking sector can only occur once a central government and its accompanying financial arms are functioning and stable. A formal banking sector will provide a long-term solution to the need for domestic regulation mechanisms, bring fiscal stability to the country, and bring compliance with international financial rules and regulations to the sector.[6]

With the self-regulation aspect firmly in place in the SFSA, transferring this mechanism to the Ministry of Finance and central bank should make the introduction of a formal banking sector possible. The formal financial sector will encompass remittance companies, remittance companies that have transformed into banks, new Somali banks, and, it is hoped, international banks. This new functional sector will allow for major boosts in investment, trade, employment, and the economy as a whole. Once this transition has occurred, the self-regulatory aspects will be replaced with formal, independent regulatory and monitoring mechanisms, complemented by legal and judicial systems for enforcement. This regulation will operate indefinitely, supporting the financial services sector domestically and internationally in all domains.

MOVING FORWARD

Somali remittance companies are relatively technologically advanced and are continuously working to improve the speed and efficiency of service delivery. Using their computerized systems, monies sent from countries such as Australia and the United States are delivered to recipients in remote villages in Somalia within 48 hours. The companies have developed an extensive financial infrastructure in the absence of central government, lack of a regulatory framework, and in the middle of civil war–ravaged country. Somali remittance operators are destined to lead the way for the banks and financial institutions of the future in the new Somalia.[7] For these gains to be institutionalized, the way forward must include certain commitments, discussed below, from the various stakeholders.

In continuing on the journey of increased compliance, one must still remember the domestic landscape in which the sector operates. On the surface, the landscape is one of poverty and anarchy, but underneath, it is the true entrepreneurial spirit and unification of private industry that prevails. As such, the SFSA will be able to flourish, so long as its commitment to improving the sector remains strong and the international community continues its support. Both parties, however, remain intertwined and will continue to be for the near future, as the sector recognizes its need to organize, unify, and advance itself; the international community, in recognizing the sector's critical importance to the survival of millions of people, must support the sector to keep this vital lifeline open.

Despite this commitment, the SFSA and its members still have many responsibilities to fulfill to meet this endeavor's challenges. Perhaps one of the most significant demonstrations of the commitments the sector has made is the willingness of individual players to collaborate to further their mutual interests. This commitment must be developed to its fullest extent. This collaboration will ensure that advocacy efforts are rewarded, because there will be coordinated efforts by all stakeholders to work toward implementing compliance measures. Without full cooperation by SFSA members to self-regulate in an organized, unified fashion, actual self-regulation cannot be achieved, and any efforts to improve the sector's reputation will be undermined.

With continued collaboration in hand, the SFSA must aggressively pursue training for itself and its members and actively work to improve the tarnished image of the Somali remittance sector in the wake of the closure of Al-Barakat in 2001. Through the values and enforcement mechanisms detailed in its Code of Conduct, the SFSA must strictly enforce its membership and compliance guidelines, regardless of community and familial ties. Strict enforcement will enable it to boldly announce its commitment to the international community and uphold the principles it supports.

The bulk of the responsibility for success remains with the SFSA and its members. Their tremendous tasks are to sustain the current remittance industry, improve its standards, expand its services, and assist the formal banking sector's entrance into Somalia. This task can be accomplished through its members' continued commitment and the willingness of international partners and stakeholders to recognize the SFSA's self-regulation and support this new association's quest to achieve its goals.

The host country regulators also have responsibilities to fulfill to assist the remittance sector in meeting regulatory compliance needs. This assistance serves dual purposes: first, to encourage and support new immigrants in their newly established small business enterprises; and second, to familiarize immigrants with the financial rules and regulations of their new home countries. This assistance will also safeguard these services from money laundering schemes and groups and individuals using them to conduct terrorist financing. It is in the interest of both the Somali operators and host country regulators to safeguard these services so that the Somali people can continue receiving this vital support and host country governments can adequately monitor these activities.

The sectoral entry point for the international donor community is on behalf of the millions of Somali people who rely on remittances from the diaspora for their livelihoods. The intent is to keep this lifeline open and encourage the entrepreneurial spirit of the Somalis. The donor community is committed to supporting the development of the Somali financial services sector into the fully functioning, formalized sector that it needs to be, as witnessed particularly by UNDP's initiatives in this arena over the period 2001–2005. Through coordinated donor support and industry efforts, the Somali remittance sector will thrive, and proper steps can be taken to ensure that in the future, a formal, regulated domestic banking sector can emerge, thus providing all Somali and international stakeholders with future prospects for collaboration and cooperation.

NOTES

1. Indirectly, the private sector is perhaps the greatest contributor to peace and stability, as it is generally apolitical. The job creation, increased standards

of living, and other opportunities that it provides lead to a more content and stable population.

2. Other hard currency sources come from international aid contributions and the livestock trade.

3. Because there was limited information made public on the Al-Barakat investigation, the chapter's authors have no further details.

4. Even in jurisdictions with legislation on these matters, the regulations were rarely enforced prior to September 11. Although the companies were aware of the laws, in practice, as demonstrated over decades of operation, they were not obliged to comply. The heightened focus placed on money transfer companies in the post-September 11 world forced them to comply immediately or face closure. This unanticipated burden was costly, and, for some smaller companies such as the Somali remittance companies, there were neither the human nor financial resources to fulfill the requirements in due time. As shown in this chapter, however, they have been progressive in their approaches to complying with the regulations as quickly and as comprehensively as possible.

5. Self-regulation is in line with other sectors in the Somali economy such as the Somali Telecommunication Association, which represents the booming telecommunications industry, and the Somali Business Council, which acts as an umbrella organization for all the Somali business sectors operating in the United Arab Emirates. These associations currently perform dual functions similar to those envisioned by the SFSA, and they each have plans to transfer the self-regulatory aspect over to a central authority as soon as one is in place and able to take on such responsibility.

6. It should be noted that, although full compliance is necessary for the remittance companies to continue to operate, overregulation could also cause serious problems. For example, it will impose the administrative burdens of the formal financial sector, therefore increasing operating costs and customer costs, and will delay the process of transferring funds. This burden will force some smaller companies that are financially incapable of compliance underground, and therefore farther away from the monitoring and enforcement efforts of the host country regulators.

7. The new Somalia refers to the anticipation of a time when the civil conflict has ended, a political compromise has been reached, and a stable central government is in power. This new government will not have a centralized economy as in the old regime; instead it will continue to protect the trend of a vibrant and flourishing private sector to restore order and strength to Somalia's economic systems.

REFERENCES

Omer, A. 2004. "A Report on Supporting Systems and Procedures for the Effective Regulation and Monitoring of Somali Remittance Companies (Hawala)." Nairobi: UNDP.

SACB (Somalia Aid Coordination Body). 2001. *Donor Annual Report.* Nairobi: SACB.

_____. 2002. *Donor Annual Report.* Nairobi: SACB.

World Bank. 2003. "Somalia: Socio-Economic Survey 2002. Report No. 1. Somalia Watching Brief." Nairobi, Kenya.

Chapter 13
A Proposed Framework to Analyze Informal Funds Transfer Systems

Raul Hernandez-Coss

While informal funds transfer (IFT) systems have proven to be a resilient method of transferring value from one location to another and have been especially attractive to migrants sending remittances, the use of formal systems to send remittances significantly enhances the development potential of remittances and promotes greater transparency in the market (Ratha 2003).[1] To facilitate the shift to formal systems, this chapter offers past experience and lessons in shifting from informal to formal systems and a framework for examining funds transfer systems within an individual economy.

This chapter has two objectives: first, to identify and learn from successful bilateral initiatives and formal products and services designed to strengthen remittances through formal channels, and second, to propose a framework for analyzing funds transfer systems in a given economy by estimating informal remittance flows and identifying the incentives that influence users when deciding whether to remit through formal or informal systems.

To achieve these objectives, the chapter is divided into two sections. After describing the key regulatory aspects of IFT systems that have been developed by the Financial Action Task Force (FATF), the first section outlines a variety of bilateral initiatives and market products and services that strengthen formal sector channels. While these initiatives and products represent good micro-level examples, the number of them indicates the need for a unified approach to measuring and analyzing funds transfer systems so that policy makers can harmonize efforts and strategies at the regional level and private sector entities can understand how to compete with informal systems. Thus, the proposed framework described in the chapter's second section offers an initial approach to augment and unify attempts at shifting users from informal to formal systems. Part I of the framework offers a method for roughly estimating the magnitude of IFT flows between economies. Part II analyzes a remittance sender's perceived incentives to use formal or informal systems.

Ultimately, the framework is a step toward balancing the need for IFT systems regulation with an appreciation for the incentives IFT systems offer. IFT systems provide valuable, efficient services at low cost in places where conflict, poverty, or remote geography prevent formal financial infrastructure from being built. The formal sector can learn and adapt its practices to provide similar services. The need to strike a balance between appropriate levels of regulation and minimizing financial abuse, on the one hand, and promoting cost-efficient and accessible services on the other, is a key guiding principle for researchers and policy makers seeking to enhance the development impact of remittances in a more integrated world (Maimbo 2003).[2]

REGULATORY AND MARKET ACTIVITY
IN FUNDS TRANSFER SYSTEMS

In the formal sector, government and businesses have collaborated to create a formal remittances market. Governments contribute primarily through appropriate regulation of the financial sector, but also by devising ways to stimulate the market for formal remittances. (Different governments may weigh heavily toward one side or the other.) Private institutions, in addition to complying with government regulations, contribute by responding to market demands for new and innovative products and services for the dynamic formal remittances market.

Collaboration between government and the financial sector takes various forms. The first section below describes regulatory concerns surrounding IFT systems, with particular reference to money laundering and terrorist financing, while the second describes governmental and private sector initiatives to stimulate the use of formal sector channels and create a viable formal market for remittance services. Emerging from the discussion are some clear benefits, from both the regulatory and the market perspectives, of shifting users from informal to formal systems.

Regulatory Considerations in Funds Transfer Systems

Funds transfer systems face risk of misuse for money laundering or financing of terrorism, as do other financial sector activities. Economies need to consider the appropriate level of regulation to maintain the integrity of legitimate flows without impeding that flow, particularly for workers' remittances, given the importance they have as a source of funds for developing economies.

Why Shift from Informal to Formal Systems?

While informal methods of sending remittances might be popular among migrant workers, the use of formal methods enhances the development potential of remittances and promotes increased transparency and accountability in the remittance market. This positively affects not only the government and the financial sector, but also the individual remitters and their families.

A shift from informal systems to formal ones brings much-needed accountability and transparency to the remittance market, which can only be achieved when funds transfer systems operate openly and are subject to some form of regulation. Although most users of IFT systems are legitimate, the anonymity and secrecy of IFT systems are attractive to individuals and groups engaged in illegal activities (Schott 2003). In this manner, IFT systems constitute a weak link in nations' defenses against money laundering, terrorist financing, and their predicate crimes.[3] As a consequence, many different kinds of flows travel through remittance systems, depending on the intent of the sender.[4] Regardless of the type of flow or intent of the user, legitimate and illegitimate flows bottleneck and intermingle in remittance channels. Channeling remittances through transparent, formal systems, as opposed to opaque, informal ones, protects remittance flows from illicit flows through better monitoring and recording. Also, because migrant worker remittances are believed to comprise a substantial portion of IFT flows (Buencamino and Gorbunov 2002),[5] shifting them into formal channels enables law enforcement to better focus their efforts on the illegitimate flows remaining in the informal sector.

Opaque IFT systems also present challenges in terms of their adverse effects on the market. Banking and financial services depend on a reputation for integrity, and criminal involvement can reduce investor confidence and diminish opportunities for growth (Buencamino and Gorbunov 2002).[6] Local businesses also cannot compete with companies funded by laundered money and offering services below market rates. Broader concerns include the destabilization of financial markets, because illegal funds are an unstable deposit base; and the loss of revenue and control over economic policy, because money laundering decreases government tax revenue and, when laundered funds are invested, can distort currencies and interest rates. Economic distortion also can occur when money launderers channel money to sectors in which funds are easily hidden. Their subsequent decisions to leave the industry can cause those sectors to collapse, possibly damaging the entire economy. Because money laundering enables drug traffickers, smugglers, and other criminals to expand their operations, it obliges governments to increase spending for law enforcement and health care.

Formal methods of transferring remittances are also preferable to informal ones because of their increased ability to foster development. The development aim to encourage savings and investment, or more specifically, the channeling of remittances into savings and investment mechanisms, can be best facilitated and streamlined through formal channels that offer these financial services in conjunction with remittance delivery. In addition, these remitting customers represent a business opportunity. By developing formal remittance channels that are competitive with informal ones, the formal financial sector has an incentive to develop and benefit from the overall opportunity to grow and expand through the remittances market. Individual remitters also come out ahead because remittance services competitive to those in IFT systems are available but with additional benefits that formal transfer systems afford, such as protection from the flow of illicit proceeds.

The International Financial Action
Task Force against Money Laundering

As the international standard-setter in anti-money laundering and combating the financing of terrorism (AML/CFT), FATF addresses IFT sys-
tems in its Special Recommendations on Terrorist Financing (Special
Recommendation VI) (FATF 2001). The Special Recommendation is sup-
plemented by an Interpretative Note and a note on International Best
Practices adopted in June 2003 (box 13.1). In 2000, the FATF identified
IFT systems as an area of concern in anti-money laundering efforts
(FATF 2000). The report discusses some of the general attributes of IFT
systems and describes several IFT systems—the Black Market Peso
Exchange in the Western Hemisphere, the informal *hawala* system in the
Middle East, and IFT systems operating in China and East Asia. FATF's
goal with regard to IFT systems is to ensure that they are not abused by
criminals and become a weak link in a nation's AML/CFT regime.

Initiatives: Understanding the Funds Transfer Market Through
Micro-Level Policies and Market Products

Various private sector entities and a handful of governments have implemented new products, incentives, and policies to encourage individuals
and institutions to use formal remittance systems. The initiatives include
card-based programs, international networking initiatives, and banking-
and account-based programs. The following section details these initiatives as examples of practical measures taken by businesses, organizations, and governments to meet the remittance needs of migrant workers
while regularizing funds transfers.

Bilateral Initiatives to Strengthen
Remittance Services in the Formal Sector

Recognizing the need for cooperative measures to manage the flow of
remittances, some countries have made bilateral arrangements to
improve methods of money transfer. Essentially, these agreements are
initial attempts to streamline the remittance process. Following are
some examples of the policy initiatives undertaken to promote funds
transfer through formal funds transfer (FFT) systems and foster sound
economic cooperation.

   U.S-Mexico Partnership for Prosperity. The U.S.-Mexico Partnership
for Prosperity, a private-public alliance launched in September 2001, is
an action plan to promote economic development in the poorer regions
of Mexico and reduce immigration to the United States. One of its goals
is to lower the cost of remittances from Mexican migrants to their families.[7] According to the U.S. Treasury, Mexican immigrants spent more

---

BOX 13. 1 FATF's SPECIAL RECOMMENDATIONS ON
TERRORIST FINANCING

Recommendation VI of FATF's Special Recommendations on Terrorist
Financing addresses alternative remittance systems.

Alternative Remittance

Each country should take measures to ensure that persons or
legal entities, including agents, that provide a service for the
transmission of money or value, including transmission
through an informal money or value transfer system or network, should be licensed or registered and subject to all the
FATF Recommendations that apply to banks and non-bank
financial institutions. Each country should ensure that persons
or legal entities that carry out this service illegally are subject to
administrative, civil or criminal sanctions.

Specifically, the objective of Special Recommendation VI is to
increase the transparency of payment flows by ensuring that
jurisdictions impose consistent AML/CFT measures on all
forms of funds transfer. The Interpretative Note to Special Recommendation VI states:

Special Recommendation VI consists of three core elements:

a) Jurisdictions should require licensing or registration of
   persons (natural or legal) that provide money/value
   transfer services, including through informal systems;
b) Jurisdictions should ensure that money/value transmission services, including informal systems are subject to
   applicable FATF Forty Recommendations (in particular,
   Recommendations 10-21 and 26-29) and the Eight Special
   Recommendations (in particular SR VII); and
c) Jurisdictions should be able to impose sanctions on
   money/value transfer services, including informal systems, that operate without a license or registration and
   that fail to comply with relevant FATF Recommendations.

Source: FATF 2003.

---

than US$1 billion to send money home in 2001 (U.S. Department of
State 2002). The U.S. Federal Reserve is working to expand its Federal
Reserve Automated Clearing House (FedACH) International[8] service
to support two-way credit transactions between the two countries.[9] At
the beginning in the fourth quarter of 2003, the Federal Reserve and
Banco de México, Mexico's central bank, allowed U.S. banks to send a
payment to Mexico for a surcharge of approximately US$0.67 per item,

plus the standard FedACH domestic processing fees. The service was offered initially on a limited basis but opened to all banks in the second half of 2004. Lower-cost payments from Mexico to the United States also were introduced in 2004. The key driver in offering this service is the shared vision of the Mexican and U.S. governments as set forth in the Partnership for Prosperity initiative, which encourages the financial industry to work to lower the cost of remittances sent by Mexican migrants to their families. The clearinghouse system, along with competition among the banks, should lower fees, ensuring that more money reaches families in Mexico—thereby strengthening both economies (Silver 2003).

Mexican Consular Identification Card (Matrícula Consular). Mexican Consular Identification Cards (CICs), issued in the United States since 1871, are similar to other types of identity documents (Cuevas 2003). Consular registration constitutes the official record of individuals living abroad, and the CIC is a legal proof of registration. More than 1.4 million were issued in the United States in 2002. Originally designed to identify people involved in accidents or crimes, CICs are becoming an accepted form of identification for opening U.S. bank accounts—thus introducing migrants to the formal financial sector. As of 2004, 70 banks and 56 credit unions, including Citibank, Bank of America, U.S. Bancorp, and Wells Fargo accepted the CIC (NCSL 2004). Wells Fargo estimates that it has opened over 70,000 new accounts since it began accepting CICs in November 2001 (O'Neil 2003).

To get a CIC, Mexican nationals in the United States must provide an original birth certificate, official photo identification acceptable in Mexico or an official U.S. photo identification, and proof of residence within the consular jurisdiction.

After the terrorist attacks in the United States on September 11, 2001, the Mexican government took steps to strengthen the security of the CIC. The improved version has nearly a dozen security features designed to deter falsification (Bair 2002). The Mexican government is developing an online database that will enable its consulates to verify if applicants have previously received a CIC card from another consulate and to coordinate issuance.[10]

U.S.-Philippines. The U.S. Treasury Department and the Philippines Ministry of Finance have created an initiative to reduce the costs of overseas remittance services (through greater competition and efficiency), enhance access to FFT systems, and ensure compliance with AML/CFT standards (U.S. Treasury 2003). In collaboration with the U.S. Federal Deposit Insurance Corporation and the Federal Reserve, the U.S. Treasury Department works with its Filipino counterparts to correct deficiencies in remittance channels, understand the role of the private sector, strengthen the infrastructure that supports remittances, minimize vulnerabilities in that infrastructure, promote financial literacy, and ensure proper implementation and full compliance with international best practices.

Singapore. On June 30, 2003, the Monetary Authority of Singapore announced that it would allow banks subject to branching restrictions to set up new branches specifically to provide remittance and money changing services. Since the time it was implemented, this measure enhanced access to FFT systems in Singapore and provided foreign workers with more choices and increased convenience in remitting funds to their home countries.[11]

Latin America–Spain. In January 2003, the Inter-American Development ment Bank (IDB) and Caja de Ahorros y Pensiones de Barcelona (La Caixa), a Spanish savings institution, agreed to cooperate to enhance the development impact of remittances sent from Spain to Latin America and the Caribbean (IDB 2003). The IDB's Multilateral Investment Fund (MIF) aims to reduce the cost of remittances by stimulating competition among service providers, increasing awareness of remittance services, and improving regulatory frameworks for financial services. MIF helps microcredit and savings institutions in Latin America and the Caribbean design remittance-related products and services that encourage development and participation in the formal financial sector.

Malaysia. In March 2002, a company endorsed by Nepal's central bank was given permission to organize the collection and remittance of their country's workers wages through a Malaysian bank to the company's bank in Nepal.[12] The company's office in Nepal would then arrange to send the money directly to the respective recipient's families.

Private-Sector Initiatives to Improve Remittance Services

Along with effective government regulation, private-sector initiatives—and investments—are key to developing a market in which formal remittance services are competitive, efficient, and widely available. A market that meets those criteria will increase the likelihood that money is held, invested, and transferred through intermediaries that adhere to AML/CFT standards and other financial sector regulations. The efforts of several companies to capture portions of the remittance market are described below.

This section focuses on products and services being offered or introduced in the remittances market. It does not assess those products and services for compliance with international AML/CFT standards and best practices.

Card-Based Innovations. Card-based services provide senders and recipients with convenient and affordable remittance products. Because they do not require customers to open and maintain an account, they offer great flexibility. Services offered through automated teller machines (ATMs) bring the convenience of ATM service to the remittance market.

The Morgan Beaumont MoneyCard is a prepaid package of two cards, available for $49.95 in convenience stores and $29.95 on the Internet (Bézard 2002). No identification is necessary to purchase the cards,[13] which can be sent or given to a friend or family member anywhere in the world. Targeted at Hispanic, Asian, and East European immigrant communities in the United States, the MoneyCard can be used to withdraw cash from over 750,000 ATMs and to pay for goods and services at 5.5 million points of sale worldwide. It can be replenished as often as desired. The card also can be used to build credit history.

International Networking Initiatives. Businesses and organizations representing businesses have taken steps to create an international infrastructure dedicated to remittance services. Most of the participants are nonaccount holding institutions, but the similarities among the participants end there. The new networking initiatives are making business partners out of companies with widely varying goals.

- Independent Community Bankers of America (ICBA) and Travelex agreed to launch a new money transfer service in July 2002 (ICBA 2002). The program enables ICBA's member banks to provide remittance services to customers and community members through Travelex's Worldwide Money Division, which provides Internet-enabled money transfers for about US$9 (Bair 2002). Travelex has over 650 retail branches at airports, seaports, rail stations, and tourist and business centers around the world.
- Through an agreement with 7-Eleven and Citibank Hong Kong, China, the Philippine National Bank (PNB) enables overseas Filipino workers to remit money to the Philippines through any of 7-Eleven's 480 stores in Hong Kong, China, as well as through the eight PNB branches in Hong Kong, China (Sanchez 2003). Additionally, PNB's Hong Kong, China, remittance unit has teamed up with Indonesia's Bank Mandiri to provide remittance services to Indonesian workers in Hong Kong, China. PNB hopes to duplicate the arrangement in Singapore and Taiwan.
- FedACH is a bank-to-bank mechanism developed as part of a family of international electronic funds transfer services that offer financial institutions and their customers access to an efficient and inexpensive means of processing payments in batches between the United States and other economies.[14] First introduced in 1999 for transactions to Canada, FedACH's international service expanded to include Mexico and five countries in Western Europe.[15] FedACH improves upon existing international payment processes and practices by offering shorter end-to-end clearing and settlement processing, enhancing funds availability to recipients, and providing certainty with regard to the payment amount (no fees are deducted from the principal). It also offers

reliability and stability, an established legal framework and rules, standard formats, and universal access. See box 13.2 for a description of FedACH's international model.

- Orient Commercial Joint Stock Bank (ORICOMBANK), based in Ho Chi Minh City, has a contract with the United Kingdom's First Remit to act as a money remittance service agent in Vietnam.[16] First Remit offers services in more than 50 economies worldwide. First Remit transfers money to ORICOMBANK, which remits the money to the beneficiaries in Vietnam for a fee. According to the

---

Box 13.2 FedACH's International Model

The FedACH International model enables U.S. banks to originate and receive international transactions. Using the National Automated Clearinghouse Association (NACHA), the FedACH model enables cross-border payments to be settled in U.S. dollars for the originator and receiver. The model also employs the following features:

Gateway Approach. A participant in the national payment system, or another entity acting as an agent for that participant, serves as the gateway into each economy's banking system, providing access to financial institutions there. FedACH is headquartered at the Federal Reserve Bank of Minneapolis, the gateway operator for the United States. It contracts with a gateway operator in each participating economy. When payments are flowing out from the United States to a foreign gateway operator, the foreign gateway is referred to as the receiving gateway operator.

Format Conversion. The foreign gateway operator in Canada and Mexico, or the foreign gateway agent in the case of transatlantic service, performs the conversion from the National Automated Clearinghouse Association cross-border PBR/CBR[a] format into the payment format used locally.

Foreign Exchange Conversion. The foreign gateway operator or its agent for payments from the United States accepts incoming payments in U.S. dollars and performs the foreign exchange function using competitive rates (for example, an interbank rate), applying basis points to that rate to cover its costs. For transactions to the United States, the gateway operator accepts local currency and performs the necessary exchange into U.S. dollars.

a. PBR/CBR are the NACHA standard entry class codes for cross-border transfers. PBR is a consumer cross-border ACH transaction and CBR is a corporate cross-border ACH transaction. These codes appear in the electronic record format as processing instructions.

Source: Interview with Federal Reserve Bank officials, August 2004.

bank, this fee is about 40 percent lower than fees offered by other remittance services.

- By some estimates, Western Union has approximately 12 percent of the remittance market. Its network has 165,000 agent locations in 195 countries and territories, including outlets in banks and post offices that make up more than 70 percent of the network.[17] The network allows remitters to transfer money in cash; recipients, who often have no bank account, can pick up their money in cash, in person. The cost of transferring money varies by location. Western Union invests in marketing throughout the world, raising brand awareness among communities of immigrants. Its Loyalty Card Program rewards loyal customers with faster transactions, discounts, and telephone time (First Data 2003). The company has tested a direct-to-bank service from the United States to Poland that allows a customer to send a transfer from a Western Union location to a recipient's bank account.

  In July 2003, Western Union signed a memorandum of understanding for a strategic partnership with the Vietnam Bank for Agriculture and Rural Development (VBARD). Under the agreement, Western Union's services are offered at all VBARD branches in Vietnam. With 1,660 branches covering rural and remote locations, VBARD maintains the largest branch-banking network in Vietnam. Western Union has signed a similar memorandum of understanding with Industrial and Commercial Bank, which has a network of over 1,300 locations in Vietnam through Asia Commercial Bank, Eden Trading Co., and VP Bank.[18]

- The World Council of Credit Unions' International Remittance network (IRnet) provides money transfers from some 185 credit unions with 800 locations in 35 U.S. states to 42 countries on five continents (Grace 2002). Using IRnet, up to US$1,000 can be sent for US$10, available in minutes in El Salvador and Guatemala. Foreign recipients are not charged for the transfers, and exchange rates are disclosed and guaranteed at the time of the transaction. Recipients are introduced into the financial system when they receive their funds at local credit unions. See chapter 8 of this book for more information.

Banking and Account-Based Programs. New banking and account-based programs are often by-products of the existing banking infrastructure. Banks simply create programs for money remittance that are easily operated through their banking services network. Such programs may require customers to maintain an account; in fact, they are often tied to incentive-based programs designed to encourage money-remitting customers to open accounts.

- The People's Network (L@Red de la Gente) is a cooperative between a network of credit unions, savings and loans, and other independent financial organizations in Mexico in partnership with Banco del Ahorro Nacional y Servicios Financieros (BANSEFI) (Gavito 2003). The commercial alliance offers remittance services, as well as other financial services, to people without access to commercial banks. L@Red de la Gente has 760 branches throughout Mexico. For a fee of US$6, account holders can send money to a recipient's account through numerous companies, including U.S. Bank, MoneyGram, and Giromex. Through savings accounts, customers also gain access to other products, such as insurance and home services.

- In April 2002, Bank of America launched SafeSend, a card-based money transfer service that operates between the United States and Mexico (Bézard 2002). As of 2004, the service was being provided to other immigrant communities. Up to US$1,500 can be transferred per transaction for US$10. The money is available in Mexico in less than six minutes. The recipient receives a money withdrawal card, which is used with a personal identification number at any of the 20,000 ATMs connected to Visa's PLUS Network. The service is available to any Bank of America customer and to noncustomers holding a Visa or MasterCard debit or credit card. Money can be added to the card on the Internet, by phone, or in person. Although a U.S. Social Security number is listed as a requirement for enrollment in the program, a toll-free number is provided for those who do not have one. [19]

- Banorte offers Dispersa Envíos, a remittance service between the United States and Mexico. [20] The product supports funds transfers through the Banorte branch network. Using Banorte's Internet banking system, Banorte works with more than 20 money transfer services to process transactions. The service provides payment orders of up to 30,000 Mexican pesos (US$267) and account-to-account credit transfers. If the beneficiary has a Banorte account, credit is made directly to the account and funds can be accessed at any ATM or point of sale. According to Banorte, the bank offers competitive prices and conditions.

- Citibank Global Transfers is a money transfer service that allows Citibank North America clients to send funds to Banamex customers. [21] Citibank's customers can initiate a transaction from a Citibank ATM or from Citibank On-Line. The funds arrive in a Banamex account immediately. The transfer fee for each transaction is US$5 and the exchange rate is 2 percent over wholesale bank exchange rates. Citibank's customers have full disclosure of the amount deducted from his or her account, the amount debited to the receiving account, fees, and exchange rates.

- U.S. Bank offers two remittance services for sending money to family and friends in Mexico: Secure Money Transfer at the ATM and Secure Money Transfer with the People's Network.[22] For the first service, customers sign up for a Secure Money Transfer ATM card at any of the 2,200 branches of U.S. Bank. They must provide a valid form of identification (U.S. Bank accepts the CIC) as well as name and address of the remittance recipient. The ATM-only card is sent to the recipient in Mexico, who can access funds at any of the 20,000 PLUS Network ATMs in Mexico. The cost for U.S. Bank account holders is US$8 for up to US$1,000; those without an account pay US$10 for up to US$1,000.

  The second remittance service offered by U.S. Bank uses the People's Network (L@ Red de la Gente). From any U.S. bank location, customers can send money to any of the 760 People's Network branches in Mexico. U.S. Bank account holders can transfer up to US$1,000 into a People's Network account for a fee of US$6 or, for US$8, transfer up to US$1,000 for cash pick-up at a People's Network branch.

- Targeting the U.S.-Mexico remittance market, Wells Fargo offers the InterCuenta Express account, a sweep account that transfers funds on a nightly basis to the Bancomer account of a recipient in Mexico.[23] The cost of opening an account is US$10, and there is a US$10 annual fee. Wells Fargo accepts the Mexican CIC to open accounts. The account-to-account transfer fee is US$10 for up to US$1,000 per day. Funds can be deposited through a Wells Fargo ATM, over the phone, or online. Recipients can pick up funds at a Bancomer ATM or branch and can use an ATM card for point-of-sale transactions in Mexico.

  Wells Fargo's Dinero al Instante program enables people in the United States who do not have bank accounts to transmit cash wires to Mexico without opening an account. By providing identification and a confirmation number, the recipient can pick up the funds immediately at some 2,000 Bancomer branches and 200 Tiendas Singer locations. Tiendas Singer is an appliance store that serves as a distribution agent for Bancomer, with longer hours than banks. A flat fee of US$10 covers up to US$1,000 transferred in a single day.

- Bumiputra-Commerce Bank Berhad of Malaysia and PT Bank Niaga of Indonesia (BN) jointly launched an electronic remittance service in August 2003 that enables beneficiaries to be paid within 24 hours.[24] BN currently has 160 branches throughout Indonesia, and this fast remittance service is an incentive for Indonesian workers to use this secure formal remittance service provided at a minimal cost of RM20 (US$5.25) for any amount remitted.

- State and private banks from India, Portugal, Pakistan, and Morocco have devised programs to capture a share of the remittance market by reaching out to their diaspora communities in other nations (Orozco 2003). By remitting money and opening accounts through a bank based in their home country, emigrants can offer their family members benefits such as home financing, tax breaks, low-interest loan packages, or even public housing preferences and special preferences to fill quotas in public universities. Other benefits such as expedited passport renewals, preferred traveling accommodations, and favorable exchange rates at banking branches are available for the senders.

    Bangladesh reported a 22.43 percent increase in formal remittances in the 2002–3 fiscal year. The increase boosted remittances from US$2.5 billion in the previous year to US$3.1 billion with Saudi Arabia and the United States topping the list of sending countries. The surge in formal remittances has been attributed to measures taken by the Bangladesh Bank that encourage expatriates to remit through formal channels instead of remitting through the unauthorized informal *hundi* system. Some of the steps taken by the Bangladesh Bank include expediting remittances for fast delivery and setting up foreign exchange clearance houses abroad to facilitate operations, as well as implementing AML guidelines (Xinhua News Agency 2003).

PROPOSED FRAMEWORK AND PRELIMINARY APPLICATION

On a micro level, private-sector entities and some governments have recognized the IFT phenomenon and become involved in the funds transfer market, as detailed in the previous section. While some governments have recognized the need to address the IFT issue comprehensively—as a way of formulating development strategies and of monitoring money flows for security purposes—the obscurity that surrounds IFT systems has prevented governments from adopting effective policies and regional strategies to regulate them. The comprehensive framework described in this section represents an initial attempt to gauge the scope of IFT activity from a quantitative and qualitative perspective. (Figure 13.1 presents a diagram of the framework.) Such an exercise is relevant for

- governments to harmonize regulatory policies toward IFT systems;
- governments to create bilateral initiatives that streamline the formal remittance process to strengthen FFT systems;
- private sector institutions to identify incentives, helping them compete with IFT systems.

Developing a Framework

This is a first attempt to develop a framework to understand the economic, regulatory, and social aspects of IFT systems. The exercise has evolved into a new methodology that focuses on remittance corridors, keeping the emphasis on delivering policy recommendations concerning how to shift from informal to formal remittance channels.

Blending Degrees of Formality

Informal and formal systems are generally distinguished by whether they operate "formally through the regulated financial system or informally through entities that operate outside the regulated system" (FATF 2003). Formal systems are those recognized as banking or credit institutions or nonbanking financial institutions specifically included in the formal category. IFT systems are generally deemed to operate outside the regulated financial sector.

However, the reality is that the barrier between formal and informal channels is not a firm one; there are blending degrees of formality (Maimbo 2003).[25] A formal system—an FFT system associated with the regulated financial sector—may very well use informal channels to conduct some or even all of its money transfers. Similarly, IFT systems may use formal channels at different stages of the transfer and settlement process. Thus, funds transferred through formal channels must be considered when estimating the magnitude, direction, and nature of IFT flows.

Quantitative and Qualitative Analyses

Part I of the framework described in this chapter proposes a method of estimating the unrecorded flows of money traveling between nations. For this exercise, a quantitative economic analysis in which flows through formal and informal systems are blended is considered. The analysis reveals gaps in data—red flags for further analysis. The gaps may be the result of

- unidentified flows in formal channels;
- inward and outward flows through the formal and informal channels (including legal channels that are not part of the formal channels);
- inadequate estimates of total flows (formal and informal).

Once total flows are properly estimated and recording errors or omissions in formal flows are corrected, the territory lying between formality and informality can be isolated and examined. In the process,

FIGURE 13.1 DIAGRAMMING THE FRAMEWORK

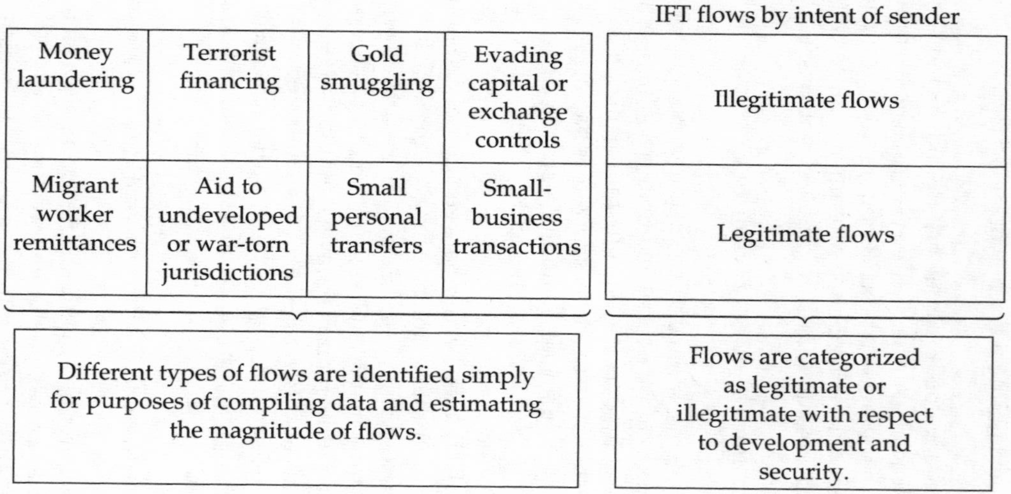

IFT flows by intent of sender

Money laundering	Terrorist financing	Gold smuggling	Evading capital or exchange controls	Illegitimate flows
Migrant worker remittances	Aid to undeveloped or war-torn jurisdictions	Small personal transfers	Small-business transactions	Legitimate flows

Different types of flows are identified simply for purposes of compiling data and estimating the magnitude of flows.

Flows are categorized as legitimate or illegitimate with respect to development and security.

Source: Author's research.

Note: BOP = Balance of Payments. MTO = Money Transfer Operator.

(Continues)

Figure 13.1 Diagramming the Framework (*Continued*)

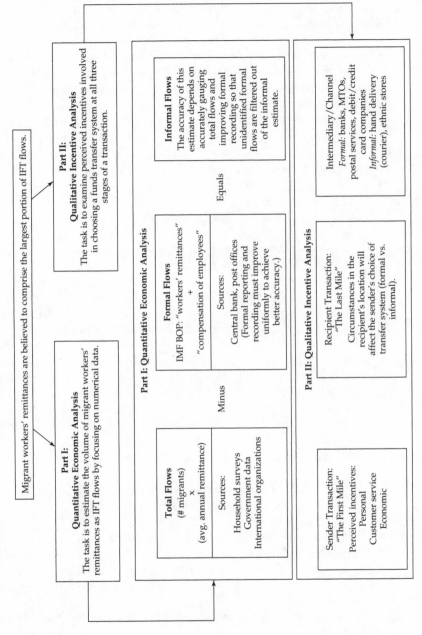

estimates of the amount of money traveling through the informal sector will become far more accurate and reliable.

Part II of the proposed framework deals with analyzing the qualitative features of the data gap and determining why senders may choose to remit through informal channels. The key task in this exercise is to stand in the shoes of the money sender. What goes through the mind of a money remitter when he or she decides to send money abroad? What sort of benefits and burdens do they consider? These are the money remitter's perceived incentives. Regulations and other government behavior toward funds transfers must be considered when analyzing these incentives because they can drastically affect the perceived incentives faced by remitters as they choose their remittance method.

The Framework

This framework represents a first attempt to apply a uniform methodology for more extensive research that will take into account the particulars of individual economies. Formal cross-border transfers as reported in the IMF's balance-of-payments statistics (table 13.1) provide a good starting point for applying the framework. However, they do not reflect the actual volume of flows between nations because they do not include remittances that are not reported to central banks during the preparation of the balance-of-payments statistics. For illustrative purposes, table 13.1 compares recorded formal flows for the 21 Asia-Pacific Economic Cooperation (APEC) member economies.

IMF's balance-of-payments statistics distinguish between workers' remittances and compensation of employees. Combined, the two categories make up the "official remittance flows" used as the point of reference for estimating informal flows in Part I of the framework.[26]

Part I: Quantitative Economic Analysis
(Estimating Informal Money Flows)

Part I draws on the concept of "indirect estimation," using triangulation to estimate total flows and, by extrapolating from known formal flows, to estimate flows in unrecorded channels, including informal channels. Problems with trying to estimate informal transfers are reviewed in box 13.3.

The methodology for estimating total flows has been well established by the IMF:

> While it is difficult—in the absence of data—to estimate [workers remittances], estimates . . . may be developed via data models. . . .
> If the compiler knows the number of foreign workers in the . . .
> economy and can develop (perhaps through a survey) an estimate

TABLE 13.1 FORMAL CROSS-BORDER TRANSFERS, 2001
US$ million

Economies	Workers' remittances (under current transfer)		Compensation of employees (under income)		Migrants' transfers (under capital account)		Reported total	
	Credit[a]	Debit[b]	Credit[a]	Debit[b]	Credit[a]	Debit[b]	Credit[a]	Debit[b]
Australia	—	—	501	–547	1,389	–484	1,890	–1,031
Brunei Darussalam	—	—	—	—	—	—	—	—
Canada	—	—	—	—	—	—	—	—
Chile	—	—	—	–16	—	—	—	–16
China	1,679	–223	674	–950	—	–50	2,353	–1,223
Chinese Taipei	—	—	—	—	—	—	—	—
Hong Kong, China	—	—	2	–2	—	—	2	–2
Indonesia	1,259	—	—	—	—	—	1,259	—
Japan	950	–2,410	180	–270	690	–670	1,820	–3,350
Korea, Rep. of	26	–232	519	–50	36	–1,115	581	–1,397
Malaysia	—	–3,081	435	–745	—	—	435	–3,826
Mexico	9,814	—	1,215	—	—	—	11,029	—
New Zealand	213	–175	—	—	1,100	—	1,313	–175
Papua New Guinea	—	—	—	—	—	—	—	—
Peru	705	—	—	—	—	–110	705	–110
Philippines	192	–37	7,171	—	—	–21	7,363	–58
Russian Federation	123	–296	704	–507	423	–931	1,250	–1,734
Singapore	—	—	—	—	—	—	—	—
Thailand	—	—	1,380	—	—	—	1,380	—
United States	—	–22,990	3,160	–8,400	—	—	3,160	–31,390
Vietnam	—	—	—	—	—	—	—	—

Source: IMF, *Balance of Payments Statistics Yearbook,* 2001, 2002.
Note: — = Not available. For a full description of the IMF Balance of Payments and the three components displayed in the table: "workers' remittances," "compensation of employees," and "migrants' transfers," see IMF 1996, pp. 77, 91, 93.
a. Credit refers to incoming flows.
b. Debit refers to outgoing flows.

of average remittances per worker, he could then estimate worker remittance credits by multiplying the number of workers by average remittances. (IMF 1995, pp. 142–144)

Indirect bilateral estimates of informal flows can be derived by subtracting the amount of flows in all formal channels from total flows. Three estimates are required.

Official Remittance Flows. The first side of the triangle comes from recorded remittance flows. These are the bilateral flows of funds between sending and recipient economies. The source for these official remittance flows is IMF balance-of-payments statistics (see table 13.1).

Box 13.3 Preliminary Obstacles to Estimating IFT

A number of obstacles are encountered when estimating informal funds transfers.

Blending Degrees of Formality. A multitude of transfer channels, a multitude of actors, and many bilateral relationships make up the formal funds transfer sector. Although FFT actors usually use official channels, they may also use informal or unrecorded channels to conduct business. Because transactions carried out through such channels are not reflected in official statistics, the volume of FFT flows may be seriously underestimated.

Incomplete Recording and Estimate Discrepancies. What is recorded as "official" is, in most cases, only what the major banks in each country report to the economy's central bank (sometimes information about remittances through post offices is also recorded).[a] Beyond this, very little is known. According to the research conducted for this chapter, the information produced by most central banks does not detail all sources of funds. For example, the reported figure may reflect the activity of all institutions considered part of the regulated financial sector, or just a few (IMF Committee on Balance of Payments Statistics 2002).[b] Furthermore, migration estimates and wage data can vary depending on the source of data, creating disparate quantitative figures.

FFT Systems Transparency. The fact that a funds transfer agent operates in the formal sector does not necessarily mean that its business operations are transparent. FATF has led the international effort to create standards of transparency for formal financial agents (such as "know-your-customer" policies and reporting of suspicious transactions). Still, one cannot assume that all FFT systems adhere to local regulations, let alone international best practices. Anecdotal evidence suggests that FFT business activity moves in and out of the informal sector, but nontransparency and gaps in recording prevent authorities from knowing how frequently this occurs.

Legal and Administrative Obstacles. Legal and administrative requirements may discourage reporting. Taxes and other constraints on flows may prevent otherwise legitimate transactions from being reported and recorded. In some cases, the trade and capital accounts may include unrecorded flows. For example, an exchange rate control regime may be circumvented by over- and underinvoicing products, thus creating unrecorded flows. Significant "errors and omissions" in the capital account can be indications of unrecorded flows. Consequently, trying to identify informal remittances is a daunting task, one that can only be accomplished through a systematic enhancement of information collection throughout the entire balance-of-payments system.

BOX 13.3 PRELIMINARY OBSTACLES TO ESTIMATING IFT
(Continued)

a. For example, balance-of-payments statistics for the recording of "workers' remittances" for the Philippines incorporates only the banking sector while Malaysia's also includes postal offices.
b. The IMF Committee on Balance of Payments Statistics, established in 1992, aimed to reduce discrepancies in global balance-of-payments statistics published by the IMF as well as to foster greater coordination of data collection among economies.

Source: Discussions with World Bank staff.

Derived Workers' Remittances. The second side of the triangle is provided by estimating actual worker remittances. The estimate is derived from bilateral data on the number of migrant workers abroad, the average wage of migrant workers abroad, and the percentage of wages sent by migrant workers to their home economy. These three amounts, multiplied, give us the derived value of workers' remittances. Because workers' remittances are confidently assumed to be the largest component of international funds transfers, this figure is the appropriate one from which to triangulate the third side.

Data on the number of migrant workers comes from several sources, primarily governments and the International Organization for Migration (IOM), the International Labour Office (ILO), and the Organisation for Economic Co-operation and Development (OECD). The sources for estimating the wages of migrant workers and the percentage of wages sent home are surveys, government data, and anecdotal evidence.

Estimate of Funds in Informal Channels. Calculating the final side of the triangle is simply a matter of subtraction. Official remittances minus worker and wage remittances results in an estimate of unrecorded flows traveling through various channels. This unrecorded flow may be composed of a blend of transfers from formal channels that have not been properly identified with transfers from informal channels excluded from recording altogether.

Part II: Qualitative Incentives Analysis: the First Mile, the Last Mile, and the Intermediary

The second part of the framework anticipates the isolation of IFT channels from the general flow of funds in the formal sector, part of which are already recorded in official statistics and part of which remain unrecorded. By identifying perceived incentives that lead people to choose IFT over FFT channels, previously opaque activity becomes clearer. The analysis may be broken down into three stages: the sender's transaction, or first mile; the recipient's transaction, or last mile; and the intermediary.[27]

The First Mile. Because a sender must initiate every transaction, one of the keys to solving the IFT puzzle is to think like a sender of informal remittances. Several factors and perceived incentives need to be considered to develop an understanding of the sender's point of view. Foremost among these are the sender's perceived incentives in choosing a funds transfer system. The character and intent of the sender also play important roles.

The Last Mile. Senders will choose to remit in a fashion that makes it possible for the recipient to receive the funds. Thus, the features of the recipient economy will loom large in the sender's decision making. If, for example, the recipient relative, friend, or acquaintance lives in a rural area with no FFT outlets, the sender may well choose an IFT system, even though he or she may have preferred to use an FFT system.

The Intermediary. The nature of the intermediate channels is also an important factor in mapping IFT flows. Because formal and informal channels may blend, a remittance through an FFT system may involve money being sent through an informal network somewhere along the way. IFT intermediaries may settle accounts among themselves through established accounts in formal institutions, such as banks. The behavior of intermediaries is also deeply affected by legal considerations, notably whether their operation is legal or illegal, the level of law enforcement, or whether they are remitting on behalf of criminal customers.

The Perceived Incentives in Choosing a Funds Transfer System

Money remitters choose IFT systems over FFT systems for many reasons, including those set out below.[28] Some incentives may be unique to particular economies or societies and may not be listed here. Others may not apply to a given jurisdiction or funds transfer system. However, at least some of the incentives described below will certainly apply at some point in the decision making process of every sender. Because much will depend on transactional considerations, each jurisdiction must investigate its own landscape in more detail to discover which incentives are most influential. The groupings have been constructed for convenience and do not represent a strict division. Many incentives will overlap.

Personal Incentives

Anonymity and Secrecy. IFT transactions require no identification, except perhaps a recipient password, and no formal policy governs recordkeeping. The anonymity of IFT transactions is a benefit that should not be understated. For example, illegal immigrants may believe that using a formal institution for their remittances poses a risk of discovery and deportation. Migrant workers may find it too difficult and expensive to navigate the bureaucracy to obtain official identification. These obstacles are circumvented by using IFT systems. Anonymity also attracts the business of illegal enterprises. As long as criminals profit from illegal activity, they will continue to seek out secret and obscure methods of transferring and laundering money. The absence of recordkeeping and the practice of anonymous transfers make IFT systems prime candidates for use by criminal elements.

Cultural Familiarity. IFT systems predate FFT systems in many societies throughout the world. Money remitters may choose IFT systems out of comfort and familiarity. Formal institutions can scare away potential clients, particularly when language or procedures pose obstacles. IFT systems are adapted to the cultures in which they operate.

Personal Contacts. IFT systems that cater to particular ethnic groups thrive on networks of personal and family contacts. As a result, remitters may choose to use IFT systems operated by friends or relatives, or certain IFT channels may become widely recognized or recommended among the members of a particular ethnic community. In such cases, personal connections may outweigh other perceived incentives.

Customer Service Incentives

Dispute Resolution. Differences between the customer and intermediary may also be easier to manage through IFT systems that do not have layers of management or bureaucracy. Because IFT intermediaries often rely on trust and reputation to maintain business, they are less likely to make dispute resolutions inconvenient and more likely to do whatever it takes to maintain their good reputation in their particular network.

Accessibility. FFT agents may be widely available to the sender, but not to the recipient. IFT systems may be better able to reach places where FFT systems have not been established.

Discrimination. Unskilled migrant workers may be compelled to use IFT systems because of class division and discrimination. Sometimes formal institutions, such as banks, view servicing lower class workers as detrimental to their prestige. If no one fills the resulting void, remitters may be forced to use informal means.

Versatility and Resilience. IFT systems can survive civil wars and conflicts, economic crises, weak and unreliable financial sectors, economic sanctions, and other events that can affect the formal economy and national infrastructure.

Economic Incentives

Speed. According to some estimates, an informal transfer can take as few as six hours between major international cities. If the recipient lives in an underdeveloped rural area, informal transfers can normally be completed within 24 hours (El-Qorchi, Maimbo, and Wilson 2003).

Cost. IFT costs have been estimated at 2 percent to 5 percent of the transferred amount. Formal systems range in cost, but even the cheapest formal money remitters struggle to charge a competitive rate. Because IFT systems do not devote resources to regulatory compliance, they generally can charge cheaper rates. This is not the case everywhere, however. In some places, banks and other FFT systems charge competitive prices and offer other incentives and benefits that IFT systems cannot, such as housing preferences or low-rate home financing. Also, anecdotal evidence suggests that some IFT channels will knowingly charge higher rates when making transfers connected to illegal activity because the intermediary is assuming a greater legal risk and knows that the sender will pay more to avoid formal channels.

Secondary Benefits. Some institutions have specifically targeted money remittances as a market to be captured. Consequently, they will offer deals and incentives to encourage people to remit through their institutions. Incentives include programs whereby money remitters abroad can confer certain benefits on recipients, and discounts for frequent or large remittances (Orozco 2003). Formal institutions are in a better position than informal actors to develop secondary benefits because they are usually better equipped to network with other legitimate businesses and government entities.

Legal and Regulatory Environment. Whether IFT systems are legal or illegal can play a significant role in the market. The right laws and regulations, properly enforced, can deter illegitimate IFT activity. Under such circumstances, remitters will perceive a greater risk in using an informal channel, and intermediaries will be more cautious and selective with their customers, resulting in a general depression of the IFT market. Although IFT systems have proved difficult to regulate, some notable successes have drastically altered certain markets (El-Qorchi, Maimbo, and Wilson 2003).[29] On the other hand, liberalizing the market and easing regulations may force FFT systems to compete with IFT systems, creating a self-regulating market based on competition (El-Qorchi, Maimbo, and Wilson 2003).[30]

Figure 13.2 roughly illustrates how the framework may be applied to a specific economic situation. In this case, the illustration reflects Mexican migrant workers in the United States remitting back to Mexico. Although limited in its application at this initial stage, the framework reveals a descriptive analysis of some critical issues regarding Mexico's shift from informal to formal systems.

FIGURE 13.2 ILLUSTRATING THE FRAMEWORK

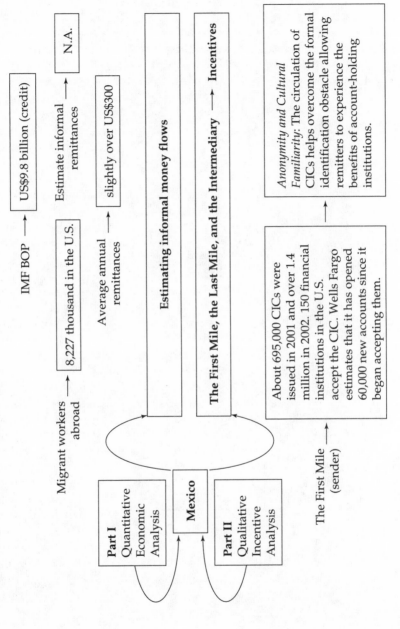

Source: Author's research.
Note: BOP = Balance of payments. CIC = Consular identification card.

(Continues)

FIGURE 13.2 ILLUSTRATING THE FRAMEWORK (*Continued*)

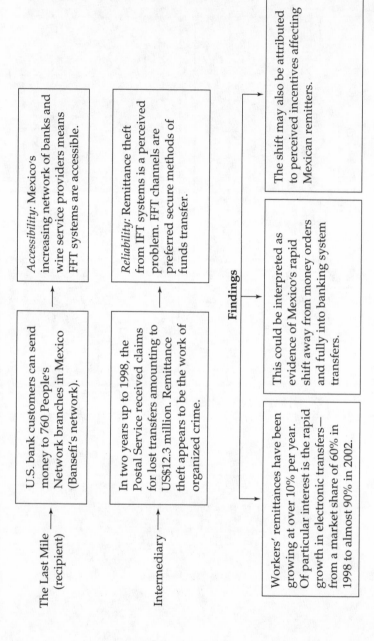

CONCLUSIONS

The framework is intended to be a first step in helping researchers go from identifying broad features and concepts in funds transfer systems to analyzing specific economic jurisdictions and their actual funds transfer landscape. In doing so, the international community can begin to map out the actual landscape of international IFT systems, based on evidence and data gathering instead of anecdotes and guesswork, thus understanding the issues involved in creating a shift from informal to formal systems. The following observations, drawn from using the framework in a limited fashion while preparing the initial APEC Alternative Remittances Systems (ARS) Initiative report, offer an initial indication of critical issues in shifting users from informal to formal systems.

Legal and regulatory provisions affect the funds transfer market and the perceived incentives faced by senders; governments must therefore strike an appropriate balance in their level of regulation. Onerous requirements can burden formal systems or create enforcement obligations for the government that cannot be feasibly implemented,[31] whereas private-sector competition and targeted government cooperation can shift the balance of incentives in favor of FFT systems.[32]

Government initiatives can help by improving the infrastructure used to transfer funds between financial institutions at low cost. Effective initiatives can incorporate ideas such as automated clearing houses and private settlement and clearing channels, and facilitate the entry of nonbank financial institutions such as credit unions and microcredit institutions into the workers' remittance market.[33]

Understanding the motivation of the sender is also of utmost importance in devising ways to increase FFT services. Different societies and jurisdictions are likely to find that remitters are affected by very different incentives.[34] Perceived incentives are shaped by the cultural, social, and economic characteristics of each sending and receiving economy. Furthermore, migrant workers' remittances can be lured into FFT systems through incentives. By identifying the perceived incentives—personal, customer service, and economic—that influence the choices of participants in the remittance process, governments and financial service companies can gear their initiatives toward those incentives.

Finally, rural areas represent a potential market opportunity for the financial sector. Governments should also engage the private sector to build up financial infrastructure, while educating and acclimating migrant workers and their families to the benefits and processes of formal financial institutions. This process of "banking the unbanked" is crucial to any effort designed to bring about a shift from informal to formal systems.

Given that the proposed framework is at an initial stage, there are clearly improvements to be made on the framework itself. Many such improvements will be apparent as the framework is put to the test. However, even before such tests are done, the framework can be augmented by filtering the unidentified flows revealed in Part I of the framework. Informal flows need to be distinguished from formal flows that are escaping recording mechanisms, through improvements to the transparency of the balance-of-payments statistics reported for each economy and detailing the components that make up the reported number.

Because the framework is designed to help researchers go from broad to specific, it must be utilized in the context of economy-specific case studies that analyze incentives outlined in Part II. For instance, important lessons can be learned by applying the framework to economies at various stages of shifting from informal to formal systems so as to map out the successful process of balancing regulations and incentives that have advanced such a shift. Ultimately, without follow-up research that focuses on individual economic jurisdictions, the framework's potential cannot be realized.

NOTES

1. The development potential for remittances is described in detail in the *Global Development Finance 2003* report (World Bank 2003).

2. IFT systems have provided an invaluable means of moving funds in Afghanistan in the absence of formal channels. Nongovernmental organizations, humanitarian groups, and families use these services. The situation in Afghanistan, which calls for a balanced approach, has practical lessons for all jurisdictions where the formal financial sector is weak or nonexistent.

3. Experts agree that IFT systems are not intrinsically "bad," and often fill a legitimate need for financial services where formal ones do not function. However, the FATF acknowledges that IFT systems present an area of concern for anti-money laundering and combating the financing of terrorism (AML/CFT), due largely to their clandestine nature. Features that may make these systems popular (no identification requirements, no recordkeeping, no visibility for regulators and authorities) also leave them vulnerable for abuse by criminals. Law enforcement efforts in many regions of the world have uncovered links between some IFT operations and illegal activity, such as drug trafficking and money laundering. The FATF includes these systems in its 1999-2000 "Report on Money Laundering Typologies" (FATF 2000).

4. Personal remittances, such as migrant worker remittances, are one type of transfer, and have not been widely associated with money laundering schemes. Larger transfers, such as those related to trade, generally have higher utility for money laundering schemes than do personal transfers of small amounts.

5. Researchers have estimated global IFT flows at between US$100 billion to US$300 billion annually. At a World Bank discussion on worker remittances in

May 2003, economist Richard Adams estimated that worker remittances in IFT systems were roughly equal to remittances through formal channels, which would equal approximately US$80 billion for 2002.

6. Research indicates that reputation fallout due to banking system failure or collapse in nations with developing financial sectors is a significant factor in driving people from formal systems toward informal systems.

7. Information provided by Federal Reserve Bank officials in author interviews.

8. "FedACH International" is a registered service mark of the Federal Reserve Bank. All information regarding FedACH was provided by Federal Reserve Bank officials in author interviews.

9. The Federal Reserve Automated Clearing House (FedACH International) service model was first introduced for transactions to Canada in 1999. (See the description of FedACH International in box 13.2. The service supports the flow of commercial credit and debit transactions from the United States to Canada. The Federal Reserve Bank offers this service to U.S. banks and originating depository financial institutions for a per-item surcharge of US$.039 in addition to standard FedACH domestic processing fees (origination, addenda, and input file processing fees).

10. Information provided by officials from Mexico's Secretaría de Relaciones Exteriores in author interviews.

11. Information provided by Singapore government officials in author interviews.

12. Information provided by Malaysian officials in author interviews.

13. An identification process is required for compliance with international best practices according to FATF criteria. See box 13.1.

14. Information provided by Federal Reserve Bank officials in author interviews.

15. The Eurogiro Network A/S (EGN) will provide access to the gateway operator in each economy: BAWAG/P.S.K. Group in Austria, Deutsche Postbank AG in Germany, ING Bank in The Netherlands, Swiss Post-PostFinance in Switzerland, and Girobank PLC in the United Kingdom.

16. Information provided by the World Bank country office in Vietnam in author interviews.

17. Information in this section was provided by Western Union officials in author interviews.

18. Information provided by the World Bank country office in Vietnam in author interviews.

19. Bank of America's SafeSend service is described at http://www. bankofamerica.com/safesend/?lang=en.

20. Information provided by Banorte officials in author interviews.

21. Information provided by Citibank/Banamex officials in author interviews.

22. Information provided by U.S. bank officials in author interviews.

23. Information provided by Wells Fargo officials in author interviews.

24. Information provided by Malaysian officials in author interviews.

25. The Afghan money-changers represent a remittance system that raises many interesting issues regarding degrees of formality.

26. "Migrant's transfers" refers to the value that is attached to a migrant when he or she moves out of one economy into another. Because migrants' transfers do not represent transactions, they create no flow in the sense of value transferred through a channel or intermediary. Consequently, the value captured under the rubric of migrants' transfers is of limited use in analyzing the magnitude and characteristics of channels used by remitters to transfer funds. For that reason, it is omitted from the framework for estimating informal money flows.

27. The "first mile" is a figure of speech used to describe the initial obstacles that a user of a network must overcome to benefit from existing network infrastructure. In regard to funds transfer systems, it refers to the obstacles that a remittance sender faces when trying to gain access to FFT systems. Similarly, the "last mile" problem refers to the difficulties a remittance recipient faces in accessing transferred funds.

28. Many of these incentives also appear in El-Qorchi, Maimbo, and Wilson, 2003.

29. Following a government corruption scandal involving bribes through IFT systems, India explicitly prohibited the practice with some notable success.

30. Afghanistan's money remitters are organized into a self-regulated body similar to a union or fraternity of registered dealers. Formal institutions in the Philippines have adopted many IFT systems-style practices, such as door-to-door service, to compete with informal money remitters.

31. One of the six APEC economies examined through the framework showed that AML/CFT enforcement can occur in the informal sector while legitimate worker remittances continue to increase.

32. One of the six APEC economies examined through the framework revealed a notable shift from informal to formal channels in recent years.

33. Three of the APEC economies examined showed positive signs that formal systems were able to compete with and win over clients from informal systems when programs and initiatives were created by the government and the private sector that addressed significant factors affecting incentives.

34. One of the APEC economies examined is unique in that it has a highly organized labor-export industry that drastically affects the landscape for remittance systems including incentives. Another APEC economy previously examined appears to defy the popular assumption that cost is the biggest perceived incentive that affects money remitters. In this particular economy, remitters appear to use more expensive formal means, rather than less expensive informal means, because the formal systems are more reliable.

REFERENCES

Bair, Shelia C. 2002. "Improving Access to the U.S. Banking System Among Recent Latin American Immigrants." Multilateral Investment Fund, University of Massachusetts, Amherst.

Bézard, Gwenn. 2002. *Global Money Transfers: Exploring the Remittance Gold Mine.* New York: Celent Communications.

Buencamino, Leonides, and Sergei Gorbunov. 2002. "Informal Money Transfer Systems: Opportunities and Challenges for Development Finance." DESA Discussion Paper 26, United Nations, New York.

Cuevas, Jose Luis. 2003. "Heartland: A New Horizon." Paper presented at a conference entitled "An Informed Discussion of the Financial Assimilation of Immigrants," sponsored by the Federal Reserve Bank of Chicago and Proteus, Inc., Des Moines, IA, June 24.

El-Qorchi, Mohammed, Samuel Maimbo, and John F. Wilson. 2003. "Informal Funds Transfer Systems: An Analysis of the Hawala System." IMF Occasional Paper No. 222, International Monetary Fund and World Bank, Washington, DC.

FATF. 2000. "Report on Money Laundering Typologies (1999–2000)." Paris: OECD.

————. 2001. "Special Recommendations on Terrorist Financing and Interpretative Notes, Special Recommendation VI." Paris: OECD

————. 2003. "Combating the Abuse of Alternative Remittance Systems: International Best Practices," Special Recommendation VI. Paris: OECD.

First Data. 2003. "Payment Services." http://www.firstdata.com/index.jsp.

Gavito, Javier. 2003. "Banking the Unbanked." Paper presented at a conference entitled "An Informed Discussion of the Financial Assimilation of Immigrants," sponsored by the Federal Reserve Bank of Chicago and Proteus, Inc., Des Moines, IA, June 24.

Grace, David. 2002. "Wooing the Unbanked on Both Sides of the Border." *Credit Union Opportunities* 2(2). World Council of Credit Unions. National Credit Union Administration.

ICBA (Independent Community Bankers of America). 2002. "ICBA and Travelex to Enter $15 Billion Hispanic International Money-Transfer Market." July 17. Washington, DC: ICBA.

IDB (Inter-American Development Bank). 2003. "IDB and Caixa of Barcelona to Cooperate on Cutting Costs of Remittances Sent by Latin American Migrants." Press release January 23. http://www.iadb.org/exr/PRENSA/2003/cp1203e.htm.

IMF (International Monetary Fund). 1995. *Balance of Payments Compilation Guide.* Washington, DC: IMF.

————. 1996. *Balance of Payments Textbook.* Washington, DC: IMF

————. 2001. *Balance of Payments Statistics Yearbook.* Washington, DC: IMF.

————. 2002. *Balance of Payments Statistics Yearbook.* Washington, DC: IMF.

IMF Committee on Balance of Payments Statistics. 2002. *Annual Report.* Washington, DC: International Monetary Fund.

Maimbo, Samuel. 2003. "The Money Exchange Dealers of Kabul: An Analysis of the Hawala System in Afghanistan." Working Paper 26972, World Bank, Washington, DC.

NCSL (National Conference of State Legislatures). 2004. "Consular Identification Cards." Denver, CO: NCSL.

O'Neil, K. 2003. "Consular ID Cards: Mexico and Beyond." Washington, DC: Migration Policy Institute.

Opportunity International (United Kingdom). 2003. "Global Charity and Global Corporation to Partner to Improve Cross-Border Money Transfer Remittances Which Aid World's Poorest." Press release, May 28.

Orozco, Manuel. 2003. "Worker Remittances in an International Scope." Working Paper, Multilateral Investment Fund of the Inter-American Development Bank, Remittances Project, Washington, DC.

Ratha, Dilip. 2003. *"Worker's Remittances: An Important and Stable Source of External Development Finance.* In *Global Development Finance 2003.* Washington, DC: World Bank.

Sanchez, Elizabeth L. 2003. "PNB Targets Remittance Tie-ups with Singapore, Taiwan Entities." *Asia-Africa Intelligence Wire.* June 18. *InfoTrac OneFile Plus.* University of Virginia Libraries.

Schott, Paul Allan. 2003. *Reference Guide to Anti-Money Laundering and Combating the Financing of Terrorism.* Washington, DC: World Bank and IMF.

Silver, Sara. 2003. "Cost of Sending Dollars to Mexico." *Financial Times,* June 11, p. 1.

U.S. Department of State. 2002. "U.S.-Mexico Partnership for Prosperity." Press release, March 22.

U.S. Treasury. 2003. "U.S. Strengthening Remittance Channels to the Philippines." Press release, May 20.

World Bank. 2003. *Global Development Finance 2003.* Washington, DC: World Bank.

Xinhua News Agency. 2003. "Remittances to Bangladesh Reach Record High in fiscal 2002–2003." August 21.

Part V
Migration, Development, and Remittances

Chapter 14
The Impact of International Migration and Remittances on Poverty

Richard H. Adams Jr. and John Page

At the start of the twenty-first century it was estimated that about 175 million people—roughly 3 percent of the world population—lived and worked outside the country of their birth (United Nations 2002). This chapter studies the impact of international migration and remittances on poverty in a broad cross-section of developing countries. Several earlier studies have examined the effect of international migration and remittances on poverty in specific village or country settings,[1] but none seem to deal with the broader impact of these phenomena on poverty in developing countries. Two factors appear to be responsible for this scholarly reluctance to take the broader view. The first is a lack of poverty data—it is difficult to estimate accurate and meaningful poverty headcounts in a broad and diverse range of developing countries. The second relates to the nature of data on international migration and remittances. Few developing countries publish records on migration flows, while many of the developed countries that do keep records tend to undercount the large number of illegal migrants living within their borders. At the same time, the available data on international remittances do not include the large (and unknown) sum of remittance monies that move through private, unofficial channels. As a result of these data problems, key policy questions remain unanswered. Exactly what is the impact of international migration and remittances on poverty in the developing world? How do international migration and remittances affect poverty in different regions of the developing world?

This chapter proposes to answer these, and similar questions by using a new set of data from 74 developing countries. This data set includes all low- and middle-income developing countries for which reasonable information on poverty, international migration, and remittances could be assembled. To ensure the results are representative, the data set includes countries in each major region of the developing world: East Asia, Europe and Central Asia, Latin America and the Caribbean, the Middle East and North Africa, South Asia, and Sub-Saharan Africa.

The chapter is organized as follows: The first section sets the stage by reviewing the findings of recent village- or country-level studies on the relationship between international migration, remittances, and poverty. The second section presents the new data set. The third section describes how this data set uses new sources of information to calculate the relevant migration, remittances, and poverty variables. The fourth and fifth sections describe the main econometric findings in the developing world as a whole and in various geographic regions. The final section draws conclusions.

INTERNATIONAL MIGRATION, REMITTANCES, AND POVERTY

The literature includes little agreement and scant information concerning the impact of international migration on poverty. Stahl (1982), for example, writes that migration, particularly international migration, can be an expensive venture and it is therefore the better-off households that will be more capable of migration. Similarly, Lipton (1980), in a study of 40 villages in India that focuses more on internal than international migration, found that "migration increases intra-rural inequalities . . . because better-off migrants are 'pulled' toward fairly firm prospects of a job (in a city or abroad), whereas the poor are 'pushed' by rural poverty and labor-replacing methods" (p. 227).

Other analysts, however, suggest that the poor can and do benefit from international migration. For example, Stark (1991, p. 140) finds that in rural Mexico "relatively deprived" households are more likely to engage in international migration than are "better off" households. In a similar vein Adams (1991, 1993) uses a poverty line and predicted income functions to estimate the income status of households in rural areas of the Arab Republic of Egypt before and after international migration. Using this framework Adams finds that the number of poor households declines by 9.8 percent when household income includes international remittances, and that remittances account for 14.7 percent of total income of poor households (1991, p. 74).

While the findings of these past studies are instructive, their conclusions are of limited use due to a small sample size. Stark's findings, for instance, are based on 61 households from two Mexican villages, while those of Adams are based on 1,000 households from three Egyptian villages. Clearly, the scope of these studies needs to be extended to see if their findings hold for a larger and broader collection of developing countries.

A NEW DATA SET ON INTERNATIONAL MIGRATION, REMITTANCES, AND POVERTY

This evaluation of the impact of international migration and remittances in developing countries is based on a new empirical data set that includes complete data on international migration, remittances, and poverty for as many developing countries and time periods as possible. Initially the goal was to include all 157 countries classified as low income or middle income by the World Bank in the *World Development*

Report 2000/2001.[2] However, it proved impossible to find migration, remittances, and poverty data for many of these developing countries. Because similar data problems have constrained past work on the topic, it is useful to spell out the nature of the difficulties.

Few, if any, of the major labor-exporting countries publish accurate records on the number of international migrants they produce. Therefore, migration stocks and flows must be estimated by using data collected by the main labor-receiving countries. For the purposes of this chapter, two main labor recipients are used: the United States and the European countries of the Organisation for Economic Co-operation and Development (OECD). The following 21 countries are included in OECD (Europe): Austria, Belgium, the Czech Republic, Denmark, Finland, France, Germany, Greece, Hungary, Ireland, Italy, Luxembourg, the Netherlands, Norway, Poland, Portugal, the Slovak Republic, Spain, Sweden, Switzerland, and the United Kingdom. Unfortunately, no data are available on the amount of migration to the third and fourth most important labor-receiving regions in the world: the Arab states of the Persian Gulf and South Africa.

Because of their importance to labor-exporting countries, remittance flows tend to be the best-measured aspect of the migration experience. For instance, the International Monetary Fund (IMF) keeps annual records of the amount of worker remittances received by each labor-exporting country.[3] However, as noted above, the IMF reports data only on official worker remittance flows, that is, remittance monies transmitted through official banking channels. Because a large (and unknown) proportion of remittances move through private, unofficial channels, the level recorded by the IMF underestimates the actual flow to labor-exporting countries.[4]

Finally, with respect to poverty, many developing countries—especially those with smaller populations—have not conducted the nationally representative household budget surveys that are needed to estimate poverty. For example, of the 157 countries classified as low or middle income by the World Bank, 76 (48 percent) have not published the results of any household budget survey.

Given these data limitations, this chapter uses data from 74 low- and middle-income developing countries. All had relevant international migration, remittance, and poverty data dating back to 1980. In line with other cross-sectional analyses of poverty (Ravallion and Chen 1997; Adams 2003), 1980 was selected as a cutoff point because previous poverty data are far less comprehensive.

The countries, regions, poverty, migration, and remittances indicators of the new data set are presented in table 14A.1 in annex 14A. The data set includes a total of 190 observations from the 74 developing countries, an observation being any year for which complete data on poverty, migration, and remittances exist. The data set is notable in that it includes 42 observations (from 21 countries) in Sub-Saharan Africa, a region for which migration and poverty data are relatively rare. It also includes observations from countries in all other regions of the developing world.

CALCULATION OF POVERTY, MIGRATION, AND REMITTANCE VARIABLES

Table 14A.1 reports three different poverty measures. The first, the poverty headcount index, set at US$1.08 per person per day, measures the percentage of the population living beneath that poverty line at the time of the survey.[5] However, the headcount index ignores the depth of poverty, that is, the amount by which the average expenditures[6] (income) of the poor fall short of the poverty line. Therefore the poverty gap index is also reported. A poverty gap of 10 percent, for example, means that the average poor person's expenditures (income) are 90 percent of the poverty line. The third poverty measure—the squared poverty gap index—indicates the severity of poverty. The squared poverty gap index possesses useful analytical properties, because it is sensitive to changes in distribution among the poor.[7]

To measure inequality, table 14A.1 uses the Gini coefficient. In the table this measure is normalized by household size. The distributions are weighted by household size so that a given quintile (such as the lowest) has the same share of population as other quintiles across the sample.

The remaining variables in table 14A.1—migration as a share of country population and remittances as a share of country gross domestic product (GDP)—are of key importance to this study. Because these two variables must be estimated using some rather heroic assumptions, it is crucial to discuss each variable in turn.

In the absence of detailed records on international migration in the labor-exporting countries, the migration variable in this study is estimated by combining data from the two main labor-receiving regions of the world: the United States and OECD (Europe). The migration variable is constructed using three steps. The first uses data from the 1990 and 2000 U.S. population censuses on the "place of birth for the foreign-born population." Although these data are disaggregated by country of birth for about 50 different labor-exporting countries, it is not at all clear whether all of these "foreign-born" people are, in fact, international migrants. For example, people born in Mexico and brought to the United States as infants would probably not consider themselves migrants. Moreover, it is also not clear how many of those who enter the United States illegally are, in fact, included in the "foreign-born" population figures. As some observers have suggested, the U.S. census data may be undercounting by 20 to 30 percent the actual migrant population living—legally or illegally—in the United States.[8]

The second step in calculating the migration variable is to estimate the number of "foreign-born" living in the OECD (Europe).[9] The OECD (Europe) data are not as detailed as the U.S. census data and differ from the U.S. data in several key ways. Most basically, the OECD (Europe) data classify immigrants differently. Because U.S.-born children of immigrants have U.S. citizenship, the United States defines an immigrant as a person who was born abroad to non-U.S. citizens. Most OECD (Europe) countries, however, follow an ethnicity-based definition of immigration status. This method classifies a person on the basis of the ethnicity of the parent, rather than on place of birth. Thus, a child of Turkish parents born in Germany is typically classified as an immigrant. This different way of classifying immigrants has the net effect of increasing the stock of immigrants in any particular OECD (Europe) country, and perhaps biasing the estimates here by including "migrants" who were born, raised, and educated in that country. Another key difference between the OECD (Europe) data and the U.S. data has to do with the number of labor-exporting countries recorded. While the U.S. census data can be used to count the number of "foreign-born" (or migrants) from about 50 different countries, the OECD (Europe) data record the number of "foreign-born" (or migrants) in each European country coming from just 10 or 15 countries. While this is not a significant problem for large labor-exporting countries (Turkey, for example), which send many migrants to Europe, it is a problem for countries that export fewer migrants, such as Brazil or Sri Lanka, where the actual number of migrants to any particular European country might not be recorded at all.

The final step in calculating the migration variable is to take the sum of the foreign-born from each labor-exporting country who are living in either the United States or the OECD (Europe), and divide this sum by the population of each developing country. These figures—"migration as share of population"—are the ones that appear in table 14A.1. In all likelihood, these figures underestimate the actual number of international migrants produced by any given labor-exporting country, because they do not include the large number of illegal migrants working in the United States and the OECD (Europe). These figures also do not count the unknown number of international migrants working in other labor-receiving regions (like the Arab states of the Persian Gulf).

The process of calculating the remittances variable in table 14A.1 is more straightforward, but it also involves one heroic assumption. All remittance data come from the IMF's *Balance of Payments Statistics*

Yearbook. As noted above, the main problem with these data is that they count only remittance monies that enter through official banking channels; they do not include the large (and unknown) amount of remittances sent home through private, unofficial channels. For example, in one major labor-exporting country—Egypt—it has been estimated that unofficial remittances amount to one-third to one-half of total official remittances (Adams 1991). For this reason, it is likely that the "official remittances" figures recorded in table 14A.1 are gross underestimates of the actual level of remittances (official and unofficial) entering each labor-exporting county.[10]

ECONOMETRIC MODEL AND RESULTS

This section uses the cross-country data to analyze how international migration and remittances affect poverty in the developing world. Using the basic growth-poverty model suggested by Ravallion (1997) and Ravallion and Chen (1997), the relationship to estimate can be written as

$$\log P_{it} = \alpha_i + \beta_1 \log \mu_{it} + \beta_2 \log (g_{it}) + \beta_3 \log (x_{it}) + \varepsilon_{it} , \tag{14.1}$$

where i = country $1, .., N$; and t = year $1, .., T_i$. In equation (14.1), P is the measure of poverty in country i at time t, α_i is a fixed effect term reflecting differences between countries in distribution, β_1 is the elasticity of poverty with respect to mean per capita income given by μ, β_2 is the elasticity of poverty with respect to income distribution given by g, β_3 is the elasticity of poverty with respect to variable x (such as international migration or remittances), and ε is an error term that includes errors in the poverty measure.

The income variable in equation (14.1) can be measured in two different ways: first, as per capita GDP, in purchasing power parity units, as measured from national accounts data; and second, as per capita income (expenditure), as calculated from household budget surveys done in the various developing countries. As Deaton (2001) and others have shown, these two measures of income typically do not agree. Income (expenditure) as measured by household surveys is calculated from the responses of individual households. However, income as measured by GDP data come from national accounts, which measure household income as a residual item, so that errors and omissions elsewhere in the accounts automatically affect the calculation of household income (expenditure). Because the national accounts data also include many items (such as the expenditures of nonprofit organizations and the imputed rent of owner-occupied dwellings) that are not included in the household surveys, it is little wonder that the two measures of income do not correspond.

For the purposes of this study, equation (14.1) is estimated using both measures of income. This allows the robustness of the findings to be tested against different definitions of income.

In the literature, equation (14.1) is often measured in first differences, to deal with possible correlation problems between the variables, because the dependent and independent variables are drawn from a single source of data (household budget surveys). However, when equation (14.1) is estimated in first differences, neither of the variables of concern—migration as a share of country population and remittances as share of country GDP—are statistically significant. Two possible reasons exist for this outcome. First, neither the migration nor the remittances variable shows much variation over time. Second, in taking first differences, there is an increase in the ratio of measurement error to information, and this increase in measurement error leads to the estimation of less precise coefficients for the migration and remittances variables. For these reasons, this study will estimate equation (14.1) as a level equation because the correlation problem between variables is not that great, with the dependent and independent variables being drawn from different sources of data—the dependent variable coming from household budget surveys and the independent variables (for migration and remittances) from various other sources. The basic estimation technique is ordinary least squares. Using the migration data, ordinary-least-squares estimates of equation (14.1) are presented in table 14.1. Because all the variables are estimated in log terms, the results can be interpreted as elasticities of poverty with respect to the relevant variable.

In table 14.1 the coefficients for both income variables—GDP and survey mean income—are of the expected (negative) sign and statistically significant in all cases. However, the results for the model as a whole are better and more precise when estimated using survey mean income: the R^2 coefficients increase from the 0.4 to 0.5 range to 0.6 to 0.7. We will therefore focus on the results obtained by using survey mean income.

In table 14.1 the poverty elasticities with respect to income inequality (Gini coefficient) are positive, as expected, and their magnitude is consistent with other recent analyses of poverty reduction.[11] The latter outcome suggests that countries with higher income inequality also have higher poverty.

When the dependent variable in table 14.1 is poverty headcount or poverty gap, the results for the migration variable are negative and statistically significant. However, when the dependent variable is squared poverty gap, the share of migrants in the country's population has no significant impact on poverty. For the poverty headcount measure, the estimates using survey mean income suggest that, on average, a 10 percent increase in the share of migrants in the country's population will

TABLE 14.1 ELASTICITY OF POVERTY, ESTIMATED USING
INTERNATIONAL MIGRATION DATA

	Dependent variable = poverty headcount (percentage living on US\$1.08/person/day or less)		Dependent variable = poverty gap		Dependent variable = squared poverty gap	
	Equation					
Variable	*(1)*	*(2)*	*(3)*	*(4)*	*(5)*	*(6)*
Per capita GDP (constant 1995 U.S. dollars)	−1.178 (−8.84)**		−1.349 (−8.82)**		−1.417 (−7.51)**	
Per capita survey mean income (expenditure)		−2.336 (−16.85)**		−2.623 (−15.24)**		−2.660 (−11.49)**
Gini coefficient	3.396 (6.88)**	4.025 (12.08)**	4.170 (7.89)**	4.798 (11.60)**	4.600 (6.88)**	5.002 (9.29)**
Migrants as share of country population[a]	−0.156 (−2.49)**	−0.188 (−4.48)**	−0.120 (−1.68)*	−0.153 (−2.93)**	−0.029 (−0.27)	−0.048 (−0.69)
Constant	13.549 (10.94)**	16.273 (19.75)**	14.089 (9.96)**	17.397 (16.55)**	14.021 (8.03)**	16.827 (12.03)**
Number of observations	109	106	109	106	106	100
Adjusted R^2	0.494	0.767	0.481	0.722	0.399	0.598
F-Statistic	36.11	116.09	34.41	92.0	22.91	50.12

Note: Estimates were obtained using ordinary least squares. All variables are expressed in logs. T-ratios are shown in parentheses. Number of observations reduced for certain equations because of missing values. See table 14A.1 for countries and survey dates.
a. Migrants measured as number of immigrants from country recorded as living in the United States or OECD (Europe).
* Significant at the 0.10 level.
** Significant at the 0.05 level.

lead to a 1.9 percent decline in the share of people living on less than US\$1 per person per day. This means that, for a "representative" country, if exactly one-half of the population lives below the poverty line of US\$1 per person per day, a 10 percent increase in migration will bring the proportion living in poverty down to about 49 percent, holding the level and distribution of income constant. International migration, therefore, has a small but statistically significant impact on poverty reduction, independent of the level of income and its distribution.

Table 14.2 shows the results when equation (14.1) is estimated using remittances data. The remittances variable—remittances as a share of country GDP—has a negative and significant impact on all

TABLE 14.2 ELASTICITY OF POVERTY, ESTIMATED USING INTERNATIONAL REMITTANCE DATA

	Dependent variable = poverty headcount (percentage living on US$1.08/person/day or less)		Dependent variable = poverty gap		Dependent variable = squared poverty gap	
	Equation					
Variable	*(1)*	*(2)*	*(3)*	*(4)*	*(5)*	*(6)*
Per capita GDP (constant 1995 U.S. dollars)	−1.197 (−9.10)**		−1.432 (−9.67)**		−1.416 (−8.77)**	
Per capita survey mean income (expenditure)		−2.278 (−16.85)**		−2.652 (−15.90)**		−2.534 (−14.05)**
Gini coefficient	2.845 (5.56)**	3.256 (9.38)**	4.167 (7.22)**	4.641 (10.84)**	4.760 (7.76)**	5.053 (11.05)**
Official remittances as share of country GDP	−0.116 (−1.98)*	−0.160 (−3.64)**	−0.205 (−3.11)**	−0.172 (−3.18)**	−0.214 (−2.88)**	−0.211 (−3.68)**
Constant	13.144 (11.12)**	15.786 (19.47)**	14.611 (10.99)**	17.396 (17.39)**	14.130 (9.75)**	16.342 (15.21)**
Number of observations	104	99	104	99	93	92
Adjusted R^2	0.443	0.746	0.499	0.733	0.517	0.722
F-Statistic	28.29	97.23	35.19	90.77	33.84	79.94

Note: Estimates were obtained using ordinary least squares. All variables are expressed in logs. T-ratios are shown in parentheses. Number of observations reduced in table because of missing values. See table 14A.1 for countries and survey dates.
* Significant at the 0.10 level.
** Significant at the 0.05 level.

three measures of poverty: headcount, poverty gap, and squared poverty gap. As was the case with the migration model, the size of the elasticity of poverty with respect to remittances is small. On average, the point estimates for the poverty headcount measure using survey mean income suggest that a 10 percent increase in the share of remittances in country GDP will lead to a 1.6 percent decline in the share of people living on less than US$1 per person per day. Controlling for the level of income and income inequality, the more sensitive poverty measures—poverty gap and squared poverty gap—suggest that international remittances will have a slightly larger impact on poverty reduction. The point estimates for the poverty gap and squared poverty gap suggest that, on average, a 10 percent increase in the share of remittances will lead to about a 2 percent decline in the depth of poverty.

It is useful to speculate on the reasons why international migration and remittances have such a small—albeit statistically significant—impact on poverty reduction. As noted at the outset, both variables are probably underestimated. The variable "migrants as share of country population" is underestimated because it does not include those people who illegally migrate to the United States or the OECD (Europe); also, it does not include the large number of migrants who go to work in other labor-receiving regions (such as the Arab States of the Persian Gulf or South Africa). Similarly, the variable "remittances as share of country GDP" does not include the large (and unknown) amount of money that is remitted through private, unofficial channels. Because workers who migrate illegally are more likely to be poor and to remit through unofficial channels, it is likely that the variables used in this study underestimate the true impact of international migration and remittances on poverty in labor-exporting countries. If, in the future, it were possible to get more accurate estimates of the number of legal and illegal migrants and their official and unofficial remittances, it is likely that international migration and remittances would have an even stronger statistical impact on poverty reduction in the developing world.

Data problems notwithstanding, the results provide an intriguing puzzle and point to an important area for future work. Remittance flows can be treated analytically in the same way as any other increase in national income. Their poverty-reducing impact derives from two sources: first, from an increase in per capita GDP or survey mean income (given the distribution of income); and second, from any contemporaneous change in the distribution of income that occurs as a result of the receipt of remittances by different income groups. If the distributional bias of remittance income to households is progressive, the poverty-reducing impact of the increase in income will be greater than it would have been if the distribution had remained unchanged. A regressive bias will result in the opposite outcome.

In our econometric specifications we control for the level of per capita income and for its distribution. Yet the analysis still finds a significant independent poverty-reducing impact of both migration and (more convincingly) remittances on the poverty headcount and on some measures of depth and severity. Looking at the picture another way, rather than expressing surprise at the small magnitudes of the elasticity of poverty reduction with respect to the migration and remittance variables, we might be surprised that they are significant at all. Is there perhaps a third channel by which incomes remitted affect the level and severity of poverty in developing countries?

Our data do not permit us to move beyond speculation, but one conjecture, at least, is consistent with the data. Because the distributional data related to income change less frequently than the poverty and income data, the migration and remittance variables may be picking up the effect of a progressive bias in the distribution of remittance income among households. In this case, while the main channel by which remittances reduce poverty is the income variable, their distributional impact is captured by the independent migration or remittances variable. The fact that the elasticity of the measure with respect to remittances is greater in the cases of the poverty gap and the squared poverty gap than it is for the poverty headcount may lead some credence to this hypothesis.

REGIONAL RESULTS

Because international migration and remittances reduce poverty in the developing world as a whole, it is useful to see if they also reduce poverty in different geographic regions. Table 14.3 prepares for such an analysis by presenting mean values for the relevant poverty, migration, and remittance variables in each of the six regions of the developing world: East Asia, Europe and Central Asia, Latin America and the Caribbean, the Middle East and North Africa, South Asia, and Sub-Saharan Africa.

Table 14.3 shows that mean values for the migration variable (migration as share of country population) are highest in two regions: Latin America and the Caribbean, and the Middle East and North Africa. In the table, mean values for the remittances variable (official remittances as share of country GDP) are highest in the Middle East and North Africa, and South Asia. However, it should be noted that in all regions both the migration and the remittances variables are quite small, typically 4 percent or less of country population or GDP.

In theory, it should be possible to estimate equation (14.1) using migration and remittance data for the poverty headcount measure in each of the six geographic regions of the developing world. However, in practice the number of observations for some regions (for example, East Asia, the Middle East and North Africa) is just too small to estimate meaningful econometric relationships. For this reason, it is best to group the regions together on the basis of their main labor-destination area (the United States or OECD [Europe]), and then estimate equation (14.1) to examine the underlying relationships between migration and poverty, and remittances and poverty.

The results of this approach are shown in table 14.4, where it is assumed that two regions—East Asia, and Latin America and the Caribbean—send all their migrants to the United States and that the

TABLE 14.3 REGIONAL SUMMARY OF MEAN VALUES FOR POVERTY, INEQUALITY, MIGRATION, AND REMITTANCES

Region	Number of observations	Poverty headcount (percentage living on US$1/person/day or less)	Poverty gap (percent)	Squared poverty gap (percent)	Gini coefficient	Migration as share of country population	Official remittances as share of country GDP (constant 1995 U.S. dollars)
East Asia	13	15.46	3.14	0.92	0.401	0.72	0.34
Europe and Central Asia	46	2.49	0.69	0.31	0.306	0.54	0.09
Latin America and the Caribbean	55	15.01	5.69	3.09	0.509	3.62	1.29
Middle East and North Africa	14	2.51	1.07	0.22	0.382	1.91	9.60
South Asia	20	34.67	9.06	2.53	0.324	0.50	2.59
Sub-Saharan Africa	42	40.87	17.27	9.64	0.464	0.03	0.63
Total	190	18.87	6.88	3.47	0.414	1.43	1.55

Note: All figures are mean values calculated from data in table 14A.1.

TABLE 14.4 ELASTICITY OF POVERTY BY REGION, ESTIMATED USING
INTERNATIONAL MIGRATION AND REMITTANCE DATA

Dependent variable = poverty headcount
(percentage living on $1.08/person/day or less)

Variable	Full Sample		East Asia, Latin America and the Caribbean		Europe and Central Asia, Middle East and North Africa, South Asia, Sub-Saharan Africa	
			Equation			
	(1)	*(2)*	*(3)*	*(4)*	*(5)*	*(6)*
Per capita GDP (constant 1995 dollars)	−1.147	−1.197	−0.957	−0.926	−0.952	−1.841
	(−8.60)**	(−9.10)**	(−5.61)**	(−5.15)**	(−4.05)**	(−10.71)**
Gini coefficient	3.563	2.845	2.004	2.036	2.538	1.556
	(7.26)**	(5.55)**	(3.43)**	(3.55)**	(3.70)**	(2.34)**
Migrants as share of country population[a]	−0.181		−0.062		−0.669	
	(−2.93)**		(−1.14)		(−4.51)**	
Official remittances as share of country GDP		−0.116		−0.162		−0.063
		(−1.98)*		(−2.62)**		(−0.91)
Constant	13.427	13.144	11.155	10.898	10.089	15.601
	(10.96)**	(11.12)**	(7.45)**	(7.11)**	(5.27)**	(11.53)**
Number of observations	109	104	62	46	47	58
Adjusted R^2	0.504	0.443	0.338	0.394	0.772	0.663
F-Statistic	37.63	28.29	11.38	10.77	53.08	38.45

Note: Estimates were obtained using ordinary least squares. All variables are expressed in logs. T-ratios are shown in parentheses. Number of observations reduced for certain equations because of missing values. See table 14A.1 for countries and survey dates.

a. Migrants measured as number of immigrants from country recorded as living in the United States or OECD (Europe).

* Significant at the 0.10 level.
** Significant at the 0.05 level.

other four regions send all their migrants to the OECD (Europe). The results are mixed. While the coefficients for the migration and remittance variables all have the correct (negative) sign, in only two of four cases do the variables have a statistically significant impact on poverty. The point estimates for the statistically significant variables suggest that, on average, a 10 percent increase in the share of remittances will lead to a 1.6 percent decline in the poverty headcount in East Asia and Latin America, whereas a 10 percent increase in the share of migrants will lead to a 6.7 percent decline in the poverty headcount in the other four regions.

In table 14.4 it is interesting to note that the adjusted R^2 in equations (3) and (4) is much lower than that in equations (5) and (6), which means that the regression equation explains far less of the variance in the level of the poverty headcount ratio in East Asia and Latin America and the Caribbean than in the other four regions of the developing world (Europe and Central Asia, Middle East and North Africa, South Asia, and Sub-Saharan Africa). A possible explanation for this difference may be that there are a larger number of illegal (and thus uncounted) migrants working in the United States as opposed to the OECD (Europe), and this has a negative impact on the "fit" of the regressions in equation (3). However, this does not explain why the remittances variable in equation (6) is also poorly estimated. Evidently, more work is needed to uncover the reasons for these anomalies.

CONCLUSIONS

This chapter used a new data set of 74 low- and middle-income developing countries to examine the impact of international migration and remittances on poverty. Five key findings emerged.

First, international migration—defined as the share of a country's population living abroad—has a strong, statistically important impact on reducing poverty in the developing world. On average, a 10 percent increase in the share of international migrants in a labor-sending country's population will lead to a 1.9 percent decline in the share of people living on less than US$1 per day.

Second, the study finds that international remittances—defined as the share of official remittances in country GDP—has a negative and statistically significant effect on all three poverty measures used in the analysis. On average, the point estimates for the poverty headcount measure indicate that a 10 percent increase in the share of remittances in country GDP will lead to a 1.6 percent decline in the share of people living on less than US$1 per day. However, the more sensitive poverty measures—the poverty gap and squared poverty gap—suggest that international remittances will have a slightly larger impact on poverty reduction. The point estimates for the poverty gap and squared poverty gap suggest that a 10 percent increase in the share of remittances will lead to about a 2 percent decline in the depth and severity of poverty in the developing world.

Third, while an analytical decomposition of the impact of remittance flows on poverty would suggest that they should have their primary poverty-reducing impact through increases in per capita incomes or changes in income distribution, the empirical results find a significant independent poverty-reducing effect. This finding, which is not incon-sistent with other empirical decompositions of poverty dynamics that find a relatively large unexplained residual in the income-distribution decomposition (Ravallion 1997), raises a major area for future research to identify the channels by which remittances affect the level and dis-tribution of income in developing countries.

Fourth, the impact of international migration and remittances on poverty seems to vary by region of the developing world. For example, controlling for the level and distribution of income, while international migration does not have a statistically significant impact on poverty reduction in the developing regions of East Asia and Latin America and the Caribbean, it does have a significant impact on poverty reduction in other regions of the developing world (Europe and Central Asia, the Middle East and North Africa, South Asia, and Sub-Saharan Africa). One possible reason for these differences may be that there are a larger number of illegal (and thus uncounted) migrants coming from East Asia and Latin America, and that the poverty effects of these illegal migrants are not considered in this analysis. This points to the need for better esti-mates of the numbers of undocumented international migrants in vari-ous regions of the world, and for increased study of the impact that these uncounted migrants have on poverty in labor-exporting countries.

The final finding is more a plea than a conclusion. From the stand-point of future work on this topic, far more attention needs to be paid to collecting and publishing good data on international migration and remittances. With respect to migration, it would be useful if developing countries would start publishing records on the number and destina-tion of their international migrants. In many developing countries these data are already being collected, but they are not being pub-lished. With respect to international remittances, the IMF should make greater efforts to count the amount of remittance monies that are trans-mitted through private, unofficial channels. Because poor people are more likely to remit through informal, unofficial channels, a full and complete accounting of the impact of remittances on poverty in the developing world needs more accurate data on the large and currently unknown level of unofficial remittance transfers.

NOTES

1. See, for example, Adams 1991, 1993; Taylor 1992; Gustafsson and Makon-nen 1993; Taylor, Zabin, and Eckhoff 1999; Stark 1991.

2. The full list of these 157 countries appears in World Bank 2001, p. 334.

3. The IMF records annual international remittances in its publication *Bal-ance of Payments Statistics Yearbook*.

4. A recent IMF study (El-Qorchi, Maimbo, and Wilson 2003) estimated that informal transfers of remittance monies could amount to US$10 billion per year.

5. To ensure compatibility across countries, all the poverty lines in table 14A.1 are international poverty lines, set at estimates of US$1.08 per person per day in 1993 purchasing power parity (PPP) exchange rates. The PPP exchange rates are used so that US$1.08 is worth roughly the same in all countries. PPP values are calculated by pricing a representative bundle of goods in each country and comparing the local cost of that bundle with the U.S. dollar cost of the same bundle. In calculating PPP values, the comparison of local costs with U.S. costs is done using conversion estimates produced by the World Bank.

6. Generally, expenditure is more readily measured than income, due to the ability of households to smooth their expenditure over time in the face of income fluctuations arising from seasonality or shocks.

7. Although a transfer of expenditures from a poor person to a poorer person will not change the headcount index or the poverty gap index, it will decrease the squared poverty gap index.

8. For more on this point, see U.S. Census Bureau (2001) and Warren (2000).

9. The data on the "foreign-born" population living in the OECD (Europe) come from OECD, *Trends in International Migration* (various years).

10. In a draft paper based on 71 developing countries, Adams and Page (2004) estimate that unofficial remittances—defined as those remittances passing through private, unrecorded channels—are about 75 percent larger than the volume of official remittances.

11. See, for example, Ravallion (1997) and Adams (2003).

REFERENCES

Adams, Jr., Richard. 1991. "The Effects of International Remittances on Poverty, Inequality and Development in Rural Egypt." Research Report 86, International Food Policy Research Institute, Washington, DC.

————. 1993. "The Economic and Demographic Determinants of International Migration in Rural Egypt." *Journal of Development Studies* 30(1): 146–57.

————. 2003. "Economic Growth, Inequality, and Poverty: Findings from a New Data Set." Policy Research Working Paper 2972, World Bank, Washington, DC.

Adams, Jr., Richard, and John Page. 2004. "International Migration, Remittances, and Poverty in Developing Countries." Policy Research Working Paper 3179, World Bank, Washington, DC.

Deaton, Angus. 2001. "Counting the World's Poor: Problems and Possible Solutions." *World Bank Research Observer* 16(2): 125–47.

El-Qorchi, Mohammed, Samuel Maimbo, and John F. Wilson. 2003. "Informal Funds Transfer Systems: An Analysis of the Hawala System." IMF Occasional Paper 222, International Monetary Fund, Washington, DC.

Gustafsson, Bjorn, and Negatu Makonnen. 1993. "Poverty and Remittances in Lesotho." *Journal of African Economies* 2(1): 49–73.

IMF (International Monetary Fund). Various years. *Balance of Payments Statistics Yearbook.* Washington, DC.

Lipton, Michael. 1980. "Migration from Rural Areas of Poor Countries: The Impact on Rural Productivity and Income Distribution." *World Development* 8(January): 1–24.

OECD (Organisation for Economic Co-operation and Development). Various years. *Trends in International Migration: Annual Report.* Paris.

Ravallion, Martin. 1997. "Can High-Inequality Developing Countries Escape Absolute Poverty?" *Economics Letters* 56: 51–57.

Ravallion, Martin, and Shaohua Chen. 1997. "What Can New Survey Data Tell Us About Recent Changes in Distribution and Poverty?" *World Bank Economic Review* 11(2): 357–82.

Stahl, Charles. 1982. "Labor Emigration and Economic Development." *International Migration Review* 16(4): 869–99.

Stark, Oded. 1991. *The Migration of Labor.* Cambridge, MA: Harvard University Press.

Taylor, J. Edward. 1992. "Remittances and Inequality Reconsidered: Direct, Indirect, and Intertemporal Effects." *Journal of Policy Modeling* 14(2): 187–208.

Taylor, J. Edward, Carol Zabin, and Kay Eckhoff. 1999. "Migration and Rural Development in El Salvador: A Micro-Economywide Perspective." *North American Journal of Economics and Finance* 10(1): 91–114.

United Nations. 2002. *International Migration Report 2002.* Department of Economic and Social Affairs, Population Division, New York.

U.S. Census Bureau. 1990. *Population Census.* Washington, DC.

———. 2000. *Population Census.* Washington, DC.

———. 2001. "Profile of the Foreign-Born Population in the United States: 2000." Washington, DC.

Warren, Richard. 2000. "Annual Estimates of the Unauthorized Immigrant Population Residing in the United States and Components of Change: 1987 to 1997." Office of Policy and Planning, U.S. Immigration and Naturalization Service.

World Bank. 2001. *World Development Report, 2000/2001: Attacking Poverty.* Washington, DC: World Bank.

ANNEX 14A. DATA SET SUMMARY

TABLE 14A.1 SUMMARY OF DATA SET ON POVERTY, INEQUALITY, INTERNATIONAL MIGRATION, AND REMITTANCES

Country	Survey year	Region	Poverty headcount (percentage living on US$1/person/day or less)	Poverty gap (percent)	Squared poverty gap (percent)	Gini coefficient	Migration as share of country population	Official remittances (millions of U.S. dollars)	Official remittances as share of country GDP (constant 1995 U.S. dollars)
Algeria	1988	Mid. East & N. Africa	1.75	0.64	0.48	0.414	2.77	379	0.97
Algeria	1995	Mid. East & N. Africa	1.16	0.23	0.094	0.353	2.01	1,101	2.63
Bangladesh	1984	South Asia	26.16	5.98	1.96	0.258	0.04	527	2.19
Bangladesh	1986	South Asia	21.96	3.92	1.07	0.269	0.04	497	1.9
Bangladesh	1989	South Asia	33.75	7.72	2.44	0.288	0.05	771	2.68
Bangladesh	1992	South Asia	35.86	8.77	2.98	0.282	0.06	848	2.55
Bangladesh	1996	South Asia	29.07	5.88	1.6	0.336	0.09	1,217	3.16
Belarus	1988	Eur. & Cent. Asia	0	0	0	0.227	0	0	0
Belarus	1993	Eur. & Cent. Asia	1.06	0.13	0.03	0.216	0	0	0
Belarus	1995	Eur. & Cent. Asia	2.27	0.71	0.46	0.287	0	29	0.27
Bolivia	1990	L. America & the Caribbean	11.28	2.22	0.6	0.42	0.47	2	0.03
Botswana	1985	Sub-Saharan Africa	33.3	12.53	6.09	0.542	0	0	0
Brazil	1985	L. America & the Caribbean	15.8	4.69	1.82	0.595	0.05	25	0.01
Brazil	1988	L. America & the Caribbean	18.62	6.78	3.22	0.624	0.05	19	0.01
Brazil	1993	L. America & the Caribbean	18.79	8.38	5.01	0.615	0.08	1,123	0.17
Brazil	1995	L. America & the Caribbean	13.94	3.94	1.46	0.6	0.09	2,891	0.41
Brazil	1997	L. America & the Caribbean	5.1	1.32	0.5	0.517	0.11	1,324	0.17

(continues)

TABLE 14A.1 SUMMARY OF DATA SET ON POVERTY, INEQUALITY, INTERNATIONAL MIGRATION, AND REMITTANCES (Continued)

Country	Survey year	Region	Poverty headcount (percentage living on US$1/person/day or less)	Poverty gap (percent)	Squared poverty gap (percent)	Gini coefficient	Migration as share of country population	Official remittances (millions of U.S. dollars)	Official remittances as share of country GDP (constant 1995 U.S. dollars)
Bulgaria	1989	Eur. & Cent. Asia	0	0	0	0.233	0.2	0	0
Bulgaria	1992	Eur. & Cent. Asia	0	0	0	0.308	0.2	0	0
Bulgaria	1995	Eur. & Cent. Asia	0	0	0	0.285	0.2	0	0
Burkina Faso	1994	Sub-Saharan Africa	61.18	25.51	13.03	0.482	0	80	3.83
Central African Rep.	1993	Sub-Saharan Africa	66.58	40.04	28.56	0.613	0	0	0
Chile	1987	L. America & the Caribbean	10.2	2.25	0.66	0.564	0.4	0	0
Chile	1990	L. America & the Caribbean	8.26	2.03	0.73	0.56	0.42	0	0
Chile	1992	L. America & the Caribbean	3.91	0.74	0.23	0.557	0.44	0	0
Chile	1994	L. America & the Caribbean	4.18	0.65	0.15	0.548	0.46	0	0
Colombia	1988	L. America & the Caribbean	4.47	1.31	0.57	0.531	0.8	448	0.65
Colombia	1991	L. America & the Caribbean	2.82	0.75	0.32	0.513	0.86	866	1.14
Colombia	1995	L. America & the Caribbean	8.87	2.05	0.63	0.574	1.02	739	0.8
Colombia	1996	L. America & the Caribbean	10.99	3.16	1.21	0.571	1.06	635	0.67
Costa Rica	1986	L. America & the Caribbean	12.52	5.44	3.27	0.344	1.43	0	0

TABLE 14A.1 SUMMARY OF DATA SET ON POVERTY, INEQUALITY, INTERNATIONAL MIGRATION, AND REMITTANCES (Continued)

Country	Survey year	Region	Poverty headcount (percentage living on US$1/person/day or less)	Poverty gap (percent)	Squared poverty gap (percent)	Gini coefficient	Migration as share of country population	Official remittances (millions of U.S. dollars)	Official remittances as share of country GDP (constant 1995 U.S. dollars)
Costa Rica	1990	L. America & the Caribbean	11.08	4.19	2.37	0.456	1.41	0	0
Costa Rica	1993	L. America & the Caribbean	10.3	3.53	1.79	0.462	1.58	0	0
Costa Rica	1996	L. America & the Caribbean	9.57	3.18	1.55	0.47	1.71	122	1.03
Côte d'Ivoire	1985	Sub-Saharan Africa	4.71	0.59	0.1	0.412	0	0	0
Côte d'Ivoire	1987	Sub-Saharan Africa	3.28	0.41	0.08	0.4	0	0	0
Côte d'Ivoire	1993	Sub-Saharan Africa	9.88	1.86	0.54	0.369	0	0	0
Côte d'Ivoire	1995	Sub-Saharan Africa	12.29	2.4	0.71	0.367	0	0	0
Czech Republic	1988	Eur. & Cent. Asia	0	0	0	0.194	1.73	0	0
Czech Republic	1993	Eur. & Cent. Asia	0	0	0	0.266	1.53	0	0
Dominican Republic	1989	L. America & the Caribbean	7.73	1.51	0.42	0.504	4.89	301	2.91
Dominican Republic	1996	L. America & the Caribbean	3.19	0.71	0.26	0.487	7.08	914	7.13
Ecuador	1988	L. America & the Caribbean	24.85	10.21	5.82	0.439	1.38	0	0
Ecuador	1995	L. America & the Caribbean	20.21	5.77	2.27	0.437	1.92	382	2.13

(continues)

TABLE 14A.1 SUMMARY OF DATA SET ON POVERTY, INEQUALITY, INTERNATIONAL MIGRATION, AND REMITTANCES (Continued)

Country	Survey year	Region	Poverty headcount (percentage living on US$1/person/day or less)	Poverty gap (percent)	Squared poverty gap (percent)	Gini coefficient	Migration as share of country population	Official remittances (millions of U.S. dollars)	Official remittances as share of country GDP (constant 1995 U.S. dollars)
Egypt, Arab Rep. of	1991	Mid. East & N. Africa	3.97	0.53	0.13	0.35	0.15	2,569	4.99
Egypt, Arab Rep. of	1995	Mid. East & N. Africa	5.55	0.66	0.13	0.283	0.18	3,279	5.45
El Salvador	1989	L. America & the Caribbean	25.49	13.72	10.06	0.489	9.06	228	3.39
El Salvador	1996	L. America & the Caribbean	25.26	10.35	5.79	0.522	11.67	1,084	11.22
Estonia	1988	Eur. & Cent. Asia	0	0	0	0.229	0	0	0
Estonia	1993	Eur. & Cent. Asia	3.15	0.91	0.51	0.395	0	0	0
Estonia	1995	Eur. & Cent. Asia	4.85	1.18	0.39	0.353	0	0	0
Ethiopia	1981	Sub-Saharan Africa	32.73	7.69	2.71	0.324	0.07	0	0
Ethiopia	1995	Sub-Saharan Africa	31.25	7.95	2.99	0.399	0.09	0	0
Gambia, The	1992	Sub-Saharan Africa	53.69	23.27	13.28	0.478	0	0	0
Ghana	1987	Sub-Saharan Africa	47.68	16.6	7.81	0.353	0.11	1	0.02
Ghana	1989	Sub-Saharan Africa	50.44	17.71	8.36	0.359	0.12	6	0.11
Ghana	1992	Sub-Saharan Africa	45.31	13.73	5.61	0.339	0.18	7	0.12
Ghana	1999	Sub-Saharan Africa	44.81	17.28	8.71	0.327	0.32	26	0.37
Guatemala	1987	L. America & the Caribbean	47.04	22.47	13.63	0.582	2.09	0	0
Guatemala	1989	L. America & the Caribbean	39.81	19.79	12.59	0.596	2.34	69	0.59

TABLE 14A.1 SUMMARY OF DATA SET ON POVERTY, INEQUALITY, INTERNATIONAL MIGRATION, AND REMITTANCES (Continued)

Country	Survey year	Region	Poverty headcount (percentage living on US$1/person/day or less)	Poverty gap (percent)	Squared poverty gap (percent)	Gini coefficient	Migration as share of country population	Official remittances (millions of U.S. dollars)	Official remittances as share of country GDP (constant 1995 U.S. dollars)
Honduras	1989	L. America & the Caribbean	44.67	20.65	12.08	0.595	2.11	35	1.05
Honduras	1992	L. America & the Caribbean	38.98	17.74	10.4	0.545	2.74	60	1.65
Honduras	1994	L. America & the Caribbean	37.93	16.6	9.38	0.552	3.23	85	2.23
Honduras	1996	L. America & the Caribbean	40.49	17.47	9.72	0.537	3.66	128	3.12
Hungary	1989	Eur. & Cent. Asia	0	0	0	0.233	2.02	0	0
Hungary	1993	Eur. & Cent. Asia	0	0	0	0.279	1.75	0	0
India	1983	South Asia	52.55	16.27	NA	0.32	0.04	2,311	1.25
India	1986	South Asia	47.46	13.92	NA	0.337	0.06	2,105	0.99
India	1988	South Asia	47.99	13.51	NA	0.329	0.07	2,402	0.98
India	1990	South Asia	45.95	12.63	NA	0.312	0.09	1,875	0.68
India	1995	South Asia	46.75	12.72	NA	0.363	0.11	7,685	2.17
India	1997	South Asia	44.03	11.96	NA	0.378	0.12	10,688	2.7
Indonesia	1987	East Asia	28.08	6.08	1.78	0.331	0.01	86	0.07
Indonesia	1993	East Asia	14.82	2.98	0.39	0.317	0.05	346	0.2
Indonesia	1996	East Asia	7.81	0.95	0.18	0.364	0.08	796	0.39
Indonesia	1998	East Asia	26.33	5.43	1.69	0.315	0.1	959	0.4
Iran, Islamic Rep. of	1990	Mid. East & N. Africa	0.9	0.8	NA	0.434	0.63	1	0.01

(continues)

TABLE 14A.1 SUMMARY OF DATA SET ON POVERTY, INEQUALITY, INTERNATIONAL MIGRATION, AND REMITTANCES (Continued)

Country	Survey year	Region	Poverty headcount (percentage living on US$1/person/day or less)	Poverty gap (percent)	Squared poverty gap (percent)	Gini coefficient	Migration as share of country population	Official remittances (millions of U.S. dollars)	Official remittances as share of country GDP (constant 1995 U.S. dollars)
Jamaica	1988	L. America & the Caribbean	5.02	1.38	0.67	0.431	17.03	76	1.73
Jamaica	1990	L. America & the Caribbean	0.62	0.03	0.01	0.418	19.07	136	2.75
Jamaica	1993	L. America & the Caribbean	4.52	0.86	0.29	0.379	21.8	187	3.39
Jamaica	1996	L. America & the Caribbean	3.15	0.73	0.32	0.364	24.4	636	11.46
Jordan	1987	Mid. East & N. Africa	0	0	0	0.36	0.87	939	16.72
Jordan	1992	Mid. East & N. Africa	0.55	0.12	0.05	0.433	0.93	843	14.46
Jordan	1997	Mid. East & N. Africa	0.36	0.1	0.06	0.364	0.94	1,655	23.08
Kazakhstan	1988	Eur. & Cent. Asia	0.05	0.02	0.01	0.257	0	0	0
Kazakhstan	1993	Eur. & Cent. Asia	1.06	0.04	0.01	0.326	0	0	0
Kazakhstan	1996	Eur. & Cent. Asia	1.49	0.27	0.1	0.354	0	10	0.05
Kenya	1992	Sub-Saharan Africa	33.54	12.82	6.62	0.574	0	0	0
Kenya	1994	Sub-Saharan Africa	26.54	9.03	4.5	0.445	0	0	0
Kyrgyz Republic	1988	Eur. & Cent. Asia	0	0	0	0.26	0	0	0
Kyrgyz Republic	1993	Eur. & Cent. Asia	22.99	10.87	6.82	0.537	0	2	0.1
Kyrgyz Republic	1997	Eur. & Cent. Asia	1.57	0.28	0.1	0.405	0	3	0.17
Latvia	1988	Eur. & Cent. Asia	0	0	0	0.225	0	0	0
Latvia	1993	Eur. & Cent. Asia	0	0	0	0.269	0	0	0
Latvia	1995	Eur. & Cent. Asia	0	0	0	0.284	0	0	0

TABLE 14A.1 SUMMARY OF DATA SET ON POVERTY, INEQUALITY, INTERNATIONAL MIGRATION, AND REMITTANCES (*Continued*)

Country	Survey year	Region	Poverty headcount (percentage living on US$1/person/day or less)	Poverty gap (percent)	Squared poverty gap (percent)	Gini coefficient	Migration as share of country population	Official remittances (millions of U.S. dollars)	Official remittances as share of country GDP (constant 1995 U.S. dollars)
Latvia	1998	Eur. & Cent. Asia	0.19	0.01	0	0.323	0	3	0.05
Lesotho	1987	Sub-Saharan Africa	30.34	12.66	6.85	0.56	0	0	0
Lesotho	1993	Sub-Saharan Africa	43.14	20.26	11.84	0.579	0	0	0
Lithuania	1988	Eur. & Cent. Asia	0	0	0	0.224	0	0	0
Lithuania	1993	Eur. & Cent. Asia	16.47	3.37	0.95	0.336	0	0	0
Lithuania	1996	Eur. & Cent. Asia	0	0	0	0.323	0	2	0.03
Madagascar	1980	Sub-Saharan Africa	49.18	19.74	10.21	0.468	0	0	0
Madagascar	1994	Sub-Saharan Africa	60.17	24.46	12.83	0.434	0	11	0.35
Mali	1989	Sub-Saharan Africa	16.46	3.92	1.39	0.365	0	76	3.49
Mali	1994	Sub-Saharan Africa	72.29	37.38	23.06	0.505	0	103	4.43
Mauritania	1988	Sub-Saharan Africa	40.64	19.07	12.75	0.425	0	9	1.04
Mauritania	1993	Sub-Saharan Africa	49.37	17.83	8.58	0.5	0	2	0.2
Mauritania	1995	Sub-Saharan Africa	30.98	9.99	4.59	0.389	0	5	0.47
Mexico	1984	L. America & the Caribbean	12.05	2.65	0.78	0.54	1.86	1,127	0.47
Mexico	1989	L. America & the Caribbean	16.2	5.63	2.75	0.551	4.66	2,213	0.87
Mexico	1992	L. America & the Caribbean	13.31	3.23	1.04	0.543	6.1	3,070	1.07
Mexico	1995	L. America & the Caribbean	17.9	6.15	2.92	0.537	7.39	3,673	1.28
Moldova	1988	Eur. & Cent. Asia	0	0	0	0.241	0	0	0

(continues)

TABLE 14A.1 SUMMARY OF DATA SET ON POVERTY, INEQUALITY, INTERNATIONAL MIGRATION, AND REMITTANCES (Continued)

Country	Survey year	Region	Poverty headcount (percentage living on US$1/person/day or less)	Poverty gap (percent)	Squared poverty gap (percent)	Gini coefficient	Migration as share of country population	Official remittances (millions of U.S. dollars)	Official remittances as share of country GDP (constant 1995 U.S. dollars)
Moldova	1992	Eur. & Cent. Asia	7.31	1.32	0.32	0.344	0	0	0
Morocco	1985	Mid. East & N. Africa	2.04	0.7	0.5	0.392	4.38	967	3.81
Morocco	1990	Mid. East & N. Africa	0.14	0.02	0.01	0.392	4.02	1,336	4.24
Mozambique	1996	Sub-Saharan Africa	37.85	12.02	5.42	0.396	0	0	0
Namibia	1993	Sub-Saharan Africa	34.93	13.97	6.93	0.743	0	8	0.25
Nepal	1985	South Asia	42.13	10.79	3.75	0.334	0	39	1.43
Nepal	1995	South Asia	37.68	9.74	3.71	0.387	0	101	2.3
Nicaragua	1993	L. America & the Caribbean	47.94	20.4	11.19	0.503	4.38	25	1.47
Niger	1993	Sub-Saharan Africa	41.73	12.43	5.29	0.361	0	13	0.74
Niger	1995	Sub-Saharan Africa	61.42	33.93	23.66	0.506	0	6	0.32
Nigeria	1997	Sub-Saharan Africa	70.24	34.91	NA	0.505	0.09	1,920	6.37
Pakistan	1988	South Asia	49.63	14.85	6.03	0.333	0.11	2,013	4.56
Pakistan	1991	South Asia	47.76	14.57	6.04	0.332	0.16	1,848	3.62
Pakistan	1993	South Asia	33.9	8.44	3.01	0.342	0.18	1,562	2.78
Pakistan	1997	South Asia	30.96	6.16	1.86	0.312	0.22	1,409	2.19
Panama	1989	L. America & the Caribbean	16.57	7.84	4.9	0.565	3.53	14	0.25
Panama	1991	L. America & the Caribbean	18.9	8.87	5.48	0.568	3.55	14	0.21
Panama	1995	L. America & the Caribbean	14.73	6.15	3.39	0.57	3.61	16	0.2

TABLE 14A.1 SUMMARY OF DATA SET ON POVERTY, INEQUALITY, INTERNATIONAL MIGRATION, AND REMITTANCES (Continued)

Country	Survey year	Region	Poverty headcount (percentage living on US$1/person/day or less)	Poverty gap (percent)	Squared poverty gap (percent)	Gini coefficient	Migration as share of country population	Official remittances (millions of U.S. dollars)	Official remittances as share of country GDP (constant 1995 U.S. dollars)
Panama	1997	L. America & the Caribbean	10.31	3.15	3.67	0.485	3.67	16	0.19
Paraguay	1990	L. America & the Caribbean	11.05	2.47	0.8	0.397	0	43	0.56
Paraguay	1995	L. America & the Caribbean	19.36	8.27	4.65	0.591	0	200	2.21
Peru	1985	L. America & the Caribbean	1.14	0.29	0.14	0.457	0.33	0	0
Peru	1994	L. America & the Caribbean	9.13	2.37	0.92	0.446	0.89	472	0.96
Peru	1997	L. America & the Caribbean	15.49	5.38	2.81	0.462	1.03	636	1.08
Philippines	1985	East Asia	22.78	5.32	1.66	0.41	1.26	111	0.21
Philippines	1988	East Asia	18.28	3.59	0.94	0.407	1.49	388	0.64
Philippines	1991	East Asia	15.7	2.79	0.66	0.438	1.69	329	0.49
Philippines	1994	East Asia	18.36	3.85	1.07	0.429	1.86	443	0.62
Philippines	1997	East Asia	14.4	2.85	0.75	0.461	2	1,057	1.28
Poland	1987	Eur. & Cent. Asia	0	0	0	0.255	1.89	0	0
Poland	1990	Eur. & Cent. Asia	0.08	0.027	0.02	0.283	1.84	0	0
Poland	1992	Eur. & Cent. Asia	0.08	0.031	0.02	0.271	1.81	0	0
Romania	1989	Eur. & Cent. Asia	0	0	0	0.233	0.62	0	0
Romania	1992	Eur. & Cent. Asia	0.8	0.34	0.31	0.254	0.77	0	0

(continues)

TABLE 14A.1 SUMMARY OF DATA SET ON POVERTY, INEQUALITY, INTERNATIONAL MIGRATION, AND REMITTANCES (Continued)

Country	Survey year	Region	Poverty headcount (percentage living on US$1/person/day or less)	Poverty gap (percent)	Squared poverty gap (percent)	Gini coefficient	Migration as share of country population	Official remittances (millions of U.S. dollars)	Official remittances as share of country GDP (constant 1995 U.S. dollars)
Romania	1994	Eur. & Cent. Asia	2.81	0.76	0.43	0.282	0.88	4	0.01
Russian Federation	1994	Eur. & Cent. Asia	6.23	1.6	0.55	0.436	0.34	0	0
Russian Federation	1996	Eur. & Cent. Asia	7.24	1.6	0.47	0.48	0.35	0	0
Russian Federation	1998	Eur. & Cent. Asia	7.05	1.45	0.39	0.487	0.36	0	0
Senegal	1991	Sub-Saharan Africa	45.38	19.95	11.18	0.541	0	105	2.54
Senegal	1994	Sub-Saharan Africa	26.26	7.04	2.73	0.412	0	73	1.71
Sierra Leone	1989	Sub-Saharan Africa	56.81	40.45	33.8	0.628	0.18	0	0
South Africa	1993	Sub-Saharan Africa	11.47	1.83	0.38	0.593	0.14	0	0
Sri Lanka	1985	South Asia	9.39	1.69	0.5	0.324	0.06	292	3.45
Sri Lanka	1990	South Asia	3.82	0.67	0.23	0.301	0.12	401	4
Sri Lanka	1995	South Asia	6.56	1	0.26	0.343	0.3	790	6.06
Tanzania	1991	Sub-Saharan Africa	48.54	24.42	15.4	0.59	0	0	0
Tanzania	1993	Sub-Saharan Africa	19.89	4.77	1.66	0.381	0.17	0	0
Thailand	1988	East Asia	25.91	7.36	2.73	0.438	0.21	0	0
Thailand	1992	East Asia	6.02	0.48	0.05	0.462	0.24	0	0
Thailand	1996	East Asia	2.2	0.14	0.01	0.434	0.25	0	0
Thailand	1998	East Asia	0	0	0	0.413		0	0
Trinidad and Tobago	1992	Latin America	12.36	3.48	NA	0.402	10.5	6	0.12

TABLE 14A.1 SUMMARY OF DATA SET ON POVERTY, INEQUALITY,
INTERNATIONAL MIGRATION, AND REMITTANCES (*Continued*)

Country	Survey year	Region	Poverty headcount (percentage living on US$1/person/day or less)	Poverty gap (percent)	Squared poverty gap (percent)	Gini coefficient	Migration as share of country population	Official remittances (millions of U.S. dollars)	Official remittances as share of country GDP (constant 1995 U.S. dollars)
Tunisia	1985	Mid. East & N. Africa	1.67	0.34	0.13	0.434	3.12	271	2.11
Tunisia	1990	Mid. East & N. Africa	1.26	0.33	0.16	0.402	3.01	551	3.71
Turkey	1987	Eur. & Cent. Asia	1.49	0.36	0.17	0.435	4.18	2,021	1.56
Turkey	1994	Eur. & Cent. Asia	2.35	0.55	0.24	0.415	4.13	2,627	1.66
Turkmenistan	1988	Eur. & Cent. Asia	0	0		0.264	0	0	0
Turkmenistan	1993	Eur. & Cent. Asia	20.92	5.69	2.1	0.357	0	0	0
Uganda	1989	Sub-Saharan Africa	39.17	14.99	7.57	0.443	0	0	0
Uganda	1993	Sub-Saharan Africa	36.7	11.44	5	0.391	0	0	0
Ukraine	1989	Eur. & Cent. Asia	0.04	0	0	0.233	0	0	0
Ukraine	1992	Eur. & Cent. Asia	0	0.01	0.01	0.257	0	0	0
Ukraine	1996	Eur. & Cent. Asia	0	0	0	0.325	0	0	0
Uruguay	1989	Latin America	1.1	0.47	0.4	0.423	0	0	0
Uzbekistan	1988	Eur. & Cent. Asia	0	0	0	0.249	0	0	0
Uzbekistan	1993	Eur. & Cent. Asia	3.29	0.46	0.11	0.332	0	0	0
Venezuela, R. B. de	1981	L. America & the Caribbean	6.3	1.08	0.25	0.556	0.08	0	0
Venezuela, R. B. de	1987	L. America & the Caribbean	6.6	1.04	0.22	0.534	0.14	0	0
Venezuela, R. B. de	1989	L. America & the Caribbean	8.49	1.77	0.49	0.557	0.19	0	0

(*continues*)

TABLE 14A.1 SUMMARY OF DATA SET ON POVERTY, INEQUALITY, INTERNATIONAL MIGRATION, AND REMITTANCES (*Continued*)

Country	Survey year	Region	Poverty headcount (percentage living on US$1/person/day or less)	Poverty gap (percent)	Squared poverty gap (percent)	Gini coefficient	Migration as share of country population	Official remittances (millions of U.S. dollars)	Official remittances as share of country GDP (constant 1995 U.S. dollars)
Venezuela, R. B. de	1993	L. America & the Caribbean	2.66	0.57	0.22	0.416	0.29	0	0
Venezuela, R. B. de	1996	L. America & the Caribbean	14.69	5.62	3.17	0.487	0.36	0	0
Yemen, Republic of	1992	Mid. East & N. Africa	5.07	0.93	NA	0.394	0	1,018	28.49
Yemen, Republic of	1998	Mid. East & N. Africa	10.7	2.42	0.85	0.344	0	1,202	23.77
Zambia	1991	Sub-Saharan Africa	58.59	31.04	20.18	0.483	0	0	0
Zambia	1993	Sub-Saharan Africa	69.16	38.49	25.7	0.462	0	0	0
Zambia	1996	Sub-Saharan Africa	72.63	37.75	23.88	0.497	0	0	0
Zimbabwe	1991	Sub-Saharan Africa	35.95	11.39	4.56	0.568	0	0	0

Sources: All poverty and inequality data are from World Bank, Global Poverty Monitoring database. Migration data from U.S. Population Census and OECD, *Trends in International Migration*. Remittance data from IMF, *Balance of Payments Statistics Yearbook*.

Note: NA = Not available.

Chapter 15
Transnationalism and Development:
Trends and Opportunities in Latin America

Manuel Orozco

Within the framework of globalization, new transnational networks have emerged from the consolidation of migration ties. Migration networks, based on household-to-household relationships, are now contributing significantly to the integration of countries into the global economy. Expressions of that integration include immigrant-based donations, small and large investments, trade, tourism, and unilateral transfers of worker remittances. This chapter addresses those concepts and their relationship to development.

In addition to the sending of remittances, the mobilization of migrant (and their relatives') savings and investments at home (through acquisition of land, property, or small businesses) is spurring economic growth in areas—especially rural areas—traditionally neglected by the private and public sectors. Communication among and between households has generated dramatic revenue flows to businesses in the United States and Latin America, as seen, for example, in the increasing demand for telephone services.

These transnational migration patterns—involving money transfers, tourism, transportation, telecommunications, and nostalgic trade,[1] together known as the "Five Ts"—pose important policy questions about the relationship between transnationalism and development. Those relationships are becoming increasingly relevant for people and development.[2] In practical terms, a typical immigrant's economic link with the home country extends to at least four practices that involve spending or investment: family remittance transfers, demand for services (such as telecommunications, consumer goods, or travel), capital investment, and charitable donations to philanthropic organizations raising funds for the home country's community.

Attention to the positive effects of family remittances on household and national economies is slowly translating into development strategies, such as offering financial services to individuals in transnational households. However, other areas of transnational relationships remain underexplored.

TRANSNATIONAL COMMUNITIES
LINKING HOMES AND COUNTRIES

The number of the world's transnational families—defined as groups that maintain relationships and connections with home and host societies—is growing with continued international migration.[3] These dynamics of migrant cross-border engagements encompass a range of activities including, but not limited to, remittance sending, social networks, economic relationships, cultural practices, and political participation. In turn, the origin and the depth of the transnational ties that migrants maintain with both the sending and receiving communities can determine the creation and success of social groups like hometown associations (HTAs) (Andrade-Eckhoff and Silva-Avalos 2003).

These transnational family relationships have an economic aspect that goes beyond the scope of remittances. The analysis that follows is based on five surveys conducted among remittance senders from 12 different countries of origin in New York; Los Angeles; Chicago; Washington, DC; and Miami. This analysis focuses on assessing the extent of transnational ties using the Five Ts as units of analysis (see the survey methodology at the end of this chapter).

Gauging the extent of transnational ties depends on the type of transnational engagement. For example, Levitt (2004) cites Portes (1999) who argues that possibly only 10 percent or less of U.S. migrants participate in regular transnational economic and political activities.

As the chapter results show, immigrants are more connected. The analysis of the Five Ts shows that 60 percent of immigrants send remittances on a regular basis, that is, 12 times a year; one-third of them travel once a year, 65 percent call home weekly, and 68 percent buy home-country goods.

Transnationalism is relevant with respect to the interplay between microeconomic relationships and macroeconomic ones. Mittelman (2000) explains that the current anatomy of the global political economy is a spatial reorganization of production among the continents of the world, large-scale flows of migration among and within them, complex networks that connect production processes and buyers and sellers, and the emergence of transnational cultural structures that mediate among these processes. He goes on to stress that increased competition among and within continents, mediated by such micropatterns as ethnic and family networks, accelerates cross-flows of migrants. In turn, this cross-flow of migration produces economic effects in the labor-exporting country.

Do these micropatterns affect the home country's economic growth? Can the movement of people become an indicator of economic development? The flow of remittances suggests positive answers. Furthermore, when other characteristics of the Five Ts are included in the analysis, the impact may be greater than previously expected.

Taking one region as an example, countries in Central America and the Caribbean have sought to integrate themselves into the world economy through four dynamics: nontraditional exports, the *maquiladora* phenomenon,[4] immigration, and tourism. As it has diversified in these four areas, Central America has ceased to be an exclusively agro-exporting region or a so-called after-dinner economy—that is, an exporter of coffee, sugar, and rum. Rodas-Martini (2000) stresses this point in the relation between integration into the global economy and integration with the north. This is reflected in terms of "the commercial flows (man-ufactures, agricultural products, and tourism) and the flow of factors of production (illegal migration and foreign investment)" (p. 17).

From a more critical perspective, Robinson (2001) argues that global changes in the form of flexible capital accumulation and the global division of labor have "resulted in an increased heterogeneity of labor markets in each location" (p. 529). In more specific terms, Robinson argues that one form of transnational accumulation is observed based on the entrance of new activities mixed with the model of global accu-mulation. For Robinson, the transnational model in Central America is observed through "production of export-processing factories (of clothes in particular), transnational services (especially tourism), export of non-traditional agricultural products, and remittances sent by Central Americans working in the United States" (p. 539).

In fact, in most countries of the region, almost half of the gross domestic product (GDP) depends on these four factors, which have had a multiplying effect on other areas (see table 15.1). Within the con-text of migration, however, little is known about the effects of the other components of the Five Ts—money transfers, tourism, transportation, telecommunications, and nostalgic trade.

As this analysis will show, Central America's economic interdepen-dence operates in part as a function of migrants who reside abroad and serve as the primary source of tourism for countries such as Honduras, Nicaragua, and El Salvador. Immigrants generate much of the demand for air travel to the region, and their telephone calls to relatives account for the majority of U.S.–Central American telecommunications. They are also the ones who transfer at least US$5 billion annually in remit-tances. There is also trade, or nostalgic commerce, which will grow in importance with liberalization of trade with the United States. These Five Ts become key determinants of transnational engagement.

TABLE 15.1 CENTRAL AMERICA IN THE GLOBAL ECONOMY, 2002
US$ millions

Sector	Guatemala	El Salvador	Honduras	Nicaragua	Costa Rica	Dominican Republic
Remittances	1,775	1,995	735	600	206	2,044
Merchandise exports (not including maquiladora)	2,960	3,287	1,344	582	5,352	719
Maquiladora	373[a]	543	546	102[a]	1,221[a]	1,875
International tourism	606	254	251	157	936	2,609
Gross domestic product	22,476	14,598	6,683	2,498	16,652	21,000

Source: Inter-American Development Bank, country profiles; for data on official develop-ment assistance, World Bank, *Global Development Indicators 2003*; CEPAL 2003.
a. Figures are for 2000 for these countries.

Transportation

One key source of communication among immigrants and their families is the use of air transportation. Relatives in Latin America visit family members in the United States, or immigrants travel home to visit their relatives. The end result is a significant amount of air travel among family members.

From John F. Kennedy International airport alone, annual flights to Santo Domingo carry nearly 140,000 people. Another 95,000 travel from Miami annually. The majority of these travelers are Dominican tourists and business people engaged in the Dominican Republic. The situation is similar in El Salvador. Grupo Taca, an airline carrier that serves Central America, flies 21 times a day from the United States to El Salvador (Orozco 2002b). At least 70 percent of its customers are Central Americans. Air travel to Central America has increased significantly—the demand for flights has spread throughout the United States. Several U.S.-based airlines, including American Airlines, Continental, Delta, and United have established daily operations in Central America.

Thirty percent of remittance-sending immigrants indicate that they travel to their home country at least once a year. Immigrant groups vary with regard to travel, with Ecuadorans, Dominicans, and Guyanese traveling more often than other immigrants (table 15.2). Ecuadorans are among the most frequent travelers to their country, with 12 percent traveling twice a year and almost 40 percent once a year. More than one in 10 Dominicans travel three times a year, two in 10 travel twice, and one in three travels once a year.

The immigrants who have not traveled back to their country tend to have lived in the United States for only a short time. More than 60 percent of those living in the United States fewer than six years have not traveled back to their home country (table 15.3). This finding is consistent with other research showing that recent immigrants tend to send less money home due to lower incomes and the obligations of settling into a new country.

Tourism

Economic connectivity between migrants and their native country has become a regular practice. Tourism in El Salvador and the Dominican Republic is heavily weighted toward nationals living abroad. In the Dominican Republic, for example, more than 500,000 tourists visiting the country are Dominicans living abroad, predominantly in the United States (table 15.4). Most stay 15 days or more and spend around US$65 a day. In the Salvadoran case, well over 40 percent of arrivals in El Salvador are Salvadorans. This community has produced a demand for new goods and services that local and international tourism companies are seeking

TABLE 15.2 FREQUENCY OF IMMIGRANT TRAVEL TO HOME COUNTRY
percent

Country of origin	Three or more times a year	Twice a year	Once a year	Once every two years	Once every three years	Travel little	Never traveled
Ecuador	0	12.2	39.2	35.1	4.1	9.5	0
Dominican Republic	11.6	24.5	33.3	10.9	3.4	16.3	0
Guyana	5.8	12.1	26.7	18.4	10.7	26.2	0
El Salvador	1.5	5.6	20.4	5.6	8.7	23.5	34.7
Mexico	2.5	5.0	20.1	4.6	6.3	14.6	46.9
Colombia	2.0	7.0	13.0	6.0	0	15.0	57.0
Nicaragua	2.0	6.0	11.3	13.3	3.3	12.7	51.3
Cuba	0	2.3	10.9	4.0	1.7	13.1	68.0
Honduras	0	5.5	6.8	12.3	2.7	12.3	60.3
Guatemala	0.9	3.7	4.6	3.7	0.9	15.6	70.6
Weighted average	3.0	8.2	19.1	10.1	5.0	17.0	37.7

Source: Data from author's 2003–4 survey of immigrants in New York; Los Angeles; Washington, DC; Chicago; and Miami; administered by Emmanuel Sylvestre and Associates. Partial results reported in Orozco 2004a; see survey methodology at end of chapter.

TABLE 15.3 FREQUENCY OF TRAVEL TO HOME COUNTRY AND
          YEARS LIVING IN THE UNITED STATES
percent

Frequency	Less than 6 years	7 to 12 years	More than 12 years
Three or more times a year	1.6	2.2	7.7
Twice a year	5.2	8.6	15.0
Once a year	11.9	24.8	25.3
Once every two years	5.6	16.4	9.5
Once every three years	2.4	6.8	8.1
Travel little	11.7	19.8	23.8
Never traveled	61.6	21.2	10.6
Average for all immigrants	46.6	34.5	18.9

Source: Data from author's 2003–4 survey of immigrants in New York, Los Angeles, and Miami, administered by Emmanuel Sylvestre and Associates. Partial results reported in Orozco 2004a.

to supply by offering tour packages, trips, and real estate in coastal regions. A similar pattern is observed in Nicaragua and Honduras. Even the Jamaican economy, which relies heavily on international tourism, reflects a demand for tourist services from Jamaicans living abroad. Although official figures indicate that six percent of Jamaican tourism is from the diaspora (table 15.4), government officials stress that this figure is low because Jamaicans do not report on the immigration forms as Jamaican citizens but as foreign nationals, thus skewing the statistics.

TABLE 15.4   NATIONALS AS A PERCENTAGE OF TOURISTS IN THE
DOMINICAN REPUBLIC, JAMAICA, AND MEXICO

	Nationals	Percentage	Year
Dominican Republic	523,588	15	2003
Jamaica	57,428	6	2004
Mexico	2,203,100	22	1997

Source: Banco Central, Republica Dominicana, http://www.bancentral.gov.do/; Bank of
Jamaica, *Statistical Digest,* October 2004; Banco de Mexico, www.mexico-travel.com.
Note: Jamaican government officials stress that the percentage reported is at least half of
the actual trend: Jamaicans living overseas do not fill out the forms as nonresident
Jamaicans, so statistical records underestimate their actual volume.

Visiting the home country entails more than staying with relatives.
Immigrants who return home to visit are also tourists who spend considerable amounts on entertainment with their families. The visits take
place on various occasions, from Christmas and New Year's, to Easter
and other religious holidays. Other immigrants go on special trips to
their hometowns for weddings, birthdays, deaths, or other emergencies.

Immigrants typically spend at least US$1,000 per stay. Ecuadorans
again are the most notable group, in that they not only travel more
often, but also spend the most. Other Latinos tend to spend similar
amounts, around US$1,000 to US$2,000 (table 15.5).

Guyana offers an interesting example of the extent of economic contacts. Forty percent of Guyanese who send remittances visit the home

TABLE 15.5   HOW MUCH IS SPENT PER TRIP?
percent

	Less than US$1,000 per stay	Less than US$2,000 per stay	Over US$2,000 per stay
Colombia	82.9	17.1	0.0
Cuba	50.0	26.9	23.1
Ecuador	9.6	39.7	50.7
El Salvador	43.6	48.2	8.2
Guatemala	51.6	35.5	12.9
Guyana	45.8	41.1	13.1
Honduras	56.7	33.3	10.0
Mexico	33.9	38.4	27.7
Nicaragua	72.7	21.2	4.5
Dominican Republic	35.8	50.7	13.4
Average	43.9	38.9	17.0

Source: Data from author's 2003–4 survey of immigrants in New York; Los Angeles;
Washington, DC; Chicago; and Miami; administered by Emmanuel Sylvestre and Associates. Partial results reported in Orozco 2004a, see survey methodology at end of chapter.

country at least once a year (see table 15.2). This number represents a potentially lucrative and relatively untapped market. Guyanese immigrants visiting their home country spend on average US$1,000 a stay. This adds up to at least US$25 million left in the country. Thus, these contributions to the economy may be almost as important as remittances, which are estimated at over US$100 million (Orozco 2004a).

Telecommunications

Telecommunications connects migrants living abroad with their home countries. The volume of calls to Central America and the Caribbean increased as connectivity improved, opening opportunities for business expansion and investment in cellular telephony, the Internet, and cable transmission. Companies such as AT&T, Bell South, and Motorola have set up economic infrastructure to facilitate communication between the members of the diaspora and their homelands, benefiting local enterprises.

Home-to-home phone calls may be responsible for most of the revenue generated in international long-distance telecommunications. Central Americans living in the United States maintain significant contact with their home countries—and telephone calls are a major form of transnational family contact. Over 60 percent of Central Americans call at least once a week and spend at least 30 minutes a week on the phone with relatives abroad, totaling 120 minutes a month (tables 15.6 and 15.7).

Immigrant contacts account for a substantial share of telephone companies' revenues on service between the United States and Latin America. Half of the call minutes from the United States to Central America and the Dominican Republic, for example, are household to household (table 15.8).

Trade

Another important feature of contemporary migration is consumption of home-country goods. Migrants have become a new market for exports from their home country. Ethnic imports to the United States—called nostalgic trade and including items such as beer, rum, cheese, and other foodstuffs—are gaining attention among producers in Central America and the Caribbean.

Purchasing nostalgic goods is a way of maintaining cultural traditions from the home country while generating revenue for the home country. In the comparative survey carried out by the author, Latinos were asked whether they buy products from home. The large majority answered positively. Only Cubans offered a low response rate, due to the fact that

TABLE 15.6 FREQUENCY OF INTERNATIONAL
         LONG-DISTANCE TELEPHONE CALLS MADE
         TO HOME-COUNTRY RELATIVES

percent

	Two or more times a week	Once a week	Once every two weeks	Once a month	Seldom call
Colombia	39.0	38.0	16.0	6.0	1.0
Cuba	11.9	35.7	32.1	16.7	3.6
Ecuador	55.0	43.0	2.0	0	0
El Salvador	23.8	34.3	27.6	11.4	2.9
Guatemala	21.1	34.9	26.6	12.8	4.6
Guyana	16.6	25.3	30.4	20.7	6.9
Honduras	23.0	33.8	25.7	10.8	6.8
Mexico	28.3	44.4	14.3	9.0	3.9
Nicaragua	29.1	40.5	20.3	8.1	2.0
Dominican Republic	60.7	16.7	11.3	8.0	3.3
Total (wtd. avg.)	29.1	34.7	21.3	11.2	3.7

Source: Data from author's 2003–4 survey of immigrants in New York; Los Angeles; Washington, DC; Chicago; and Miami; administered by Emmanuel Sylvestre and Associates. Partial results reported in Orozco 2004a; see survey methodology at end of chapter.

TABLE 15.7 AVERAGE DURATION OF INTERNATIONAL
         LONG-DISTANCE TELEPHONE CALLS MADE TO
         HOME-COUNTRY RELATIVES

percent

	Less than 5 minutes	6 to 10 minutes	11 to 20 minutes	20 to 30 minutes	More than 30 minutes
Colombia	2.0	10.0	15.0	32.0	40.0
Cuba	4.6	21.1	39.4	21.1	9.7
Ecuador	0	4.0	45.0	37.0	13.0
El Salvador	0.5	4.3	11.4	22.4	59.0
Guatemala	0	1.8	9.2	18.3	64.2
Guyana	3.4	15.3	39.0	22.0	7.6
Honduras	4.0	14.7	20.0	25.3	29.3
Mexico	2.5	3.2	7.8	29.4	55.7
Nicaragua	0.7	9.3	24.7	36.0	26.0
Dominican Republic	0.7	6.7	13.3	35.3	44.0
Average	2.0	8.9	22.0	27.3	35.7

Source: Data from author's 2003–4 survey of immigrants in New York; Los Angeles; Washington, DC; Chicago; and Miami; administered by Emmanuel Sylvestre and Associates. Partial results reported in Orozco 2004a; see survey methodology at end of chapter.

TABLE 15.8 PHONE CALLS BETWEEN THE UNITED STATES AND SELECTED CENTRAL AMERICAN COUNTRIES

Country	Total minutes (2002)	U.S. revenue (US$)	Payment to country	Household-to-household minutes (2003)
El Salvador	659,528,740	185,825,580	68,190,716	492,510,153
Guatemala	909,056,312	300,132,848	77,585,373	305,441,973
Honduras	338,475,478	108,026,709	77,177,514	169,417,799
Dominican Republic	1,005,737,128	149,761,218	41,348,782	660,806,085

Source: Data from author's 2003–4 survey of immigrants in New York; Los Angeles; Washington, DC; Chicago; and Miami; administered by Emmanuel Sylvestre and Associates. Partial results reported in Orozco 2004a; see survey methodology at end of chapter. United States Census Bureau 2000; *2001, 2002 International Telecommunications Data,* Federal Communications Commission, December 2001, and January 2003.

Note: Computation based on an average of four calls a month at 5, 8, 15, 25, and 30 minutes per call. Formula was sum of phone calls = annual minutes × percent calling × immigrant percent remitting (from 2000 U.S. census).

they travel less and have much less contact with Cuban institutions. The U.S. embargo on Cuba hampers the acquisition of home-country goods. However, more than 70 percent of other Latinos reported that they bought goods from their country of origin (table 15.9).

When asked what products they bought, most immigrants pointed to six core products: rum, cigars, tamales, bread, tea, and cheese, although Guyanese immigrants, for example, identified more than 20 different items imported from Guyana to meet household needs (table 15.10).

TABLE 15.9 DO YOU BUY HOME-COUNTRY PRODUCTS?

percent

	Yes	No
Colombia	81.0	19.0
Cuba	28.6	71.4
Ecuador	95.0	5.0
El Salvador	55.7	44.3
Guatemala	50.5	49.5
Guyana	82.2	15.7
Honduras	74.3	25.7
Mexico	76.2	23.8
Nicaragua	83.3	16.7
Dominican Republic	65.3	34.7
Average	68.4	31.3

Source: Data from author's 2003–4 survey of immigrants in New York; Los Angeles; Washington, DC; Chicago; and Miami; administered by Emmanuel Sylvestre and Associates. Partial results reported in Orozco 2004a; see survey methodology at end of chapter.

TABLE 15.10 TOP SIX HOME-COUNTRY PRODUCTS PURCHASED
BY EMIGRANTS

percent

	Rum	Cigars	Tamales	Bread	Tea	Cheese
Colombia	9.0	13.0	35.0	26.0	24.0	34.0
Cuba	16.0	13.7	3.4	11.4	4.6	7.4
Ecuador	3.0	n.a	3.0	81.0	6.0	26.0
El Salvador	6.2	6.2	22.4	38.6	10.0	34.8
Guatemala	6.4	7.3	23.9	24.8	13.8	29.4
Guyana	41.5	21.2	n.a	n.a	n.a	n.a
Honduras	21.3	21.3	38.7	30.7	17.3	48.0
Mexico	10.6	9.9	37.9	41.1	13.8	48.2
Nicaragua	12.7	7.3	28.0	28.7	14.0	60.7
Dominican Republic	36.0	4.7	2.7	14.7	3.3	32.0
Average	17.5	10.7	18.8	27.7	9.6	30.8

Source: Data from author's 2003–4 survey of immigrants in New York; Los Angeles; Washington, DC; Chicago; and Miami; administered by Emmanuel Sylvestre and Associates. Partial results reported in Orozco 2004a; see survey methodology at end of chapter.
Note: n.a. = Not applicable.

The magnitude of these dynamics has macroeconomic effects. According to the Ministry of Economy of El Salvador (Batres-Marquez, Jensen, and Brester 2001) and CEPAL (2003), these products are estimated to represent at least 10 percent of total exports from El Salvador to the United States, or US$450 million. Salvadoran foods such as tortilla flour, red beans, *loroco, semita,* cheese, and *horchata* are important exports (Batres-Marquez, Jensen, and Brester 2001). The Batres-Marquez study and other experiences encouraged the government to seek to bring these items into the trading agenda during negotiations on the proposed Central American Free Trade Agreement (CAFTA). In fact, El Salvador was the only government with an agenda explicitly including its ethnic market. For example, exports to the United States of El Salvadoran beer ballooned from US$1 million to US$3.5 million between 1999 and October 2001 (United States Trade Representative 2002). Many home-country producers have established businesses in the United States to cater to the migrant community.

Guyanese-Americans have a demand for goods such as rum, fish, and tea—and profits from such products represent an important share of total exports. Imports of spices, for example, which more than 60 percent of immigrants reported buying from Guyana, have grown substantially in the past five years, from less than US$1,000 to US$35,000 (Orozco 2004a).

Healthy demand for nostalgic goods has induced migrants to invest in home-country manufactures of foodstuffs such as cheese, fruits, and vegetables. Migrants residing in the United States have set up businesses back in their home countries to establish stores of various kinds. An example is Roos Foods, Inc., a food manufacturer that produces and sells processed milk products in Central America and to Central Americans and Mexicans living in the United States. Roos operates in the United States but with franchises in Nicaragua and El Salvador. This trend of migrant investment in home countries is likely to continue.

TRANSFER OF REMITTANCES AND HOMETOWN ASSOCIATION DONATIONS

Remittances also constitute an important source of economic activity. Latin ethnic stores still account for as much as 60 percent of the money transfer business to Latin America, but competition has become significant. The money transferred to Latin America (which as of 2004 was US$45 billion) has had multiplier effects, generating profits and wealth.

According to a survey carried out by the Inter-American Development Bank, 60 percent of immigrants send remittances every month and 70 percent at least eight times a year (MIF-IADB, 2004). Immigrants sending remittances are the key players in transnationalism. With incomes below U.S. averages—US$21,000 a year on average, with 25 percent living below the U.S. poverty level (table 15.11)—they send at least US$2,500 annually as part of their commitment to relatives. Although figures vary from country to country and from year to year, the overall trend is that they remit at least US$200 a month, or 15 percent of their income (table 15.12). Their low income relates to their low educational attainment and the types of jobs they hold. According to the U.S. Census Bureau (2000), 62 percent of Central Americans and Mexicans do not have a high school diploma, and only 5 percent have a bachelor's degree or higher.

As a result of family remittances, a growing financial stream flows from low-income individuals to Latin America. This flow is spreading dramatically in both size and scope. Countries in Latin America and the Caribbean receive nearly one-third of global remittances, the highest

TABLE 15.11 HOUSEHOLD INCOME BY RACE
percent; US$

	Household income		
Group	Less than $20,000	$20,001 to $35,000	More than $35,000
Hispanic/Latino	31	25	44
Non-Hispanic White	21	18	60

Source: U.S. Census Bureau 2000. http://www.census.gov/population/socdemo/hispanic/ppl-171/tab12-1.xls.

TABLE 15.12 AVERAGE MONTHLY AMOUNT REMITTED BY LATIN AMERICANS IN THE UNITED STATES

US$

Country	2002	2003	2004
Argentina	198	226	212
Bolivia	276	244	235
Brazil	376	300	541
Chile	303	288	279
Colombia	256	267	220
Costa Rica	350	348	301
Dominican Republic	199	186	176
Ecuador	295	303	293
El Salvador	287	394	339
Guatemala	269	271	363
Guyana	n.a.	n.a.	179
Haiti	162	161	123
Honduras	257	246	225
Jamaica	263	262	209
Mexico	378	369	351
Nicaragua	146	149	133
Panama	222	208	196
Paraguay	304	281	263
Peru	191	173	169
Uruguay	n.a.	203	198
Venezuela, R. B. de	228	161	138

Sources: National Money Transmitters Association 2005; data provided to the author.
Note: n.a. = Not available.

share of all world regions. Remittances are more than quadruple the total of official development assistance to the region (tables 15.13 and 15.14).

Although important for Latin America as a whole, remittances are most significant for the small and poor countries of Central America and the Caribbean.

Some of the major changes in remittance flows involve the range and number of countries sending and receiving remittances, the intensity of flows, and the scope of economic links between the home and host countries.

A greater number of countries are receiving money from their migrant diasporas. The magnitude of these changes is observed in the increased flow into South America. For example, in 2002 Mexico accounted for a third of all remittances to the region, down from 50 percent just four years before. The significance of these flows is also reflected in the increasing volumes relative to the immigrant population from each country and region. Many traditional recipient countries are seeing substantial increases in overall amounts. It seems clear that remittances are becoming part of a broader process of economic interchange.

TABLE 15.13 REMITTANCES, INVESTMENT, AND FOREIGN AID IN
LATIN AMERICA, 1996 AND 2001

US$ thousand

	1996			2001		
	Remittances	FDI	ODA	Remittances	FDI	ODA
Mexico	4,224	9,186	287	8,896	24,731	75
Central America	1,819	1,102	1,827	3,567	2,018	2,095
Caribbean	2,359	733	744	4,526	2,706	478
South America	1,716	9,266	809	4,021	8,170	1,047
Total	10,118	20,287	3,667	21,010	37,625	3,695

Source: Remittances, central bank of each country; foreign investment and aid, World Bank, *Global Development Indicators,* 1996, 2001.
Note: FDI = Foreign direct investment. ODA = Official development assistance. ODA here excludes loans from the World Bank or IMF.

TABLE 15.14 FOREIGN-BORN LATINOS IN THE UNITED STATES
AND REMITTANCES TO LATIN AMERICA, 2000

Region	Population in United States	Percent of Latino immigrants	Remittances (millions of U.S. dollars)	Percent
Mexico	9,177,487	57	10,502	33
Caribbean	2,953,066	18	5,749	18
Central America	2,026,150	13	5,555	17
South America	1,930,271	12	10,202	32
Latin America	16,086,974	100	32,000	100

Source: United States Census Bureau 2000; Inter-American Development Bank estimates.

Argentina, Colombia, and República Bolivariana de Venezuela all have registered increased inflows of remittances. Economic and political crises in these countries have prompted their nationals to migrate in search of stability and a better quality of life. The case of Colombia is illustrative of a growing trend in which the flow of remittances has surpassed all major sources of export revenue, including oil. Remittances to Colombia grew from US$0.5 billion in 1995 to more than US$3 billion in 2002. Similarly, thousands of Venezuelans have migrated in the past five years, since 2000. The economic crisis in Argentina spurred a massive emigration to Europe (Spain and Italy) and the United States, dramatically increasing remittance flows. Although the Central Bank of Argentina has not been able to quantify the magnitude of the flows with any precision, at least US$200 million is entering the country from the United States. One money transfer company alone probably remits about US$130 million from the United States to Argentina.

Despite economic and political difficulties in the host countries, the flows continue to grow significantly. Continued recession and tightened immigration laws in the United States have not reduced flows to the main recipient countries. Flows have not followed cyclical economic dynamics in either the sending or receiving economies.

Intensity: Deepening Flows in Guatemala and Peru

Remittance flows are also growing in intensity—in Guatemala and Peru as elsewhere. Guatemala experienced a major increase—from US$600 million in 2001 to US$2.1 billion in 2003. In Peru, remittance flows grew from US$700 million to US$1.1 billion in that same period. Improved statistical tracking accounts for a large part of this growth, but the increase is also reflected in the fierce competition for new customers and niches in the money transfer business.

In a series of projections done for the Pew Hispanic Center, Lowell stressed that because transfer costs will continue to decline in an increasingly competitive market, it is more likely that per capita remittances will continue to grow. Both the medium and high projections assume that the market will "shake out" in the next five years, after which the level of per capita remittances reached will remain fixed into the future. The author concluded that a most preferred projection is one that will show an annual increase in remittances of more than 8 percent (Lowell 2002).

The Lowell projections were looking at transfers to Mexico and Central America, but if the emerging flow of emigrants from South America and the increases reported in some countries are added to the equation, the growth potential for the hemisphere will be greater than what Lowell predicted.

Money transfers, telecommunications, tourism, trade, and transportation—all five sectors have experienced new business opportunities and opportunities for trade and investment due to migration.

Hometown Associations

The trend of remittances and other relationships is also accompanied by various forms of collective organization that translate into the formation of hometown associations, or HTAs. HTAs, organizations of immigrants that raise funds for the betterment of their places of origin, are growing in importance in Latin America and the Caribbean due to the sheer size of the support to their communities (Orozco 2004b). They illustrate an example of the relationship between transnationalism and development. This relationship is complex, reflecting a combination of initiatives and motivations: cultural, economic, political, and social.

One key aspect of these organizations is their ability to promote equity, an important component of the development philosophy. These migrant associations seek to promote small social changes with a concern for the community, particularly toward vulnerable sectors, such as children and the elderly. Thus, although primarily philanthropic in nature, HTA work sometimes overlaps with economic development activities, and in this way represents an important link between countries of origin and emigrants. It addresses the need for economic aid in migrants' home countries, strengthens cultural ties, and improves the quality of life for home communities.

In the United States, there are thousands of Latin American and Caribbean HTAs. According to the Mexican consulates, there are over 700 registered Mexican clubs (although government officials in Mexico and Latino community leaders estimate a much higher and increasing number). Figure 15.1 shows the increase in Mexican HTAs based in Chicago alone since 1994.

However, HTAs are not just a Mexican phenomenon. Most Latin American immigrants are organized into HTAs with the purpose of helping their communities. Salvadoran HTAs, for example, have grown in numbers since the 1990s; in Washington, DC, Salvadorans from eastern El Salvador are organized in more than 20 groups to raise money for assistance in areas like San Miguel province. The Comunidad Unida de Chinameca, created in 1991, is a typical Salvadoran HTA: it began its activities in the city of Chinameca by constructing the school's water tower and 12 restrooms; and from there it went on to construct a laundry facility and recreational park for the town, and painted and built a

FIGURE 15.1 GROWTH OF MEXICAN CLUBS (HTAS) IN CHICAGO

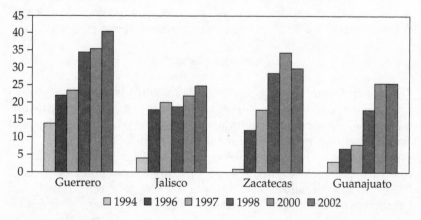

Source: Orozco 2003.

roof for the local church. The Comunidad raises some US$30,000 annu-
ally, mostly through fundraising events. After the 2001 earthquake in El
Salvador, the Comunidad received donations of construction material
from the French Embassy to build a wall for the Red Cross, and the
town participated by donating labor (Orozco 2004c).

Guyanese HTAs focus on projects similar to those in Central America
and Mexico. These associations are based in Canada and the United
States—New York in particular—and have long-standing organiza-
tional bases. Guyana Watch, founded in 1992 and based in Queens, New
York, conducts an annual medical outreach clinic in Guyana, whereby a
group of 20 to 25 doctors and nurses travel to three different cities in
Guyana (Essequibo, Demerara, and Berbice) and work at a clinic for one
day, attending to between 2,500 and 3,000 people (Orozco 2004a).

Whereas remittances are received by at least one-quarter of the
households in a Mexican home town, HTAs can become important to
improving the quality of life of all households. They can facilitate
projects that would otherwise be impossible for the receiving communities to implement. The contributions are even more striking
when compared to the municipal public works budgets. In towns
with fewer than 3,000 people, HTA donations are equal to over 50
percent of the municipal public works budget. For localities with
populations under 1,000, the HTA donations can amount to up to
seven times the public works budget (see table 15.15). Thus, HTAs
accomplish projects that would otherwise be impossible for these
communities to implement.

Although HTA impact is significant when it happens, it is interesting
to note that unlike the other components of the Five Ts, the number of
people who are members of these kinds of associations is relatively
small compared to the total immigrant population. Table 15.16 shows

TABLE 15.15 MEXICO: BUDGET ALLOCATION, HTA DONATIONS,
AND POPULATION

Population range	Average HTA donation (US$)	Average ratio of HTA donation to public works budget	Average population of community
Under 999	8,648	7.1	407
1,000 to 2,999	11,999	0.5	1,686
3,000 to 4,999	8,397	0.1	4,014
5,000 to 9,999	9,602	0.1	7,328
10,000 to 14,999	11,072	0.0	12,405
Over 15,000	14,589	0.0	57,248
Total Average	9,864	3.5	5,283

Source: Orozco 2003.

TABLE 15.16 REMITTANCE SENDERS WHO BELONG TO AN HTA

Country of origin	Remitters who belong to an HTA (percent)
Colombia	5.6
Ecuador	10.0
El Salvador	1.5
Guatemala	2.8
Guyana	26.3
Honduras	6.7
Mexico	2.1
Nicaragua	4.0
Dominican Republic	3.3
Bolivia	1.4
Mean	5.5

Source: Data from author's 2003–4 survey of immigrants in New York; Los Angeles; Washington, DC; Chicago; and Miami; administered by Emmanuel Sylvestre and Associates. Partial results reported in Orozco 2004a; see survey methodology at end of chapter.

that the percentage of people belonging to HTAs is relatively small, amounting to about 5 percent of total remitters.

POLICY OPTIONS FOR DONORS AND GOVERNMENTS IN LINKING MIGRATION AND DEVELOPMENT

The trends and patterns observed with regard to the ties immigrants have with their home countries show that the relationship is significant. The implications for businesses and the policy environment are also important. Nine policy options are summarized below that relate to reducing transactions costs, leveraging the capital potential of remittances through banking and financing, promoting tourism and nostalgic trade, and establishing a state policy that recognizes the country's diaspora.

Cost reduction. Remittances are an important source of income in Latin America, representing between 3 percent and 20 percent of national incomes. Fees and commissions for sending money are expensive, a concern to development agencies, immigrants, and other interested parties. Technology already exists through which money transfers can (and do) cost next to nothing for savvy senders and recipients—but how can these advantages be extended to immigrants and their relatives? Possible options to reduce costs include the formation of strategic alliances between money transfer companies and banks and between banks in Latin America and in North America (for example, using debit card technologies that rely on automated teller machines); the use of software platforms designed for money transfers; and transfers from credit union to credit union (see chapter 8).

Enabling policy and regulatory environments. Expanding sending methods, increasing competition, and educating customers about charges all help reduce costs associated with money transfers. In Latin America, money transfers need to be facilitated. A comprehensive effort to support senders and recipients should foster an environment in which remittances are less costly and can also have developmental leverage. This includes detecting unfair business practices.

Banking the unbanked. Only 60 percent of Latin American immigrants in the United States use, or consider themselves to have meaningful access to, bank accounts. Moreover, in Mexico and Central America, fewer than 20 percent of people have access to a bank account. The effects of being unbanked are significant. The unbanked not only face higher costs and other difficulties on a daily basis, they also lack the ability to establish credit records and obtain other benefits from financial institutions. Helping senders and recipients to participate in the banking industry would help ensure lower transfer fees. Governments and private institutions already engaged in that effort could devise a strategy linking remittance transfers with banking options as a way to attract migrants into the financial system.

Investment and microenterprise incentives. Studies have shown that, on average, between 5 percent and 10 percent of remittances are saved or invested. Some people are in a position to use their money for an enterprising activity. Both private sector and development players can insert themselves as credit partners for these potential investors. The effect is the provision of remittance-backed credit in local communities that lack active credit markets and production networks. Tying remittances to micro-lending has great potential to enhance local markets.

Tourism. Currently, a significant percentage of immigrants visit their home country as tourists, yet there is no tourist policy aimed at members of the diaspora. That void reflects government neglect and a lost opportunity. Governments and the private sector can participate in joint ventures to offer their migrants tour packages to discover and rediscover their home countries. They can also work out investment alliances with migrants interested in partnering to establish joint ventures relating to tourism.

Reaching out to the diaspora. An outreach policy to the community residing abroad is key to any migrant-sending country's economic strategy. Currently no such policy is in place in most countries, and governments could gain significantly from such an approach.

Nostalgic trade. Significant demand exists for so-called nostalgic goods, and many of the small businesses created by migrants rely on the importation of such goods. Governments, development agencies, and the private sector, particularly artisans' businesses, find a natural opportunity to enhance their productive and marketing skills by locating their products with small ethnic businesses in North America, where strong demand exists.

Hometown associations as agents of development. The philanthropic activities of HTAs have proven development potential. Some of the infrastructural and economic development work performed by these associations provides momentum for development agents to partner in local development. Governments in Central America and the Caribbean could work with international organizations and HTAs to design income-generation schemes for their local communities.

Remittances and new technologies. A key partnership opportunity among development players and the private sector lies in tying technology to remittance transfers, including through microfinance institutions. One emerging technology, Wi-Fi (wireless fidelity), allows rural residents to place telephone calls through low-cost wireless Internet telephony, using low-cost computer servers and terminals. Wi-Fi–enabled computers send and receive data securely, reliably, and quickly, through radio technology—indoors and out, anywhere within the range of a base station. A Wi-Fi network can be used to connect computers to each other, to the Internet, and to wired networks. The technology has strong potential to be used by microfinance institutions to manage money transfers. Linking Wi-Fi technology to remittances and microfinance institutions offers an advantage to local businesses and, more important, opens financial windows for new markets. Remittance-receiving households have a demand for savings and credit, and internationally connected microfinance institutions could provide the necessary service to that sector.

TRANSNATIONALISM AND DEVELOPMENT IN PERSPECTIVE

Economic development is a complex process that involves integrating a range of actors and institutions to implement sound long-term strategies. The process may involve integrating new players and accommodating changing realities. The complex nature of development and the ability to adapt policies to variations over time, and to focus on country-specific realities are critical issues in the field of social change and within the current context of a globalized world.

This complex reality takes on critical importance in Latin America and the Caribbean, where the shifting dynamic of transnational migration affects the economies of this region. Migration in Latin America to the United States, Canada, Europe, Japan, and other areas of the world is largely a consequence of the failures of development but also of the impact of globalization (Orozco 2002). The prevailing trend of inequality—a pervasive historical reality—has provoked large emigrant populations. However, the economic activities that

TABLE 15.17 DIMENSIONS OF TRANSNATIONAL ENGAGEMENT

	Percentage of migrants who remit	*Percentage of remitters engaged with home country*
Send remittances	60	100
Travel once a year or more		32
Spend more than US$1,000 each visit		57
Call home once a month or more		65
Buy home country goods		68
Belong to an HTA		6
Have a bank account in home country		24
Have financial obligations		10
Support family with other finances		21

Source: Data from author's 2003–4 survey of immigrants in New York; Los Angeles; Washington, DC; Chicago; and Miami; administered by Emmanuel Sylvestre and Associates. Partial results reported in Orozco 2004a; see survey methodology at end of chapter.

immigrants engage in with their home countries reposition their roles in more concrete ways, while simultaneously helping their home country economies stay afloat.

As this chapter has shown, there is a significant level of engagement between remittance senders and their homelands (see table 15.17). The chapter focused predominantly on the extent of transnational ties between senders and recipients; it did not analyze those immigrants who do not send remittances and yet do maintain other kinds of contacts. This group includes many community leaders and members of HTAs who, in lieu of sending money to their families, seek to help their hometowns and raise funds for that effort.

Given the reality of transnationalism and the policy opportunities laid out in the previous section, increased dialogue and engagement among migrants, governments, the private sector, civil society, and the international community are imperative. Just as the economic contributions of migrants to their home countries are significant, their participation in the policy debate should make them development stakeholders with voice and authority.

About the Survey

Surveys were conducted of remittance senders from 12 countries in Latin America living in New York; Los Angeles; Miami; Washington, DC; and Chicago. These individuals were approached at remittance outlet stores, from which people typically send their remittances. A total of 2,800 men and women remittance senders were interviewed. The procedure was random and the survey was administered during the months of May and July 2003, and February to April 2004. Participation was voluntary.

The demographic distribution was chosen using statistical data from money transfer businesses that provided company information about main locales where people send or receive remittances. This methodology has proven more effective than other random surveys because it captures only the remittance sender groups. In that sense, one obtains a better universe for analysis. The data is part of a project on transnational communities funded by the Rockefeller Foundation.

NOTES

1. Nostalgic trade is the import and export of goods by and for migrants with their countries of origin, such as traditional spices, handicrafts, and clothing.

2. Development economics has long considered foreign savings key to increasing a country's capital-output ratio. Within that context, four factors have been considered: foreign direct investment, official development assistance, foreign trade, and the transfer of technology. Remittances are also foreign savings of significant magnitude.

3. There are a range of definitions of transnationalism, for example, "groupings of migrants who participate on a routine basis in a field of relationships, practices and norms that include both places of origin and destination" (Lozano 1999). The trend of ties is spreading everywhere north-south, as well as south-south with significant regional migration patterns.

4. Establishing offshore plants (in Mexico, for example) that carry out part or all phases of an industrial process for the parent company (perhaps located in the United States). This phenomenon often reduces the costs of production-costs of labor, energy, water, and raw materials.

REFERENCES

Andrade-Eckhoff, Katharine, and C. Marina Silva-Avalos. 2003. "Globalization of the Periphery: The Challenges of Transnational Migration for Local Development in Central America." Working Document, FLACSO, El Salvador.

Batres-Marquez, S. Patricia, Helen H. Jensen, and Gary W. Brester. 2001. "Salvadoran Consumption of Ethnic Foods in the United States." Working Paper 289, Center for Agricultural and Rural Development, Iowa State University.

CEPAL (Comisión Económica para América Latina y el Caribe). 2003. "Pequeñas Empresas, Productos Etnicos y de Nostalgia: Oportunidades en el Mercado Internacional: Los casos de El Salvador y México." Mexico: CEPAL.

Federal Communications Commission (FCC). International Telecommunications Data (1996–2002). Washington, DC. www.fcc.gov/wcb/iatd/stats.

Levitt, Peggy. 2004. "Transnational Migrants: When 'Home' Means More Than

One Country." Migration Policy Institute, Washington, DC. http://www.migrationinformation.org/Feature/display.cfm?id=261

Lowell B. Lindsay. 2002. "Remittance Projections: Mexico and Central America, 2002–2030." In *Billions in Motion: Latino Immigrants, Remittances and Banking.* Washington, DC: Pew Hispanic Center.

Lozano-Ascencio, F., and B. Roberts. 1999. "Transnational Migrant Communities and Mexican Migration to the U.S." *Ethnic and Racial Studies* 2 (2): 238–69.

Mittelman, James H. 2000. *The Globalization Syndrome: Transformation and Resistance.* Princeton: Princeton University Press.

MIF-IADB. 2004. "Survey of Latino Remittances from the United States to Latin America by U.S. State." Washington, DC: MIF-IADB. Survey results released by the MIF-IADB in May.

Orozco, Manuel. 2002a. "Globalization and Migration." *Latin American Politics and Society* 44(2): 41–66.

———. 2002b. *Attracting Remittances: Practices to Reduce Costs and Enable a Money Transfer Environment.* Washington, DC: Multilateral Investment Fund of the Inter-American Development Bank.

———. 2003. "Hometown Associations and their Present and Future Partnerships: New Development Opportunities?" Inter-American Dialogue, Washington, DC.

———. 2004a. "Distant but Close: Guyanese Transnational Communities and Their Remittances from the United States," Inter-American Dialogue, Report commissioned by the U.S. Agency for International Development, Washington, DC.

———. 2004b. "Mexican Hometown Associations and Development Opportunities." *Journal of International Affairs* 57(2): 31–52

———. 2004c. "The Salvadoran Diaspora: Remittances, Transnationalism and Government Responses." Paper commissioned by the Tomas Rivera Policy Institute, Washington, DC.

Portes, Alejandro, William Haller, and Luis Guarnizo. 2002. "Transnational Entrepreneurs: The Emergence and Determinants of an Alternative Form of Immigrant Economic Adaptation." *American Sociological Review* 67 (2): 278–98.

Robinson, William I. 2001. "Transnational Processes, Development Studies and Changing Social Hierarchies in the World System: A Central American Case Study." *Third World Quarterly* 22(4): 529–563.

Rodas-Martini, P. 2000. "Centroamérica: Una Estrategia para Insertarse con Exito en la Economía Mundial en el siglo XXI." In *Central America 2020.* Florida: FIU.

United States Census Bureau. 2000. "United States Census 2000." Washington DC: United States Census Bureau.

United States Trade Representative (USTR). 2002. "2002 Trade and Policy Agenda and 2001 Annual Report." Washington DC: USTR.

World Bank. various years. *Global Development Indicators.* Washington, DC: World Bank.

Chapter 16
Remittances: The New Development Mantra?

Devesh Kapur

A s the existence of this book confirms, workers' remittances are generating considerable excitement in financial circles and among practitioners of economic development. After exploring the reasons for that excitement, this chapter subjects it to critical scrutiny, drawing attention to some conclusions that may prove simplistic or overoptimistic, particularly in view of the poor quality of available data on remittances.

FINANCIAL REMITTANCES:
SIZE, SOURCES, AND DESTINATIONS

Five features of the remittance picture merit special attention.

Significant Source of Financing for Developing Countries

Remittances are an increasingly significant source of external financing for developing countries.[1] In the decade to 2004, remittances have emerged as the second largest source of net financial flows to developing countries. Their growth is in contrast to net official flows (aid plus debt), which have stagnated if not declined. The total volume of remittances to developing countries in 2001 was US$72.3 billion, nearly one-and-a-half times net official development assistance (ODA) in that year of US$57.5 billion (table 16.1). Once one examines the figures for net transfers—the bottom line after deducting profit repatriation, interest

TABLE 16.1 NET FLOWS OF EXTERNAL FINANCE TO DEVELOPING COUNTRIES, 2001

| US$ billion | | | | | Remittances to net flows |
Region	Private flows	Official flows	Remittances	Total net flows	(percent)
East Asia and Pacific	36.4	5.7	10.4	52.5	20
Europe and Central Asia	30.9	10.2	8.9	50.0	18
Latin America and the Caribbean	62.8	23.4	22.6	108.8	21
Middle East and North Africa	8.3	2.0	13.1	23.4	56
South Asia	2.9	6.0	14.9	23.8	63
Sub-Saharan Africa	11.6	10.2	2.4	24.2	10
Total	152.9	57.5	72.3	282.7	26

Source: World Bank, *Global Development Finance 2003.*
Note: Official flows include lending from multilateral banks, the IMF, and bilateral loans and grants. Private flows include equity (foreign direct investment and portfolio investments), and both long- and short-term debt.

payments, and remittance outflows (most developing countries have some outflows as well)—the true significance of remittances for developing countries is much more apparent: remittance flows then are 10 times net transfers from private sources and double those from official sources in 2001 (table 16.2). While this reflects in part the large stock resulting from flows of private and official finance in previous years, it is precisely the "unrequited" nature of remittances that makes this big difference—all other sources have a corresponding claim on the receiving country, and this claim can be substantial.

The welfare and growth effects from these different sources are in all likelihood quite different. However, if one is interested in the financial bottom line, remittances were clearly the most important source of net foreign exchange flows to developing countries in 2001. For reasons discussed in the next section, the growing importance of remittances relative to other sources of external finance is likely to continue. Aid levels declined in the 1990s, and a more-than-modest upturn is unlikely, despite assurances from donor governments. Private capital flows are unlikely to reach the euphoric pre–Asian-crisis levels anytime soon.

Which countries contribute most to remittance outflows and which are the principal recipients? The 10 largest sources and recipients in the last decade include both developed and developing countries (table 16.3). The United States, unsurprisingly, is the largest source, and four countries in the Middle East (Saudi Arabia, Israel, Kuwait, and Oman)

TABLE 16.2 NET TRANSFERS OF EXTERNAL FINANCE TO
DEVELOPING COUNTRIES, 2001

US$ billion Region	Private transfers	Official flows	Remittances	Total net flows	Remittances to net flows (percent)
East Asia and Pacific	−9.1	−2.7	10.3	−1.5	695
Europe and Central Asia	10.9	3.0	6.7	20.6	33
Latin America and the Caribbean	5.8	14.6	20.9	41.3	51
Middle East and North Africa	−5.4	−1.6	−3.6	−10.6	34
South Asia	−0.5	3.6	14.8	17.9	83
Sub-Saharan Africa	3.5	8.6	1.3	13.4	9
Total	5.2	25.5	50.4	81.1	62

Source: World Bank, *Global Development Finance 2003.*
Note: Official transfers include lending from multilateral banks, the IMF, and bilateral loans and grants. Private transfers include equity (foreign direct investment and portfolio flows), and both long- and short-term debt flows.

TABLE 16.3 LARGEST SOURCES AND RECIPIENTS OF REMITTANCES,
ANNUAL AVERAGE, 1992–2001

US$ billion

Source country	Amount	Recipient country	Amount
United States	20.7	India	7.7
Saudi Arabia	15.4	France	6.9
Germany	8.8	Mexico	5.7
Switzerland	8.1	Philippines	5.0
France	4.9	Germany	4.1
Italy	2.2	Portugal	3.8
Israel	2.1	Egypt, Arab Rep. of	3.8
Belgium/Luxembourg	1.8	Turkey	3.7
Kuwait	1.4	Spain	3.0
Oman	1.4	Greece	2.7

Source: IMF, *Balance of Payments Statistics Yearbook,* various years.

are among the 10 largest. Three G-7 members (Canada, Japan, and the United Kingdom) do not make this list, while several smaller countries (Belgium/Luxembourg and Switzerland) do.[2]

The general impression is that remittances are a phenomenon affecting poor countries, but that is only partly true. Of the 10 largest recipients of remittances in the 1992–2001 period, seven were Organisation for Economic Co-operation and Development (OECD) countries and two of the top five were G-5 countries (France and Germany). Of the US$111 billion in total remittances in 2002, about three-fourths (or US$80 billion) accrued to developing countries. The share received by developing countries has ranged from less than half in the late 1980s to about three-fourths in 2000. Might those fluctuations reflect poor data? (See box 16.1.) The largest 10 recipients have been quite stable over the decade, except that Morocco has replaced Greece in recent years.

Remittances are less concentrated than other private flows. Whereas the top 10 recipients of foreign direct investment (FDI) had a 70 percent share of FDI flows to developing countries in 2001, the share of the top 10 recipients of remittances was 59 percent.

Destination of International Remittances

The bulk of international remittances do not accrue to the poorest countries. Nearly half of all remittances received by developing countries are received in lower-middle-income countries, while the other half flows about equally to upper-middle-income and low-income countries (figure 16.1).

BOX 16.1 THE LIMITATIONS OF REMITTANCE DATA:
A SERIOUS CAVEAT

Considering their volume and relative importance, the quality of data on remittances is quite poor. The most striking feature of a basic table of remittance inflows and outflows by country and year is the number of zeros—usually an indication of missing or unreported data. Even considering only those countries with a population greater than 1 million (the absolute volume of remittances is likely to be modest for smaller countries), the lack of data is unusually severe, even today (see table). The data used in this chapter should be interpreted keeping in mind severe limitations with regard to their quality.

REMITTANCE FLOWS: PERCENTAGE OF CELLS FOR WHICH
NO DATA IS AVAILABLE

Year	1970–79	1980–89	1990–99	2000–1
Inflows	77	53	39	34
Outflows	77	52	43	45

Source: World Bank, *Global Development Finance 2003.*
Note: A cell is a country-year data point.

The International Monetary Fund's (IMF's) balance-of-payments (BOP) data—which it gets from member countries—has many gaps in the matter of remittances. The most troubling are in precisely those countries (Afghanistan, Haiti, and Liberia) where economic collapse makes remittances a critical source for household consumption and social insurance. Even countries like Cuba and Vietnam show zero remittance inflows, while Hong Kong (China), Singapore, and Canada show zero or very little outflow, despite the large diasporas of the former and large numbers of migrant workers in the latter. Most receiving countries have incomplete data for several years over the last two decades, making it difficult to do rigorous analysis. Different countries use different techniques to capture remittances, and it is unclear how comparable the reported data are.

The reasons for the differences in data quality are not too difficult to understand. The institutional channels through which financial capital flows from North to South have a strong interest in maintaining good data. Creditors are relatively few in number and have both greater capabilities as well as greater power to ensure that data mandates are adhered to. Moreover, poor data on international financial flows has been implicated in numerous financial crises—among them the Latin American debt crisis and the various other financial crises of the 1990s. Because such systemic crises have repercussions for global financial stability, mainly in the

(Continues)

Box 16.1 THE LIMITATIONS OF REMITTANCE DATA: A
SERIOUS CAVEAT *(Continued)*

industrial countries, each has resulted in an improvement in data quality. By contrast, the individual sources of remittances are numerous, and the recipient countries—mostly developing countries—lack the capabilities and perhaps even the incentives to ensure better data.

The very definition of remittances creates problems. The narrowest definition of remittances—unrequited transfers—refers narrowly to money sent by migrants to family and friends on which there are no claims by the sender, unlike other financial flows such as debt or equity flows. The data in this chapter include two additional categories that are recorded separately in a country's balance-of-payments statistics: "migrant transfers," which arise from the migration (defined as change of residence for at least a year) of individuals from one economy to another and are equal to the net worth of the migrants; and "compensation of employees," funds sent back by temporary workers (who work abroad for less than a year). The World Bank recently adopted this practice as well. See *Global Development Finance 2003*, annex to chapter 7 (World Bank 2003).

FIGURE 16.1 REMITTANCE INFLOWS TO DEVELOPING COUNTRIES

US$ billion

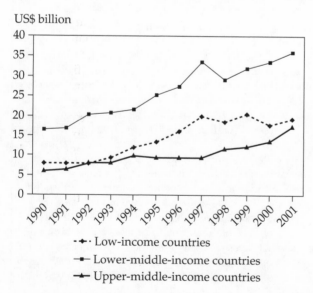

- -◆-· Low-income countries
- -■- Lower-middle-income countries
- -▲- Upper-middle-income countries

Source: World Bank, *Global Development Finance*, various years.

Remittances benefit some regions more than others. Latin America (particularly the Andean countries, Central America, and Mexico), South Asia, the Middle East and North Africa, and some parts of East Asia (especially the Philippines and Indonesia) are disproportionate beneficiaries. The fact that Sub-Saharan Africa receives the smallest amount of reported remittances and (unlike trends in other regions) has shown virtually no growth in remittances in the period 1998–2003 is a sobering indication that this source of finance is unlikely to change the external financing problems of the region.

The limited remittance inflows to Africa reconfirm that geography does matter. Migrations from African countries are large, but civil strife in the region sends migrants across borders to other impoverished African countries rather than to rich countries. Geographical contiguity to rich countries (clearly important, especially for illegal migration) privileges Mexico, Central America, and the Maghreb. The lack of geographical proximity is less of a hindrance to nationals of Latin American countries who enjoy access to European labor markets because of prior migrations to Latin America from Europe. With the Middle East likely to suffer increasing curbs on net migration, South Asia, which receives a large volume of remittances from that region, will witness a decline unless migration to other regions rises.

The two countries with the largest global migrations, China and India, report substantial differences in remittances. Surprisingly, China receives comparatively little—about US$1 billion annually in the period 1992–2001, about one-eighth of India's receipts (US$7.7 billion annually over the same period). These large differences are probably less the result of fundamental differences in the characteristics, size, or vintage of migrations from the two countries, than of differences in incentives (especially tax policies) and economic opportunities in the two countries. In contrast to the remittance figures, the figures for FDI from overseas nationals of the two countries are the reverse, with overseas Chinese investing 10 to 20 times more than overseas Indians (the figures vary considerably depending on the status of investments from Hong Kong, China, and assumptions regarding the magnitude of so-called round-tripping (domestic funds outflows that are legally or illegally brought back to the country). However, a large fraction of FDI in China—about a quarter—is invested in real estate (Tseng and Zebregs 2002). Because this type of investment is common to the deployment of remittances as well, it reinforces the suspicion that there is a not inconsiderable statistical overlap between remittances and FDI. If the two (that is, remittances and migrant FDI) are combined, financial inflows from emigrants from the two countries are more comparable—with inflows into China being two to four times those into India.

Stable Source of Financial Flows

Remittances have emerged as the least unstable source of financial flows for countries afflicted by shocks and constitute the single most important source of insurance for many poor countries. Remittance flows are much more stable than private capital flows, which exhibit strong herd-like behavior, amplifying the boom-bust cycles in many emerging markets. Consequently, remittances can be viewed as a self-insurance mechanism for developing countries, whereby overseas migrants help in diversifying sources of external finance. This role, strengthened by the low risk correlation between the country of residence and the country of origin, is especially important for poor countries because, like poor people, poor countries find it difficult to get insurance. Not surprisingly, remittances have emerged as a critical insurance mechanism for residents of countries afflicted by economic and political crisis (Lebanon during its civil war, and Haiti's political crisis in the 1990s), natural disasters (Central America in the aftermath of Hurricane Mitch), international sanctions (Cuba), or failed state authority (Somalia).

In the late 1990s, Ecuador experienced its worst economic crisis of the century. The resulting political chaos, social upheaval, and economic collapse led to the largest emigration in the country's history (particularly to Spain). In just two years, more than a quarter million Ecuadorans left the country. Remittances jumped from US$643 million in 1997 to more than US$1.4 billion in 2001 (10 percent of gross domestic product [GDP]), emerging as the second largest source of foreign exchange after petroleum exports (Jokisch and Pribilsky 2002).

Cuba's attitude toward remittances changed when the collapse of the Soviet Union in the early 1990s left the country without a geopolitical benefactor to prop up its inefficient economy. Not only did overseas assistance dry up, but the global price of its principal export (sugar) collapsed as the United States tightened its embargo of the island. Until that time the country had curbed overseas remittances from its rich diaspora, who were in large part deeply hostile to the regime. However, with Soviet aid gone, the Cuban government took steps to attract remittances by offering numerous incentives to residents receiving U.S. dollars. By 1995 remittances were approximately US$530 million (from just US$50 million in 1990). At a time when foreign aid and FDI combined were only about US$100 million and exports just US$1.1 billion (Eckstein 2003)—and an acute foreign exchange crisis threatened to take the country the way of the Democratic People's Republic of Korea—remittances provided a crucial lifeline.

Primary Income Source for Smallest Countries

For the many small countries—especially island economies in the Caribbean and the Pacific—remittances, along with foreign aid and tourism, have become the only viable sources of income. In Cape Verde, around two-thirds of families receive money from abroad.[3] For many families, remittances offer the only source of income, not surprising in a country where, in 2000, only 435,000 citizens lived on the island and twice as many abroad. Such high levels of migration and remittance might well indicate that these countries are simply nonviable economic entities, but given political realities they will continue to exist—surviving to a considerable extent on the labors of their overseas populations.

Just a Fad?

As with the euphoria surrounding private capital flows in the mid-1990s, the attractiveness of remittances is in part a reaction to failures of earlier development mantras. Development thinking has been as prone to fads and fashions as private capital is alleged to be. Remittances strike the right cognitive chords. They fit in with a communitarian "third way" and exemplify the principle of self-help. People from poor countries can just migrate and send back money that not only helps their families, but the host and recipient countries as well. Immigrants, rather than governments, become the biggest provider of foreign aid. The general feeling appears to be that such private foreign aid is much more likely to go to people who really need it. On the sending side it does not require a costly government bureaucracy; on the receiving side far less is likely to be siphoned into the pockets of corrupt government officials. It appears to be good for equity and for poverty and yet imposes few budgetary costs. What could be better? Are these hopes valid?

WHY HAVE REMITTANCES GROWN?

What explains the growth of remittances in recent years? The most obvious factor is the steady growth of its underlying cause, namely migration, especially to rich countries. Even though annual flows of legal migrants have grown in fits and starts, illegal migration and the stock of emigrants has certainly grown. The United Nations estimates that roughly 175 million people were living outside their country of birth or citizenship in 2000, up from 120 million in 1990 (United Nations 2002; Martin and Widgren 2002). An analysis of the 2000 U.S. census reveals that of the foreign population in the United States in that year, nearly half (47 percent) had entered the country in the past decade. Elsewhere, the foreign population in 17 European economies tracked by the OECD (OECD 2001) rose from 15.8 million in 1998 to 21.7 million in 2001—an increase of 37.2 percent. In the oil-exporting Persian Gulf States, foreign workers continue to represent more than 50 percent of the labor force in all countries, and 70 percent of the labor force of 10 million in Saudi Arabia (Martin and Widgren 2002).

The frequency and intensity of economic and financial crises in many developing countries since 1985 has not only spurred migration but also increased the need for social safety nets, amplifying the demand for remittances.

Some of the reported increase in remittances is, in all likelihood, a statistical artifact. For one thing, data quality has improved (as evidenced by the declining number of zeroes in the table in box 16.1). Furthermore, changes in the economic policies of many developing countries, especially with regard to foreign exchange controls, have sharply reduced the black market premium for foreign exchange. As a result, part of the increase in officially recorded remittances reflects a shift from informal to formal channels.

A less obvious factor driving the growth in remittances is burgeoning infrastructure that has helped ease the movement of money across borders. For a long time, the remittance business was dominated by specialized money transfer companies. In 2002, for example, Western Union alone conducted almost US$700 billion in transfers and payments worldwide through 68 million customer-to-customer transactions (and another 173 million customer-to-business transactions). In 1994 it had 24,000 agents worldwide, of which two-thirds were in North America. By mid-2003 this figure had increased nearly sevenfold (to 165,000), of which 70 percent were based outside the United States.

The exorbitant costs of remittances (about 10 percent to 12 percent of the estimated US$25 billion transferred from the United States) and the implied large profits, have drawn new service providers. The most significant change has been in the strategies of major commercial banks, which had been slow to recognize that the remittance business was a potential source of significant new opportunities. Portuguese banks realized this in the early 1980s, when they established branches in areas with concentrations of immigrants (like France) and offered free transfer services along with arrangements with local agents for home delivery. By the late 1990s, deposits from emigrants represented about 20 percent of the total deposits in Portugal. In the Americas, the collapse of the Mexican banking system after the "Tequila" crisis (Latin American Banking crisis of 1994–95) opened up the Mexican banking sector to FDI. As major Spanish and U.S. banks began buying Mexican banks, remittances gradually moved to the center of their strategies.

The new players began to buy complementary U.S. assets and to cement alliances with other banks to leverage the remittance business.[4] It soon became evident that users of remittance services could become full banking customers—spearheading a large expansion of retail banking to two severely underserved groups on both sides of the border. The banks have also been surprised by the relative wealth of Mexican customers. The transfer business is already paying dividends. Bank of America has found that 33 percent of its U.S.-Mexican remittance customers have opened an account. Citigroup is using its transfer business to attract customers for other products—and one way to do that is to lower fees on transfers between Citigroup accounts in the United States and Mexico. Banks are now extending the products and technologies developed in the Mexico-U.S. remittance business to other Hispanic remittance markets in the United States, Spain, and Spanish North Africa.

Despite the growth of formal transfer mechanisms, substantial amounts of remittances continue to flow through informal (and sometimes underground) channels, outside the purview of government supervision and regulation. These informal value transfer (IVT) systems go back centuries, particularly in Asia. Examples include *hawala* and *hundi* (South Asia), *fei chien* (China), *phoe kuan* (Thailand), *Hui* (Vietnam), and *casa de cambio* (South America). Informal systems flourish in countries with economic controls, political instability, and low levels of financial development. Using rudimentary technologies, they rely more on trust than violence, riding on the social capital of ethnic groups. They transfer millions of dollars globally, offering speed, easy access, low costs, and anonymity. Senders present money to an IVT system agent (usually in an ethnic neighborhood), who calls or faxes instructions to a counterpart in the region where the money is to be sent. The counterpart makes the payment within a few hours. Settlements are made either with a transfer in the opposite direction or by over- or underinvoicing of cross-border trade. (For more information on the operation of IVT systems, see chapter 11.)

These services transfer funds are derived from both legitimate and illegitimate activities—including corruption, tax evasion, drugs, terrorism, and funds deployed by intelligence agencies. However, there is more speculation than evidence on the scale of illegitimate activity (Passas 1999). Attempts by western governments to regulate IVT activities have arisen in the context of anti-money-laundering measures and terrorist financing (see chapter 14).

EFFECTS OF FINANCIAL REMITTANCES

Remittances finance consumption, land and housing purchases, and philanthropy; they are an important source of social insurance in lower-income countries; and they provide liquidity for small enterprises in the absence of well-functioning credit markets. They also finance capital investments—in equipment, land, wells and irrigation works, and education—with long-term implications for economic development.

The complex effects of remittances are a function of the characteristics of migrants and the households they leave behind. These household transfers may be seen as an expression of altruism, or as an implicit intrafamily contractual arrangement or family loan. The relative importance of motives appears to vary with the institutional setting (Foster and Rosenzweig 2001).

However, at this point it is important to dispel one myth surrounding remittances—that they compensate for emigration of the most highly qualified, or brain drain. It is often argued that although poor countries may lose the scarce human capital that is critical for development, they gain another scarce factor, namely financial resources in the form of remittances. The two are not substitutes. Although, as will be noted later, emigrants are positively selected, remittances are not a trade-off for brain drain—for several reasons. The real detrimental effects of brain drain for developing countries arise from the migration of the upper end of human capital distribution—engineers, scientists, physicians, professors, and so on. This scarce human capital is usually drawn from the upper decile of the income distribution rather than the middle. Although there are exceptions (for example, temporary skilled migrants such as technology workers admitted to the United States with H-1B visas), for the most part these households are in less need of remittances, unless the country of origin undergoes a major crisis. Indeed, if the brain drain is a response to political repression or economic and political instability, rather than simply better economic opportunities abroad, human capital flight and financial capital flight complement each other. Instead of one form of capital outflow being "compensated for" by another type of capital inflow, the migration simply precipitates the outflow of financial capital as well. Countries such as Afghanistan, Colombia, Ghana, Haiti, and República Bolivariana de Venezuela, as well as Cuba in the late 1950s and early 1960s, which have witnessed violent regime changes and civil wars, are examples of this phenomenon. This is not to say that the brain drain of professionals might not have other benefits for the country of origin, such as business and commercial networks or investment flows and philanthropy, but those effects are distinct from financial remittances.

REMITTANCES AS SOCIAL INSURANCE

As noted earlier, remittances play a critical insurance role—with significant impact on both poverty and equity. For people in failed states, remittances are critical for personal consumption. In Haiti, remittances were about 17 percent of GDP in 2001. In Somalia following the collapse of a formal government in the early 1990s, remittances from the Somali diaspora based in the Persian Gulf States, several European countries, the United States, and Canada became a critical survival resource for many Somali families. In particular, remittances helped many urban families cope during the harsh years of the 1990s. By the end of the decade, with remittances between 25 percent and 40 percent of GDP (all figures are approximate), in some pockets, such as southern Somalia, these resources began to be invested in construction and commerce (Salah 1999).

A country that suffers a macroeconomic shock generally receives greater remittances. The many recent economic and financial crises have resulted in two simultaneous shocks that affect remittances: a positive income shock to the remitter because of devaluation and a negative income shock to the recipient because of the economic downturn. Both predict an increase in remittances (in domestic currency terms). Countries that suffered an economic shock (defined as a decline in GDP of 2 percent or more) were chosen and remittances relative to private consumption were examined in the years preceding and following the crisis. If the insurance hypothesis holds true, the share of remittances in private consumption would be expected to increase. Due to the unavailability of consistent annual data on remittances for the countries suffering a shock, this issue was examined in both an unbalanced panel (figure 16.2) and in a balanced panel (figure 16.3). In the latter, data were analyzed for a set of countries for which annual data are available for three years preceding and following a shock. In both cases there is a sharp increase in the ratio: remittances increase when a country suffers a macroeconomic shock.

Why does this matter? Its importance lies in the emerging consensus that, with globalization, factor markets are of crucial importance for poverty alleviation. Households tend to be much more specialized in income (or factor earnings such as land, labor, or capital) than they are in consumption. Hence, it is the source of income rather than the pattern of expenditure that affects the poor relative to the average household (Winters 2000; Reimer 2002). Remittances provide social protection to poor households, reducing vulnerability to shocks. Although the immediate impact of remittances is on transient poverty, the long-term effects should not be underestimated. For instance, it is now recognized that transient poverty is a serious obstacle to human capital investment. The impact on school attendance of an income shock is consistently larger for daughters than sons (Sawada 2003). Thus, even if remittances affect only transient poverty, the effect on human capital investment, especially in girls, could be quite substantial. Of course, for beneficial effects to occur the remittances should

FIGURE 16.2 UNWEIGHTED AVERAGE OF REMITTANCES AS A
SHARE OF PRIVATE CONSUMPTION, UNBALANCED

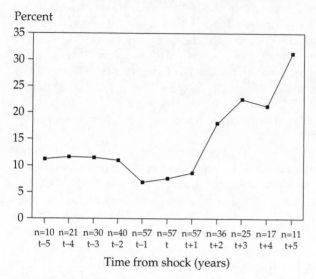

Source: Author's calculations.

FIGURE 16.3 UNWEIGHTED AVERAGE OF REMITTANCES AS A
SHARE OF PRIVATE CONSUMPTION

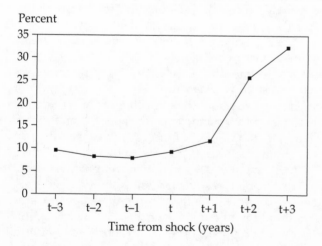

Source: Author's calculations.

Note: Fourteen countries are included: Barbados 1988–94, Colombia 1985–91, Comoros 1985–91, Ghana 1983–89, Guinea-Bissau 1988–94, India 1980–86, Jamaica 1992–98, Mauritania 1989–95, Mexico 1991–97, Morocco 1989–95, Panama 1984–90, Trinidad and Tobago 1989–95, Tunisia 1989–95, and Turkey 1990–96.

accrue to poor households in the first place, which in turn depends on whether the international migrants from that country are drawn from such households.

The particular characteristics of who migrates—so-called selection effects—are equally important for equity. While in both cases the eventual effects are strongly mediated by labor-market effects of migration, the distributional consequences are more complex given the uneven access to such flows across households, ethnic groups, communities, and regions. Households that receive remittances rapidly attain standards of living greater than those that do not have family members working abroad. Households with more diversified portfolios—both in financial assets and human capital assets—will gain relative to those with purely domestic portfolios in the event of a domestic economic shock that results in a devaluation and economic downturn. The income stream from the overseas portfolio increases in domestic currency terms after a devaluation, thereby increasing the holder's income relative to lower-income groups. If remittances flow to poorer households concentrated in a particular region, it might reduce inequality within the region even while widening it among different regions. Research in the Philippines shows that households with overseas migrants have done substantially better in the years since the Asian crisis than those that had no members abroad. This is to be expected, because migration is a form of coinsurance and results in families having diversified portfolios. Indeed, even where households have members who are migrants abroad, those families above a certain income threshold are found to use remittances for investment (in the case of the Philippines, in human capital that would make it easier to migrate abroad), while those below this threshold use it for subsistence consumption (Yang 2003). This is particularly true during a crisis, when households face substantial financial and economic stress and resultant pressure on consumption.

Migrants are rarely drawn randomly from the population. Instead they are drawn selectively from specific communities—regional, ethnic, or religious—as well as from specific educational and income levels. These selection effects mediate between migration, remittances, and poverty and equity outcomes in the country of origin. The average level of education of emigrants is greater than the average level in the country of origin—often substantially so (figure 16.4).

In the Latin American case it has been shown that while only about one-fifth of Latin Americans have completed high school or college, a little over half of the Latino immigrants in the United States have a secondary education or better. Well-educated Latin Americans are at least two-and-a-half times more likely to be found in the United States than in their home country populations. In their analysis of Mexican migration to the United States, Chiquiar and Hanson (2002) find that Mexican

FIGURE 16.4   POPULATION (AGE 25 AND OLDER) AT HOME AND
              OVERSEAS WITH TERTIARY EDUCATION

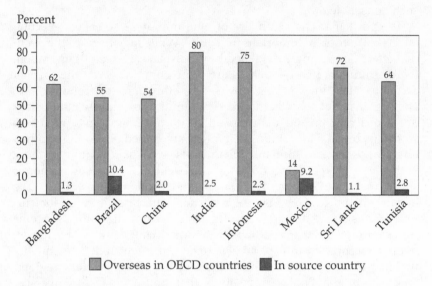

■ Overseas in OECD countries   ■ In source country

Source: Bureau of Labor Statistics and Bureau of the Census, various years; OECD, *Trends in International Migration,* various years.

Note: Data are for different years for different countries.

immigrants, while much less educated than U.S. natives, are on average more educated than residents of Mexico. If Mexican immigrants in the United States were paid prevailing wages for those skills in Mexico, they would tend to occupy the middle and upper portions of Mexico's wage distribution. In contrast to earlier work that posits a negative-selection hypothesis (Borjas 1987), these findings suggest that in terms of observable skills there is intermediate or positive selection of immigrants from Mexico. The results also suggest that migration abroad may raise wage inequality in Mexico.

The fact that migrants are not being drawn from the poorest households in their country of origin means that while remittances are poor-friendly, their direct effects on the poorest groups may be limited. Instead, the effects on structural poverty are likely to occur through substantial indirect effects: the demand for labor-intensive services (such as construction workers when remittances are used for home building), and perhaps even redirecting government social expenditures from areas benefiting from remittances to those that are not.

These results are likely to be less representative of the many illegal immigrants, who are much more likely to come from poorer households. Large-scale illegal immigration occurs mainly where there is geographical proximity—for example, from Mexico and Central America to the United States, intra-Asian migration (Myanmar to Thailand, Nepal to India), and from the Maghreb to Europe. Strong anecdotal evidence indicates that the many poor people who do make it across borders incur substantial debt in making the often-illegal journey. In such cases they become indentured laborers who then have to work to pay off the loan (often to criminal syndicates), reducing their remittances. On balance, however, if migrants are low-skill or unskilled workers, the beneficial impact on poverty and inequality is maximized for the migrant-sending country. It is not just that the ensuing remittances are directed at poorer households, but that the supply of unskilled labor in the source country is reduced, thereby increasing wages of unskilled workers left behind.

The evidence regarding the direct impact of remittances on economic development and growth is limited. It is common to hear officials in remittance-receiving countries lament that the bulk of remittances is spent on consumption. In the case of poor families, it is hardly surprising that remittances are used to augment subsistence consumption, and that therefore little is saved and very little invested in projects that could stimulate economic growth. Nonetheless, insofar as remittances finance the consumption of domestically produced goods and services such as housing, there are wider multiplier effects. Moreover, additional consumption also increases indirect tax receipts (Desai, Kapur, and McHale 2003). There is some suggestion that the propensity to save is higher among remittance-receiving households than in others (Orozco 2003). If true, this suggests that remittances leverage broader economic development by augmenting national savings.

To take another example, it has long been recognized that capital and liquidity constraints are critical for small-enterprise development, especially in poorer communities with imperfect capital markets. For instance, an analysis of capital constraints on investment levels of microenterprises in Mexico found that remittances from migration by the owner or family members working in the United States were responsible for almost 20 percent of the capital invested in microenterprises throughout urban Mexico—additional cumulative investment capital of nearly US$2 billion. Within the 10 states with the highest rate of migration from Mexico to the United States, almost a third of the capital invested in microenterprises was associated with remittances (Woodruff and Zenteno 2001). Insofar as remittances are driving the retail banking strategies behind foreign investment in Mexican banks, an inadvertent but potentially far-reaching effect of remittances on Mexico could be the transformation of its banking system. Fewer than one in five Mexicans has a bank account, and many rural areas of central Mexico, source of the most migrant laborers to the United States, lack any bank branch. Weak formal credit markets have been particularly inimical to Mexico's small and medium enterprises. If the remittance-driven postmerger banking strategy in Mexico leads to the transformation of retail banking in Mexico, the long-term economic benefits of remittances may be great indeed.

More recently, immigrant communities have sought to pool remittances and channel them for public purposes. For instance, in the last decade, Hispanic immigrants across the United States have organized themselves into hometown associations (HTAs) that finance public works projects and small businesses in the towns from which they have migrated. The Mexican government has taken the initiative to leverage these remittances by creating a "three-for-one program," whereby all HTA remittances used to improve infrastructure or establish businesses are matched dollar for dollar by the Mexican federal, state, and local authorities (Alarcon 2000). This three-fold leveraging has had some notable successes at the local level, but the cumulative impact remains limited.

Often communities do not have the resources to maintain what has been built through these contributions. Hype notwithstanding, HTAs have not so far been used significantly to fund direct income-generating projects. In particular, it is unclear if they are creating jobs so that Mexicans do not have to emigrate, or instead simply subsidizing future migration through improved training. Perhaps the biggest benefit is that the HTAs become a glue for local collective action in both the sending and the receiving country. For migrants, these associations help maintain ties to their hometown, which in turn may help sustain private remittances.

SO WHAT'S THE PROBLEM?

It is interesting that when examining the impact of remittances, micro-level studies (principally by anthropologists) are less sanguine about its effects than more macro-level studies (usually by economists). A common theme in the former is the duality of greater wealth but fewer economic opportunities for those left behind—a Pyrrhic victory. So-called "migravillages" in Latin America have in many cases been physically transformed; but often the handsome new houses are empty because their owners live in the United States. Likewise, remittances have helped build better schools, but enrollment has been declining. In regions where remittances were initially a consequence of migration, over time they have emerged as its principal driver, as the very money that increased the material wealth of the villages gradually undermines their future. What is good for individual migrants and households, in other words, may not be as beneficial for the communities. Whether economic development is more about the former or the latter is something that can be reasonably debated.

Even at the household level, remittances can have ambiguous effects. Consider the case of home-care workers such as Jamaican nannies in New York or Filipino nannies in Hong Kong. In many cases, these are mothers who have left their own children behind to take care of children in richer households. The household in the home country has a higher consumption level due to remittances, but the children of these workers grow up without the presence of their mother. We could take the migration decision of the mother as a "revealed preference" of an improvement in household welfare. Why would she leave otherwise? However, we do not have an independent analysis that this is indeed the case.

In communities heavily dependent on remittances, a culture of dependency often sets in. In a variety of contexts it has been observed that household members simply stop working and wait from month to month for the overseas remittance. Such negative incentives—a form of moral hazard—also result in an increase in the reservation wage. Young men prefer to remain unemployed and wait for the possibility that they themselves will migrate, rather than take up jobs at the local market-clearing wage. That remittances increase consumption much faster than production raises issues of long-term sustainability, given an inevitable decline as migrants settle in new communities and links with their home communities gradually erode. Of course, this issue is moot if most people leave the community.

Similar negative incentives can also act at the national level. If remittances are relatively large, and if a large share is spent on nontradeables—housing and land are particularly favored—the country is likely to suffer from "Dutch disease."[5] Effectively this results in an appreciation of the real exchange rate, rendering exports less competitive. The country's principal export—labor—could replace labor-intensive products as the cheap factor. At an aggregate level, remittances constitute a form of rent. Exporting products requires painstaking effort to build the institutions and infrastructure that help develop necessary productive capacity. Exporting people, on the other hand, occurs in most cases by default rather than by design. Nonetheless, if the latter also results in large foreign exchange receipts, the pressure to undertake reforms needed for export-led growth are considerably attenuated. For instance, countries can maintain larger fiscal deficits in the context of international migration and remittances. In the absence of remittances, high fiscal deficits would imply higher current-account imbalances and hence greater reliance on foreign savings (assuming the deficit is not monetized—less likely given that central banks are relatively more independent today), resulting in higher capital-account inflows.[6] However if remittances are high, current-account deficits will be lower, thereby reducing the likelihood that high fiscal deficits will precipitate a balance-of-payments crisis—the most common trigger for economic reforms in developing countries. Thus, countries with high levels of remittances can sustain higher fiscal deficits—while keeping international financial institutions like the IMF and the World Bank at bay.[7] Increasing politicization of these institutions has meant that potential borrowers have transitioned from coinsurance through these institutions to self-insurance in the form of higher foreign exchange reserves and international migration and remittances.

POLITICAL EFFECTS

Money buys influence. It should not be surprising, therefore, that in countries where remittances are important, the political effects are not inconsequential. In countries such as the Dominican Republic (where remittances are 10 percent of GDP), presidential candidates campaign in the United States. From Mexico to India, the lucre of remittances has led politicians to switch positions with regard to their diaspora—from benign neglect to active courtship. Regimes in socialist economies like Cuba and the Democratic People's Republic of Korea have used remittances to augment scarce hard-currency resources and thereby to strengthen themselves in the short term. Cuba draws remittances from its U.S.-based diaspora, while the Democratic People's Republic of Korea earns remittances mostly from *pachinko* parlors run by Koreans living in Japan. However, insofar as these remittances sow the seeds of economic transformation, they can begin to quietly erode the political system. In Cuba access to remittances has increased inequality in a political system that draws its legitimacy from its commitment to equity. Remittances have a strong racial bias as well, since the diaspora is predominantly white while the island is mostly black. Blacks gained under Castro and were therefore less likely to emigrate, but now they have less access to the informal dollarized economy. Furthermore, access to remittances is also heavily urban and regional; Havana, with 20 percent of the island's population, receives approximately 60 percent of all remittances. Thus, rural-urban inequality is also likely to widen.

It is possible to view remittances as a political weapon of the weak. Rather than simply react to state policies, international migration and remittances have forced states to accommodate new realities. In lieu of political voice, migration becomes an exit strategy, and remittances either fuel further exit or empower political voice by making resources available to new groups. In several Latin American countries, even as economists debated the relative merits of dollarization, the influx of "migradollars" were rendering the debate moot.

The political impact is not just confined to home countries. In host countries, remittances have been quietly reshaping immigration policies. In 2002, the Mexican government negotiated with banks and wire transfer agencies in the United States to make it easier and cheaper for immigrants to send money home. The Mexican government began to distribute consular identification cards (*matrículas consulares*) and persuaded U.S. banks to accept them as identification cards for the purpose of opening bank accounts, irrespective of the legality of the bearer's immigration status.[8] Major U.S. banks, attracted by the high fees and volume, began to accept these cards. The remittance market was also a good complement to U.S. banks' strategy of expanding operations in Latin America by buying local banks in the region. After all, if a bank could get a customer to step inside and make a deposit (in the United States) or a withdrawal (in, say, Mexico), it might interest him or her in other financial products. In turn, by simply offering to do business with any illegal foreign resident who got a consular identification card, U.S. banks have quietly reshaped their country's migration policy toward illegal immigrants from Latin America. As Mexican consulates began to be flooded with applications for identification cards, local governments and law enforcement agencies in the United States began accepting them in support of applications for other forms of identification such as driver's licenses, making the lives of illegal migrants less onerous.

Because international remittances are a form of cross-border financial flows, it should not be surprising that they also have international political effects. In many countries the importance and concentration of remittances affect bilateral relationships and foreign policy. While remittances affect politics at the local level, causality runs the other way at the macro level—it is politics that affects remittances. To the extent that sources of remittances for some receiving countries are heavily concentrated in regions and countries that suffer from political instability, the remittance-receiving countries are especially vulnerable. The emergence of "remittance communities" creates source-destination dyads that increase covariant shocks and can become a coercive instrument on the part of migrant-destination countries. Remittances from migrants in Côte D'Ivoire accounted for a quarter of GDP in Burkina Faso, and the civil war in 2002 in the former rapidly reverberated to the latter.

The oil shocks and the Gulf crisis in the Middle East in the early 1990s not only affected oil-producing countries but had a regional contagion effect through their demand for labor. A similar phenomenon was observed in Southeast Asia during the Asian crisis in the late 1990s, when the expulsion of Indonesian labor from Malaysia and Thailand exacerbated the crisis in Indonesia, increased tensions between the countries, and weakened the Association of Southeast Asian Nations. Following the 1991 Gulf War, the Gulf countries punished workers from Jordan and Yemen, especially Palestinians, for supporting Saddam Hussein, expelling them from their countries. In all these cases, remittances from family members earning money in the

Persian Gulf states were crucial. The heavy price paid then and the continued dependence on remittances from the Gulf account for the opposition of some countries to the U.S.-led invasion of Iraq in 2003.

Control of remittances as a form of economic warfare has been most evident in the Israeli-Palestinian conflict. In September 2000, Israel began revoking the work permits of Palestinians because of security concerns. At that time, some 100,000 Palestinian workers from the West Bank and Gaza Strip crossed into Israel every day. By January 2002, only 25,000 Palestinian workers and 8,000 merchants had permits to enter, a number that has continued to drop. In their place, Israel began to import foreign workers (an estimated 230,000), largely from China, Thailand, Africa, and the Philippines to work in agriculture and construction. As a result remittance outflows from Israel tripled from less than US$1 billion in the early 1990s to nearly US$3 billion in 2001. The economic effects on the West Bank and Gaza have been devastating. Gross national income per capita fell by 11.7 percent in 2001 and a further 18.7 percent in 2002, as poverty levels jumped from 21 percent in 1999 to 46 percent in 2002. The drop in remittances had larger indirect effects as well, because the loss of income resulted in depressed demand for Palestinian goods and a sharp decline in imports from Israel—in turn adversely affecting Israel's economy (World Bank 2002).

As with much else in the contemporary world, remittances changed in the aftermath of September 11, 2001. For Pakistan, a front-line state caught in this vortex, where remittances were around US$1 billion in 2000 (about a third of their peak in 1982–83), this proved a blessing. Many Pakistanis with savings in offshore accounts repatriated their funds, fearful of being caught in U.S.-led investigations into terrorist financing. Under pressure from the United States, the Pakistani central bank tightened controls on the web of money-changers (locally known as hundi operators), and introduced a law restoring immunity from disclosure of the sources of income for holders of foreign-currency accounts. As a result, the difference between the official and market rates narrowed to less than 1 percent, and remittances to Pakistan exceeded US$3 billion in 2002.

In contrast, the effects were disastrous for Somalia—a country with no recognized government and without a functioning state apparatus. After the international community largely washed its hands of the country following the disastrous peacekeeping foray in 1994, remittances became the inhabitants' lifeline. With no recognized private banking system, the remittance trade was dominated by a single firm (Al-Barakat).[9] In 2001, the United States shut down Al-Barakat Bank's overseas money remittance channel, labeling the bank "the quartermasters of terror." With remittances representing 25 percent to 40 percent of total gross national product, closure of this channel was devastating. The humanitarian impact of money frozen in transit was considerable.

Remittances provided many times what the aid agencies were providing to rebuild the deeply impoverished country. Although little evidence of Al-Barakat's backing for terrorism has been discovered,[10] the effects of the ban on the country's well-being were significant.

POLICY OPTIONS

The Somali case emphasizes two issues. First, there is little doubt that remittances are an important potential mechanism to fund terrorism, civil wars, and liberation struggles. From the support for the revolutionary council of the Free Aceh Movement in Sweden, to the Liberation Tigers of Tamil Eelam in Canada and the Kashmiri cause in the United Kingdom, there is no shortage of examples. In Somalia itself a large portion of remittances went to supply arms to the rural guerrillas who toppled the government in January 1991. For the peoples of the conflict-afflicted countries of Afghanistan, the Democratic Republic of Congo, and Somalia, and for nationalities without states (Kurds, Palestinians, and pre-independence Eritreans and East Timorese), overseas remittances are the oxygen essential not just for family survival and household consumption, but also to finance militant causes and support leaderships that may use the struggle to maintain their hold on power. In other cases, such as Armenia and Croatia, remittances underwrote long-distance nationalism, boosting hard-line regimes and complicating efforts to resolve regional conflicts.

Second, the Somali case illustrates the need for greater efforts to create an acceptable international money transfer system in the growing number of countries where the state has collapsed, where international aid is scarce, and where desperate nationals are trying to do more for themselves. No greater challenge faces the international community than the responsibility to address the well-being of people living in such states. Currently, the international community is relying principally on a "big stick" approach—proscriptions and sanctions against countries and financial intermediaries. For instance, in 2003 the United States considered sanctions to cut off remittances to the Democratic People's Republic of Korea. With the Paris-based Financial Action Task Force, the United States is pressuring countries to start monitoring door-to-door remittances, fearing that this unregulated flow of money could be used for terrorist activities. New legislation is forcing money transmitters to install expensive new compliance technologies. It is certainly the case, as the United Nations Development Programme (UNDP) found in Somalia, that current money transfer systems in that country do not meet acceptable international standards, lacking the means to identify suspicious transactions and money laundering schemes. International efforts will be more meaningful, however, if they are directed toward building a financial architecture rather than just wielding the blunt instrument of sanctions. The UNDP's initiative to work with foreign governments and Somalia's remaining money transfer and remittance companies to comply with standard financial rules and regulations and help firms institute standard bookkeeping, auditing, and reporting, is an example of such an alternative policy option.

The international community can best address the channels through which remittances are transmitted by helping construct a financial architecture that reduces the transactions costs of intermediation and increases its transparency. Recently the World Council of Credit Unions launched the International Remittance network (IRnet) to facilitate remittance transfers from the United States (see chapter 8). IRnet does not charge recipients any fee and offers better exchange rates—but as yet its services are confined to members. The Inter-American Development Bank is helping create a common electronic platform between sending and receiving countries in the Latin American region and within receiving countries (Buencamino and Gorbunov 2002). Much more could be done. In particular, the international community should fund a much more substantial effort to underwrite the development and maintenance of a common electronic platform that would facilitate remittance transfers. If the facility were maintained under the aegis of a multilateral organization (UNDP, for example), it could ensure both greater transparency and lower transactions costs. By allowing registered IVT systems operators as well as Interpol access to such a platform at a low cost, many of the advantages of informal banking would be coupled with the transparency of such a central facility. It should be remembered that public subsidies for such an endeavor would in all likelihood be much less than the high costs involved in policing and monitoring, as well as less than the greater transactions costs now being incurred.

Another step to help lubricate international remittance transfers would be to work on transforming the role of post offices, the single biggest global distributional channel. The U.S. Postal Service began a program called Dinero Seguro (safe money) for sending remittances, but with charges at nearly 10 percent of the face amount it has had little success. Postal "giro" payment systems are widely used in Europe and Japan. Linking the postal giro systems worldwide would facilitate international postal transfers, paralleling the agreement for the exchange of mail among member countries of the Universal Postal Union.

What can receiving-country governments do to enhance the development impact of remittances? First, they should get a better handle on the magnitudes and sources of these flows. In contrast to the massive effort devoted to monitoring and managing foreign aid flows, governments for the most part devote little attention to remittances. Effective monitoring would require creating a spatial map of the country's overseas communities, not just by destination country but by specific locations within those countries. This would allow financial intermediaries to better target these communities. Moreover, they should, with the efforts of international financial institutions, get data on remittance outflows from sending countries. This would allow them to cross-check inflows, as is currently done with trade flows.

Second, increasing the long-term productive impact of remittances requires greater competition and a carrot-and-stick approach to increase the penetration of formal financial intermediaries, especially banks, in areas with higher levels of emigration. This is especially the case if the propensity to save is higher in remittance-receiving households than in others, which would suggest that the presence of an extensive network of financial intermediaries in these areas could help leverage remittances for broader economic development and help augment national savings rates. Remittances could also be used to underpin mortgage markets,[11] or be securitized as future receivables to augment foreign credit ratings (Ketkar and Ratha 2001).

Third, governments need to monitor and regulate labor market intermediaries more actively, because they often cheat potential migrants. Intermediaries lubricate flows—but they also can divert a substantial stream of income to themselves.

Finally, governments should be aware that active attempts to encourage or require investment of remittances are unlikely to have significant economic benefits. The best way for recipient-country governments to ensure that a greater proportion of remittances are productively invested (rather than spent on immediate consumption) is to have a supportive economic environment for all forms of investment. Countries such as India and Turkey have tried to increase remittances by offering various preferential schemes (such as tax-free status) under the capital account. Such preferential treatment inevitably leads to round-tripping. Instead, governments should direct their efforts toward improving the financial sector.

A NEW DEVELOPMENT PARADIGM, OR JUST ANOTHER DESTABILIZING FORCE OF GLOBALIZATION?

Remittances are one of the most visible—and beneficial—aspects of the way in which international migration is reshaping the countries of origin. In a variety of settings remittances are quietly transforming societies and regions and are the most visible example of self-help undertaken by poor households in the global arena. Their role is particularly important in augmenting private consumption and alleviating transient poverty in receiving countries. However, their effects on structural poverty and long-term economic development are less well understood. Given their importance, rigorous data and research on the effects of remittances is surprisingly limited, in stark contrast to the substantial body of literature on the other principal sources of development finance—foreign aid, flows from the International Monetary Fund and the World Bank, and FDI and private debt flows.

Unlike foreign aid, remittance flows do not put any burden on taxpayers in rich countries. Nonetheless, remittances occur only to the extent that emigrants from poor countries can work in richer countries. It is clear that countries that are much more open to immigration are also the principal sources of remittances. Insofar as remittances constitute substantial sources of external finance to poorer countries, should they not be counted as part of a country's contribution to poor countries?[12] When they are counted, the U.S. contribution to development finance increases substantially (but not as much as that of Saudi Arabia), while the contribution of more immigrant-resistant countries such as Japan falls. The critical difference between foreign aid and remittances is that the former consists primarily of transfers from public entities in the donor country to public agencies in receiving countries; even when it is directed to civil society actors such as nongovernmental organizations, it goes to organized entities. Remittances, of course, simply go directly to households, and in that sense their immediate impact on poverty—through increased consumption—can be greater than traditional foreign aid, depending on the income characteristics of the receiving household. The transactions costs are lower and there is less leakage to rent-seeking bureaucracies and consultants. However, their long-term impact may be more questionable, especially if few productive assets are being created. Thus, it would appear that remittances are a better instrument to address transient poverty, which arises due to shocks (to individual households or whole nations), rather than structural poverty. To alleviate structural poverty, broad economic transformation may still require external financial resources in the form of budgetary support for governments in many poor countries.

If remittances are to become the principal mechanism by which resources are transferred to poor countries, more liberal immigration policies will be required in industrial countries. Perhaps in the new round of global bargaining, developing countries might add to the slogan "trade not aid" the coda "migration not aid." In the ongoing trade negotiations under the Doha Round, developing countries would do well to press for greater levels of temporary migration and concentrate less on foreign aid. Such an approach might be better for all sides, in fact, but it is unclear that many governments, rich or poor, have the incentive to embrace it, because rich-country governments would lose potential leverage on developing-country governments, while the latter lose a source of rents. Indeed, it is likely that foreign aid and bilateral trade agreements will increasingly be used to persuade developing countries to check migrant outflows.

Finally, it is worth asking whether a less visible, quantifiable, and tangible form of remittances—namely, social remittances and the flow of ideas—have a more critical impact than their pecuniary counterpart. The overseas experience must have some cognitive effect on migrants. At the same time, the communications revolution has led to an exponential growth of transnational telephone calls and e-mail, as well as a sharp increase in international travel. As a result, not just elites but social groups at the lower end of the social spectrum are exposed to new information, not just new ways of making or selling things, but also new views of what is acceptable in terms of service standards, the role of the state, or the behavior of politicians. The cumulative effect of millions of conversations—akin to filling a pond one drop at a time—is interesting to speculate on. Perhaps it is here that the real effects of remittances will be felt. But that is another story.

NOTES

1. I am grateful to Dilip Ratha of the World Bank for the data used in this section and discussions related to the same. Also see Ratha 2003.

2. Data for Belgium and Luxembourg are usually combined.

3. Data are drawn from Cape Verde 2002.

4. Thus Spain's Banco Bilbao Vizcaya Argentaria bought Bancomer and then emerged as a dominant player in the electronic transfer business. Its volume grew from 657,000 transactions in 1999 to 12.65 million in 2001 thanks largely to the alliance it started in 2000 with Wells Fargo and the U.S. Postal Service, and to links with money transfer services in the New York area. Following Citbank's purchase of Banamex in 2001, it introduced a single account that can be operated on either side of the border, using branches of either Citibank or Banamex. In 2002, Bank of America, the biggest U.S. retail bank, took a stake in Santander Serfin, the third-largest Mexican bank, which was controlled by Spain's Santander Central Hispano. The remittance business also drove Hong Kong Shanghai Banking Corporation's decision to buy Grupo Financiero Bital, a large Mexican retail bank along with Household International, a consumer credit lender with branches across the United States, as a base for remittance business.

5. Dutch disease is an economic phenomenon in which the discovery and exploitation of natural resources deindustrializes a nation's economy. In the given scenario, the value of the country's currency rises (making manufactured goods less competitive), imports increase, exports decrease, and productivity falls. The phenomenon was first observed in the Netherlands in the 1960s, when large reserves of natural gas were first exploited.

6. Moreover, the general trend of greater trade openness and increasing domestic liberalization means that excess demand has much less effect on inflation.

7. For instance, India has maintained exceedingly high fiscal deficits (about 10 percent of GDP) even as inflation is modest (about 5 percent). In part this is because its current account—buoyed by remittances exceeding US$12 billion (2.5 percent of GDP)—is positive. For a more elaborate discussion, see Kapur and Patel (2003).

8. The cards are digitally coded and check an applicant's information against computerized census and voter rolls in Mexico. The accounts allow immigrants to send automated teller machine cards to relatives back home, so rather than spending US$25 to send US$200 at a typical money transfer counter, immigrants can give their families access to U.S. funds for about US$3 per transaction.

9. Al-Barakat operated in 40 countries, was the country's largest private employer, handled about US$140 million a year from the diaspora, and offered phone and Internet services.

10. By early 2003, only four criminal prosecutions had been filed, and none involved charges of aiding terrorists.

11. This is being attempted in Mexico with the assistance of Fannie Mae and JP Morgan.

12. A new research initiative currently underway by the Center for Global Development and *Foreign Policy* magazine, on the impact of an array of rich country policies on poor countries, does take this into account.

REFERENCES

Alarcon, Rafael. 2000. "The Development of Home Town Associations in the United States and the Use of Social Remittances in Mexico." Inter-American Development Bank, Washington, DC. http://www.thedialogue.org/publications/alarcon.pdf.

Borjas, George. 1987. "Self Selection and the Earnings of Immigrants." *American Economic Review* 77(4): 531–53.

Buencamino, Leonides, and Sergei Gorbunov. 2002. "Informal Money Transfer Systems: Opportunities and Challenges for Development Finance." DESA Discussion Paper 26, United Nations, New York.

Bureau of Labor Statistics and Bureau of Census. Various years. Current Population Survey. Washington, DC. http://www.bls.census.gov/cps/cpsmain.htm.

Cape Verde, Ministry of Finance and Planning. 2002. "Interim Poverty Reduction Strategy Paper." Praia, Cape Verde.

Chiquiar, Daniel, and Gordon H. Hanson. 2002. "International Migration, Self-Selection, and the Distribution of Wages: Evidence from Mexico and the United States." NBER Working Paper 9242, National Bureau of Economic Research, Cambridge, MA.

Desai, Mihir, Devesh Kapur, and John McHale. 2003. "The Fiscal Impact of High Skilled Emigration: Flows of Indians to the U.S." Weatherhead Center for International Affairs, Working Paper 03-01, Harvard University, Cambridge, MA.

Eckstein, Susan. 2003. "Diasporas and Dollars: Transnational Ties and the Transformation of Cuba." Rosemarie Rogers Working Paper 16, Massachusetts Institute of Technology, Cambridge, MA.

Foster, Andrew, and Mark Rosenzweig. 2001. "Imperfect Commitment, Altruism and Family: Evidence from Transfer Behavior in Low-Income Rural Areas." *Review of Economics and Statistics* 83(3): 389–407.

IMF (International Monetary Fund). Various years. *Balance of Payments Statistics Yearbook.* Washington, DC: IMF.

Jokisch, Brad, and Jason Pribilsky. 2002. "The Panic to Leave: Economic Crisis and the 'New Emigration' from Ecuador." *International Migration* 40(4): 75–102.

Kapur, Devesh, and Urjit Patel. 2003. "Large Foreign Currency Reserves: Insurance for Domestic Weakness and External Uncertainties?" *Economic and Political Weekly* 38(11): 1047–53.

Ketkar, Suhas, and Dilip Ratha. 2001. "Development Financing During a Crisis: Securitization of Future Receivables." Policy Research Working Paper 2582, World Bank, Washington, DC.

Martin, Philip, and Jonas Widgren. 2002. "International Migration: Facing the Challenge." *Population Bulletin* 57(1): 1–43.

OECD (Organisation for Economic Co-operation and Development). 2001. *Trends in International Migration.* Paris: OECD.

OECD. Various years. *Trends in International Migration.*

Orozco, Manuel. 2003. "The Impact of Migration in the Caribbean and Central American Region." FOCAL (Canadian Foundation for the Americas), FPP–03-03, Ottawa.

Passas, N. 1999. "Informal Value Transfer Systems and Criminal Organizations: A Study into So-Called Underground Banking Networks." The Hague: Ministry of Justice (the Netherlands).

Ratha, Dilip. 2003. "Worker's Remittances: An Important and Stable Source of External Development Finance." In *Global Development Finance: Striving for Stability in Development Finance,* 157–75. Washington, DC: World Bank.

Reimer, Jeffrey J. 2002. "Estimating the Poverty Impacts of Trade Liberalization." GTAP Working Paper 20, Center for Global Trade Analysis, Department of Agricultural Economics, Purdue University, Lafayette, Indiana.

Salah, Idil. 1999. "Peace and Development in Northern Somalia—Opportunities and Challenges." Som-Can Institute for Research and Development, Canadian International Development Agency.

Sawada, Yasuyuki. 2003. "Income Risks, Gender, and Human Capital Investment in a Developing Country." CIRJE F-Series, Faculty of Economics, University of Tokyo. http://d.repec.org/n?u=RePEc:tky:fseres:2003cf198&r=dev.

Tseng, Wanda, and Harm Zebregs. 2002. "Foreign Direct Investment in China: Some Lessons for Other Countries." IMF Policy Discussion Paper PDP/02/03, IMF, Washington, DC.

United Nations. 2002. *International Migration 2002.* Population Division, United Nations, New York.

Winters, L. Alan. 2000. "Trade, Trade Policy and Poverty: What Are the Links?" Research Paper 2382, Centre for Economic Policy Research, London.

Woodruff, Christopher, and Rene Zenteno. 2001. "Remittances and Microenterprises in Mexico." Working paper, University of California, San Diego.

World Bank. 2002. "Fifteen Months—*Intifada*, Closures, and Palestinian Economic Crisis: An Assessment." Washington, DC: World Bank.

———. 2003. *Global Development Finance.* Washington, DC: World Bank.

Yang, Dean. 2003. "Remittances and Human Capital Investment: Child Schooling and Child Labor in the Origin Households of Overseas Filipino Workers." Gerald R. Ford School of Public Policy, University of Michigan, Ann Arbor, MI.

Index